A taxonomy of state capitalism

Emerging Markets Studies

Edited by Joachim Ahrens, Alexander Ebner, Herman W. Hoen, Bernhard Seliger and Ralph Michael Wrobel

Vol. 7

PETER LANG

Axel Wölk

A taxonomy of state capitalism

The developmental phases of Russia, Kazakhstan, South Korea and Singapore - a comparative institutional analysis

PETER LANG

Bibliographic Information published by the Deutsche Nationalbibliothek
The Deutsche Nationalbibliothek lists this publication in the Deutsche Nationalbibliografie; detailed bibliographic data is available in the internet at http://dnb.d-nb.de.

Library of Congress Cataloging-in-Publication Data
A CIP catalog record for this book has been applied for at the Library of Congress.

ISSN 2190-099X
ISBN 978-3-631-84908-8 (Print)
E-ISBN 978-3-631-85308-5 (E-Book)
E-ISBN 978-3-631-85339-9 (E-Pub)
E-ISBN 978-3-631-85340-5 (E-Mobi)
DOI 10.3726/b18336

Peter Lang – Berlin · Bern · Bruxelles · New York · Oxford · Warszawa · Wien

This publication has been peer reviewed.

www.peterlang.com

For Judit with my unconditional love

Preface

This book is a slightly edited version of my dissertation which has been submitted to, accepted by and successfully defended at the Universit of Groningen. Furthermore, this book is part of the project Governance in Emerging Economies (GEE), which was funded by the Volkswagen Foundation.

Contents

List of Abbreviations

BTI	Bertelmann Transformation Index
CEO	Chief Executive Officer
EDB	Economic Development Board
EPB	Economic Planning Board
et al.	et alii
FDI	Foreign Direct Investment
GCC	Golf Cooperation Council
GDP	Gross Domestic Product
GIC	Government of Singapore Investment Corporation
GLC	Government-linked Corporations
GNI	Gross National Income
HCI	Heavy and Chemical Industry
HDI	Human Development Index
i. e.	id est
ICT	Information and Communication Technologies
ILO	International Labour Organization
KPI	Key Performance Indicators
MNC	Multi-national Corporations
MOF	Ministry of Finance
NIC	Newly Industrialized Countries
NIE	New Institutional Economics
NGO	Non-Governmental Organization
OECD	Organization for Economic Cooperation and Development
PAP	People's Action Party
R&D	Research and Development
SASAC	State-owned Assets Supervision and Administrative Commission
SME	Small and Medium Enterprises
SOE	State-owned Enterprises
SPIK	Spezialni Investnij Kontrakt
SWF	Sovereign Wealth Funds
TFP	Total Factor Productivity
UNDP	United Nations Development Program
WEF	World Economic Forum

1 Introduction

"History is the unfolding of miscalculations."

Barbara Tuchman

Abstract
In this introduction the research question is formulated and the scientific relevance of analyzing the phenomenon of state capitalism demonstrated. As a matter of fact, the research question can be formulated as follows: "What is state capitalism and how can its profound performance differences be explained?" This topic is to be tackled with the theoretical framework of New Institutional Economics (NIE). So far, in the literature no theoretically based definition of state capitalism has been given and the literature is also largely reticent on reasons for the performance differences. In the course of this introductory chapter there are also antecedents of state capitalism and a short synopsis of the developmental trajectory of Russia and China illustrated.

Keywords: Research question, Performance differences, New Institutional Economics, Developmental trajectory of Russia and China, Antecedents

1.1 Overview

With the fall of the Berlin Wall in 1989 and the demise of the Soviet Union in 1991 there seemed to be no alternative to a market capitalist economic model anymore. In every conceivable way, the possibility of erecting a communist economic and political rule seemed to be outmoded. Some observers even saw a new era coming, where there was no competition between economic systems.

In this regard Fukuyama (1992) even proclaimed the end of history. He argued that market capitalism will be the sole surviving economic order until the end of mankind. In a rather similar fashion Diamond (2018) presented a theory that proclaimed that the course of history is to an overwhelming degree defined by our biology. This extended even to Marshall (2016), seeing topography as providing for the rising and failing. For instance, the rise of China escalating from around the millennium cannot be accounted for with theories of among others Fukuyama. It is especially, the rise of China and its growing competition with the US throughout the world that has highlighted grave differences in the respective economic systems of those rivalling two globally dominant nations (see Dow Jones, 28th of June 2019).

Overall, the economic systems of the US and most other Western societies differ from those of a number of other countries. Similar to the era of the Cold War both sides are convinced that their economic system is superior to the other one. This time the economic system of state capitalism competes with market capitalism. Countries such as China and Russia promote their politico-economic systems in foreign countries similar to market capitalist countries such as the US, Germany or Great Britain propagating their orders abroad. This becomes evident in Africa, where both sides seek to convince respective regimes of their economic system. In a number of instances, foreign aid is made conditional on adopting elements of the politico-economic order of the donour country.

Thus, a new rivalry between two politico-economic systems appears to emerge again. Market capitalism seems to be well analyzed and understood, since it has been in the focus of economists at least after Smith (1776) dealt with the "wealth of nations". But for state capitalism the literature appears to be rather scant. In the same vein, the entire concept of state capitalism is characterized by a high degree of fuzziness. It is one of the main aims of this study to increase clarity of what state capitalism is and how it differs from market capitalism.

First of all, it is essential to note that state capitalism is a global phenomenon with a number of commonalities among countries adopting this economic order. At the same time, structure, policies, but especially economic performance of this economic order differ significantly between the respective countries. This does not only relate to the growth rates of real gross domestic product (GDP), but also other development indicators such as income and wealth distribution, life expectancy, literacy, a health indicator such as infant mortality and poverty rates. This divergence could possibly be the outcome of variations in the economic orders of the respective state capitalist countries. So, the research question that is posed is the following: What is state capitalism and how can its significant performance differences be explained?

In the course of this study, before this question is tackled, there is subsequently a comparison of Russia and China as typical examples of state capitalism with widely diverging development trajectories. Afterwards antecedents of modern state capitalism are identified. For reasons of space looking back at prior forms of state capitalism will be done in a rather concise manner, but sufficiently comprehensive to underline that state capitalism is not a completely new phenomenon.

In order to seek for answers to the research question a theoretical basis is needed. Here elements of New Institutional Economics (NIE) are chosen. This is due to the fact that in state capitalism institutions play such a crucial role. In general, there are numerous rules and the respective economies are highly regulated. By the same token growth, or more generally development, hinge crucially on institutions. Since it is the aim of this monography to relate structures and policies to performance, an institutional approach is all the more warranted.

Generally speaking, state capitalism is far from a system with a minimalist or *Nachtwächter* state, where the corporate sector acts largely unconstrained. Markets do not work frictionless. Transaction costs are ubiquitous in economic systems, but tend to be even higher in state capitalism with its less perfectly functioning markets compared with market capitalism. In order for markets in state capitalist countries to function at all the state needs to provide the regulatory setting or order policy, but also intervenes into the economy quite frequently and significantly with process policy in the terminology of Eucken (1990). In order to analyze these rules and interventions it seems to be inevitable to apply an institutional approach.

For this purpose, different elements of NIE are applied. First of all, institutions need to be defined, but also their functions and their role in institutional change are of quintessential importance. Since the research question relates to performance and therefore development, it is essential to understand how institutions changed in the course of time. Performance differences appear to be at least partially the outcome of differences in institutional change.

After the introduction and the theoretical part, the next section deals with state capitalism itself from the viewpoint of previous literature. The state of research is illustrated. It will be shown, how state capitalism is looked upon in the literature. This entails different concepts of state capitalism. Numerous scientists have defined state capitalism differently and this includes the fact that they have placed divergent emphasis on central elements of state capitalism. After this comprehensive look into the literature, it becomes evident what state capitalism is in the eyes of different scientists. As becomes obvious by then, no scientist has so far stringently applied theoretical tools in order to analyze state capitalism. So far, no politico-economic model for state capitalism exists, let alone in an NIE setting.

Basic elements of NIE are then to be included in the subsequent models of market and state capitalism. Here the social order approach of North et al. (2009) with mature natural states as examples of models for state capitalism is integrated as well. In this regard, it will be argued that the relatively lower degree of the rule of law is the most evident difference between state and market capitalism when looking at the institutional framework. Based on this difference other key dissimilarities emerge, helping to explain how constituting factors differ from market capitalism. For reasons of juxtaposition a model of market capitalism is provided as well as a reference model and differences as well as similarities are highlighted.

This is one of the key aspects, where this study seeks to contribute to existing research. Based on a NIE approach it theoretically defines and explores the basic characteristics of state capitalism. Therefore, the constituting principles of state capitalism are to be identified, differences between state and market capitalism are observed and commonalities as well as cleavages of different variants of state capitalism are to be identified. Here such factors as market protection, innovativeness, state ownership and state financing are taken into account.

Concerning bureaucratic capacities and a penchant for industrial policy state capitalist countries differ from market capitalist ones, too. The same holds true in general for institutional divergences. But at the same time state capitalist countries allow for the coordination mechanism of the market with an acceptance of private property rights. These seven elements of state capitalism are to follow from the model of state capitalism. In this sense state is differentiated from market capitalism as well as socialism and thereby an insight should be gained, as to what state capitalism is in the reasoning of this study.

In a second step, with regard to significant performance differences among state capitalist countries, which have rather heterogenous structures, it should be established, how the respective forms of state capitalism are constituted. As mentioned above, it is the aim of this monography to give explanations as to why state capitalism worked in a number of countries and in a number of other countries obviously not. Here with regard to methodology a qualitative – interview-based –, grounded and comparative approach is chosen. In order to achieve this, it is first of all essential to build a taxonomy of different forms of state capitalism.[1] This taxonomy will be based on four constituting principles. As a matter of fact, this approach serves to increase the degree of the taxonomy's theoretical foundation, since the constituting principles are derived from the previously developed model.

It is a key goal of this project to develop a varieties of state capitalism proposal. In this regard, the seven constituting principles are applied to explore diverging structures and policies in respective state capitalist categories. In the end, typical archetypes of state capitalism shall be identified. In all probability, single state

1 Taxonomies are an essential and indispensable part of scientific work. In essence this refers to all fields of science. One relatively recent example is quantum physics, which ultimately only gained relevance and became the core pillar of modern physics after Gell-Mann (1996) at the end of the 1960s classified the myriads of elementary particles that had been detected in various experiments (Resag, 2017, 267–270). Thus, in economics it appears to be obligatory, to do research on a classification of state capitalism in order to establish this widely applied economic order in mainstream economics. That said, even in the world of fashion meticulous attention is given to categorize the textiles worn by models and every-day-people (Barthes 2010).

capitalist countries do not fit perfectly into one of the groups, but there is to be an evident proclivity for a country to plausibly fall into one of the categories.

After having differentiated state from market capitalism and developed a taxonomy, these concepts are to be applied to the real world. Therefore, it will be assessed, which countries among upper middle income countries of the World Bank Development Indicators are state capitalist and which ones are not. This approach is chosen for reasons of scope. Taking into account all countries of the world, would exceed the scope of this study by far. As a matter of fact, research (see for instance Bremmer 2010 and Kurlantzick 2016) hints to the fact that state capitalist countries are significantly overrepresented among middle income countries. Then, in an ultimate step based on the idea of different varieties of state capitalism the economic performance of separate state capitalist groups will be compared.

Thus far, there is a short-coming in the line of argumentation. The respective forms of state capitalism are derived from a number of figures and a first qualitative approach. These findings need to be substantiated through a more thorough input. For reasons of scope and space this analysis needs to be confined to a limited number of cases studies with countries from separate varieties of state capitalism. Here the four countries of South Korea from the 1960s to the 1990s, Singapore from the 1960s, Russia and Kazakhstan from the 1990s are chosen.

For this purpose, a qualitative approach for the latter two is chosen with the technique of interviews. A number of experts from both countries will be interviewed and thus a comprehensive picture of the form of state capitalism in those cases should emerge. Interviews clearly display perceptions and views. They are not molded into hard figures. This gives a qualitative analysis the reputation of being rather soft evidence. But overall agents tend to base their decisions on perceptions and views. Second, in a number of cases no documents exist, which refer for instance to bureaucratic quality, for example when it comes to corruption. Third, de jure rules often differ tremendously from how these rules de facto work. Since the trajectories of the developmental states of South Korea and Singapore are very well researched – some even say over-researched – an analysis of the literature is chosen for these two countries.

In the end, there should be four distinct case studies giving an in-depth analysis of those countries. This should pave the way for illustrating structural and policy differences among varieties of state capitalist countries and explaining their diverging development trajectories. Should this not be the case, it is obligatory to partially or entirely resort to different countries. Under the positive scenario this study will thus help to explain, which structural, policy and performance varieties exist in state capitalism and furthermore which elements of state capitalism are development-enhancing and which ones are not.

1.2 A Tale of two Countries

According to Fukuyama (1992) we have reached the end of history. Even according to less dramatic accounts, in our times we observe a certain tendency towards convergence of economic systems (see Streeck 2009, p. 161–162). Both arguments are at least debatable and will be put into doubt with the following tale of two state capitalist countries. In the subsequent section two state capitalist countries will be highlighted that both differ considerably from market capitalism. But China and Russia also differ in a lot of respects significantly from each other. Their similarities, but also their structural, policy and performance differences will be the subject of this section.

As a matter of fact, in some regards Russia and China display similar characteristics. Both emerged from a socialist system, which called itself communist and had no private ownership of the means of production. In effect, almost the entire corporate sector was state-owned. In both countries existed one-party rules by communist parties. Competition in the political field was limited to intra-party feuds and sometimes even purges. In the economic sphere competition was greatly inhibited, too. Indeed, a quota system was in place that constrained enterprises to fulfill certain production targets. Planning was key to the command economy. However, budget constraints – especially if politically well-connected enterprise managers were involved– tended to be soft, even in case of target failures. To exacerbate the problem the quota systems were manipulated in a lot of regards by politicians, bureaucrats and enterprise managers for personal gain.

As a result of ubiquitous inefficiencies, the call for institutional change in both countries became urgent towards the end of the 1970s. Nevertheless, change did not come about through structures constraining political leaders to pursue a certain policy approach. There was for instance no imminent economic or political urgency for Mikhail Gorbachev to embark on glasnost and perestroika when he came to power in 1985 (McFaul 2001). The institutional framework did not determine the initiation and even less the final outcome of institutional change. Change in the instances of both countries can be attributed to political leaders, Gorbachev in the case of the Soviet Union and Deng Xiao-ping in the case of

China. This serves as an important argument for an actor-centered approach in portraying the development trajectories of both countries.[2]

However, even though structures, policies and performances of both communist countries resembled each other initially, and in both cases institutional change was initiated by communist political leaders, in the course of history Russia and China developed very differently. In Russia Gorbachev simultaneously liberalized the economy up to a certain extent with the means of perestroika and allowed for political change through glasnost.[3]

China: Partial Liberalization of the Economy – Continuation of Autocracy in Politics

Deng opted for a different approach. He never questioned the one-party-rule of the Communist Party and quelled calls for democratic reforms, culminating in the massacre of Tiananmen square in 1989 during the student protests. Deng always defended the primacy of politics vis-à-vis the economic sphere and likewise the superiority of autocracy compared to democracy. Nevertheless, he increasingly allowed for private property rights, epitomized in his famous statement that it is glorious to become rich.

During his tenure and afterwards the structure of the corporate sector changed rapidly. While at first state-owned enterprises (SOEs), mostly in traditional industrial sectors such as coal and steel, dominated, gradually new politically well-connected players entered markets. In this regard, national champions even in high-tech-sectors were formed, where China utilized its comparative advantage of low labour costs versus industrialized nations.

Simultaneously, China improved on its bureaucratic capacities and capabilities. New agencies were formed, especially to regulate rapidly evolving markets such as financial and housing markets. This was also done in order to increase bureaucratic competence, for instance by creating a lead agency such as the

---

2 In a similar fashion Vennewald (1994, p. 10) argues that political developments and economic strategies depend on political and economic actors. Those who control the strategic resources of a society have a chance to put the country on an intended developmental trajectory.

3 Much has been written about Gorbachev's motives to allow for more political freedoms, especially freedom of speech. The most convincing argument is that with this approach he intended to use public opinion as a means to break resistance in the Communist party. In the end however, this very glasnost also swept him away from power as his adversary Russian president Boris Yeltsin became more popular (Treisman 2012).

State-owned Assets Supervision and Administration Commission (SASAC) for managing SOEs on behalf of the state council.

At the same time, the government allowed for more coordination among enterprises through business and sectoral associations. But this was mostly permitted for SOEs, whereas in the rest of the corporate sector there is a relatively low degree of organization among entrepreneurs. However, up to a certain extent the government sees advantages in delegating the costs of coordination to the business sector (Heilmann 1999). But until now there are no powerful business associations, which can act as an effective counterweight to decision-makers in Beijing.

However, this does not stifle China in constantly upgrading its industrial base and moving up the value chain by utilizing industrial policy through identifying strategic sectors, where the country wants to compete on world markets. With subsidies, access to cheap credits from state-owned banks in the official banking system and tax credits enterprises are guided into engaging in activities in sectors with a higher value-added. These moves are occasionally supported by strict regulations, favouring domestic enterprises over competitors from abroad.[4]

As a matter of fact, the government steers these strategic sectors effectively, but leaves national champions a certain leeway. In other non-strategic sectors, the government applies less regulation and conducts less formal as well as informal guiding. It also does not act as an enterprise-owner to the same extent as it does in strategic sectors.

Thus, in China the government allows for some private activities on markets. But especially in strategic sectors markets are highly regulated and also shielded from foreign competition. There rules a strong hand of the Communist government in strategic sectors such as high technology, steel, defense or telecommunication. By the same token, politically no organization or individual is allowed to challenge the supremacy of the Communist Party.

---

4 In this regard Beijing has recently selected batteries for electric cars as a strategic sector. Here, China applies rigorous methods to create national champions. In order to form world market leaders, Chinese policymakers virtually shut out globally leading foreign companies in battery technology such as Samsung and Panasonic from domestic markets. The Ministry of Industry and Information Technology in the same vein initiated a subsidy program for promoting domestic production of electric vehicles' main component, which according to analysts constitutes one of the key markets of the future (Wall Street Journal 2017).

Russia: Progressing from Gorbachev to Putin

Here, observers note a different developmental trajectory in Russia. Shortly after the first steps of Perestroika were undertaken in the Soviet Union, Gorbachev allowed for open discussions in the society about the economic and political course of the country. Gorbachev had a vision of democratic socialism, which he never sketched out in concrete terms. As a result, the government seemed to be in a constant mode of improvisation and even retreatment. This contrasts with China, where the government allowed for some economic experimentation, but never ceded any of its political powers (Heilmann 2011, p. 62).

The key problem for Gorbachev was always his indecisive stance concerning private property rights. Ideologically, he seemed to be strongly opposed to some entrepreneurs becoming rich. Therefore, he only cautiously liberalized the economy, starting with hybrid forms of private ownership such as cooperatives. As Gorbachev's reforms progressed, the standard of living of the population deteriorated instead of as promised by the reformers starting to improve. Moreover, centrifugal forces within the multi-ethnic Soviet Union started to endanger Gorbachev's reform agenda. In most of the 15 Soviet republics demands for independence became vocal, especially in the Baltics. In the end, in a certain sense Gorbachev had failed. Politically, he had initiated the dissolution of the Soviet Union. And economically he had to give in to radical reformers, propagating a shock therapy into market capitalism, which in structure and policies differed completely from his intended democratic socialism.

Under the new – now Russian – president Boris Yeltsin reformist Yegor Gaidar was assigned to usher in radical change for the economic system. Politically, Russia had become a democracy, even if very fragile, as demonstrated by the standoff between the Supreme Soviet and Yeltsin in 1993. Economically, a system emerged, which Russians themselves called "wild". Most parts of the corporate sector were privatized, even in natural resources. In a relatively short time-frame some individuals, the so-called oligarchs, thus became very rich. This led to tremendous discontent among the population, so that the successor of Yeltsin, Vladimir Putin, embarked on a course of renationalizing parts of the corporate sector and emphasizing the primacy of politics vis-à-vis the economic sphere.

Even under Putin there is a relatively high degree of concentration in the economy to be observed. Relatively large parts of the corporate sector are in the hands of a few oligarchs. As a matter of fact, still today the economy is very much dependent on natural resources, even though oligarchs by now also engage in retail, machinery or banking (see Treisman 2016). In contrast to China observers note more collective action among entrepreneurs, who in a number of cases use business associations as a means to protect themselves from property rights violations by the state or even by raiding from private sector competitors.

In terms of bureaucracy relatively low capabilities are identified. There are no pilot agencies and corruption is ubiquitous. This appears to be one of the reasons why industrial upgrading and diversifying away from natural resources has never been accomplished to as much of an extent as in China. Whereas in China national champions come from a number of industries – also in sectors high up on the value chain such as telecommunications, IT and defense – in Russia both national champions Gazprom and Rosneft do engage in the extraction and distribution of natural resources. A clearly discernible industrial policy with targets and potential subsidies is only slowly emerging in Russia, for instance with the projected innovation city Skolkovo south of Moscow. But so far whereas there existed a successful industrial policy in China, this was not the case in Russia.

The structural and policy differences of both countries also result in diverging performances. Whereas China has conquered export markets – even in finished goods – and is one of the most successful export nations of the world, Russia predominantly still relies on the export of its natural resources, being subject to fluctuating prices on world commodity markets. This has an effect on state budgets. In Russia tax revenues depend to a large extent on the world market oil price, whereas in China the economy is far more diversified and less vulnerable to asymmetric shocks. This diverging development trajectory is also evident when looking at economic growth rates. From 1995 to 2015 real gross domestic product in China increased on average by 9.5 percent per year. The corresponding value for Russia is just 3.1 percent.

Thus, while starting from relatively similar initial conditions both countries had a widely diverging development trajectory. This is possibly due to some key differences in their structural and policy frameworks. Obviously both countries lag behind industrialized nations – but also peer groups from other state capitalist countries – with regard to rule of law. But as a matter of fact, the state in China has managed to overcome resulting property rights and therefore incentive problems. This is not the case in Russia. Therefore, two countries have been illustrated that in their state capitalist systems vary significantly from market capitalism, but also from each other. This is another clear indicator to refute Fukuyama's claim of an end of history.

1.3 Antecedents of State Capitalism

Historically the term state capitalism has been an amorphous concept. A vast number of terms has been applied in order to analyze this phenomenon – from interventionist state to corporatism to orchestrated capitalism (Krug 2015, p. XIV). One author has even coined the phrase "neoliberal" state capitalism with regard to quantitative easing of the most important central banks after the financial crisis of 2008/09 (see Kellogg 2017, p. 56).

In 2011 economist Niall Ferguson rather provocatively proclaimed that "we are all state capitalists now" (Ferguson 2011, p. 1). He referred to bail-outs during the financial crisis of 2008/09 and China's economic rise. But is an overarching role for the state in the economic sphere indeed such a new phenomenon? This subsection illustrates that throughout history a number of state capitalist forms already existed.

To begin with, state capitalism can at least be traced back to the era of mercantilism prior to and during the times of Adam Smith.[5] Mercantilism indeed involved a prominent role for the state in steering the economy. The state regulated guilds and manufactories strictly. In a number of cases the state acted as owner and manager of enterprises. Where private enterprises gained a prominent position in the economy – such as the British East India Company – they were expected to pursue national goals besides pursuing the private interest of reaping profits. In this predecessor of state capitalism, a high degree of political control was exerted with little leeway for private entrepreneurs. This can to a great extent be attributed to a number of regulations, but also direct interventions by politicians and bureaucrats. Both factors tended to prevent enterprises from growing in size and reaping economies of scale. Lack of size was not only due to pre-modern technology.

The most – especially by Adam Smith (1776) – criticized aspect of mercantilism was its utter emphasis on maximizing the exports of goods in order to promote imports of gold, among others as a means to finance frequently occurring wars. This at the same time also served economic purposes. In general, the mercantilist state with the means of maximizing exports and minimizing imports – among others through deterring economic agents from utilizing

5 In our times, the supposedly state capitalist country China is regularly accused of applying mercantilist policies, especially in trade. Today no serious economist would term himself as mercantilist. The entire term "mercantilism" has become derogative. In this sense, referring to this formerly widely adopted economic order also serves as a severe accusation against state capitalists of modern times (see for instance Bremmer 2010).

import products –, pursued the goal of securing jobs on their home markets (Schneider 2012, p. 121). In this regard, the strong job-securing position of the mercantilist state resembled that of the Keynesian state. Whereas the former endeavours to promote its labour market through trade, the latter concentrates on deficit spending and more general to foster aggregate demand.

Since in mercantilism one country's loss of gold reserves was another one's gain, exchange between nations was seen as a zero-sum-game (Bremmer 2010, p. 39). The same reasoning prevailed with regard to the labour market, where promoting exports to the detriment of an import country was deemed to result in more jobs on the home market and the same net loss of jobs in the importing country. Economists of those times had not yet discovered the mutual benefits of trade in the form of welfare gains and comparative advantages, which became widely popular with the works of David Ricardo.

It is striking that mercantilism – especially in France – coincided with the emergence of absolutist, national states. This facilitated the strong position of the state in mercantilist economies. Some observers in this regard point to the fact that a number of modern state capitalist countries are ruled autocratically and not democratically (see below). Bremmer (2010, p. 41) argues that this state dominance over the economy resulted in a general disregard for economic principles such as consumer choice.

The mercantilist state was indeed characterized by an industrial policy, which in many ways resembled modern state capitalism and intentionally distorted prices. Thus, for instance in Prussia in the 18th century the state pursued an industrial policy defining for instance silk as a strategic sector, culminating in an import ban on silk worms. Much in the same vain, the iron ore industry in Silesia was defined as a priority and with investments by the state strongly supported. The same holds true for a ship wharf in Stettin or the company Splittgerber & Daum, which specialized on the sale and procurement of foreign armory. This company even obtained generous state contracts and was as a private company protected from competition. Furthermore, the state cooperated significantly with the private sector in some rudimentary forms of public private partnerships. Instruments of the Prussian state in its industrial policy were export subsidies, import duties and tax privileges. Some observers in this regard even complained about the lack of quality of products, for instance of a state-supported plant for watches. Such failures in investment were among others possible, since there existed a constant exchange between state and entrepreneurs. Some entrepreneurs for instance served in municipal councils, raising their voices as well as concerns and even government ministers occasionally conferred with these entrepreneurs.

Nevertheless, it needs to be maintained that the Prussian state with these means managed to form some internationally competitive industries, which otherwise would not have come into existence. It is doubtful, whether private agents would have had the economic resources to build an entire industry such as in iron ore. By initiating the creation of this industry, the Prussian state managed to crowd in private investments after a certain time lag had lapsed and thus many observers credit the Prussian state with having successfully industrialized sizable parts of its territory (Clark 2008, p. 201–206).

Even after the heyday of mercantilism state activism remained a central pillar in the world economy and even economic development. This became evident especially in the argumentation of German economist Friedrich List, who in the 19th century spoke out against laissez-faire capitalism and among others advocated the nurturing of infant industries in order not to fall further behind the leading national economy of Great Britain (Schneider 2012, p. 121). It is remarkable that even in the developmental phases of presumably strongly pro-market Great Britain and the US significant traces of state protection were evident (Chang / Rowthorn 1995, p. 4).

For instance, the US shielded its markets from foreign competition through relatively high tariffs. This was explicitly designed to abet the country in building up an own industrial base. The US initially was not able to compete with its former mother country in textiles – the cornerstone of early industrialization. Especially in textile machines domestic manufacturers had less capacity than British producers.

The US needed to build up domestic technology, so that it did not become dependent on imports of machinery and remain trapped in the position of a cotton exporter. In order to move up in the value chain US politicians adopted a trade legislation with tariffs of up to 25 percent. Congress also perceived an urge to such policies due to lower labour costs on the other side of the Atlantic. By the same token, tariff revenues served as a key source of income for the newly erected government. With this income important prerequisites for industrialization such as education were financed.

Even after its early industrialization phase the US did not abstain from applying policies, which resemble state capitalist measures, although they were termed differently. As a matter of fact, in times of crisis the United States repeatedly reverted to a strong position for the state, not least of all during the early New Deal under President Franklin D. Roosevelt in the 1930s (Skocpol / Finegold 1982, p. 255–278). Roosevelt for instance pushed through legislation providing for public works projects. Furthermore, he subsidized agricultural production and even enforced a number of trade measures. He also regulated the financial sector in a draconian manner and in discord with the opinion of liberal economists. Thus, the Glass-Steagall act – legislated in 1933 – in effect separated investment from deposit banks.

Socialism, which started with the October revolution in 1917, can be seen as another precursor of state capitalism.[6] Here the state is to own all means of production, so that no value added remains in the hands of private capitalists. With its overarching role for the state in the economy socialism has some parallels to state capitalism, but the latter – at least up to a certain extent – allows for private commercial activities, as will be seen later on.

In socialism planning is the key for the economy. Hierarchies and not markets are the accepted coordination mechanism. Large ministries determine production and consumption plans. Information is gathered by bureaucrats as opposed to private entrepreneurs, who in a Hayekian sense could possibly far better in a trial and error manner explore consumer demands. The sheer size of ministries and the general tendency to centralization lead to grave information losses. At the same time, the problem of asymmetric information between the state and private agents was never solved. As a matter of fact, the fall of socialism has proven that gradually the state was not able to control and steer the economy in an efficient manner. Prohibitively high welfare losses resulted and eventually communism collapsed.

Haynes (2011) categorizes the economic system of the former Soviet Union as state capitalist. In this regard Haynes emphasizes that in the Soviet economy exploitation of the working class existed to appropriate the surplus, as it occurs in the eyes of Marxists under every capitalist system (Haynes 2011, p. 40–42). But it was appropriated by the state, which in the eyes of Haynes consisted of a clique of self-interested socialist leaders, who accumulated personal wealth to the detriment of non-elites. At the same time, German economist Friedrich Pollock used the term "state capitalism" as an antithesis to Western capitalism, equating it with socialism (Pollock 1973, p. 1–45). Both authors disregard the fact that in state capitalism private enterprises are not outlawed and some value added always remains with the private sector. But this semantic divergence can at least in the case of Pollock possibly be accounted for through semantic changes in the course of history for the term state capitalism. As mentioned above modern state capitalism is no equivalent to socialism – neither semantically nor in content.

6 Here the author refrains from the term "communism", since it was a Marxian ideal, which as most observers claim was never realized and only on paper declared to have been achieved by Soviet leaders.

But evidently there is a degree of communism's legacy involved when looking at today's state capitalism. Thus, it is striking that a number of supposedly state capitalist systems such as in Russia and China emerged from communism. In a sense, the overarching role of the state under the former regimes facilitate the transition to a state capitalist system, which to a high degree still relies on planning for the corporate sector.

After the Second World War a number of East Asian Newly Industrialized Countries (NIC) adopted among the staunchest of all anti-communist rhetoric. But in reality, they relied to a significant degree on state intervention (Chang / Rowthorn 1995, p. 5). This so-called developmental state as it excelled among others in Japan, South Korea, Singapore and Taiwan achieved record economic growth rates and with its far-reaching industrial policy served as a model for other developing countries. All of these regimes relied on significant state ownership of the corporate sector as in most examples of prior forms of state capitalist policies. They took the role of an active state and pursued the goal of constant technological upgrading. These nations among others succeeded by relying on reverse engineering, emulating foreign technology from Western countries. With the passage of time many of these states became industrialized nations themselves.

As a matter of fact, state capitalism is by far no completely new phenomenon. Arguably, in the course of recent history some argue that in Europe France with the planification and Finland opted for state capitalism post 1945. This serves to illustrate the fact that the history of state capitalism would be a project on its own account. This overview is not intended to be comprehensive, but seeks to underline the fact that state capitalism is an economic order with a relatively long history.

All the mentioned historical forms of state capitalism share a high degree of state intervention into the economy – be it through direct state ownership, the enforcement of industrial upgrading or a restrictive trade policy. Therefore, it becomes evident that state capitalism has a number of antecedents in history. At the same time, even some parallels to socialism can be found. This introduction intended to give a clearer picture of the rather fuzzy phenomenon state capitalism with an overview, a comparison of state capitalist China and Russia as well as this abbreviated historical account. Now that a first insight into state capitalism has been presented, it should be possible to progress with a more in-depth analysis by modeling state capitalism. This will be done by utilizing the NIE.

2 Modeling State Capitalism

> *"In order to seek truth, it is necessary once in the course of our life, to doubt, as far as possible, all things."*
>
> René Descartes

Abstract

By now an overview of state capitalism has been given. But it is the aim of this study to understand state capitalism and explain its puzzling performance differences with the help of a theoretical framework. This will be presented below in the form of foundations of NIE. Subsequently, a more thorough look into the current state of the literature on state capitalism is taken. A model of state capitalism will be developed and, as a reference model, a model of market capitalism will be presented. This serves not only to differentiate state from market capitalism, but also allows for the creation of a taxonomy of state capitalism. This is a first step to understand performance differences in state capitalist variations. Finally, institutional change within, towards and away from state capitalism can be observed. These phenomena are addressed in the concluding section.

Keywords: New Institutional Economics, Literature on State Capitalism, Model of Market Capitalism, Theory of State Capitalism, Constituting Principles, Institutional Change

2.1 Fundamentals of New Institutional Economics

An institutional approach appears to be fruitful for analyzing politico-economic systems, because institutions are ubiquitous. Economic activity is to an utmost extent about economic exchange.[1] And reality reveals that this exchange almost never works frictionless. Transaction costs abound, i.e. the costs for searching, processing and monitoring contracts. Here institutions play a key role by having a significant impact on transaction costs. Especially in analyzing state capitalism it appears to be necessary to take institutions into account, because according to the third strand of literature dealt with below for the better or worse political

---

1 This exchange is according to the tenets of economics conducted by two utility or more concrete wealth maximizing individuals, thus the homo oeconomicus. Other sciences lean in marked contrast to this economic model for human exchange to the theoretical construct of homo ludens, who exchanges goods and services for the sole purpose of utility improvement. The outcome of the exchange does not matter to such an extent as for the homo oeconomicus, rather it is the mere fact of having established an exchange that matters according to this theory (see Huizinga 2004).

leaders of this economic system seek development as a goal. But likewise, without institutional change and a lowering of transaction costs no development tends to be possible.

Therefore, the emergence of NIE – initiated at first through the article "The Nature of the Firm" by Coase (1937) – served as a breakthrough for aligning economics more with reality. The first subsection lays the foundations for an institutional analysis. Subsequently, the functions of institutions are investigated. The last subsection addresses the important topic of institutional change.

2.1.1 Methodological Individualism, Bounded Rationality and Institutions

In order to progress with an institutional analysis, it needs to be clarified how actions of political and economic agents are shaped, i.e. whether they act and decide more as individuals or more as members of a social group. In this regard, the author will subsequently introduce the concept of methodological individualism, which is situated in the middle of both extremes. After having introduced methodological individualism and dealt with limitations in the computational faculties of economic agents, institutions will be defined as the smallest building block of the subsequent analysis.

Methodological Individualism

The theory of methodological individualism is considered to be the most successful doctrine in explaining social phenomena (Mantzavinos 2004, p. 3–4). It is most widely associated with the work of Karl Popper. He conceded that for individuals social conditioning as much as structural constraints are central. Therefore, no human being can act or even exist in a solipsistic setting. Individuals do not act atomistically, i.e. in an isolated way, but are embedded into phenomena such as culture, traditions, customs and habits. Their actions cannot be reduced to isolated motives which are completely loose from any social context. According to Popper there are shared collective beliefs and a degree of intersubjectivity (Di Iorio 2016, p. 357–359). Individuals therefore share common mental models so that it is clearly possible to form groups and engage in collective action.

But at the same time methodological individualism refutes the idea of social determinism. It denies that only social entities have a real existence and deserve to be endowed with original social essence (Di Iorio 2016, p. 355). Individuals can act autonomously without their actions being solely determined by their social background. In such a manner, it is possible to analyze individual bureaucrats and politicians rather than their organizations as relevant actors, maximizing their own utility (Stark 2012, p. 14–15). Moreover, such an approach makes it possible to look at bureaucrats and politicians in their social and even historical context and better understand how they form decisions.

Bounded Rationality

In order to make choices, institutions are essential. Likewise, in a perfect, frictionless functioning world, actors gather and process all relevant information for making best choices. No limits to their computational capacities exist. But reality clearly reveals that we can never digest all relevant information. There is so much informational input that we have to rationalize on relevant information. We assume that some information is necessary, some is not and some we are not even aware of. In such a way, we are bounded in our rationality (Simon / Egidi 1992). This also corresponds to methodological individualism, where tradition, customs and habits give economic agents an orientation in their choices. Besides methodological institutionalism bounded rationality is also postulated as an assumption for this study.

Consequently, individual actors make decisions without considering all information. But economists – whether from the neoclassical mainstream or NIE – tend to agree that in our intentions we are always rational. At the same time, we will not always have acted rationally, when we look back at the outcomes of our decisions, since we were not able to compute all relevant information. But overall, we generally strive to rationally maximize our own utility (Williamson 1985, p. 45).

Institutions

The entire political, economic and social intercourse in a given society is shaped by institutions, i.e. formal and informal rules including their enforcement characteristics (North 1990). Formal rules are usually established and enforced by the state, whereas informal rules like habits, conventions or customs gradually evolve within society mostly through private agents (Voigt 2009, p. 31). These rules are privately enforced. They cannot be altered abruptly, but transform only slowly. The state has no decisive levers to modify informal institutions (North 1990, p. 45).

Institutions can be understood either as the result of a game or as the rule of a game (Voigt 2009, p. 26). Some authors argue (for instance Schotter 1981) that institutions constitute regularity in social behavior, which all members of a society have agreed upon in recurring situations. According to this reasoning institutions are the outcome of interactions between members of society after for instance economic exchange took place. But such an approach does not explain how among others a constitution evolved which in its essence sets the rules for a playing-field, but is not a playing-field in itself.

Williamson (1985, p. 15) argues rather in the same vein, when he states that "firms, markets and relational contracting are important economic institutions". Here the outcome of an exchange may be in itself an institution as well. One example are negotiations between an employer and an employee that result in a work contract as the basis of any firm, which Williamson assumes to be the sum of numerous institutions.

In contrast to that North (1990, p. 73) sees firms as organizations. Likewise, they are not agglomerations of institutions, but in essence players acting within an institutional framework and not the result of interactions between various players. North also differs from Williamson's more micro-economic transaction cost approach by stressing the importance of enforcement. This is essential, since rules have no meaning in real life, if individuals choose not to comply with them. North (1990, p. 3) states, that "Institutions are the rules of the game in a society or, more formally, are the humanly devised constraints that shape human interaction (…) The rules and informal codes are sometimes violated and punishment is enacted" (North 1990, p. 3–4) This definition includes enforcement characteristics as well as incentives in human exchange.[2]

In much the same vein Mantzavinos (2004, p. 83) sees institutions as "normative social rules, that is, the rules of the game in a society, enforced either through law or (…) social control". In the following the definitions of North and Mantzavinos are utilized. This approach has the advantage of facilitating a clear analysis of human interaction as it occurs in state capitalist systems. The author thus avoids the danger of mixing outcomes with rules. There exists an institutional framework, in which politicians, bureaucrats and actors of corporate organizations act in order to maximize their utility. In this sense, formal and informal institutions are seen as exogenous in the short run and can for the most part be changed by individual actors or organizations only in the long run.[3] At the

2 Aoki (1996, p. 12) hints at the fact that institutions can also be self-enforcing. But this does not apply to all sorts of institutions, since in a number of cases actors maximize their utility by violating an institution, if it is not enforced privately or by the state.

3 Greif (2008, p. 14–15) adopts a game theoretic approach, where institutions are endogenous, among others since a significant number of them are self-enforcing and no third party enforcement is needed.

same time especially in game-theoretic settings institutions can be endogenized as much as institutional change (Aoki 2007, p. 1). Furthermore, enforcement is clearly included in the definition, which helps to better understand politico-economic developments in state capitalist countries. But for such an analysis it needs to be illustrated which functions institutions serve in the political and economic sphere, how they can enhance or inhibit growth and development.

2.1.2 Functions of Institutions

The primary function of institutions is to determine how goods or services are exchanged. This exchange is in the center of any sustained economic development. Only by exchanging productive factors as well as goods and services can a country reap the fruits of specialization, which is the essential conditio sine qua non for prosperity (North 2005, p. 72–73). In order to realize these benefits, institutions have to diminish expectation uncertainty. They need to stabilize expectations so that economic agents are confronted with an institutional framework that minimizes risks and therefore fosters incentives for specialization and investing (Voigt 2009, p. 25). Some formal as well as informal institutions ease exchange and lower transaction costs. They economize on transaction costs (Ahrens 2002, p. 58). Others inhibit exchange and therefore economic development. Overall, the developmental path a country follows is in this regard decidedly influenced by its institutions (North 1990, p. 107).

Orthodox neoclassical theory only sees the endowment of a country with the productive factors labour, capital and – according to recent research – human capital and technology as decisive. Adherents to the NIE do not deny that the output of an economy depends on the input of production factors. But in order to accumulate production factors, to increase productivity, and to initiate growth, institutions are of critical importance. At the same time, it does not suffice to raise massive inputs of production factors and let frictionless working markets provide for their efficient allocation as neoclassical economists recommend. Institutions shape the exchange of goods and services among economic actors. The more efficiently they function the more efficiently are production factors allocated.

It is the overarching function of institutions to ease economic exchange through a predictable business environment that allows for specialization.[4] But

4 Hall and Soskice (2001, p. 10–11) view the functions of institutions in a different manner. For them institutions serve to provide capacities for the exchange of

this overall function needs to be broken down into more operable sub-functions. Institutions have at least five specific functions: promoting the flow of information, securing property rights, fostering competition (World Bank 2002, p. 10), solving the problem of conflicts in society (Mantzavinos 2004, p. 83) and reducing violence by redistributing wealth (Greif / Iyigun 2013, pp. 3–4). These will now be dealt with in more detail.

First, adequate and sufficient information – such as the exact price and quality of a good – is important before an exchange takes place. If the contract partners are well informed a priori, the risk of welfare losses through deception is minimized. This holds true for contract enforcement a posteriori as well. Thus, the cost of transacting is relatively low compared to a situation with a paucity of information. Institutions can enable information flows in a number of ways. One example is their regulatory capacity to coerce all contract parties to faultlessly publish relevant information.

Second, institutions define and protect property rights. These are among others codified in patent laws, corporate governance, bankruptcy laws, auditing or financial reporting rules (Chang 2003, p. 83–91). In this regard, property rights have important incentive characteristics. Only if one party has a clearly defined title to a property, it can exchange this good without a high amount of frictions and possibly earn a profit. Formal and informal institutions set these titles. Thereby, institutions affect transaction costs. They can increase transactions costs, when economic activity, thus economic exchange, is dominated by economic actors being guided by the informal institution of opportunistic behaviour.

When economic actors operate in an institutional setting where opportunistic behaviour is prevalent, monitoring costs and thus transactions costs increase. But in this context, institutions can also have the development enhancing function to suppress opportunistic behavior (Ahrens 2002, p. 55). For instance, formal and informal institutions can increase the probability that the government hands over control and possession of an SOE to the management, when certain pre-defined innovation targets are fulfilled, to thereby keep a commitment made before.

Third, institutions can foster competition. Optimally they ease the entry and exit of market participants. Furthermore, they are able to provide for transparency on markets and establish the rules by which rival companies compete. One

---

information, monitoring behavior, sanctioning defections and assisting in encouraging actors to strive for collective action.

example is trademark protection law. A company is liable to deliver trademarks it promises to offer. Thereby competition is strengthened and entry into a market regulated. Companies then have fewer incentives to manipulate the market. If they violate market rules and deliver fake products, courts have the power to punish them. But as will be seen later on state capitalist governments manipulate markets by limiting entry and are thereby inhibiting competition. Nevertheless, this served as an effective tool of industrial policy, for instance to upgrade the industrial base. Therefore, if these institutions do not serve the function of increasing competition, this does not have to be development inhibiting.

Fourth, social conflicts are ubiquitous in society. They emerge when the utility of one individual is dependent on cooperative behaviour of other members of society. If constantly conflict resolution was lacking in society, individuals would be solitary and forms of exchange are regularly inhibited. Institutions tend to solve this problem by defining general normative patterns, which the majority of individuals complies with (Mantzavinos 2004, p. 87–88). Note that this corresponds to the theory of methodological individualism where shared mental models are essential for cooperation.

Fifth, institutions provide for income and wealth redistribution. Not only in moral, but also in purely economic terms this is an important sub-function. Redistribution can foster risk-taking and thereby innovative activities since economic agents thereby acquire a safety net, which supports them in case their enterprise fails (Greif / Iyigun 2013, p. 2) Furthermore, if vast parts of the population felt excluded from the rewards of economic development, the risk of violence would increase. The eruption of massive social unrest would ceteris paribus significantly increase transaction costs and reduce economic performance.

In a nutshell, institutions can render business environments more predictable and thereby promote development by facilitating economic exchange. This is a result of their ability to ease information flows, define as well as protect property rights, strengthen competition, solve social conflicts and redistribute wealth.

2.1.3 Institutional Change

If certain institutions serve growth and development enhancing functions, why do many countries stay poor and not utilize these formal and informal rules? To begin with, an encompassing theory of institutional change, which could also be applied in the real world, is probably impossible. People, i.e. actors, matter and consequently structures do not predetermine the trajectory a country takes (see Jackson 2009). In the end choices by political leaders tend to initiate institutional change and are not fixated by the institutional framework that the actor is confronted with at the outset of his tenure. Individuals will always have a considerable degree of discretion in their choices. Therefore, deterministic theories of institutional change are unrealistic (Mantzavinos 2004, p. 94). Second, institutions have a tendency towards hysteresis. Changing institutions entails relatively huge efforts with all the related costs of collective action. Even if formal institutions can virtually be changed ad-hoc, the impact is often weakened by the persistence of conflicting informal rules, which are far more difficult to alter. This leads to some form of path dependence, where decisions and developments in the past lock in future institutional frameworks. In such a manner, inefficient institutions can persist, although a different institutional arrangement would be more development enhancing (North 2005, p. 51).

Therefore, the flexibility of an institutional setting, i.e. its capacity to change, is an important determinant of economic growth.[5] New political or economic developments might necessitate a modification of rules. These developments could be technological, for instance the dawning of the Internet, as well as political such as alterations in the preferences of broad layers of the population or of belief systems among the elites.

Explanations of Institutional Change

Overall, institutional change can be explained through economic, socio-political and historical institutionalism. Another strand in the literature deals with legitimacy (Gilley 2008, p. 259–260). Organizations as well as individuals initiate change and in some cases even create institutions. For instance, organizations of the state such as ministries, agencies or the parliament explicitly formulate or even pass and enforce laws. At the same time, private organizations such as enterprises actively participate in setting institutions. An example is a company lobbying for new export subsidy rules. In this regard organizations are agents of institutional change (North 1990, p. 73).[6] They become a set of players within

5 In a way this creates a target conflict, since changes increase uncertainty, which in the short term tends to inhibit exchange and specialization as shown above (Voigt 2009, p. 226).

6 In an earlier work North (1981, p. 31–32) postulated that for reasons of the free rider problem institutional change will more likely come from above, since constituents due to their large number have little incentive to organize themselves in order to change the institutional framework. This corresponds to the actor-centered approach chosen in this study, where mostly political leaders initiated political change, for instance with the goal to have their respective countries embark on a developmental path. North, however, gives a caveat. Institutional change in a number of instances is possible from below

an institutional framework (Aoki 1996, p. 9). However, political leaders can also alter institutions, even setting a country on a new institutional path.

First, institutional change can take place in an economic market-oriented fashion. Institutions entail costs and benefits in very much the same way as typical economic goods. In short, an institution has a relative price when compared to another institution. In a politico-economic environment, where there is competition, state organizations for example choose the institutions with the lowest relative price. Otherwise politicians face defeat at the ballot box, since they have not acted rationally and not chosen the institution with the lowest relative price. In general, in this setting state or private organizations have an incentive – for instance re-election or higher profits – to optimize rules (North 1990, p. 78). In essence in this case the market laws of supply and demand dominate. If the demand for a modified or new institution rises, organizations will strive to provide for this supply. This has the characteristics of a market-induced institutional change. Efficient outcomes are guaranteed as long as there is perfect competition in the political and economic market. Naturally market failures have to be ruled out, for instance a lack of free elections in political markets. There needs to be a competitive liberal democracy without rent-seeking and lobbying.

Second, in a socio-political setting, where an uncompetitive environment prevails, organizations can have an incentive to modify rules regardless of their relative prices. The reason can be vested interests, such as rent-seeking. There are no market forces to rectify such a decision. In this environment, charismatic leaders of powerful organizations can occasionally alter formal institutions more or less singlehandedly. In these respects, interests and belief systems – they can be called perceptions as well – of a group or its leaders play a significant role and shape institutions (North 2005, p. 6 and 49–50).

These perceptions can change in reaction to an alteration in relative prices. Institutional change might then have the same results as under a competitive market environment. But in a number of cases belief systems are independent of relative prices and are altered through social factors.[7]

---

owing to ideology. Constituents are sometimes willing to make significant sacrifices without adequate chances of being rewarded for them, among others in a pecuniary form, for the purpose of supporting the cause of a certain ideology.

7 According to Mantzavinos (2004, p. 98) only the first two factors – economic and ideological – mentioned above motivate institutional change. He appears to overlook historical factors and change through legitimacy problems.

Third, in a historical approach at critical junctures in the path of a country institutional change tends to be facilitated. At such a juncture state and society perceive to be stalled. For instance, possibly, economic performance has considerably weakened, there is a crisis in the political leadership or societal forces critically threaten regime survival, for instance through mass protests. At these moments, where rigidities of the political and economic system are weakened, political leaders can more easily steer their nations on a preferred course.

This is an actor-centered approach for initiating institutional change at critical junctures. Eventual success of relevant actors hinges on a number of factors. As a matter of fact, for political leaders it seems to be impossible to shape and implement a new institutional framework against the preferences of a majority of the elites. Therefore, elites must up to a certain extent be embedded into the decision-making. After all, for the elites, power, i.e. political influence, and economic rents are at stake. Since in a number of instances certain elite members constitute veto players, their support needs to be garnered.

This can possibly be accomplished by credibly committing to installing a new institutional framework, where veto players of the elites receive sufficient economic rents to approve for instance of a new politico-economic system. Likewise, veto players will strive not to lose political power after such a new politico-economic system is installed. As in the case of rent distribution political leaders need to commit to heeding the interests of these elite veto players. Such commitments can consist of unequivocal public statements, elevation into powerful positions of persons clearly defending interests of veto players or safeguards in the country's constitution (see McFaul 2001).

Fourth, institutional change tends to occur, when the state suffers from a legitimacy crisis. Similar to a situation at critical junctures, especially poor economic growth and development, lack of stability and failure of granting political as well as civil rights can be highlighted (Gilley 2008, p. 271). Referring to the first point in fast growing emerging economies authoritative regimes in a number of cases guaranteed their political survival through sufficient economic performance. "Shared growth" – i.e. economic gains that are divided among broad layers of society – can support legitimacy. Therefore, economic growth can overcome a lack of stability and compensate the population for significant short-falls in political as well as civil rights.

Here it is clearly visible that institutional change can be the driving force to embark on a developmental phase. In all four state capitalist case studies dealt with below the emergence of a state capitalist system played a significant role in initiating a developmental phase. State capitalism is seen by a number of political leaders as a model for developing their respective countries.

From limited to open access Orders

Before this sub-section is concluded a model for a specific kind of institutional change is presented. It concerns the transformation from a so called limited to an open access order in the terminology of North et al. (2009). Here the social order is transformed from a situation, where the state limits access to political and economic resources for vast parts of the population to a system, where there is a minimum degree of participation in political and economic decision-making. According to North et al. (2009, p. 151) three doorstep conditions need to be fulfilled in order to realize such a transformation. First of all, the system needs to have become sufficiently depersonalized, i.e. organizations need to live perpetually and not depend on the existence of one or a number of individuals. Second, there needs to be consolidated control over the military. Third, the rule of law for elites needs to have been enacted.

According to North et al. (2009, p. 151–154) these conditions need to exist for achieving a transformation to an open access order. To begin with, only perpetually lived organizations can guarantee the durability of the state. They enable impersonal exchange on political and economic markets, which is essential for access of political and economic agents to resources. By a consolidated control of the military (or police), foremost through the defense (or interior) ministry, it is guaranteed that not one fraction of the state usurps the state monopoly on violence, i.e. the right to use physical force. Such a development would be inconsistent with a general open access to political power, when not even the state monopoly on violence is explicitly in the hands of a civilian government. Lastly, rule of law for elites is necessary in order to regularize behavior of relevant elite players and bound them to rules. This guarantees sustaining relations among elite players for long-term time horizons. Again, this facilitates impersonal exchange and therefore open access.

If all three door-step conditions were fulfilled, the state could progress from a limited to an open access order. But this is no natural, pre-determined process. When the conditions are fulfilled, political leaders may have an option, but no constraint, to install an open access order. But in order to for instance draft a new constitution, political leaders with their specific belief systems need to prefer such a system. Likewise, pressure from below through discontent among the population can support or even initiate such a transformation.

By now, NIE foundations have been laid in the form of defining institutions, their functions have been expounded on and institutional change been dealt with. As a result, it can be maintained that institutions do matter and an institutional analysis of state capitalism is warranted, since especially in this economic order institutions facilitate or hamper economic development. This analysis appears to be most fruitful with an actor-centered approach, which is conducted in a comparative fashion. The reason is that first of all actors, which tend to be political and economic organizations as a whole as well, shape the institutional framework and thereby the economic trajectory a country takes. Second, by comparing different countries with diverging institutional frameworks it can more easily be concluded, why nations differed in their economic performances. Overall, the theoretical groundwork laid in this section serves as the building block for creating a model of market and one of state capitalism. But first of all, in the subsequent sub-section the existing literature about state capitalism is discussed.

2.2 State Capitalism in the Literature

In this subsection it is illustrated how state capitalism is defined in the literature.[8] As a matter of fact, the literature is remarkably reticent as to how state capitalism emerged as such a force spanning emerging economies around the world (see for instance Nölke et al. 2014, p. 9–20).[9] At this stage in this study it will first be

8 In essence it is differentiated here between three strands of state capitalism in the literature. But as a matter of fact, a fourth strand can be identified. Since it is underrepresented in the literature it is only briefly dealt with in this footnote. As a matter of fact, repeatedly state capitalism has been equated with socialism (see for instance Pollock 1973, p. 1–45). According to German economist Alfred Wagner the latter consists of a nationalization of production enterprises, price controls instead of freely fluctuating prices and a redistributive taxation policy (Wagner 1894, cited from Pollard 2011, p. 3). Although these policies are occasionally applied in state capitalism and – rather as an exception – even used in market capitalism, these socialist interventions do not characterize capitalist systems.

As a matter of fact, in state capitalism nationalization and price controls are not applied throughout all sectors of the economy. Admittedly, companies are regularly brought under state control. But in state capitalist countries numerous privately held enterprises remain. Concerning redistribution of income and wealth, the tax system in state capitalism clearly intervenes into the financial funds of its people. Nevertheless, this does not necessarily result in a significant redistribution. However, some researchers refer to a phenomenon of welfare-state capitalism (Vallier 2019).

9 One reason for the emergence of state capitalism might be seen in colonialism. Kohli (2004, p. 17-18) argues that colonialism established a direct political control, which developing countries could build on to form state-led economies. This resulted in the formation of sizable bureaucracies. But the effects were widely different as shown by

dealt with definitions, which see state capitalism foremost as a system, where the state acts as an owner. Subsequently, approaches are presented that stress the government's interventions and especially its alleged inefficiency, domination of markets and rent-seeking. Finally, concepts of state capitalism are shown that combine state ownership with its policies vis-à-vis the corporate sector.

State Ownership as the Core Characteristic

In essence, the first strand of literature about state capitalism underlines the central role of State-owned Enterprises (SOEs). Over the last decade, the number of SOEs among the largest companies of the world has indeed increased significantly (Clo et. al. 2017, p. 61). These companies usually follow so called double bottom lines. On the one hand they strive to generate profits, especially when private investors hold ownership shares as well. Naturally, the state as an investor is interested in obtaining such returns, too, for instance in order to finance governmental tasks. But on the other hand, the state can pressure SOEs into forgoing profits to the advantage of employees and consumers, i.e. political supporters and potentially voters. Some states therefore force SOEs to keep wages above market rates or prices below market equilibrium for political purposes.

"Lacking the pressure of market investors toward profitability SOEs can be more effectively used as a source ... to meet the political objectives of governments and politicians" (Musacchio / Lazzarini 2012, p. 26). Very much in the same way observers stress inefficient operation of SOEs by the state, a penchant for corruption and frequent corporate losses (Huat 2016, p. 499). Clo et. al (2017, p. 62) contend that SOEs pursue non-commercial and political interests, are involved in anti-competitive activities and create economic distortions on the global level. Likewise, Guriev (2018, p. 115) even argues that bureaucrats supervising failing SOEs have an incentive to keep those companies solvent opposed to privatization and a recognition of the loss. In the latter case the bureaucrats would have to acknowledge their own failure, with all the ensuing sanctions by the state. As a result, the status quo is upheld and therefore competitive advantages of SOEs against private companies persist.

But apart from these rather critical accounts authors describe SOEs as the central pillar of state capitalism. Some researchers even contend that under the specific conditions of state capitalism SOEs tend to perform better than privately

---

Kohli's case studies of South Korea, Brazil, India and Nigeria with partially widely differing developmental outcomes.

held companies (see Estrin et al. 2019). In the case of China that can be attributed to favourable treatment of SOEs by the state (Li et. al. 2018). Kurlantzick (2016, p. 9) calls a country state capitalist, if the "government has an ownership stake in or significant influence over more than one-third of the five hundred largest companies by revenue". Musacchio / Lazzarini (2012, p. 4) do not go so far as to specify concrete numbers, but see state capitalism in two alternative modes: "Leviathan (i.e. the state, A. W.) as a majority investor and Leviathan as a minority investor".[10] Thus in accordance with Kurlantzick they define state capitalism as a system, where the government owns significant shares of the corporate sector.

Schneider (2012, p. 123) applies a rather different definition. He broadly sees state capitalism as a system, where the state directly or indirectly becomes an entrepreneur and tends to favour certain groups of companies. Therefore, Schneider does not take de jure ownership into account, but looks at the de facto role of the government in acting as an entrepreneur. Consequently, it becomes obvious that Schneider is going one step further than Kurlantzick and Musacchio/ Lazzarini and also looks at governmental action which he characterizes as arbitrarily favouring certain corporate entities. But in general Schneider also concentrates on the ownership role of the state.

Referring explicitly to state capitalism in China Liebman / Milhaupt (2016, p. XIV) both observe a direct state participation in the economy especially assisted by SOEs. Markets and corporations are utilized, but with a non-democratic governance structure. While these authors avoid concentrating solely on ownership in their definition – just as Schneider does –, they see SOEs as the core of state capitalism. Furthermore, they also allude to a non-negligible role of markets in state capitalism which is an important enhancement to other definitions. Also, in the context of state capitalism Clo et. al. (2017, p. 62) argue that SOEs can overcome under-investment by private companies, since these are more exposed to the risks associated with high start-up costs, uncertainty as well as adverse borrowing conditions on underdeveloped financial markets.

At the same time, it remains an open question whether state capitalism can indeed be democratic as Liebman / Milhaupt explicitly refute in their definition. Kurlantzick for instance differentiates between dictatorial state capitalism as in China or Russia and democratic state capitalism as in Brazil or India.

---

10 In the same direction, Lin (2017, p. 107–108) asserts that the state in China pursues the goal of a mixed-ownership economy, in principle meaning a preference for partial privatization. China hopes to accompany such a trend with a professionalization of management in these companies, i.e. for instance more performance-based remuneration.

To sum it up, all four definitions differ from each other up to a degree, but they all place SOEs in the center of state capitalism. The following definitions, although far from neglecting the relevance of SOEs take a different and partially more critical look at state capitalism.

State Interventions as the defining Characteristic

Whereas economists such as Kurlantzick and Musacchio / Lazzarini define state capitalism in relatively neutral terms with an overarching degree of state ownership, other approaches focus more on political motives and governmental measures. In such a direction points the most often cited definition of Bremmer (2010, p. 23): "It is a form of bureaucratically engineered capitalism particular to each government that practices it. It's a system in which the state dominates markets primarily for political gain."

This definition entails four distinct statements about the nature of state capitalism. First, measures, which the state applies are bureaucratic, obviously meaning a hierarchical fashion as opposed to market-based solutions. Second, Bremmer is more explicit than Kurlantzick and Musacchio / Lazzarini in broadly assuming state dominance of markets. As will be shown later on there are varieties of state capitalism, where the government hardly intervenes at all into certain markets. Thus, economists should treat this assumption with caution. At the same time, Bremmer points out that the type of intervention into the corporate sector could create problems such as rent-seeking. Some interventions such as pursuing a complicated licensing regime for imports and exports proved to be inefficient and burdensome for the corporate sector. But as a number of developing countries especially in East Asia illustrate, the degree of intervention as such poses no growth and development limiting factor. In general, what counts is not so much the quantity as far more the type and quality of interventions (Kohli 2004, p. 377)

Third, the motive of politicians is postulated as being political gain, for instance to avoid being unseated. This point is at least debatable, since motives are often disguised and also not clearly measurable. But possibly he just emphasizes the obvious, as is also assumed for market capitalist countries: With their economic policies politicians as a rule strive for re-election in democracies and avoiding to be toppled from power in dictatorships.

But even this could possibly be a false assumption, since some politicians might maximize their own utility function by striving for aims such as national welfare, national unity or more broadly economic development and thereby might even risk their political survival. Nevertheless, even if pure political gain was the motive of leaders in state capitalism economic development could be supported. In a number of state capitalist countries there exists incentive compatibility in a form that leaders who maximized their own utility, i.e. political gain, also pursued growth and development enhancing policies. National goals and objectives of personal utility maximization were compatible. For instance, this can be the case if the tax base increases in unison with the achievement of national development goals such as poverty reduction.

Fourth, Bremmer underlines the particularity of each state capitalist case. This is a valuable contribution to research about state capitalism, since countries such as Brazil, Russia or China – although economists call all of them state capitalist and they show a number of similarities with regard to their economic system – represent very unique varieties of state capitalism. As a matter of fact, in this study it is sought to illustrate the differences and similarities between and of state capitalism in Russia, Kazakhstan, Singapore and South Korea in the course of this study.

Based on the research of Bremmer, Aligica and Tarko define state capitalism as "a paradigmatic example of a rent-seeking society". Accordingly, with the assumption of being similar to mercantilism state capitalism is deemed to be better understood as a rent-seeking society than as any other alternative model (Aligica / Tarko 2012 p. 55–56). Bremmer's motive of state capitalist leaders' striving for "political gain" is consequently enlarged to mean rent-seeking, i.e. seeking to increase one's wealth without creating new wealth. This corresponds to the detrimental consequences of rent-seeking on the economy as postulated by economist Anne Krueger (Krueger 1974, p. 291–303). Obviously, some state capitalist countries display a high degree of rent-seeking in the form of corruption. This becomes evident when looking at rankings of Transparency International. But this reasoning overlooks that there are other examples, which during their developmental phases were far less marked by rent-seeking.

In a later paper Aligica / Tarko (2014, p. 169) differentiated between state and crony capitalism. They equate crony capitalism with a rent-seeking society and define as the legitimating basis for this economic order stealth behavior by deception by privileged groups and politicians. The ideological basis is populism, helping to overcome legitimacy deficits. At the same time both authors see state capitalism as relatively stable and in a position to utilize efficient rule by experts combined with the ideology of nationalism.

At the same time Baumol et al. (2007) assume that state capitalist leaders aim to extract wealth and other benefits from industries and firms. Furthermore, according to these authors those leaders take a position that centrally administered policies for allocating resources are best to maximize economic growth (Baumol et al. 2007, p. 63). As opposed to prior more neutral definitions here politicians are characterized as engaging in kleptocratic activities in order to enrich themselves or elites which support them. Again, such an observation is adequate for some forms of state capitalism, but not every single state capitalist country. Therefore, the position of Baumol et al. conflicts with Bremmer's principle of particularity.

Relevance of Development in State Capitalism

The previous two strands of literature illustrate two diverging views about state capitalism. The first in principle equates state capitalism with significant state ownership. Then the second puts more of an emphasis on governmental action in state capitalism, which is seen as consisting among others of political gain, market dominance, rent-seeking or even wealth extraction.

In marked contrast Ahrens et al. (2016) combine a factual description of state capitalism's elements with state interventions. In their approach state capitalism does not only consist of SOEs, but also allows for small private businesses. Nevertheless, the state does not allow markets to pick winners or losers for investing. In many ways politicians and bureaucrats claim superior judgment vis-á-vis markets. Much in the same direction the state allows for no indelible commitments to multinational corporations (MNC) and international banks. (Ahrens et al. 2016, p. 8). In a certain sense the state thereby defends its autonomy against pressure from MNC or the international banking community, but might risk being captured by the local private sector.

Furthermore, the state does not allow its currency to fluctuate freely. At the same time the state strongly restricts off-shoring and tax avoidance. Nevertheless, state capitalist countries are integrated into a globalized world economy and do allow funding of the corporate sector and even the state itself with finances from abroad. In many cases minority shares are listed on stock exchanges (Ahrens et al. 2016, p. 8).

This description of state capitalism stresses the state's role of providing a framework for the economy. It is also reminiscent of Rodrik's argumentation that the state can act to overcome coordination failures in the economy (Rodrik 2007, p. 27). This occasionally corresponds to the state reserving the right for itself to pick industries, which can compete on world markets. This clearly hints at the role of the state in a number of state capitalist countries to embark on a developmental phase. Such a reasoning is taken up by Taylor (2014, p. 342). He also alludes to the state as a chief owner applying a degree of central planning, but he then emphasizes the role of the state as formulating and implementing national goals through long-run economic development.

In this sub-section three approaches towards state capitalism have been presented. As a matter of fact, not one of them utilized a theoretical framework such as the NIE foundations presented above. Therefore, subsequently there will be a model of state capitalism presented below to fill a gap in the literature, culminating in the formulation of seven constituting principles of state capitalism. In order to have a reference model to compare with state capitalism, a model of market capitalism is at first created in the following sub-section.

2.3 Market Capitalism as a Reference Model

In this sub-section a model of market capitalism is created based on the works of Hodgson (2015) and Eucken (1990). The model is solely intended to be used as a benchmark for a comparison with state capitalism.

Market Capitalism dates back at least to the times, after Adam Smith published "The Wealth of Nations" in 1776. And indeed, there is a huge amount of literature about market capitalism (see for instance Amable 2003, Hodgson 2015, Hall / Soskice 2001, Eucken 1952/1990, Smith 1776/1910, Marx 1993, Aoki 2003, Aoki 2013, Schumpeter 1942). In the course of history market capitalism has changed its form repeatedly and by now we can observe "varieties of capitalism" with liberal and coordinated and other types of market economies (Hall / Soskice 2001)[11]. But nevertheless, it is possible and useful to discern key elements of market capitalism and how these interact with each other.

To begin with, the most basic approach in identifying market capitalism consists of referring to the existence of private property rights and markets. Furthermore, it is of importance to analyze how these elements interact with each other, for instance how the coordination mechanism works. Basically, market capitalism is grounded on the interplay of enterprises, players of the financial system, which is at least partially in private hands, political organizations and the state together with the existence of rule of law, open markets and a functioning price system.

---

11 Amable (2003, p. 172–173) even differentiates between five different models of capitalism: market-based capitalism, Asian capitalism, Continental European capitalism, Social-democratic capitalism and Mediterranean capitalism. For reasons of simplicity the author will not enlarge on this complex variety, but restricts himself to common characteristics of all forms of market capitalism. By the same token, Whitley (1999) presents six different national business systems of capitalism.

In the center of any market capitalist system stands a legal system, which guarantees the rule of law, secures private property rights as well as transfer of these rights (Hodgson 2015, p. 259). Naturally, the legal system is in public hands, so that the state plays a crucial role as the enforcer of institutions even in the most liberal market economies.[12] At the same time the state should not be seen as a single entity. It is made up of numerous individuals, who occasionally pursue conflicting goals. But in general, for reasons of simplicity the state is subsumed under its three powers government, parliament and judiciary. Apart from this the bureaucracy is taken into account as an autonomous actor. This appears to be permissible even though strictly speaking bureaucrats are part of the government – after all the bureaucracy implements government policy and typical agency problems ensue.

In this regard, the state serves as a guarantor of the rule of law and actively shapes it. Through this third-party enforcement of institutions, the state transforms economic possession, which has no legal ownership title, into secure legal property rights (Hodgson 2015, p. 103).[13] Rule of law is based on formal and informal institutions as much as formal state organizations such as courts. Doubtlessly, the rule of law is a key pillar of market capitalism, since it creates property that can be exchanged on markets. It can be seen as a development enhancing institution fostering expectations certainty. Evidently without rule of law no open markets could exist. Markets do not emerge out of nowhere, but with the help of an institutional framework (Aoki 1996, p. 3). Since problems such as asymmetric information are prevalent, markets also need to be regulated, which is one of the

12 At this point it needs to be clarified that in the literature the role accorded to the state has undergone tremendous changes. Liberal economists in the 19th century preferred a Nachtw ächterstaat that only focused on providing for the judicial system and national defence. With the rise of Keynesianism post World War II the state was supposed to intervene into the economy and for instance foster growth by deficit spending. When the states came close to being overburdened with debts and inflation rates soared, the pendulum swung in the other direction and neoliberalism gained ground in academia. Since then there is a counter movement to be observed, where economists increasingly plead for an activating state, which gives impulses and occasionally even acts as an entrepreneur in cases of market failure, but seeks not to crowd out private economic actors.

13 There is a number of economists, who criticize Hodgson for this distinction. They claim that legal property rights are not a necessary condition for the existence of economic property rights (see Barzel 2015, p. 719–723).

state's primary functions. In such an institutional framework, the functions of institutions dealt with above can be fulfilled.

Constituting principles of market capitalism

Here the constituting principles by Eucken (1990) are a useful benchmark for understanding market capitalism beyond referring solely to markets and property rights. These are open markets, primacy of monetary policy and price level stability, liability rules, contractual freedom, private property rights, and the steadiness of economic policies. Regulating principles, needed to maintain the market order, include institutions for social security, anti-trust policy and institutions for a correction of external effects. All of these factors guarantee in Eucken's theory the core principle of market capitalism, i.e. a functioning price mechanism with flexibility and adaptability. In this regard the market capitalist system, indicates the relative scarcities of goods and services. In an ideal world, this allows for an efficient allocation of production factors and enables markets to find an equilibrium.

Regarding open markets the state in market capitalism guarantees that commercial exchange can be impersonal. That means in general the exchange is not bound to one individual as such. Buyer and seller have not to be known to each other. This allows enterprises to reap advantages of scale. Likewise, Eucken sees monetary policy as essential, so that the purchasing power of the currency is maintained. Inflation is a constant risk, which needs to be subdued. According to Eucken without a minimum of macro-economic stability no market capitalist system can function.

Liability rules, contractual freedom and the existence of private property rights can all be related to the central role of rule of law as postulated to be the core constituent of market capitalism by Hodgson. Ultimately, rule of law grants economic agents all of those three rights. First of all, for incentive reasons economic agents in market capitalism are at least partially liable for their actions, so that in case of solvency problems creditors are up to a certain extent reimbursed. But at the same time economic agents also need to be able to reduce their commercial risks. As a matter of fact, creation of limited liability, for instance in the form of stock companies, was one of the key factors for promoting capitalism after the industrial revolution. This alleviated the risk of business failure without eliminating it, fostered economic development and remains a key characteristic of market capitalism until today.

Second, contractual freedom and secure property rights are a conditio sine qua non for the existence of open markets. Without clearly defined title to a property an economic agent is in no position to exchange his good on the market. Naturally, such an exchange would require the state to allow for contractual freedom, so that a buyer has the freedom of choice to in principle sell to whomever he intends to. Both constituents are pillars of open markets and thereby correspond to one of institutions' key functions mentioned above, i.e. enable exchange as the basis for specialization and therefore economic development.

By the same token, economic actors in market capitalism have another safeguard in commercial activities. They can rely on a relatively high degree of steadiness in economic policy. The judicial system prevents the state even under changes of government from sudden policy turns.[14] This stability is one of the key advantages of market capitalism, since economic actors do not have to incur high costs for hedging against sudden policy changes. As illustrated above, this is in direct correspondence with one of the core functions of institutions, i.e. diminishing expectations uncertainty.

At the same time, a minimum of social security is guaranteed for market participants. As a matter of fact, the state does not tolerate all forms of market outcomes. Through social policy the market capitalist state ensures that poverty among its citizens stays below a certain threshold. This formal institution – abetted by the informal institution of empathy – allows for a minimum of social stability. Correspondingly, it increases a propensity to take risks, which is essential for all commercial activities. If for instance an entrepreneur fails with his enterprise he still is entitled to receive certain social security benefits. In this regard, he has a social safety net. The lack of utter poverty through a system of social security is one of the factors behind market capitalism's striking resilience and stability.

Moreover, market capitalism is characterized by an anti-trust policy conducted by the government and its bureaucracy. Hardly any economist doubts the value of such an infringement on contractual freedom, since monopolies could emerge, which burden the society with prohibitively high social costs (Chang 2011, p. 478–479). Nevertheless, anti-trust policy infringes on the right to transact, i.e. contractual freedom. But even liberal market economies do not accept all conceivable market outcomes. When competition is endangered by some companies growing too large, their growth can be curtailed. For instance, in a number of cases mergers and acquisitions are forbidden. This is justified by

---

14 As a matter of fact, on some occasions even in market capitalism abrupt changes in economic policy are possible, but they tend to be rarer and less severe than in state capitalism.

alluding to a hazard for open markets. The functioning of market capitalism is effectively endangered, since there is the risk of a monopolistic market form, threatening entry to markets for other corporate actors and price rises for consumers.

Finally, Eucken sees the internalization of external effects as another regulating factor of market capitalism. The costs of commercial activities should be borne by the perpetrator. In this regard, if an enterprise pollutes a forest these costs should be internalized as to be accounted for not by the public, but by the private company. One instrument for the state are environmental laws. Concededly so far, it has in no market capitalist system been accomplished to internalize all external effects, since the task is too complex. But at least the intention exists and it has been put into law in some respects.

Political and economic actors in market capitalism

So far, the constituting and regulating principles and more generally the state have been explained as pillars of market capitalism. But in market capitalism economic organizations, such as private enterprises and political organizations, such as parties, are of critical importance, too. As North postulated, they are agents of institutional change. At the same time taking organizations into account is a useful means to adopt a more actor-centered view (Hall / Soskice 2001, p. 6).

Economic organizations operate in an institutional framework that enables them as mentioned above to transact on open markets. They are regulated by the bureaucracy. Among others rules of conduct ensure that the state's autonomy is not imperiled. In market capitalism the bureaucracy is sufficiently capable to conduct the policies planned and decided on by the government It is able to ensure consistency and regularity in its interaction vis-á-vis the corporate sector. In this regard, the institutional framework, mostly guaranteed by the rule of law, protects economic organizations from violations of their property rights either by the bureaucracy or by private partners of economic exchange.

Likewise, political organizations are protected by the rule of law as well. Curtailment of parties' rights or even its closure can be brought before the Constitutional Court. In those market capitalist states, where we observe democratic rule, this equates to an essential safeguard for political organizations as long as they are not openly endangering the democratic system. Such an institutional framework enables political competition, where ideally in the long run the best ideas and political plans are realized.

At the same time, political organizations play a significant role in guaranteeing the rule of law. For instance, they shape public opinion, which as an instrument helps to uphold the rule of law. Doubtlessly, political parties play a key role in relation to the state. There is no clear dividing line between the state and parties. Party members hold positions in all three powers: executive, legislative and judiciary. In a way this is intended, since it guarantees in the words of North et al. (2009) an open access to political tenures. Thereby, individuals have an opportunity to join a party and in this open access order assume political posts. This is another factor, which promotes political competition and consequently political markets in market capitalism.

A key role is also accorded to the financial system. It provides the economy with liquidity as in any economic system. In market capitalism, there are banks and financial markets. These are mostly in private hands. In general, the state sets the rules for the financial system. By the same token, the financial system provides the state with liquidity, for instance when the state emits government bonds on financial markets. In this regard, financial markets take over a critical role in market capitalist systems. This is even aggravated by the role the financial system plays in coordinating economic organizations. According to Hall and Soskice (2001) especially in liberal market economies capital markets in an ideal world steer financial resources into the most efficient projects of economic organizations. They regularly dominate strategic corporate decisions and take a governance function. In coordinated market economies, this role is to a larger extent taken up by the banking sector.

To sum it up, in market capitalism the rule of law prevails. Prices can react to changes in supply and demand. Price controls are absolute exceptions and have to be justified by policy-makers with market failures. The state guarantees competition on open markets, meaning that markets are contestable and entry barriers have to be sufficiently low. Incentives for economic activity are high powered due to secure property rights. Here the overarching role of the rule of law with its quintessential function as a formal institution of securing property rights stands out. Incomes through economic activity are accorded to a significant degree to the relevant economic actors and not to the state or even to bureaucrats in the form of corruption.

Naturally the state deducts income and other taxes. But these are neither so exorbitant as to amount to expropriation nor are they out of the realm of the rule of law. A tax payer has a fair chance challenging his tax burden before the courts, if he perceives to have his property rights violated. Naturally, economic actors are liable for business failure. But commercial activities are facilitated by bankruptcy laws and limited liability for a vast number of entrepreneurs. The rule of law seeks to guarantee that damages through entrepreneurial decisions have predominantly to be borne by the perpetrator.

By now a model of market capitalism has been built. Since the research question is to understand how state capitalism functions and why it apparently works in a number of cases and fails in other cases, this model of market capitalism serves as a benchmark for comparing it to a model of state capitalism, which will be developed in the subsequent sub-section.

2.4 A Model of State Capitalism

In this sub-section it is sought to identify what state capitalism is by creating a model of this economic order. To that end, at first Eucken's constituting principles for market capitalism will be applied to differentiate market from state capitalist systems. Subsequently, the most significant elements of state capitalism will be scrutinized. Finally, from this starting-point it should be possible to establish a model of constituting principles of state capitalism.

Basically, from the most simplistic perspective there are markets and private property rights in market capitalism. Strictly speaking, the same can be said of state capitalism with the caveat that markets are not in general open, private property rights are often violated and the state is a dominant actor.[15] But since this crude factual evidence proves relatively little, it seems to be fruitful to again resort to Eucken's constituting principles.

Applying constituting principles of market to state capitalism

In this regard, the primary constituent of market capitalism, i.e. a flexible price system, is already impaired in state capitalism. Prices often do not mirror scarcities on factor and product markets. In a vast number of instances, prices are intentionally wrong, to use Alice Amsden's phrase, meaning they are distorted. In the following it should become clear, why this is the case in state capitalism.

First of all, markets are only partly open. High entry barriers in a number of sectors, especially in strategic industries, are created by the state and incumbent competitors for newcomers. Newcomers are de facto barred from certain markets. The instruments applied can take numerous forms. Domestic newcomers can for instance practically be excluded from these markets by closing access

15 With reference to the state the author here solely subsumes the government and bureaucracy under this entity, since quite regularly the legislative and judicial powers play a negligible role and de facto no separation of powers exists.

to financial sources. Foreign competitors can be excluded through high tariffs or outright bans to invest in certain domestic markets. In general economies of scale matter. Thus, occasionally the government fosters infant industries for one enterprise to become a national champion and due to scale advantages at least no domestic competitor has the means to contest this market.

Markets in state capitalism regularly are not atomistic and anonymous, but function in the form of granting favours to preferred persons in exchange for other gains. In a certain sense, markets are used as tools by politicians, who seek to follow on goals such as export promotion, protectionism and product imitation. Price controls are accepted as an instrument of industrial or social policy. This corresponds to Nölke et al. (2015, p. 543–545) and their model of a state-permeated market economy. Here mechanisms of loyalty and trust between members of the elites based on personal relations are of key importance. Enterprises favoured by the government can resort to domestic sources of funding easier than other competitors and are often controlled by influential families.

As a matter of fact, the state does not place primary importance to the stability of the currency. Securing the purchasing power of economic agents is not a primary goal of the government. In contrast to that the government is willing to accept certain levels of inflation, if it facilitates fulfilling goals such as economic growth or lowering poverty.

Regarding liability, contractual freedom and secure private property rights these all relate to the rule of law. In general, in state capitalist countries no widely applied rule of law can be observed. Indeed, in state capitalism there are grave shortcomings with regard to the rule of law. Out of this situation significant legitimacy problems result (Holmes 2016, p. 234–235). In order to achieve this legitimacy and not imperil regime survival the government in state capitalism especially claims legitimacy on performance, such as development, for instance more equitable income distribution, less poverty, more competitiveness or more economic growth.[16]

But this does not alter the fact that due to a lack of rule of law private property rights are not secure. Though not continuously being imperiled by a cleptocratic state, economic agents have to incur costs to hedge risks of having their property rights violated. One instrument in this regard is capital flight, another buying political influence, for instance through donations for a certain number of members of ruling parties (see Markus / Charnysh 2017, p. 1660). Only rarely do state

16 Possibly it could also seek legitimacy by serving narrow interests, creating law and order or by suppressing political opposition.

capitalist governments outright confiscate private property. In many instances they apply informal tools of guiding the corporate sector – often through its bureaucracy. This amounts for instance to the bureaucracy hinting to an economic agent that it would be opportune for him to overstaff his enterprise, abstain among others from lay-offs and accept incurring less profit or even losses.

In this regard it becomes clear that opposed to Eucken's constituting principles contractual freedom is limited in state capitalism. Even though by law economic agents tend to be entitled to freely contract with all other economic agents, de facto a different picture emerges. Here it would in a number of cases be drastically sanctioned by the state for instance to employ political opponents to the government. Regarding liability this appears to hinge on political considerations. Since de facto no rule of law is in place, economic agents can be held liable for corporate decisions, which they did not even make. In very much the same sense, liability for politically well-connected managers of SOEs can de facto be excluded. Even criminal behaviour is under certain conditions condoned. Thus, SOE-managers often have an incentive to act in a way that does not imperil their political connections as opposed to successfully operating on relevant markets, i.e. increasing revenues or profits. In a certain sense the fact that politics tends to provide a safety net for SOE-managers, problems of moral hazard might ensue out of a lack of liability.

In state capitalism economic policy is conducted in a discretionary manner. There tends to be less steadiness in economic policy than in market capitalism. The government only insignificantly perceives to be bound by rules. This results in a number of instances in sudden policy changes. Since most state capitalist systems are autocratic, decisions can be enacted in a relatively short time-frame, for instance due to being unencumbered by time-consuming debates in the legislative branch of power. If perceptions – a form of informal institutions – of political leaders change, sometimes in a shock-wise manner, economic policy can undergo very swift and profound shifts.

On the other hand, in state capitalism elites – often as members of influential families, clans or parties – shape the economic system. Even in regime changes elites are often not substituted, but a continuity exists. For instance, in the corporate sector in a number of instances a new stock of entrepreneurs is not promoted into key positions and existing companies are shielded from competition, thereby protecting rents of the elites (see Jones / Sakong 1980, p. 171 and 176). This tends to be a stabilizing factor, alleviating the inherent tendency of state capitalist systems to sudden shifts in economic policy.

Concerning anti-trust policy political leaders in state capitalism do not feel committed to – as mentioned above – uphold open markets. They see anti-trust policy as a tool of industrial policy. Thus, if it supports development a number of state capitalist countries even actively engage in market consolidation, in a number of cases resulting in only one national champion for certain markets. One enterprise can reap more economies of scale than two competing players could. Its large size also endows this national champion with relatively significant market power and facilitates operating profitably on export markets. Such an industrial policy is often criticized by economists, since it regularly entails subsidizing national champions and thereby further distorting prices.

With regard to correction of external effects a similarity to market capitalism can be identified. A number of state capitalist countries for instance also applies environmental policies, seeking to internalize external effects such as pollution. The corresponding laws tend to be less draconian than in market capitalist countries – in content and enforcement –, but in general they exist and are applied.

Finally, social policy is not missing in state capitalist countries. Indeed, a number of state capitalist countries place an emphasis on maintaining a relatively even income distribution, coining phrases such as "shared growth". The tax system can be as much based on progressively taxing incomes of citizens as it is in market capitalism. In general, the state plays more of a patriarchal role in state than in market capitalism. But since state capitalist countries tend to have less gross domestic product (GDP) per capita than market capitalist states, they simply cannot afford a social security system as comprehensive as is common in market capitalism.

A comparison of market and state capitalism with the help of Eucken's constituting and regulating principles underlines structural and policy differences between market and state capitalism. Except for the correction of external effects, no key factor of market capitalism can be identified in state capitalism (see Table 1). In order to differentiate market further from state capitalism subsequently elements of state capitalism will be dealt with.

Tab. 1 Eucken's Constituting Principles in Market and State Capitalism

	Market Capitalism	**State Capitalism**
Flexible price-system	Yes	Impaired
Primacy of monetary policy	Yes	No primacy
Open markets	Yes	Limited
Private property rights	Yes	Limited
Contractual freedom	Yes	Limited
Liability	Yes	Partial
Constancy of economic policies	Yes	Discretionary

	Market Capitalism	State Capitalism
Anti-trust policy	Yes	Industrial policy
Correction of external effects	Yes	Yes
Social policy	Yes	Yes, but …

Source: Ahrens et al. (2017).

Elements of state capitalism

The first element of state capitalism is a high degree of state ownership of the corporate sector. This can take numerous forms. On the one hand the state can be sole owner of an enterprise with all profits or losses accruing to the state budget and the state being able to dictate relevant decisions. On the other hand, the state in a number of instances is minority owner in a publicly traded enterprise. Here the state is only entitled to his share of dividends. Furthermore, he does not control the company and can theoretically be overruled in board meetings by other investors.

Finally, the state can be majority investor. Here he is in a position to control corporate decisions and nominate the management according to his own preferences. Typical agency problems ensue, though. But it is also possible that SOE managers are chosen based on their allegiance to political leaders and not their business capabilities.

A second element is closely linked to the first. As a matter of fact, the state dominates the financial sector either as a regulator or as an owner. This refers to commercial banks, state-owned banks, development banks, SWFs and even capital markets. For instance, development banks support local infrastructure projects with long maturities. State-owned banks on a number of occasions bail out insolvent companies for political reasons. And state-owned venture funds, which are often subsidiaries of state-owned banks focus on small local companies and on small, fast-growing high-tech firms with initially low equity, high costs and little revenue (Clo et. al. 2017, p. 69).[17]

---

17 If a state capitalist system allows for foreign sources of funding, such as through global financial markets the regimes tend to risk their survival since they lose an important tool to control and weaken political challengers. Furthermore, they are more exposed to the risk of financial crises, which could magnify potentially disruptive political challenges (Carney 2015, p. 843). Nevertheless, state capitalist regimes usually at least partially allow for foreign funding, as with these resources economic growth is enhanced, which stabilizes their rule due to legitimacy claims mentioned above.

At this point, it needs to be maintained that in most state capitalist systems there is a bank-dominated financial sector. Therefore, apart from its dominance of SWFs, the state wields its power through its grasp – again by regulation or ownership – on banks. The financial sector is simultaneously of crucial importance in so far as it not only finances projects of the corporate sector, but increasingly even state budgets. Thus, the state has a strong incentive to control the financial industry as a source of finance, but also a tool for its industrial policy. In a carrot and stick fashion domestic enterprises can be incentivized to follow the industrial policy formulated and implemented by the state with the help of the financial system. Since on the curb market financing costs tend to be significantly higher than on official markets, the state has a lever to steer even privately held companies to be guided in their corporate strategy.

The third element are political organizations as stabilizing factors in otherwise entirely autocratic regimes. They rather – especially as opposition parties – have only limited access to the state and seldom can citizens participate in a political organization in order to gain access to leading positions in the government or bureaucracy. Nevertheless, these political organizations serve the purpose of giving political leaders at least minimal contact to the population. It helps to counter the tendency in state capitalism for political leaders to decouple themselves from developments occurring among political agents.

Since political organizations usually last for a considerable amount of time in state capitalism, they increase expectations certainty for economic as well as political agents and stabilize the state capitalist system. In general, they hardly serve to foster democracy, but are often a means for the government to gain legitimacy by creating the false impression of free and equal elections. Up to a degree, this can help to sustain stability. Under certain conditions this lack of democracy even facilitates credible commitments to the developmental goals mentioned above. Such credible commitments could be harder to give under a framework of repeated changes of governments in a democratic system (Ahrens / Stark 2012, p. 4).

A fourth element of state capitalism consists of a pre-eminent role for elites, who limit access to resources for broader layers of the population. Elites naturally hold key positions in the state, political as well as economic organizations, the military or even the financial sector, which makes them analytically difficult to differentiate from other entities such as enterprises and political organizations. Overall, elites stabilize state and society only as long as they are able to reap economic rents. Consequently, political leaders have to grant rents to these elites in order to stay in power. In this regard, key positions are sometimes filled with relatively incapable personnel, for instance military officers with no business acumen into management posts of SOEs (Jones / Sakong 1980, p. 161).

The political leadership forms a coalition of military, political, economic or even religious elites (Behuria 2015, p. 416). Often political leaders distribute these rents to generals or to be less specific to members of military and security services. This can consist of appointing well connected members of the elites to lucrative key positions in SOEs. Such a selection process tends to facilitate choosing less capable candidates than under a situation, where private shareholders fill managerial positions (see Kröll 1966, p. 328). Nevertheless, from a government perspective favouring, elitist candidates appears not to be utterly irrational. After all, in authoritarian state capitalist systems, which tend to be less stable than democratic market capitalist ones, elites are characterized by holding violence potential. If they become alienated from the political leadership they are likely to withdraw support and utilize their violence potential to unseat state leaders. In the extreme, this would equate to army generals orchestrating a coup. But this could also mean, elitist groups leading political organizations staging mass protests, which could result in the end of the regime.

Elitist rule further erodes the rule of law. This is due to a constant rearranging of rent distribution with regard to shifts in power. If one elitist group gains more power, it is awarded more rents, so that it has less of an incentive to utilize its increased violence potential, which would imperil regime survival (North et al. 2009, p. 47–48). Here a tendency towards hysteresis can be observed. Elites have an incentive to consolidate the status quo in order not to risk their share of rents (see Markus / Charnysh 2017, p. 1632). This is one of the factors accounting for the relative stability of state capitalist system with few regime changes.

Thus, in state capitalism as the name implies the state dominates. It acts as a sole, majority or minority owner of enterprises. By the same token it usurps control of the financial sector in order to conduct its industrial policy, steering the corporate sector beyond acting as owner or co-owner of SOEs. Nevertheless, the state allows for political organizations. Those are one means for political leaders not to lose connectivity to developments from below. On the upper side of society, elites have to be satisfied. They – among others as military or leaders of political organizations – hold violence potential, so that rents need to be distributed to them, for instance in the form of highly-paid positions in the state or corporate sector.

Constituting principles of state capitalism

After having differentiated market from state capitalism with the help of Eucken's constituting principles and sketched the main pillars of state capitalism, it now appears to be possible to formulate constituting principles for this economic order. Those are based on the existing literature, for which an overview had been given above, and the findings presented in this sub-section so far. Seven constituting principles of state capitalism can be discerned.

First, the state acts either directly or indirectly as a dominant actor. Political leaders or ministries are endowed with notable discretionary economic powers. Although there is no central planning, there are more or less pronounced forms of state control. This can take the form of profit utilization or management hiring in SOEs as well as informal guiding for the private sector.

Second, the state controls important parts of the financial sector including the banking system, for instance through state-owned commercial and development banks as a prerequisite for financing its industrial policy or to consolidate its politico-economic power with the help of sovereign wealth funds (SWF). Those invest domestically and abroad with the purpose of assisting domestic industries. At the same time, they are also utilized for averting economic crises and financing social policies.

Third, the government engages in an active industrial policy.[18] The applied instruments entail price controls, subsidized credits, subsidies, tax breaks or

---

18 As mentioned above a key characteristic of state capitalism is the government's emphasis on development. Since the state has strong levers at hand – for instance through ownership, bureaucratic capacities or its influence on the financial sector – there is an almost natural tendency to apply tools of industrial policy. In the example of Kohli (2004, p. 21) here it is essential that states and entrepreneurs are like two horses, which pull a chariot. Development and industrialization will only succeed, if both move in the same direction. Industrial policy needs an effective interplay of bureaucracy and corporate sector.

These policies can be conducted either in a vertical or horizontal approach. The former is also called targeted industrial policy, as there is a bias towards preferred industries. In this case the government selects certain industries for support. On the other hand, with horizontal industrial policy the government supports rather equally all sectors of the economy (see Lall / Teubal 1998). For the purpose of this study only targeted or selective industrial policy is of relevance. In general, it is seen as "an effort by a government to alter the sectoral structure of production toward sectors it believes offer greater prospects for accelerated growth than would be generated by a typical process of industrial evolution" (Noland / Pack 2003, p. 10).

privileged access to foreign currency. Implementing industrial policy and the affiliated economic measures is facilitated by the existence of a bureaucracy with a sufficiently large capacity. Such an industrial policy in a setting, where state capitalist countries are late-industrializers naturally in general leads to a situation, where the state favours more imitation than innovation of products and production processes (see Amsden 2001, p. 220).

Since they are lagging behind in industrialization they rely significantly on the transfer of technology from industrialized nations. This can either be conducted by investments of multinational companies or via imports, when through reverse engineering proprietary technological capabilities are developed. In this

---

First, industrial policy is according to economic theory in general justified when marginal social costs are not reflected in prices. Thus, the state can intervene into markets in order to internalize these externalities. In these cases of market failure welfare gains are to be expected, when the government intervenes with tools of industrial policy. These market failures can take the form of coordination failures.
Second, from a national point of view industrial policy can also create competitive advantages, which serve to increase employment and potentially the welfare of the entire country. But it needs to be noted that this is a zero-sum game. In an international context one country's gain is another country's loss, if one nation starts to increase its competitiveness through state interventions.
Third, real external economies can emerge. Due to these effects a firm profits from the product of another company owing to improvements in its productivity. In principle, these are knowledge spillovers and can improve the welfare of the entire nation. It would be recommendable for the state to promote the production and facilitate the purchase of this welfare-enhancing product (Noland / Pack 2003, p. 16).
Fourth, Rodrik (1996, p. 1–22) furthermore contends that multiple equilibria are possible. Emerging economies can become trapped in their specialization on labour-intensive standardized products. But they could have an opportunity to advance to the production of goods, which requires a better educated workforce. The reason for such an entrapment simply lies in coordination failures. Aoki (1994, p. 134) argues in the same vein. He is concerned that an entrapment in a bad equilibrium is possible, which is caused by a failure of coordination of cross-industrial investment. Indeed, especially in emerging economies coordination failures, especially on credit and labour markets, are widespread (Ferris / Gawande 1998, p. 4–37).
Also, according to Cimoli et. al. (2009, p. 19) industrial policy is important for development. Most of all, based on the infant industry argument it is often intended to nurture nascent industries. Especially in this regard the state intends to foster knowledge accumulation. Clearly, this can be facilitated through incentives for private actors. Nevertheless, it seems that sufficient government investments cannot be substituted through other instruments (Cimoli et al., p. 1–16).

regard state capitalist countries actively support national champions, whereas market capitalist countries refrain from such an industrial policy (FAZ 28th of October 2017). Since they usually have fewer means to their disposal than their counterparts from Western countries, it is also not surprising that in general expenses for research and development – calculated as a share of GDP – tend to be lower than in industrialized nations.

Fourth, state capitalist systems perceive the advantages of globalization and seek to actively utilize these. In a number of cases state capitalist regimes have institutionalized a strict export orientation, while at the same time applying protectionism in order to shield their domestic markets (see Bremmer 2014, p. 680). Through strategic industrial as well as trade policies successful regimes generate internationally competitive SOEs that operate as private enterprises. In order to protect their domestic economies, they impose import tariffs, grant export subsidies, restrict foreign investments into domestic companies or apply other non-tariff trade obstacles. Internationally successful companies are often part of strategic industries, which are targeted by the government and are directly or indirectly dominated by it.

In this regard, some state capitalist regimes are backward oriented and seek to conserve out-moded, non-efficient industry and enterprise structures. Other state capitalist regimes look forward and seek to identify or develop sectors that have a strategic importance in the future. In general state capitalist countries pursue an active industrial policy, through which they aim to catch-up with regard to industrialized nations with the means of imitation.

Fifth, state capitalist regimes not only utilize the advantages of globalization, but in general the advantages of a market-based coordination mechanism. This becomes evident with the co-existence of private companies as well as SOEs and the general orientation towards world market prices. By the same token, in principle they allow for the competitive functions of a flexible price system, although it is up to a certain extent – as explained above – impaired. Even though the state often intervenes into the price setting on factor and product markets through price-, wage- and interest rate controls, there is a fundamental and clear orientation of economic actors towards incentives based on prices, wages and interest rates.

This combined with the existence of private property rights on production factors implies that private actors can relatively autonomously pursue their own short and long-term goals and be incentivized to invest. Up to a certain degree "the state recognizes and enforces the rights of property and contract" (Baumol et al. 2007, p. 63). Furthermore, this results in the fact that even managers of

SOEs have to orient themselves with an eye towards domestic or world markets (Milhaupt / Zheng 2015, p. 680 and Baumol et al. 2007, p. 62–64).

Sixth, since in state capitalism industrial policy plays such a crucial role, the government essentially depends on a bureaucracy to conduct these policies. Diverging from country to country enforcement instruments are of a large variety, applying outright force, bureaucratic directives or informal controls. Therefore, the bureaucracy needs to be at least of a minimum size, since otherwise enforcement of policies is hardly possible. This relates to a minimum bureaucratic capacity in the form of authority and size that allows the state to actively intervene into the corporate sector, for instance through interventions on factor and product markets with the help of price, wage and interest rate controls. Since industrial policy is very multi-faceted, involving for instance also trust policy, there needs to be sufficient personnel in the bureaucracy to implement policies formulated by the government.

This does not necessarily translate into an equally capable bureaucracy. In a number of instances bureaucrats encumber reaching development goals by following their own utility functions, which can lead to extorting bribes or basically preventing investment projects from being realized. But at the same time, bureaucracies can also help to overcome uncertainty due to a lack of rule of law. Here economic agents have a chance to develop an embeddedness with the bureaucracy. This tends to ease the regulatory burden and can for instance facilitate access to bank loans. Embeddedness can improve coordination, create property rights, thereby lowering uncertainty and in general providing for more predictability. This can possibly lower transaction costs and enables certain, growth-enhancing forms of exchange. (Haveman et al 2017, p. 72 and 89). Which role the bureaucracy plays vis-à-vis the corporate sector is one of the key factors for explaining the research question of this study of why in a number of cases state capitalism worked and in a number of other instances failed.

One of the fundamental dilemmas facing governments is that they depend on a bureaucracy of a minimum size to implement policies. But by the same token agency problem are exacerbated as the bureaucracy grows and bureaucrats gain more leeway. Therefore, in principle governments aim to cap bureaucratic growth. But as the number of tasks for the state grows, so does the economic argument gain more weight to increase staff.

Seventh, state capitalist countries are characterized by a relatively common institutional framework. In essence, this takes the form of rule-making and rule-enforcing being conducted in a rather arbitrary manner. Discretion of the executive branch of power is relatively high. There tend to be few counter-weights installed in state capitalist systems. Thus, for instance the judiciary is notoriously weak, which results as mentioned above in property rights being regularly infringed on. In a nut-shell, opposed to for instance liberal and coordinated market capitalism a general rule of law cannot be observed.[19] Economic actors tend to be constrained to incur high costs in order to secure their property rights, some opting for exiting in the form of capital flight others for remaining in the form of buying political influence for instance through donations for governing parties or bribes for politicians in power.

To sum it up, the most striking feature of state capitalism is the dominant role of the state, resulting in most cases in only partially open markets, therefore an inhibited competition, and violations of property rights. The price system is relatively strongly distorted. From this starting point seven constituting principles of state capitalism were formulated. Those are the state as a dominant actor and owner in the economy, the state dominating the financial sector, an industrial policy utilizing imitation as a means to catch-up to market capitalist industrialized nations, the shielding of markets from competition, a bureaucracy with a minimum amount of capacity, an institutional framework marked by the absence of a rule of law and nevertheless the co-existence of private property rights on production factors.

When comparing both market and state capitalist models with each other, it becomes obvious that from an economic point of view market is superior to state capitalism, culminating among others in the fact that in state capitalism economic actors have to adapt to the possibility of having their property rights quite regularly violated due to the absence of the rule of law, which reduces incentives for economic activity (see Table 2).

Tab. 2 Constituting Principles of State Capitalism

	State Capitalism	**Market Capitalism**
State dominant economic player	Yes	Only as an exception
State dominance of financial sector	Yes	Only as an exception
Industrial policy applied	Yes	Only partially
Shielded markets	Yes	Only as an exception

19 Haggard (2011, p. 681–682) points out that lack of rule of law is not in itself correlated with inferior results in economic growth. According to his reasoning far more growth-inhibiting are constraints of widespread violence with related state failure in a number of countries.

	State Capitalism	Market Capitalism
Co-existence of private property rights	Yes	Yes
Minimum of bureaucratic capacity	Yes	Yes
Institutional framework marked by no rule of law	Yes	No

Source: Own illustration.

Thus, the question emerges, why state capitalists do not install a presumably more efficient market capitalist system and also why they have installed a state capitalist system in the first place. This leads back to the foundations of institutions, especially institutional change, presented above. Therefore, the subsequent sub-section deals with the emergence of state capitalism as well as its transformation to a market capitalist system.

2.5 State Capitalism and Institutional Change

State capitalist regimes can emerge out of a number of historical settings. But in a number of instances state capitalist systems are formed at critical junctures of the respective countries, where rigidities inherent in state and society are critically weakened. Political leaders under these circumstances perceive that political and economic development of their countries has stalled. They feel constrained to initiate institutional change, foremost since economic performance critically lags behind those of other comparative countries. Otherwise they would be confronted with the eminent risk of regime change – either through public unrest of sizable parts of the population or elitist groups. Under normal circumstances a state capitalist system can either emerge from a market capitalist or a socialist system. Essentially, only rarely has a country shifted from a market capitalist to a state capitalist system. Nevertheless, such an institutional change clearly seems to be in the realm of possibility.

From Market to State Capitalism

In such a case first of all the state strives to capture a dominant role in the economy. This is clearly inhibited by numerous vested interests. Private investors will orchestrate resistance to losing economic power. But especially, with the backing of public opinion at a critical juncture of a country's historic trajectory, political leaders can take advantage of a weakened position of private economic agents, who seek to defend their property rights.

To this end the state has several levers at his disposal. First of all, ownership is a primary aim for gaining control of the economy. The state can turn to outright confiscation and thereby basically destroy the rule of law. By the same token, the state can resort to more subtle means and preserve a veneer of respecting the legal framework. Thus, for instance, it is possible to accumulate majority shares of enterprises and squeeze minority investors out. Likewise, the state can limit itself to the role of a minority investor and aim for influencing decisions by adapting the instrument of informal guidance.

A second key component of reverting from a market to a state capitalist system lies in initiating interventions on strategic markets. As a matter of fact, the state can apply all tools described above to distort the price system. This would entail among others price controls on factor and product markets or inhibiting access to relevant markets by shielding them from foreign competition through tariff protection. Since hardly any empirical evidence exists as to whether a transformation from market to state capitalism can successfully be accomplished here it is only possible to point out that – as hinted at above – among others due to incentive reasons efficiency and welfare losses would probably ensue.

Furthermore, since in market capitalism powerful networks of corporate associations exist and through the rule of law an independent judiciary is in place, it seems to be a gargantuan task for political leaders to reverse market capitalism. The probable solution would be to install a dictatorship. In such a case, political actors would also tend to strive for making their state capitalist measures irreversible. This could entail enshrining state capitalist elements such as state ownership in strategic sectors of the economy in the constitution. Furthermore, to consolidate political power in the hands of current political leadership, it is possible to create a large dominant party, providing the opportunity of securing election victories, potentially in a number of cases even with the help of electoral fraud.

From State to Market Capitalism

But whether this serves the end of avoiding a situation, where political and economic agents strive towards reverting to a market capitalist system, is an open question. At critical junctures forces representing vested interests within state and society tend to be weakened, so that it becomes easier to initiate, install and enforce a new institutional framework. When rigidities are somehow softened, political actors can more easily cut through hindrances and veto players can lose their veto power. The problems of hysteresis and path dependence tend to be less severe.

According to the theory of North et. al. (2009) as mentioned above if three doorstep conditions – consolidated control of the military, perpetually lived organizations and rule of law for elites – were in existence, a state capitalist country as a limited access order can transform into a market capitalist nation, which tends to take the form of an open-access order. As a matter of fact, in most instances in state capitalist systems there is consolidated control of the military and security services. Economic and political organizations furthermore tend to be perpetually lived, so that their existence is not critically endangered as soon as their leaders pass away.

However, the doorstep condition, which is missing in state capitalism, is rule of law for the elites. As soon as the power distribution in state capitalist systems alters, so does rent distribution. Elites cannot count on having their property rights defended before courts. The judiciary provides no safeguards for elites to protect their property rights. Therefore, it critically hinges on the rule of law, whether a transformation to market capitalism can succeed. If this condition was met at least the political leadership of the respective country would have the chance of transforming to market capitalism, although success is not guaranteed. This is due to the fact that for market capitalism open markets with a flexible and functioning price system are inevitable. But such a framework is only possible if exchange were mostly on impersonal markets functioning regardless of the personality of economic agents. According to North et. al. (2009) such a situation can emerge, but may not emerge after all three doorstep conditions were in place.

Since as described above market capitalism is superior to state capitalism from a theoretical point of view, then why do state capitalists not transform their country towards market capitalism? As mentioned above, there are the problems of hysteresis and path dependence, which can in many instances only be overcome at critical junctures. This is illustrated by the requirement of having to fulfill three door-step conditions. Rule of law simply cannot be enacted overnight.

Second, market capitalist formal institutions – especially regarding an entire system of rule of law – tends at first to conflict with informal institutions prevalent in state and society in state capitalist countries. Such a situation could lead to instability, even violence, especially if rents of the elites are – as is common in regime changes – to be redistributed (see McFaul 2001). State and society could apprehend such a situation and therefore prefer to have the second-best option of a state capitalist system in place. By the same token, according to the World Bank (2008, p. 26–27) institutional change takes a significant amount of time for a country to reap the fruits of a transformation and in the transition period citizens must forgo consumption.

Lastly, in many cases state capitalist leaders and the elites profit from state capitalism due to a favourable rent distribution. With an eye towards a system change political leaders tend to apprehend losing their positions and therefore refrain from initiating institutional change. The same is possibly true for economic agents, especially leaders of enterprises. In general, when transforming towards market capitalist systems, most elitist groups tend to lose their rents. Thus, political leaders as well as elites in state capitalism tend to have no economic incentive to transform their system and change often only comes due to pressure from below. Elites therefore are an unlikely candidate for institutional change, as they have much to lose and protect their property rights against shocks (Markus 2017, p. 101).

From Socialism to Capitalism

In a number of cases state or market capitalism emerged from socialism. Here political leaders strove to make reforms irreversible.[20] These transformations and its ensuing problems have been dealt with in the literature extensively.[21] Especially important is the right sequencing of reforms. It facilitates the transformation, if first of all a consensus in state and society about political rules was formed. Then subsequently it becomes much easier for the country and its leadership to tackle property rights and recreate economic rules. When a consensus is formed – for instance a constitution passed – about the process, in which later on property rights are distributed, it becomes much easier for losers of such a redistribution to accept the outcome (see McFaul 2001). Acceptance would be even more facilitated, if compensations for losers were to be accounted for through establishing appropriate political rules.

Concerning specifically a transformation from socialism to state capitalism it suffices to mention that at least a certain number of key measures has to be conducted in order to realize a state capitalist system. Most of all constituting principle number five of state capitalism postulated above – i.e. existence of private property rights on production factors – needs to be fulfilled. This demands at least some sort of privatization of the corporate sector. By the same token markets need to be the coordination mechanism for at least a sizable share of the production of goods and services. If there was at least a partial privatization

20 One means to such an end is a shock therapy. For details of shock therapy in the transformation of socialism to capitalism see: Hoen (1998) and McFaul (2001).

21 See among others for instance: Ahrens (1994), Aslund (2013), Spak (1997) and Chang (1995).

and the state remained the dominant player in the economy, such a country had opted for the economic order of state capitalism.

By now foundations of NIE were laid. Furthermore, a model on market and one on state capitalism have been presented. In this regard constituting principles of state capitalism have been developed and institutional change regarding this economic order been dealt with. As the research question revolves around the topic of how to explain widely diverging performance differences in state capitalism in the subsequent part a taxonomy of different state capitalist varieties will be built. The classification accounts for differences in structure, i.e. the institutional framework, as well as polices and seeks to explain the resulting diverging performances.

3 A Taxonomy of Modern State Capitalism

"We must all obey the great law of change. It is the most powerful law of nature, and the means perhaps of its conservation."

Edmund Burke

Abstract
In its core, in this part a taxonomy of state capitalism will be presented, which builds on the theory and the constituting principles developed above. Then subsequently, there is to be a grounded part, where with the help of some quantitative data, it will be established, whether with the constituting principles state can indeed be differentiated from market capitalism as well as the different groups of state capitalism from each other. In this regard, proxies are applied for the constituting principles. Meanwhile there is also going to be a comparison of performances. This should help to clarify, whether the state capitalist groups, which were identified, also significantly diverged in their respective performances. At the same time, it will be illustrated that development is possible under state capitalist regimes. Economic growth rates of these countries on average even surpassed those of market capitalist ones. However, first of all, it will be dealt with antecedents of state capitalist classifications in the literature. Moreover, it will be shown, how institutional change is possible from one state capitalist variant to another.

Keywords: Varieties of State Capitalism, Classification, Institutional Change, Performances, Proxies for Constituting Principles.

3.1 Varieties of State Capitalism

3.1.1 Classifications of State Capitalism in the Literature

One of the key problems of state capitalism in current research is a lack of differentiation.[1] So far, in the literature diverging forms of capitalism have mostly been

---

1 Even for all economic systems of the world as a whole there are only few typologies. One exception is provided by Witt et al. (2018), who in their cluster analysis found the nine main forms of economic systems world-wide to be Highly Coordinated, Coordinated Market, Liberal Market, European Peripheral, Advanced Emerging, Advanced City, Arab Oil-Based, Emerging and Socialist Economies. Another example is Fainshmidt et. al. (2018). They are differentiating between seven different varieties of institutional systems in understudied regions. These are State-led, Fragmented with fragile state, Family-led, Centralized tribe, Emergent LME, Collaborative agglomerations and Hierarchically coordinated. For their taxonomy they apply the following five institutional dimensions: the state, financial markets, human capital, social capital

dealt within the VOC context, concentrating on developed nations. However, recently research emerged in the literature, encompassing all forms of capitalism in the world (Feldman 2019, p. 163). In the Western world state capitalism is often portrayed as a relatively homogenous economic order. Accordingly, many scientists do not distinguish between different forms of state capitalism. In that sense, it is not even surprising that CEOs of the world's top companies in the world describe state capitalism one-sided and decidedly negative as among the ten most important threats to market capitalism (Bower et al. 2011).

Musacchio and Lazzarini (2012, p. 3–5) take a more nuanced stance. In their research they distinguish between the state as a majority or minority investor. They stress that under certain conditions of market failure the economy can benefit from state activities as a minority investor. Both authors refer to the examples of Russia and China with a more direct, i.e. majority investor, form of state involvement, whereas in Brazil the state acts more as a minority investor. The performance of each system depends on the existing contingencies in each separate case, for example the degree of distortions that are created (Musacchio / Lazzarini 2012, p. 52).

Likewise, Muscacchio et al. (2015) differentiate between more forms of state capitalism. In their variety of state capitalism they postulate that there is a variety with the state as owner of SOEs, majority investor, minority investor or acting in a way to effectively steer the corporate sector with means of engaging in an industrial policy with some horizontal, but also selective measures. They stress that each of these varieties caters to different needs in the developmental phase of a state capitalist country. Thus, for instance if there was a country where the corporate sector suffered from an extreme need of financing, it could profit from the state engaging as an investor. On the other hand, if these needs are already fulfilled and the corporate sector is more in want of the state assisting in opening up new markets, granting subsidies for research and development, engaging in training the labour force or fostering product and process innovations through procurement the state often opts for the final variety of state capitalism as enunciated by Musacchio et al. (2015).

---

and corporate governance. Schneider (2013, p. 20) builds on a VOC approach and enumerates four different types of capitalism as liberal market, coordinated market, networked market and hierarchical market. On the other hand, Walter / Zhang (2012, p. 15) postulate based on social coordination and economic action the four variants of East Asian capitalism as being co-governed, state-led, networked and personalized.

Kurlantzick (2016, p. 27–30) differentiates on the one hand between autocratic and democratic state capitalist countries and on the other hand between efficient and inefficient state capitalism. In his classification, the most autocratic state capitalist countries are Saudi Arabia, Kazakhstan as well as Uzbekistan and the most democratic Brazil, Norway and India. Furthermore, he classifies Algeria, Egypt and Uzbekistan as the most inefficient. Singapore, Norway and Malaysia are singled out as the most efficient. With regard to performance the most efficient state capitalist countries display the highest degree of competitiveness and innovation (Kurlantzick 2016, p. 38 and 40).

As a matter of fact, in this study it is built in the following taxonomy on the research of Mussachio / Lazzarini (2012) and Kurlantzick (2016). State ownership is in the former taxonomy the most important constituent of state capitalism – either as majority or minority investor. But as Musacchio / Lazzarini (2012) themselves concede it is problematic to determine the respective performance of both types of state capitalism. In this study state ownership is rather seen as a constituent of state capitalism than as the sole means to differentiate between different forms of state capitalism. Kurlantzick on the other hand establishes an order of state capitalist countries according to their efficiency, but then does not provide data, which indexes for instance he applies.

Kohli (2004, p. 9–12) does not use the term state capitalism. He rather utilizes the expression "state-directed" development. In that sense, he also establishes a taxonomy with three state types: cohesive-capitalist, fragmented-multiclass and neopatrimonial. In the first most effective form, to which he counts South Korea and partially Brazil, authoritative structures reach deep down into the society and increase cohesion of numerous societal forces. There is an alliance between politics and corporate players and an effective bureaucracy exists. Nationalism or anti-communism are often applied as an ideology to gain support for embarking on a developmental path. Kohli equates the cohesive-capitalist with the developmental state, which is introduced below.

In fragmented-multiclass states public authority tends to be more fragmented. Political leaders need to make more compromises, since their power rests on numerous elitist groups. Economic growth is just one goal among many. Others are agricultural development, redistribution or national sovereignty. Policy formulation hinges on intra-elite conflicts and is not as clear-cut as in the developmental state. State capacity tends to be limited and legitimacy deficits are often countered with populist measures, for instance social policies. In certain periods of their development India and Brazil represented examples of this state type (Kohli 2004, p. 11).

Finally, in neo-patrimonial states officials tend to see public property as their personal resources. Narrow and personal interest groups inhibit development. State capacities are weak. An example is Nigeria (Kohli 2004, p. 9).

Whereas Musacchio / Lazzarini (2012) are very concrete in their classification and differentiate only according to the degree of state ownership, Kurlantzick (2016) is relatively vague. He utilizes democracy and effectiveness as differentiating criteria, which leaves some degree of discretion, when categorizing respective countries. Kohli is situated somewhere in the middle. He clearly and in detail describes differences between each type of state capitalism. In this regard, he also places an emphasis on development and industrialization. In the following taxonomy it is leant towards none of the classifications presented in this sub-section. Rather a taxonomy will be gained by in the following sub-section limiting the seven constituting principles of state capitalism to four and then further below differentiating between different forms of state capitalism.

3.1.2 Four Constituting Principles for the State Capitalist Taxonomy

As mentioned in the introductory chapter state capitalism is not a uniform phenomenon. There are numerous variations of this economic order with regional as well as ideological idiosyncrasies. While there is true to fact a significant number of similarities among economic orders of countries with a state capitalist system and in all state capitalist countries the seven constituting principles are fulfilled, apparently, at the same time there are profound differences among state capitalist countries with regard to structure, policies and performances. Therefore, in this section four archetypical principles of state capitalism are selected based on the seven constituting principles. Regarding performance differences the relevant figures will also be illustrated below.

When looking at principle number one – the state as a dominant actor in the economy – the fact tends to emerge that in general regarding state ownership of the corporate sector there is little deviation in the structure of state capitalist systems. Therefore, this principle cannot really assist in elaborating on varieties of state capitalism. The same seems to hold true for principle number two – i.e. state dominance of the financial system. Consequently, those first two principles will not be further taken into account in this section.

But coming to principles three and four – an industrial policy favouring imitation over innovation and a focus on integrating into world markets – policies in state capitalist countries diverge significantly. In a certain number of state capitalist countries, the government strives to upgrade the economy's manufacturing base and to move up the value chain. To this end products of industrialized countries are imitated – either through technology imports and subsequent reverse engineering or through foreign direct investments, where governments seek technology spillovers. Low labour costs are simultaneously utilized as a competitive advantage versus industrialized nations. Other state capitalist countries are less focused on such an industrial upgrading through imitation. They rely more heavily for instance on exporting primary goods. Nevertheless, with regard to manufacturing end products they also have to count on imitation, but as a percentage of GDP it does not play such a large role as in the formerly described state capitalist countries.

Concerning integration into world markets a relatively similar pattern in comparison with industrial policy can be discerned. Countries imitating end products most often do so for the purpose of exporting them. They strive to become integrated into the global division of labour and seek a niche at first in products with low labour costs and later on in higher quality goods. To this end up to a certain extent they make use of nurturing infant industries, for instance through slashing high import tariffs on consumer goods. Likewise, other state capitalist countries while still protecting their markets do not inhibit consumption of foreign consumer goods to such an extent. They perceive a preference among domestic economic agents for goods from abroad, which often for political reasons they do not want to restrain.

Regarding principle five about the bureaucracy all state capitalist systems are rather similar in that they endow their bureaucracies with at least a minimum size to conduct industrial policies effectively. But leaving quantity aside and looking at quality instead significant differences tend to emerge. A number of state capitalist countries has a capable bureaucracy being able to relatively efficiently implement government policies. Salaries and career paths in those bureaucracies are relatively attractive, creating high-powered performance incentives. Likewise, agency problems are mitigated to a certain extent, subduing corruption.

On the other hand, in different state capitalist countries bureaucracies are oversized, aggravating agency problems and facilitating corruption. This can lead to a situation, where the government formulates a potentially fruitful strategy of industrial upgrading only to find out that funds, which were earmarked for a respective project, virtually disappear in various echelons of the bureaucracy. By the same token, economic agents from below can find themselves basically being expropriated due to revocations of permits by lower level bureaucrats.

This directly leads over to principle number six, i.e. the absence of rule of law in the institutional framework. In certain state capitalist countries this lack is compensated for by the government. Those governments manage to in effect credibly commit themselves to at least up to a certain extent protect private property rights. This can take the form of the government committing itself to a national goal such as export promotion. Although there still is less degree of rule of law than in market capitalism and arbitrary confiscation of property is still in the realm of possibility, the fact that the government for example commits itself to export promotion can provide entrepreneurs with a safeguard, if they rationally choose to increase their production for foreign markets. The same reasoning can for instance be applied to the more general goal of economic growth.

Other state capitalist countries are less successful in credibly committing to at least minimally guaranteeing private property rights in the absence of rule of law. In a number of instances, they are not even able to rein in their own bureaucracies and prevent lower or higher-level bureaucrats from extorting bribes from the corporate sector. Thus, it becomes obvious that incentives for economic activity are relatively low in these countries, which tends to diminish developmental goals such as economic growth.

As a matter of fact, there are now four constituting principles, which can serve to distinguish varieties of state capitalism.[2] All four principles – deviations in the industrial policy and integration into world markets with regard to policies as well as quality of the bureaucracy and compensating for the absence of rule of law as more structural components of state capitalism– are interrelated and there are a number of complementarities involved, for instance a capable bureaucracy facilitates an effective and efficient implementation of a government policy to upgrade the manufacturing base by imitating higher-quality products from abroad. These complementarities will be dealt with in the subsequent taxonomy of state capitalism. This taxonomy differentiates between five varieties of state capitalism – the developmental state, dual-sector economy, crony state, petro state and predatory state capitalism. Further varieties of state capitalism could possibly also be discerned, but since in this study only archetypical forms are dealt with, such an undertaking needs to be left to future research.

3.1.3 Developmental States

In present times, the developmental state as one form of state capitalism has become such a role model that a number of less developed countries try to emulate

2 Indeed, there is still one of the seven constituting principles left to apply to this differentiation. But constituting principle number seven – co-existence of private property rights on productions factors – is unequivocally given in all state capitalist countries and therefore does not need to be dealt with further in this section.

this economic order and hope to profit from its experiences (Stark 2012, p. 3–6), although it has been seemingly discredited during the last 30 years by a number of mainstream economists (Fine 2013, p. 1). Especially for East Asian countries the term developmental state is applied, but some observers attribute its characteristics even to an African country such as Botswana (Taylor 2002, p. 1–2).

Capable Bureaucracy

One of the most striking elements of the developmental state is the existence of a capable bureaucracy.[3] Thanks to a relatively well-educated population these countries are able to recruit talented personnel for their bureaucracies. In order to attract some of the brightest minds among university graduates the civil service is made attractive, so that it can compete versus the corporate sector. For instance, there are clearly defined career paths, performance-based promotions and salaries as well as in general remunerations, which are not significantly lower than in the private sector. Adding to that the government supports efforts to create an esprit de corps among members of the civil service. This has the advantage of up to a certain degree insulating civil servants from corruption. Bureaucrats tend to be proud of serving the state and see themselves as an elite, which raises their self-esteem and their autonomy. Simultaneously it also raises the bar for commingling with the business side in illegal activities such as accepting bribes.

Nevertheless, bureaucrats are in touch with business. They are aware of problems that entrepreneurs encounter. There are quite regular meetings between both sides. In a number of instances, entrepreneurs are entitled to have their requests answered in a short time-frame. In general bureaucrats tend to be familiar with the needs of entrepreneurs. This is supported by the fact that a certain number of entrepreneurs prior to becoming business-men had been taking office in the civil service in what is called in Japanese "amakudari" or "descent

---

3 As a matter of fact, Gainsborough (2009, p. 1319–1320) argues that the entire concept of the developmental state should be looked at critically. He points out that this concept too strictly differentiates between state and society, while in reality both cannot be separated as rigorously as the concept of the developmental state does. Furthermore, he maintains that the state is no monolithic bloc. It should better be seen as consisting of numerous players. Both points deserve attention. But, in this study on a number of occasions the state is already divided into the government and the bureaucracy. Concerning, the potentially rather artificial separation of state and society, this has the advantage of allowing for analytical clarity and is thereby upheld in this study.

from heaven". This further creates an embeddedness of the bureaucracy. Evans (1995) coined the term "embedded autonomy" for bureaucracies in developmental states.[4] They communicate effectively and on a productive basis with the corporate sector strictly implementing goals set by the government without being captured by the enterprises.

In general bureaucrats tend to be highly pragmatic, concentrating on what works and what does not (Jones / Sakong 1980, p. 4 and 64–65). There are basically no ideological reasons per se that would rule out utilizing a potentially development-enhancing policy instrument. Bureaucracies of developmental states act plan rational in the terminology of Johnson (1983). Observers note a high degree of cohesion among bureaucrats and the entire elitist order and see a cohesive coalition of elitist forces uniting behind narrowly defined developmental goals (Kohli 2004, p. 23). Admittedly, bureaucracies act with a rather low level of transparency (Pirie 2008, p. 96). That situation possibly also improves cohesiveness, since a public discussion of government policies would almost certainly reveal cleavages within the state.

The entire implementation process of both policies described above requires a high degree of bureaucratic skills. Evaluation of performance in the face of complex targets is a difficult accomplishment. As mentioned above, targets have to be amended, using discretionary powers, which furthermore requires bureaucrats to be relatively immune to corruption.

Capable Bureaucracies complement Policy Goals

In general, economists and other experts quite unequivocally term bureaucracies of developmental states – as a structural constituting principle of state capitalism – as being capable. This complements the effectiveness of both policy-oriented constituting principles of state capitalism, i.e. an industrial policy to catch-up with developed nations by imitation and integration into world markets. The reason lies especially in bureaucrats' "embedded autonomy" and their skills. One means to achieve policy goals is a target-oriented implementation approach. Here bureaucrats are autonomous enough not to soften these constraints in general, but embedded enough to be flexible in case an exogenous shock makes achievement of the goal impossible.

4 As a matter of fact, Haveman et al (2017, p. 79) utilize the degree of former bureaucrats serving as executives in the corporate sector in their empirical investigation about business-state ties as a proxy for embeddedness.

Regarding policy objectives, the state expects the corporate sector among others to reach certain goals in the field of exporting imitated goods (Pirie 2008, p. 18). In case this goal is missed the typical stick can be applied, for instance in the form of not prolonging subsidized credits or no more granting export subsidies. By the same token, carrots are also used, sometimes in a classical pecuniary manner through subsidies, but occasionally even in the form of rewarding a patriotic deed, i.e. granting successful entrepreneurs a national award for having performed a patriotic duty.

At the same time the bureaucracy targets industries, where domestic enterprises are supposed to compete on a global level. Here bureaucrats have to nurture infant industries through constituting principle number three of shielding its markets. Consequently, bureaucrats – in collaboration with the corporate sector – need to elaborate specifically, which products to shield for instance with a tariff on imported goods. This requires a high amount of capability on the side of the bureaucrats, since the state risks rewarding rents to a non-competitive domestic industry. If bureaucrats lack the needed skills, the protection could last for years without the respective enterprises ever catching-up to the world market.

Credible Commitments by the State further complement Policy Goals

Thus, both policy-oriented constituting state capitalist principles are closely interlinked with the structural element of a capable bureaucracy. But this tends to be the case with regard to the government's commitment not to violate property rights drastically, too. As a matter of fact, the government has powerful levers to withdraw support from the corporate sector. This can consist of restricting access to funding on official capital markets and through the banking system, cutting or even abolishing subsidies or draining access to foreign currencies and putting severe stress on enterprises through rigorous tax audits (Jones / Sakong 1980, p. 84–85, 115 and 293).

The state can foster specific sectors with these instruments, but also punish companies for under-performance or disobedience. In a certain sense, punishing in this regard is equal to violating property rights of economic agents. Entrepreneurs having access to funding on official markets practically shut down face the risk of insolvency. Therefore, typical incentive problems ensue. Since entrepreneurs are faced with the risk of a violation of their property rights, they might decide either not to invest at all or to opt for capital flight in order to safeguard their property. In order to nevertheless incentivize economic activities, the government needs to credibly commit not to violate property rights of entrepreneurs. In the developmental state the government opts to bind itself not to violate property rights by credibly committing to national goals. In order for enterprises to cooperate in the policy targets of successfully imitating products from industrialized nations and integrating into the world economy the government credibly commits itself towards corporate players with national goals.

In a number of cases developmental goals become a form of state ideology (Taylor 2002, p. 14), and even grow into a unifying force equivalent to more widely known belief systems utilized for political purposes such as communism or state religion. It helps to convince the populace to endure a temporary decrease in living standards with the aim of a better economic future for the nation. In effect, as mentioned above the goal of development served as a credible commitment, which was possible since institutional safeguards existed, so that for political leaders, developmental goals were binding (Ahrens / Stark 2012, p. 7). In such a manner opposition to developmental policies is diminished to a degree that generally enables an effective implementation.

Indeed, since goals such as export or overall economic growth are so central to the regime and achieving them required by the government to overcome legitimacy deficits through delivering on performance targets, regime survival hinges on the cooperation of the corporate sector. The state has formulated and published national goals and placed itself in a position to have its own performance measured with these benchmarks.

If it fails to deliver, public unrest becomes more likely and in the end regime survival is at risk. Therefore, the government has arbitrarily lowered its own leverage when bargaining with the corporate sector and incurred the cost of less power. On the other hand, it has gained the benefit of not losing incentives due to insecure property rights and more general the absence of a rule of law. The corporate sector has an incentive to engage in productive activities, since the government itself has an incentive not to violate its property rights.

By the same token, if for instance export targets are not fulfilled by entrepreneurs for self-inflicted reasons, the state can still pursue a stick strategy. In this case, doubtlessly the existence of rule of law can seriously be questioned and property rights are not really secure, but rules are applied, which have been known to the enterprise a priori. Entrepreneurs can count on a low degree of generality in the formulation of targets in the sense that developmental goals such as increasing exports and upgrading industries are strictly and specifically predetermined. Only within this framework bureaucrats are allowed a relatively high degree of discretion, which increases flexibility to adapt to sudden changes in business environment. Members of the corporate sector thus again have their property rights secured in so far, that bureaucrats cannot alter the rules ex post to enterprises' detriment, which increases expectations certainty and thereby growth of investments.

By now constituting principles of state capitalism in developmental states have been highlighted, including some of their linkages. Developmental states have a capable bureaucracy and manage to overcome the problem of credibly committing not to violate property rights. Both principles have a beneficial effect on the policy principles of imitation and integration into world markets. In the subsequent sub-section, it will be dealt with the question, how this relates to the second state capitalist variant, i.e. dual economy state capitalism.

3.1.4 Dual Economy State Capitalism

The term dual economy can have a number of meanings in economics. Usually, it refers to the dichotomy of rural versus urban spaces, but also between developed and backward, export-oriented and inward-looking or agricultural and industrial sectors. Here – with regard to one form of state capitalism – the term is used to differentiate between two parts of the corporate world. The first – having gained strategic significance – is heavily influenced by the state and marked by constant interventions. On the other hand, there is a second sector, where entrepreneurs gained far more leeway in their decision-making and face fewer constraints, but also receive fewer favours by the state. This bifurcation is grasped by the Chinese doctrine of "grasping the large and letting go of the small". In this regard, central authorities control enterprises in a number of strategic sectors, whereas local authorities oversee all other industries (Haveman et al. 2017, p. 71).

Strategic Sectors

As a matter of fact, the structure of dual economy state capitalism is marked by such strategic sectors with a high degree of regulation as energy, mining, steel, banking or high technology. Here SOEs dominate and entrance barriers for newcomers are created to a significant extent, serving to increase state control. In most cases the state acts as a majority as well as minority investor in these strategic sectors (see Musacchio / Lazzarini 2012). The small number of dominant companies raises the risk of collusion, which would ceteris paribus undermine competition and increase expectations certainty (Haveman et al. 2017, p. 74).

If private companies in these strategic sectors are allowed to grow and become key players, they are under strict supervision of the state. This state attention does not have to be to the detriment of the companies concerned, since it entails support through a number of subsidies and even non-pecuniary rewards such as prevention of competition. As a matter of fact, large companies are in general in a position to negotiate better terms from suppliers and customers. They can reap economies of scale. This facilitates cost reductions and thereby competition on markets with regard to prices. In that sense, as corporate policies and strategies are connected with a search process marked by trial and error, large firms have an advantage over smaller ones, since they can more easily recover from mistakes (Haveman et al. 2017, p. 75).

Non-strategic Sectors

In general, a different picture emerges concerning non-strategic sectors. Here SOEs have less market share. There is less of a degree of concentration with a significant number of smaller players in the markets. The government in these industries concedes significant leeway to market forces, i.e. privately held enterprises, in sectors of minor importance, including farming, textiles and retail (Vakulchuk 2014, p. 8–9). In these non-strategic industries competition is far more intensive. By the same token for these companies it is often relatively difficult to influence bureaucratic processes. They have to concentrate on lower level contacts to bureaucratic agencies (Vakulchuk 2014, p. 76). Nevertheless, smaller firms profit significantly in their performance from executives and directors in their organization, who formerly served in the bureaucracy (Haveman et al. 2017, p. 95).

Entry and exit to these non-strategic sectors are far less regulated than for strategic industries. These industries are marked by private property rights and a relatively rigorous price as well as quality competition (Ahrens et al. 2016). In such a manner companies are more capable to adapt to changing market conditions. One reason for this is owing to their smaller sizes.

Relatively little Capability and Autonomy of Bureaucrats

Regarding the bureaucracy in dual economy state capitalism there tends to be less capability than in developmental states. Entry into the civil service is far less based on competitive exams. Such a motivating force as an "esprit de corps" is conspicuously missing in dual economy state capitalism. Often university graduates strive more to become well-paid managers in SOEs instead of opting to work for considerably less salary in the civil service. In general, no "embedded autonomy" such as Evans found out for the developmental state can be observed. Whereas bureaucracies tend not to lack a certain embeddedness with the business side and former civil service members quite regularly work for the corporate sector, the civil services do have relatively little autonomy versus the corporate sector. There is no notable insulation due to reputation and remuneration.

This creates the risk of capture by the business side. Indeed, corruption is a relatively sticky problem of dual economy state capitalist countries. In general, this problem is especially relevant for strategic sectors that are in the center of regulation and control by the state. Here enterprises in a number of instances collude with bureaucrats, for example in order to gain access to official capital markets or subsidized credits.

Concerning an industrial policy aiming at the imitation of products from industrialized nations, which is rigorously pursued in dual economy state capitalism as much as in the developmental state, the relatively incapable bureaucracy with little autonomy can become a burden. Bureaucrats tend to be more permissive when it comes to bending the rules with regard to target achievements. The problem is even exacerbated regarding SOEs. Here the state is often very soft on performance achievement, for instance measured in revenue or profit growth, as long as certain non-commercial, political goals such as no lay-offs of excessive staff and low prices for market participants are fulfilled. Even losses in the balance sheet are regularly accepted under these circumstances, which are dictated by politics.

Successful Integration into World Markets possible

When it comes to integration into world markets, bureaucracies tend to concentrate on large players in strategic sectors as well, which are either SOEs straight away or thoroughly influenced by the state through informal guidance or senior managers with deep links to the state.[5] These players receive incentives to gain access to export markets for instance through export subsidies, access to foreign currency and information by overseas trade information agencies.

By the same token, bureaucrats as in developmental states nurture some of these large players to become national champions in strategic sectors by applying trade policy. For certain products, where national champions are intended to gain a niche on world markets, product-specific tariffs or non-tariff trade barriers such as local content rules are enacted, so that these companies can grow on their home-markets and eventually reach sufficient scale to export on world markets.

Naturally, such a policy goal can easily backfire. Shielded from competition enterprises can reap the rents awarded to them by the bureaucracy. Even though

5 To this end CEOs are increasingly selected with an eye to their business acumen (Lin 2017, p. 108). Nevertheless, their loyalty to the ruling party and leader has to be guaranteed.

supposedly tariff and non-tariff protection are to be phased out after a certain amount of time, in a number of instances this shield is not removed even though either the respective enterprise has proven not to be capable of competing on world markets or it has become a veritable player on world markets and is in principle no more in need of protection. The reason for such an overly prolonged tariff and non-tariff protection is to be found in the peculiarities of bureaucracies in dual economy state capitalism. First, it is possible that bureaucrats lack the required skills to evaluate, when it is time to phase out the protection. As mentioned above this shield is very complex and target achievements complicated to measure. Second, it is also possible that bureaucracies have been captured by the business side. Especially on lower levels it is indeed possible for enterprises to gain a bureaucrat's favour either with pecuniary corruption or in the form of gifts.

On both fields of industrial policy – imitation of products from industrialized nations and integration into world markets – bureaucracies can become a bottleneck in successful policy implementation. Consequently, the question emerges as to why nevertheless some dual economy state capitalist countries excelled on both fields with some of their national champions becoming players on world markets. The answer can possibly be found in those countries' approach to coping with the absence of rule of law. Governments of these countries obviously managed to provide for relatively secure property rights.

Credible Commitments to secure Property Rights

As in developmental states these countries managed to credibly commit to not violating private property rights. The mechanism is relatively similar to developmental states. Regimes of dual economy state capitalist countries commit themselves to reaching explicitly specified developmental goals such as poverty alleviation, less inequality, more competitiveness, more ease of doing business and / or economic growth. Similar to developmental states, in the words of Doner et al. (2009) dual economy state capitalist countries suffer to a certain extent from "systemic vulnerability". Therefore, regimes commit to certain performance goals in order to overcome legitimacy deficits. Obviously up to a certain extent they were successful and credible in this endeavor not least of all by thus overcoming agency and skill problems with regard to their bureaucracies.

In that sense, bureaucrats have a clear incentive for not engaging too drastically and bluntly in corrupt activities or otherwise they would imperil themselves to become prone to nation-wide purges. These anti-corruption campaigns can at least partially be explained by governments' commitment to developmental goals. They cannot let the situation of occasionally incompetent and corrupt bureaucrats potentially derailing development efforts go too far. In this regard commitment to national goals serves as a mechanism to provide sufficient incentives for the corporate sector to engage in productive activities.[6]

In both forms of state capitalism dealt with so far, the state manages to overcome incentive losses, which are due to the absence of rule of law. This becomes evident when looking at the notable performance achievements of these countries' industrial policies. A different picture emerges with regard to crony state capitalism, which will be dealt with in the following sub-section.

3.1.5 Crony State Capitalism

As a third variant of state capitalism crony state capitalism will now be dealt with. In principle the term "crony capitalism" came to prominence in the wake of the "Asian crisis". But in this study the Asian "tiger states" are referred to as developmental states, whereas in crony states development for a number of reasons occasionally strongly lags behind governments' goals. In general, in crony state capitalism corruption is relatively ubiquitous, economic growth instable as well as volatile and there is hardly any development, which includes broad layers of the population. The institutional structures of those economies are much more deficient than those in developmental states (Singh / Zammit 2006, p. 220).

In crony state capitalism exchange of goods and services is often conducted through informal channels and personal relations. Anonymous markets, where buyers and sellers are basically not known to each other, exist to a far lesser extent than in the developmental state, dual economy or market capitalism. Here reciprocity in the form of gift and counter-gift plays a key role, substituting market processes up to a certain extent (May 2014, p. 90).

The problem of corruption is even more aggravating for economic agents that are in contact with the bureaucracy, for instance when registering a new company. Here significant obstacles ensue in case permits or other administrative acts have to be granted. Regularly, economic agents already fail to determine, into whose competence their case falls. Furthermore, when the bureaucrat with decision making power is determined and a payment or non-monetary gift is handed in, the act of corruption often does not correlate with the administrative act, so that this constitutes a case of dysfunctional corruption.

---

6 Here it is possible to subsume SOEs and the private sector under the corporate sector, since for SOEs incentives to contribute to the attainment of national goals can be nearly as high-powered as for private enterprises.

To a certain extent these forms of crony state capitalism can be equated with a rent seeking society. In general, there tend to be long standing relations in crony state capitalism. Without a doubt, in developmental states one key characteristic is also the close relationship between government, bureaucracy, the corporate sector and banks (Singh / Zammit 2006, p. 221). But the extent of rent-seeking in crony state capitalism is far higher and more detrimental to economic development (Kang 2003, p. 439).[7]

Low bureaucratic Quality

This is already a relatively clear indication with regard to bureaucracies' quality. As a matter of fact, as is constitutive for state capitalism, the bureaucracy is of large size relative to the size of the economy, possibly even bloated. But concerning capability economists and other scientists observe grave short-comings. Bureaucrats in a number of instances already lack basic skills required to conduct an effective implementation of industrial policy.

This has a number of reasons. For example, working for the civil service is hardly attractive compared with positions in the private sector or in SOEs. Bureaucrats have a notorious reputation and furthermore the civil service is far behind the corporate sector with regard to salaries. There are no clearly defined career paths. Bureaucrats risk dismissals for no obvious reason. Promotions and hiring are seldom performance based. They are far more contingent on personal relations to superiors, loyalty to them and furthermore loyalty to the political leadership.

Thus, it becomes close to impossible for the state to recruit the brightest minds among university graduates. The lack of skills is compounded by the absence of autonomy. Since salaries cannot compete with those on the free market, i.e. the private corporate sector, bureaucrats have a relatively high incentive to accept bribes. The threshold to engage in such activities is significantly lowered since corruption is so wide-spread in society and state, even though scorned at. In the same vein the lack of a perception of belonging to an elitist group lowers the threshold of overcoming inner resistance of becoming a corrupt state official.

---

7 A possible approach for a quantitative differentiation would consist of measuring the number of positions in the job market that are filled by these rent seeking activities rather than by market processes and comparative advantages (Aligica / Tarko 2014, p. 163). But for reasons of space and scope such a potentially fruitful differentiation cannot be conducted in this monography.

Industrial Policy relatively ineffective

This lack of capability translates into problems with conducting industrial policy. In crony state capitalism political leaders strive for imitating products from developed nations and integrating into the world economy just as much as governments in developmental states and dual economy state capitalism. But to begin with there is a lack of specific targets. Bureaucrats' and enterprises' performances can thus not be measured with the help of clear benchmarks. This creates incentive problems. For bureaucrats this amounts to having relatively unrestrained discretionary powers versus the business sector to arbitrarily formulate demands, which entrepreneurs have to fulfil.

This is especially detrimental for fostering productive business activities, since enterprises therefore have much more of an incentive to engage in rent-seeking and corruptive activities. If a performance such as mastering to imitate technology from industrialized nations for instance through reverse engineering is achieved by an enterprise, the reward be it through subsidies or non-pecuniary awards is often lacking. Contrary to that increased revenues of entrepreneurs enlarge the possibility of bureaucrats to skim of profits achieved by such a successful company.

To aggravate the absence of clearly defined targets, the lack of skills of entrepreneurs aggravates the situation. Obviously, bureaucracies display hardly any autonomy, being very susceptible to corruption by the business side. But to make matters worse there is also a lack of skills involved. Although bureaucrats appear to be embedded, keeping no arms-length towards the corporate sector, they are seldom in a position to advise on business opportunities abroad for instance in niche markets. They furthermore lack the skills, but also the incentives, to transmit their sizable discretionary powers into guiding enterprises into fruitful commercial activities. In a number of instances, they not only skim off incomes, but basically confiscate the substance of enterprises, i.e. property such as even company premises (see Markus 2015, p. 16). All this fundamentally counteracts the effectiveness of industrial policy aimed at by political leaders. Therefore, it is not even so much the lack of formulating explicit targets of industrial policy that make development almost impossible, but more the relatively inept implementation due to structural problems in bureaucracies. As a consequence, property rights in crony state capitalist countries are extremely insecure.[8]

---

8 One example is the oil industry, where especially in situations of high oil prices due to a low quality of institutions large parts of the sector are regularly nationalized (Guriev et al. 2009, p. 301).

Commitments by the state not credible

Governments seek to overcome these short-comings by just as in developmental and dual economy states credibly committing to respecting property rights. In a number of cases governments explicitly and publicly guaranteed entrepreneurs to safeguard their property rights. But these efforts tend to fail in crony state capitalism. Although political leaderships – judging by their public comments – seem to sincerely intend to relief the business side from living with the latent risk of having their property rights severely violated, they seem not to be able to rein in their own bureaucracies (Markus 2015, p. 28–29).

This is equal to a drastic form of agent predation. Governments are not able to make a credible commitment on behalf of their own agents, i.e. bureaucrats, on lower levels. Then why do governments not simply replace corrupt officials on lower levels, who are impeding businesses to engage in productive activities?

The reasons are many-fold. First of all, even if vast parts of the bureaucracy were in effect laid-off, it would be very difficult to find non-corrupt and skilled personnel instead, even if remuneration was increased. This is due to reputational effects. There is a signalling at work that tends to attract staff that is more interested in rent-seeking than in promoting for instance imitation of products and integration of national champions into world-markets. Second, bureaucrats are often chosen not so much for their qualifications but more with an eye towards their political loyalty. Thus, if the government replaces politically loyal, through non-corrupt bureaucrats, it risks to lose allegiance of these echelons of its bureaucracy.

Third, in many cases even business players no longer urge for changes in the bureaucracy. They have adapted to a situation of agent predation and with the help of corruptive activities often manage to keep competitors at bay. In effect, bureaucrats in some regards, erect entry barriers such as refusing to grant permissions in order to protect existing players on relevant markets. Therefore, in a certain sense, governments have given up on credibly committing to secure property rights.[9] They formulate national goals, but are not bound to deliver on

9 As a matter of fact, such insecure property rights due to a lack of rule of law lead to chronic legitimacy deficits in crony state capitalist countries. Whereas in developmental states these deficits are tackled with the ideology of development, in the dual economy with nationalism and partial reforms in non-strategic sectors, crony state capitalist countries resort to the ideology of populism. Economic agents appear to in many cases tolerate corruption, since they themselves can benefit from redistribution that results from the opaque rent distribution in this economic order. Another potential advantage for some economic agents in this system is that personal relationships can

these commitments. This is due to an autocratic system, where broad layers of the population have adapted to a stagnant economy with few development perspectives, but at least relatively steady income flows, for instance through selling natural resources.

3.1.6 Petro State Capitalism

The availability of sizable natural resources can be a blessing or a curse. For political leaders in petro state capitalism natural resources lower budget constraints and can increase regime legitimacy among the population owing to the possibility of financing relatively generous programs of social security. These countries have implemented a form of state capitalism, which to a high degree depends on the export of commodities. Here the state budget is financed mostly by the export of oil and gas (Hvidt 2011, p. 89). At the same time state expenses make up a significant part of GDP as is typical of state capitalism.

Those economies suffer from a strongly underdeveloped degree of diversification. Nevertheless, political leaders are aware of the risks of a one-sided economic structure, for instance an increased vulnerability to price fluctuations on world markets. Regularly, these countries are faced with revenue losses, when commodity prices fall. Furthermore, those countries are confronted with exorbitantly high-income losses as soon as natural resources are exhausted. With mixed results, political leaders try to push their economies into the direction of a diversification into industry and services (Bremmer 2010, p. 88).

Soft Budget Constraints for the Bureaucracy

One key hindrance to successfully implement a diversification strategy is a bureaucracy, that is in many respects incompetent. As much as the population's consent to autocratic rule is bought by political leaders with export incomes from natural resources, bureaucrats tend to place short-term gains for instance

---

facilitate the information flow and provide for longer time horizons in economic exchange by strengthening reciprocity and enabling some form of contract enforcement (Kang 2003, p. 440). Thus, an enforcement of property rights hinges not so much on courts and the judicial system as such, but more on loyalty within a clan and personal trust (May 2014, p. 91). Political leaders acquiesce to these benefits for a number of groups and individuals and capture support of economic agents by granting certain special privileges, justifying these with pragmatism. But those might in themselves violate the rule of law and property rights of other economic agents (Aligica / Tarko 2014, p. 171 and 173).

through accepting bribes over longer-term gains in the form of tax revenues from significantly increasing economic activity. The mentality among bureaucrats tends to be one of catching as much as one can.

Such an outcome is clearly the effect of disincentives. First of all, in a number of instances bureaucrats tend to be chosen with regard to their loyalty to the regime and not their performance or qualifications. This is aggravated by the fact that often members of the bureaucracy are also family members of political leaders. This has the added disincentive that performance becomes even less of a criterium for promotion and less-connected, but better performing members of the bureaucracy tend to be in a disadvantaged position.

Second, the abundance of funds leads to a situation with hardly any hard budget constraints. Funds can sometimes even be misappropriated without any superiors noticing it. Funds for diversifying the economy are thus in a number of cases funnelled into the coffers of bureaucrats and not utilized for productive purposes.

Third, the entire institutional setting creates a framework, where signalling deters university graduates that intend to engage in upgrading the economy from entering the civil service. Regularly, talented and goal-oriented university graduates from petro state capitalist countries prefer to move abroad and pursue their career with more job perspectives overseas. Furthermore, one key problem for the bureaucracy to recruit talented staff is due to the fact that in many instances political rulers pursue the national goal of diversification by building white elephants that in their perception increases their own prestige, but is of little economic value. This furthermore deters ambitious graduates from pursuing a career as a civil servant, who collaborates with the political leadership in diversifying the economy and giving his home country a perspective after natural resources are depleted.

Such a problem can be called the "rentier mentality", emanating from the difference between income earned by productive means and passively acquired income through rents. The connection between effort and reward is to a high degree disrupted. In state capitalist variants – such as the developmental state or the dual economy – economic agents are mostly rewarded for taking part in risky investments. In such a setting, there are strong incentives for building up manufacturing capacities, export-oriented industries and domestic savings. No such incentives exist when there are soft budget constraints due to revenues generated almost automatically from the export of natural resources (Hvidt 2011, p. 89–90).

Diversification as Industrial policy

These structural problems of the bureaucracy are linked with problems of pursuing the industrial policy goals of imitating products from developed nations and integrating into the world economy beyond exporting commodities. Petro states so far tend to pursue no consistent target-oriented strategy to diversify away from natural resources.[10] There is no clearly outlined national plan set up by the government to catch-up to industrialized nations. Therefore, there appears to be little intention to really follow in the footsteps of developmental states.

This can again be partly attributed to the abundance of funds, giving political leaders and bureaucrats little constraint to act. Another factor concerns stability among the population and bureaucrats. If political leaders and bureaucrats embarked on an ambitious diversification effort for instance with credit subsidies and sanctions, this would first of all be costly with the result of higher taxes and lower social benefits. Second, implementation would have to result in a carrot and stick strategy after the model of the developmental state. But a rigorous implementation is first of all inhibited by endemic corruption and furthermore through crony relations between those who govern and the governed. A reversal could in this regard create discontent imperilling diversification efforts all the more. These are reasons why observers note a lock-in effect that is hard to break and institutional change would presumably only be possible under the situation of a critical juncture.

Concerning rule of law observers see little movement to overcome its relative absence by credibly committing to development and protection of property rights. It appears to be a tool of political rule to grant favours and repeal them contingent on the degree of loyalty an entrepreneur or bureaucrat shows. Complete loss of wealth is always possible, but usually not as a result of a market outcome, but by losing the favour of the rulers. This situation creates an institutional framework, where incentives for productive activities are extremely low-powered and it is most rational for political as well as economic actors to engage in corruptive practices such as seeking to continue crony relations to the rulers, their families and friends. This also supports capital flight. Petro states have for a long time encountered problems to utilize their revenues for productive

10 At this point an exception has to be mentioned. The United Arab Emirates diversified into internationally competitive airline national champions and financial hubs. In this regard, they apply classical instruments of industrial policy in an approach, which is called the "Dubai model" in the literature (Hvidt 2011, p. 85). But this appears to be rather an exception than a rule and likewise involves no domestic production facilities.

purposes. Billions of dollars are placed into accounts of international banks and only passively managed (Hvidt 2011, p. 87).

Rents are foremost distributed to elites with violence potential. This helps to prevent violence and ultimately regime change in the sense of North et al. (2009). In that regard petro states with relatively high incomes through natural resources tend to have a high degree of stability with a relatively low frequency of regime change, but credible commitments to development are missing. These regimes are instead able to capture credibility for their redistribution programs, since political costs for the government not to fulfil its promises are very high in the form of influential groups reneging their support for the state. Allegiance is bought by granting special favours, for instance positions in the state bureaucracy to influential elitist individuals (Bjorvatn / Naghavi 2011, p. 740–741).

No taxes for local Economy and Dubai as a Role Model

In general, to a large extent petro states are still following the example of a rentier economy. Creation of wealth mostly depends on a small fraction of society. In such a setting the state is dislocated from wide parts of the national economy. The state finances itself with the means of oil and gas rents and is not forced to tax the local economy. Therefore, there are only few incentives for political leaders to develop an efficient economic base. Rather the state rests on distributing rents acquired through natural resource exports (Bremmer 2010, p. 87). In effect, thus a social contract emerges, where few political demands are made by the population in exchange for government services without tax levies. For such reasons, the government faces little pressure to formulate goals and objectives. Consequences are political leaders, who are aloof from local conditions, a high degree of centralization and a lack of accountability (Losman 2010, p. 429).

In general, SOEs of petro state capitalist countries are sources of national pride and employment. They often also provide for education and infrastructure. Thus, they are not solely maximizing profits or shareholder value, but pursue often incoherent political goals, among others keeping up a high degree of employment and delivering subsidized products for the domestic market, especially gas below world market prices. Occasionally, this can lead to a deficiency of investible funds and thereby imperil infrastructures, for instance of oil extractors (Losman 2010, p. 433–434 and 438).[11]

---

11 Exceptions are national champions of Golf Cooperation Council (GCC) countries, which have the advantage of directly reporting to the rulers or close associates. There tends to emerge a long-term relationship with personal trust and relatively little

Only gradually petro states are modifying their economic models to overcome the problems of a rentier economy listed above. Thus, for instance petro state capitalist countries of the Golf Cooperation Council (GCC) aim to diversify their economies into fields such as finance, tourism or the aviation industry to become less reliant on incomes from oil and gas. In this regard, they apply classical instruments of industrial policy in an approach, which is called the "Dubai model" in the literature (Hvidt 2011, p. 85). This is in accordance with the model of state capitalism presented above where a state-led development formulated by the political leadership is a central element.

By now petro states with the help of elite technocrats tend to apply targeted technology purchases, export promotion, infrastructure policies and a degree of protectionism for national champions. Authoritarianism helps to insulate bureaucrats and national champions from demands by the population that could diminish profits to a point where key corporate functions such as investing are strongly jeopardized (Hertog 2010, p. 293–294). But opposed to the developmental state there are no pilot agencies for coordinating development and diversification. This could be one of the reasons, why so far there is no significant improvement of production techniques, labour productivity, managerial innovations or high-tech innovations. Growth still mostly occurs thanks to commodity price increases. As a matter of fact, problems in the bureaucracy, policy formulation and implementation as well as no credible commitments to protect property rights are all incentives for economic actors to continue with rent-seeking instead of productive activities. There are so far – with a few exceptions – no significant changes in economic structures (Losman 2010, p. 443).

3.1.7 Predatory State Capitalism

As a final variant predatory state capitalism will be dealt with. It has been maintained that lack of rule of law is a decisive factor distinguishing state from market capitalism. As a matter of fact, this gap is most evident in the state capitalist form of predatory state capitalism. The state is in a position "to grab or appropriate

---

fluctuation in the management. The prime example in this regard is Saudi Arabian oil monopoly Aramco, which is gradually being privatized. These SOEs are in a position to have a clear mandate with few elite players intervening into daily operations or strategic goals. Thus, this has the effect of a relatively high degree of insulation from games of patronage and rent-seeking. The notorious lack of autonomy suffered by a number of SOEs is avoided for these national champions in petro states (Hertog 2010, p. 270 and 273).

coercively" (Vahabi 2016, p. 153). Evans (1995, p. 45) defines it thus: "The state preys on its citizenry, terrorizing them, despoiling their common patrimony and providing little in the way of services in return."

This type of state capitalism is in some ways similar to crony state capitalism. Here corruption is also ubiquitous and an every-day phenomenon for almost all households and companies. Ethnic favouritism and electoral malpractice do regularly occur in both forms, too. But overall, there is not such a predatory and almost criminal intention of the political leadership to be observed in crony state capitalism. Political access is restricted, power consolidated, economic competition stifled in order to generate profits for the elites and not the entire society. If elections take place they become a zero-sum game and citizens tend to turn into clients of powerful local patrons, who have themselves patrons higher up in the hierarchy (Diamond 2008, p. 43).

Cleptocratic Bureaucracy

The situation is significantly exacerbated and improvements hardly possible due to a cleptocratic bureaucracy. Here the entire term civil servant becomes a contradiction in itself. Bureaucrats serve their narrow self-interests and not those of their principal, i.e. the government or in an ulterior sense the population. Basically, incentives for becoming a bureaucrat are fundamentally misaligned. For most university graduates it is attractive to enter the civil service with the goal of extracting wealth from citizens, i.e. among others entrepreneurs.

A sense of an elitist, autonomous bureaucracy is not to be identified, so that the civil service mostly attracts graduates that intend to enrich themselves by maximizing collection of bribes. In this regard, bureaucrats tend to collude with the business sector in order to receive as many bribes as possible. The problem becomes aggravated due to lack of education. Bureaucrats in a number of instances even have no knowledge of how to apply development-enhancing policies. Thus, not only the will to pursue developmental goals is missing, but also the means.

This is all the more a reality, since the political leadership formulates no national goals. All other state capitalist variants imply at least some sort of national ambition, even if in the case of petro state capitalism the goal of diversification is often widely pursued. But in predatory state capitalism the entire aim of political leadership tends to circle around maximizing private revenues.

And since this is only possible as long as political leaders stay in office, power preservation becomes the core goal. This trickles down to the bureaucracy. The key ambition for civil servants consists in adapting to the political framework. As soon as regime change – in most cases through a coup – becomes a highly likely event, bureaucrats seek to set up relations to new political leaders. If on the other hand there is regime stability through effective political repression civil servants perceive to be relatively unconstrained in enforcing the payment of bribes.

This has severe negative side-effects for the collection of taxes and the financing of state budgets, which should officially be the source of civil servants' incomes, but also the funding of an effective industrial policy. Tax payers perceive the degree of corruption in the entire political system and resort to tax avoidance. Thus, official revenue declines even more and bureaucrats as well as politicians in this vicious circle rely all the more on bribes for their and the state's income.

The state private sector nexus, which is crucial for development, is dysfunctional. Predatory states have no effective bureaucracy and those relationships that exist are based on personal contacts with no connection to the state as a whole. A coherent industrial policy approach is notably missing. But the problem of the predatory state is not too much bureaucracy, though. Rather it is lack of it as well as the emerging weaknesses in relation to society (Evans 1995, p. 12 and 47). The regime in this regard has clear characteristics of clientelism. Interplay of government, bureaucracy and corporate sector functions through the exchange of favours between members of the state and supporters. In other forms of state capitalism rules and regulations provide for checks and balances to contain the resulting corruption. These checks and balances are effectively destroyed in the predatory state (Quimpo 2009, p. 338).

No effective Industrial Policy is conducted

These structural problems of predatory state capitalism spill over into industrial policy. Goals such as upgrading the industrial base through imitation and in general integrating into the world economy foremost through export promotion are in no conceivable way possible and due to the structural short-comings also impossible to attain. The corporate sector is stuck at the level of exporting primary goods. Not even the agrarian sector has been upgraded enough to an extent that would allow for exports.

In many instances, raw materials such as gold or diamonds are sold out to foreign investors by domestic politicians in order to enrich themselves. The formulation and implementation of a development-enhancing industrial policy is so difficult, since incentives for political leaders are not aligned with long-term development. Time horizons are very short. This is due to the fact that political leaders perceive to lose their positions if a policy change was implemented, so that they refrain from formulating it. Such an insecurity encourages capital flight in order to have a safe haven to relocate to in case of regime change.

Property Rights even for Elites completely insecure

This leads over to the dire state of property rights. These are even for the elites entirely insecure. There is an even lesser degree of rule of law in predatory state capitalism than in any other form of state capitalism. If a political or economic actor falls out of favour from the political leadership his wealth can basically be confiscated ad-hoc. He then has hardly any realistic opportunity whatsoever to pursue a trial in order to restore his property. Involuntary redistribution is conducted by expropriation, extortion or outright theft (Vahabi 2016, p. 155).

This drastic lack of rule of law is in no way diminished through credible commitments by the government. As mentioned above the state already refrains from committing to national goals and thereby securing property rights, so that it is not even the question whether they are credible or not. In this regard, even policy announcements with a low impact on the economy are not credible, since they are quite regularly reversed. There is decidedly no constancy of the economic policy.

The entire economy becomes prey to ruling elites that are often organized in clans. Economic agents react with decisively structured evasion tactics, so that black markets emerge and market coordination is substituted by alternative institutions. Much in the same vein North (1981, p. 22) argues when referring to predatory capitalism as a system, where the state sets the property rights in a way to maximize revenue of the elites, who are in power. Likewise, these political leaders pay no attention to the general level of the wealth of the society. The purpose of the government is not so much supplying infrastructure and other public goods, but to produce private goods for the elites, i.e. influential families, clans or oligarchs. In this regard, the difference between police and criminals is relatively small. The aim of the police and the judicial system is not to guarantee the rule of law, but to bend the rules so that they themselves profit from it (Diamond 2008, p. 43).

SOEs become prey to the political leadership. Managers and CEOs are appointed from the elites and their goal is to maximize revenues that flow into the coffers of corrupt politicians or business-men. In a number of cases MNCs operate in these countries and there is a clear dependence to be observed on taxing the profits of these companies (Turok 1980, p. 455). As in petro states, profitable companies to be exploited often stem from the oil or gas sector.

There is no long-term orientation in predatory state capitalism. Political leaders strive to stay in power by suppressing potential opposition with means that amount to terror. Thus, there are parallels to the basic natural state of North et al. (2009), where there is a constant threat of coups. The regimes are not embedded into society. Since they are constantly in threat of being ousted and even incarcerated political leaders pursue a strategy of grabbing as much as they can as fast as possible.

Of all forms of state capitalism, the developmental and the predatory state vary most significantly from each other. On the one hand, there is a long-term orientation with a government formulating developmental goals and a meritocratic, capable bureaucracy implementing policies, often in the form of a coherent, rule-based industrial policy.

On the other hand, there is a state that is often completely dominated by one political leader, who has no ambition of developing the country, and even if he did, had no capable bureaucracy at his disposal. In the end it needs to be maintained that the predatory state differs from failed states, though. There are in predatory states still central governments that are able to up to a certain extent collect taxes. And basic functions of the state such as defence and providing a minimum degree of infrastructure are upheld. Predatory state capitalist nations are not in the imminent process of disintegration, although there is a risk of such a fall into a failed state.

3.1.8 Democratic State Capitalism?

When looking at countries that are supposed to be state capitalist such as China or Russia, it is striking that they are mostly authoritarian or outright dictatorships. Kurlantzick (2016, p. 115–136) on the other hand sees democracy as a defining characteristic of a number of state capitalist countries and observes that the most democratic are also the most efficient state capitalist countries. But does this mean that besides the developmental state, dual economy, petro, crony and predatory state capitalism there is a category of democratic state capitalism?

An argument in favour of this view is that there are some countries such as Brazil that are considered as state capitalist and have a relatively long tradition of democracy. For example, it is almost something like a defining and typical characteristic of erstwhile state capitalist India. But here one already sees the limits of such an approach. India did not choose democracy with an eye to establishing a state capitalist system, but rather became a democracy as a result of the *satyagraha* or non-violent protest and freedom struggle against the British empire as well as the personalities leading this movement being fervent proponents of democracy.

In most state capitalist countries – even in those with democracy – there are no structural democratic and participatory elements which are reflected in the economic order. In general, patrimonial forms of coordinating economic activity tend to prevail. This becomes evident by the fact that considerable parts of the population are marginalized. Rent distribution remains a defining characteristic of state capitalism as explained in the model above. In Turkey, which could possibly qualify as being state capitalist, for instance currently democratic structures are decisively carved out and replaced by patrimonially shaped decision-making processes.

Especially in the most advanced state capitalist form of the developmental state, there are grave short-comings regarding democracy. Thus, the developmental state up to a degree is crafted after the role model of developmental authoritarianism in pseudo-parliamentary Prussia and Meiji Japan. Likewise, in a number of state capitalist countries a form of pseudo-democracy prevails (see Thompson 1996, p. 643–644).

As a matter of fact, for the success or failure of a state capitalist system democracy does not seem to be the crucial point. The value of state-business relations is not dependent on political institutions such as democratic versus authoritarian governments. What matters is the creation and sustainability of some form of a functional equivalent for the rule of law, for instance for defining and enforcing property rights, increasing transparency and accountability (Haveman et al. 2017, p. 96).

Apparently, modernization does not all by itself produce a political culture favouring democracy in most developing nations. Social mobilization and economic development in the short term rather seem to foster authoritarian structures. Even where middle classes gradually evolved, a turn to democracy was still far away. Strikingly in the developmental states in an incremental process democracy tended to progress, for instance in South Korea, Taiwan and Thailand (Thompson 1996, p. 626–627). But this occurred only after a significant amount of time elapsed, since the developmental process was initiated.

Thus, in the terminology of North et. al. (2009), as the state capitalist variant of the developmental state illustrates, there can be a tendency of some mature natural states to become open access orders. After all, they tend to develop civilian control of the military, some form of rule of law and perpetually lived organizations. Thompson (1996, p. 626–627) has come to the conclusion that the theory of a correlation between development and democratization can neither be falsified nor verified. Later on, it will be illustrated in the case studies that South Korea progressed from a dictatorship to a democracy during its developmental phase. Evidently, this country became an open access order with strong structural similarities to established democracies such as Great Britain, the United States or Germany, successively being ruled democratically by civilians since at least the 1990s.

In general, there are grave short-comings in the rule of law – depending in its extent on the respective form of state capitalism. As a matter of fact, elements of democracy have not helped to overcome the negative effects of lack of rule of law on property rights even though from a theoretical point of view these elements should have given more power to political and economic agents and strengthened their rights. However, successful state capitalist countries such as developmental states were able to credibly commit to national goals such as export growth and thus secured property to a degree as to give economic agents an incentive to engage in productive activities. In this regard, these countries also managed to reduce legitimacy deficits. Democratic elements or an emergence of democracy as such at first plays a negligible role in state capitalism. Therefore, in general it appears not to be very fruitful to include a category of democratic state capitalism to the qualitative taxonomy. Democracy appears to be no constituting factor of state capitalism nor even a category of its own.

3.1.9 Conclusion

By now all five variants of state capitalism have been illustrated. In the centre of any state capitalist system in comparison with market capitalism stands the relatively lower degree of rule of law. Whereas in developmental states and dual economy state capitalism governments are able to overcome the detrimental consequences of insecure property rights and therefore diminished incentives to engage in productive commercial activities, crony, petro and predatory state capitalist governments fail in this regard. The reason is to be found in structural problems within the bureaucracy. In crony state capitalism it is bloated, corrupt and incapable, but for political reasons almost impossible to rein in. The situation is comparable in petro state capitalism, where there is the added problem of softer budget constraints, which allow bureaucrats more leeway in pursuing narrow self-interests for instance by inhibiting development projects or shirking. In the case of predatory state capitalism, the entire bureaucracy has become dysfunctional. It is an obstacle to development and not the quintessential implementation tool.

This results in agent predation, principal expropriation, skimming and siphoning, where among others lower level bureaucrats derail development efforts by the government.[12] Consequently, industrial policy is not conducted in an effective manner. There are grave short-comings with regard to implementation, already starting with the absence of clearly defined targets. This has the effect that incentives for enterprises are relatively low-powered and are oriented more towards corruptive than productive activities.

Opposed to that, though dual economy state capitalist countries also display grave short-comings in bureaucratic capabilities, those governments manage to credibly commit to at least partially secure private property rights. Reasons for the divergence with regard to crony state capitalism can at this stage of this study not ultimately be given and need to be sought for in the case studies. But it appears to be clear that industrial policy results of dual economy state capitalism are superior to those of crony, petro and predatory state capitalism.

The most effective industrial policy is conducted in developmental states. Here a capable, elitist bureaucracy with an "embedded autonomy" (Evans 1995) effectively implements policies formulated by the governments. Indeed, even in developmental states there is less of a degree of rule of law than in market capitalism. But with relatively little corruption in the bureaucracy the corporate sector suffers only to a minor extent from agent predation, principal expropriation or skimming. If corruption takes place at all, it is mostly in the form of siphoning incomes, which tends to be disorganized and the least detrimental variant of corruption. Moreover, governments in developmental states manage to credibly commit to developmental goals. This increases the security of property rights and provides economic agents with an incentive to engage in productive commercial activities.

So far, state has been differentiated from market capitalism. And within state capitalism five different forms of state capitalism have been identified. Quite certainly, it is possible to transform from one state capitalist variant as it is possible to change from state to market capitalism and vice versa. Since the research question consists of understanding state capitalism and its performance differences, it is also important to understand, how it is possible to switch from one state

12 Agent predation consists of disorganized corruption, which infringes on ownership rights. At the same time principal expropriation also attacks ownership rights, but is organized within the bureaucracy or even political sphere. Finally, skimming is also organized, but involves only income rights. When engaging in siphoning, corrupt officials violate income rights in a disorganized manner. As a matter of fact, violating ownership rights is more detrimental than violating income rights, since with the former all future income is imperiled by the perpetrators (see Markus 2015, p. 28).

capitalist variant to another for instance with the goal of improving performance results. Institutional change between different forms of state capitalism will be dealt with in the subsequent section.

3.2 Institutional Change from one State Capitalist Variant to another

Institutional change from one state capitalist variant to another implies an upward or a downward movement along the scale of development effectiveness. This movement does not occur along a clearly defined path. Therefore, upward and downward movement will respectively be taken in its entirety and not be meticulously branched out into the respective forms of state capitalism. Still, this will entail describing how crony and petro state capitalism can switch to the developmental state with some remarks on peculiarities regarding institutional change in dual economy state capitalism. It will also be dealt with, how predatory state capitalist systems can gain more development effectiveness, although it appears to be highly unlikely that those regimes can switch to developmental states without going through the stage of for instance crony state capitalism. On the other side, downward movements appear not to be intended by policy-makers. It is more the result of a gradual erosion process, which will be described in a rather stylized manner.

Moving upwards in Development Effectiveness

If a political leader in predatory state capitalism decides to move up the ladder of development effectiveness, the first step is to improve on the civil service. It has become the center of a dysfunctional governance system, where narrow self-interests compel political and economic agents to pursue short-sighted goals of self-enrichment. Institutional change is probably only possible with a long-term approach, starting with improvements in education. If the government had a sufficiently large number of capable university graduates to choose from for positions in the bureaucracy, elements of competitiveness in the selection process could be introduced.

Education as such can serve as a tool to give more autonomy to bureaucrats vis-à-vis the business-side. An adequate educational background tends to give bureaucrats a certain sense of superiority versus the business sector. Much in the same vein a kind of "esprit de corps" can be created among civil servants and combined with sufficiently high incomes and clearly defined career paths compared to the corporate sector. This would in all probability further raise the bureaucracy's autonomy. Thus, a self-enforcing informal institution can be created that raises the bar for individual bureaucrats to engage in corruptive practices.

After such improvements in the civil service all levels of the political leadership would probably more easily switch from pursuing extractive policies to supporting productive activities, since the bureaucracy has significantly lost its capacity as a tool for collecting bribes. Furthermore, presumably the restructured civil service would take a role as a model for political leaders to follow. This could be accompanied by commitments of the government to national goals such as economic growth or the fight against poverty.

Under such a setting the commitment would have a chance to be credible due to an improved implementation process emanating from a more capable bureaucracy. This could spill over into industrial policies, becoming more target-oriented. The former predatory state capitalist country would have a chance to pursue a more realistic carrot and stick strategy at the state-business sector nexus, since the state due to its intention of gaining credibility has an incentive to set attainable goals for the corporate sector.

In this sense the nation could possibly embark on an industrial policy that promotes successful imitation of products and production processes from industrialized nations and integrates into the world economy, partially by nurturing infant industries through initially protecting domestic markets. To that end it would be indispensable for the government to credibly pursue a developmental path. But in the end, the entire described process can only work out in a gradual process, among others since informal institutions are involved which cannot be changed ad-hoc through rule modifications by the state. If a predatory state managed to partially succeed to implement some of the described changes and progress to petro or crony state capitalism this nation would have already achieved significantly much in terms of development.

If crony or petro state capitalist nations intend to enforce institutional change towards dual economy state capitalism or even the developmental state, they usually have to take advantage of critical junctures, since rent-seeking has become so endemic in these nations. The entire system of crony and petro state capitalism is so significantly marked by structural rigidities, i.e. a bloated and sclerotic bureaucracy with an equilibrium of rent distribution for elites on a relatively low developmental scale that even a charismatic leader has to utilize a favourable historical time-frame, where rigidities are somehow softened, in order to push through institutional change. This could be in time of economic or political crisis, where resistance of elitist forces tends to be diluted.

Such a political leader needs to begin with the bureaucracy. A cornerstone of reforms would consist of adding more capability and autonomy to the bureaucracy. Possible steps would include raising salaries, educating bureaucrats even after hiring, increasing fines for corruptive behaviour, introducing performance-based entry exams and promotions as well as more intangible efforts such as raising the reputation of the civil service for instance through public relations campaigns. These measures would conceivably still not be enough. Structural reforms tend to be inevitable, too. They would consist of downsizing bureaucracies, possibly decentralization, establishing smaller units, defining more competitive career paths, streamlining reporting lines and increasing accountability by unequivocally placing one civil servant in charge of one task and holding him responsible for success or failure.

This already touches on the results of industrial policy. Here direct targets would be incentive-enhancing. They could be formulated in a way that fulfillment or failure is to be clearly measurable. A carrot-and-stick approach could be introduced, where rules such as export promotion incentives as well as sanctions are rigorously implemented. This would clearly increase expectations certainty and incentivize enterprises to pursue more productive objectives – such as exploring new markets, increasing market share, revenue and profit – instead of redistributive goals such as rent-seeking. In the case of the petro state diversification could become a national ambition and industrial policy oriented towards this goal. Here targets could be specified in a way to reward successful efforts to diversify into industrial and service sectors instead of natural resource.

In order to opt for dual economy state capitalism a political leader of crony or petro state capitalism would have to define strategic sectors, where he intends to create national champions. At least for these sectors the government needs the bureaucracy to relatively capably implement industrial policy. This would entail improving on the quality of the civil service with the means described above. But finding strategic sectors, where imitation of products and export promotion are promising – is by far easier said than accomplished. There would have to be a fruitful interplay of government, bureaucracy and the business sector. Most of all this is important for efficient information flows. Before any decision can be taken, information about market potential has to flow from the business side upward to the bureaucracy and government. But such flows are only possible as long as structural changes have been implemented. This would consist of having established a more capable, goal-oriented bureaucracy that takes up signals from the business sector even on lower levels and transmits it up to higher echelons and to political decision makers.

Obviously, such a state- business nexus is missing in crony state capitalism. This is also due to the fact that governments do not manage to credibly commit to developmental goals. Such a credible commitment is contingent on a number of factors. But first of all, governments need to have a history of keeping promises made to the corporate sector. This increases the reputation and likewise provides for a chance to credibly commit on certain goals. In crony state capitalism one of the key problems is that on lower levels of the bureaucracy commitments made by the government are not kept. Far more often here bureaucrats do use their discretionary powers to extort bribes and engage in siphoning or even agent predation. But having made the structural changes with regard to the bureaucracy described above, it would be facilitated for the government to credibly commit on developmental goals, thereby alleviating the relative absence of rule of law, establishing more secure property rights and consequently increasing expectations certainty as the key function of any institutional framework.

Basically, what has been illustrated for an upward movement starting from crony state capitalism can be maintained for dual economy state capitalism as well. This variant of state capitalism needs to improve on its bureaucratic capability in order to become a developmental state. This makes structural changes and a more goal-oriented industrial policy necessary. By the same token in dual economy state capitalism the government has at least partially managed to credibly commit on developmental goals.

It has acquired a reputation of keeping promises such as securing property rights. It has already created some national champions in strategic sectors, which it could continue to support even in the system of a developmental state. However, the state would have to forgo systematically discriminating against non-strategic sectors. There would have to be some form of level playing field with facilitated entry and exit of corporate players. At the same time that does not mean the state has to step back from its industrial policy. Those instruments could even be strengthened to upgrade the industrial base and integrate more into the world economy, even exporting finished goods.

The entire process of moving up in development effectiveness is marked by trial and error. Political leaders and civil servants need to be willing to experiment. In that sense the institutional framework is in the best case characterized by what North (1990) calls "adaptive efficiency". Development and institutional change cannot be enacted overnight. There are set-backs and there is no clearly delineated development path to follow. What counts is the commitment of the state to follow through on pro-development measures.

Moving downwards in Development Effectiveness

Moving down from the developmental to dual economy or crony and petro state capitalism or from those forms to even predatory state capitalism entails a process of erosion. As in the upward movement it will progress in stages, so that a developmental state will hardly lapse straight into a predatory state. All in all, the quality of the institutional framework becomes gradually eroded. This can have a number of reasons. But most of all the process seems to start from above. The political leadership loses its grip on the state-business sector nexus. Bureaucracies tend to insulate themselves more and more from the government. They also have a tendency to grow. But increasing size does not result in more capability. The opposite seems to be true.

Bureaucrats are less and less accountable to their principals, i.e. the government. They tend to pursue goals, which are independent of their political principals. This does not necessarily consist of self-enrichment for instance through agent predation. It can also be outright attentism. Bureaucrats can decide to engage in shirking, reducing their work-load to a minimum. All that would in itself erode the characteristics so remarkable of the developmental state – a capable bureaucracy, target-oriented industrial policy and credible commitments regarding developmental goals.

The bureaucracy would quite naturally become less capable. An erosion of bureaucratic quality due to short-comings in political leadership would significantly reduce the reputation of the civil service. Ceteris paribus this translates into unfavourable signaling. Increasingly, only less talented university graduates would be attracted to apply for positions in the civil service. At the end of this process, the typical "esprit de corps" and elitist self-perception of the civil service is lost. This would almost automatically equate to a loss of autonomy versus the corporate sector and more susceptibility for engaging in corruptive activities. Consequently, incentives for corporate players change as well – away from engaging in productive activities.

Industrial policy can due to the lack of bureaucratic quality not be conducted as effectively as before anymore. It becomes difficult to give the corporate sector realistic targets, when there are no capable bureaucrats to assess the appropriate target level. Also, if shirking was involved, bureaucrats could have an incentive to set unambitious targets, which are not difficult to reach for corporate players. The reasons are first of all that performance of bureaucrats is measured by target achievement as well and second that civil servants can collude with the business sector in order to collect bribes. Thus, in a long process the effectiveness of industrial policy is undermined and a goal such as keeping up integration into the word economy and its division of labour is subverted.

By the same token, with the erosion of bureaucratic quality, it becomes increasingly hard for the government of developmental and dual economy states to credibly commit on national goals. First of all, these goals are much more difficult to achieve with a low-quality bureaucracy, which makes them less credible. Second, agency problems with regard to the bureaucracy ensue. It becomes problematic to credibly commit to a national goal, when the bureaucracy as the implementing force of policies is either not capable enough anymore or even obstructs goal achievement with enriching itself for instance through agent predation. This results in perceptions by the corporate sector that property rights become less secure with all the ensuing incentive problems.

Therefore, the former developmental or dual economy state has become stuck in a vicious circle, starting from a political leadership, which relaxed its grip on the civil service. Admittedly, other scenarios are also conceivable, such as a government, which has turned into a predatory regime, trying to squeeze out the corporate sector with the help of a temporarily still capable bureaucracy. But here the credible commitment on national goals would also be lost.

The lapse from petro or crony state capitalism into predatory state capitalism would be a gradual process as well. As in the formerly described process, this would also involve a relatively strong government turning into a weak regime, which has lost its impact on the civil service and the corporate sector. It would probably entail some form of decentralization. Decision-making would be delegated to lower levels and thereby open the door for capture by the business sector of lower level bureaucrats that tend to be more embedded with the corporate sector and thereby more prone to collusion.

Again, this deterioration of the quality of the bureaucracy results in less effectiveness for the industrial policy. In this case it would probably not be possible to speak of a meaningful industrial policy anymore. There are numerous reasons for civil servants to engage in cleptocratic practices. The first is the lack of strict governance by political leaders and higher-level bureaucrats. Second, it is possible that political leaders and higher echelons of the civil service themselves engage to an exorbitant degree in predatory activities. This would serve as an incentive for bureaucrats to emulate such a behaviour and extract wealth from the corporate sector. Third, it is conceivable that there was an erosion of the tax base a priori and bureaucrats did not receive their full salaries anymore, resulting in an incentive to collect bribes in order to compensate income losses.

Moreover, this unfavourable institutional change can also come straight from the government. For instance, a new generation of political leaders can gain political power and pursue predatory practices of self-enrichment. But it is also conceivable that the belief systems of current political leaders change. Then, the civil service can even become a tool for wealth extraction, culminating in an institutional setting where there are informal targets of how many bribes have to be collected by the bureaucracy and handed over to the regime. Here all forms of an industrial policy, such as aiming to integrate into the world economy, vanish. If correspondingly nevertheless goals existed, they would solely serve the function of a pretext for applying sticks to extract wealth from the corporate sector. Targets have lost their meaning as incentives for instance to upgrade the industrial base.

But such a detrimental institutional change can also as an exception to some extent emanate from the business side. Corporate players can have become so politically and economically powerful that they capture the civil service. Then the bureaucracy would become a tool of the business side to pursue policies, which favour certain industries and corporate players to the detriment of competitors as well as overall development. This can result in some form of "piranha capitalism" (Markus 2015), where the state aids powerful actors of the corporate sector to destroy rivals or even acquire state property for below market prices. Here again the state has become weak and is most of all completely unable to protect property rights – even those of the state itself.

By now, institutional change within state capitalism has been illustrated. It has been shown, how state capitalist regimes can change from one form to another. In the extreme this can mean that a developmental state gradually regresses in stages to the level of a predatory state. But institutional change can likewise result in a predatory state capitalist country step by step moving up to become a developmental state. The taxonomy of state capitalism as well as institutional change have all been deduced from the theory and the constituting principles of part two. Subsequently, in a grounded approach it is intended to use some data as a means to use the constituting principles with the help of proxies to differentiate market from state capitalism. Furthermore, in a stylized manner it is also sought to discern the different variants of state capitalism.

3.3 Determining State Capitalist Countries

This section consists of three parts. First of all, it is referred back to part two, where seven constituting principles for state capitalism have been identified. Now, in a first step those constituting principles are operationalized with the help of proxies. The selection of these proxies will likewise be explained. Second, relevant data will be presented to show, which countries among upper middle income countries of the World Bank qualify as state capitalist. In the same vein it will be illustrated that according to the chosen methodology widely assumed market capitalist US, Germany and Japan indeed do not qualify as state capitalist. Third, after having identified state capitalist countries their performance in terms of economic growth will be compared with those of industrialized nations of the Organization for Economic Cooperation and Development (OECD) over the last 20 years. This shall serve as an indicator whether in catch-up processes of development state capitalism is really inferior to market capitalism, as a number of neoclassical economists argue.

3.3.1 Proxies for State Capitalist Constituents

Economists and political scientists sometimes refer to state capitalism without a general understanding of what specifically constitutes such an economic order. Most authors stress the relevance of state ownership (e. g. Musacchio / Lazzarini 2014). Other scientists see the emergence of sovereign wealth funds (SWF) as the most striking characteristic of state capitalism (e.g. Bremmer 2010). Certainly, both characteristics are the most obvious signs for a state capitalist system. Nevertheless, these could be necessary, but not sufficient elements for state capitalism. For instance, most authors would agree that Norway is a market-led economy firmly rooted in the Western world. But Norway's SWF is the largest of the world and the country maintains a high degree of state ownership in the corporate sector. By the same token the economy is relatively deregulated with less government intervention than for instance in the state capitalist country par excellence, China. Therefore, Norway would obviously be classified more as market led than state capitalist.

In order not to fall into such a trap of concentrating on too few criteria for discerning state capitalism, seven constituting principles of state capitalism have been identified in part two, so that state capitalist countries can more adequately be categorized. These were the state as the dominant economic actor, a state dominance of the financial sector, application of industrial policy especially in the form of imitating products from industrialized countries, shielding domestic markets, the co-existence of private property rights, a minimum of bureaucratic capacity and an institutional framework, which is marked by a relatively strong absence of rule of law.

Although these principles were sufficiently concrete to differentiate state from market capitalism and create a taxonomy of state capitalism, in order to more precisely argue whether a country is state capitalist or not, it helps to use measurable figures. To apply those data, it is obligatory to operationalize the state capitalist constituents with proxies, for instance indexes of think tanks. These will now be developed in a systematic fashion.

For the first constituting principle the state as the dominant actor in the economy it is referred to state activity in the economy, especially by SOEs. Where there are sizable numbers of SOEs the state is able to exert strong influence on the corporate sector. Admittedly, this can beyond pure ownership further be compounded by means such as informal guidance. The state – i.e. government and bureaucracy – directly or indirectly act as an economic decision-maker. In so far, states are endowed with a significant degree of discretion. There is no central planning organization as in socialism, but a high degree of governmental control. This becomes evident when looking at state-owned or parastatal companies, where recruitment or utilization of profits are decisively influenced by the state.

One approach to incorporate state control and dominance of the economy is to look at state ownership of the corporate sector, be it as a majority or minority investor.[13] But one should be aware of the fact that ownership not necessarily equates to control. One example is China where a number of state-owned enterprises act more autonomously than some privately held corporations (Milhaupt / Zheng 2015, p. 680).

Nevertheless, for the purpose of this study data from the Economic Freedom Index of the Fraser Institute are selected as a proxy. In this regard the sub-index "Government Enterprises and Investment" is chosen. It measures the extent to which nations utilize SOEs and state resources in order to direct resources. This sub-index is created by using data from the International Country Risk Guide,

---

13 For this first criterion, however, it appears to be the first-best solution to find an indicator which directly shows, how much the state is involved in the economy. One such indicator would be public expenditures as a percentage of GDP (Lombard 2017, p. 2), another would be tax revenue as a percentage of GDP. However, both indicators have grave shortcomings in common. An observer could for instance possibly surmise that a high state expenditure quota would be an adequate indicator. But this quantifiable figure gives no allusion about the underlying structure of an economy and its coordination mechanisms. For instance, for Russia the state expenditure quota is only 37.5 percent whereas Germany with a relatively low quota compared to other EU countries displays 44.7 percent (Kisoudis 2015, p. 90). But no observer would seriously doubt that Russia is structurally state capitalist as opposed to Germany. A similar picture emerges when looking at tax revenue as a percentage of GDP.
As a matter of fact, this data does not account for the fact that rising incomes per capita require more state expenditures for governmental policies relative to the size of the economy, for instance in the fields of infrastructure and social security.

the Global Competitiveness Report and the World Bank's Doing Business Index. Subjective considerations of Fraser analysts thus do not play a role.

Concerning the second constituting principle, the state is in control of and dominates vast parts of the financial sector, i.e. especially the banking system. But there again is no clear cut, hard data for dominance. One could resort to market share of state owned financial firms as a proxy. But this would create the problem of how to define the financial market. Its size could possibly be measured in loans outstanding. But this would completely exclude equity financing from the analysis.

But, as a matter of fact, the financial sector of state capitalist countries tends to be foremost dominated by commercial banks, development banks and SWFs (Musacchio /Lazzarini 2014 and Bremmer 2010). Here it appears to be useful to apply the same yardstick as with constituting factor number one and equating dominance with ownership. As a rule, development banks and SWFs are state-owned. Thus, if at least an SWF, a development bank or state-owned commercial banks exist, the constituting factor of state dominance of the financial sector is fulfilled. This data is gained by looking at the ownership structures, which in cases of public companies can for instance be gained by analyzing regulatory filings. Regarding the existence of SWFs, the relevant data can be accessed from the SWF Institute.

Third, globally successful domestic companies are often part of strategic sectors that aim to imitate products from industrialized nations. In this regard governments engage in an active industrial policy. There are a number of instruments available, among others price controls, subsidized credits, tax breaks, access to foreign currency or ceilings for foreign control and ownership of domestic competitors. With these measures most state capitalist countries – with the notable exception of predatory state capitalism – seek to catch-up with developed nations.

Since they tend to be late industrializers they rely on technology from more advanced economies. There is more imitation than innovation in the development of new products or in the production process (Amsden 2001, p. 220). Since state capitalist countries are usually latecomers in industrialization, they significantly depend on technology transfer from industrialized nations. Such a transfer can take numerous forms, e.g. through investments by multinational corporations (MNC) or imports. In the latter case technological capabilities are developed with the help of reverse engineering. But no data is available to directly measure the degree of imitation an economy pursues, not even in the World Competitive Index of the World Economic Forum (WEF). However, in general measured as a percentage of GDP expenses for research and development could be lower for state capitalist countries than in industrialized states. Therefore, as a second-best option this bench-mark is chosen. Relevant data is available from the World Bank.

Fourth, modern state capitalist regimes seek to reap the benefits of globalization and actively pursue to utilize them (World Bank 2008, p. 21). In a number of cases these countries are very export-oriented, while they protect their own industries for instance through tariffs (Bremmer 2014, p. 680). With the help of industrial as well as trade policies successful state capitalist regimes in a number of cases generate internationally competitive SOEs, which act as if they were privately owned. These countries levy import tariffs for protection of their domestic economy, grant export subsidies, limit foreign ownership of domestic companies and in general utilize other non-tariff trade obstacles. But especially ceilings on foreign ownership can inhibit technology transfer. In order to account for all of these factors again data from the Fraser Institute is chosen. Here, the sub-index "Freedom to trade internationally" is chosen, since it incorporates such criteria as tariffs, income from import taxes or restrictions on foreign ownership.[14]

Fifth, state capitalist regimes not only reap the advantages of globalization, but also utilize advantages, which are open to them through functions of market capitalist coordination mechanisms. That becomes obvious through their orientation towards world market prices and a partial integration of competitive functions, which flexible price systems offer. Admittedly, in a number of cases the state intervenes into this mechanism with tools of price, wage and interest rate control, taxes and subsidies. In this way, price mechanisms on goods and factor markets are distorted. But in general, economic agents are confronted with incentives emanating from prices on goods and factor markets and interest rates.

---

14 Here it is important to note that indeed a number of state capitalist countries are placing an emphasis on exports. They try to gain access to world markets. On the other hand, they try to protect their own markets as to develop their domestic industries. In general, economists would resort to data about openness for this criterion. But as a matter of fact, openness is mostly inversely related to the size of the economy. Thus, countries such as China and Brazil are relatively concentrated on their own markets, whereas smaller countries such as Kazakhstan are far more open. Therefore, such data is of limited value for the purpose of this study. At the same time, it appears to be fruitful to concentrate on state capitalist countries protecting their own markets. Therefore, it appears to be fruitful to apply the Fraser data, since they also incorporate tariffs and therefore domestic market protection.

Not only in market capitalist countries but also in state capitalism these incentives are of primary importance. This implies that in combination with the existence of private property rights for the means of production private economic agents act relatively autonomously. They can pursue their own short and long-term economic goals, which are shaped by market and state incentives to invest. Even managers of SOEs have at least partially to play by the rules of (world) markets and act accordingly (Milhaupt / Zheng 2015, S. 680 and Baumol et al. 2007, S. 62–64).

In order to identify, whether a country allows for private property rights in critical cases it is most appropriate to look at the de jure and the de facto situation in the respective country. In this regard the constitution serves as a first yard-stick to find out whether private property rights are allowed. If then de facto the state also creates significant obstacles for obtaining private property rights on the means of production, a country does not qualify as state capitalist.

Sixth, a minimum size of the bureaucracy is quintessential to conduct an industrial policy. And such an industrial policy is an essential part of state capitalism regardless of the eventual success of respective industrial policy programs. Therefore, it is obligatory to find a proxy for this constituting principle as well. But in this regard, it is difficult to obtain data solely for civil servants, who are operating at the state-business sector nexus. It is beyond the scope of this study to isolate bureaucrats conducting industrial policy from other civil servants. Therefore, here the indicator of size of the civil service is measured by public sector employees in relation to overall employees in the entire economy. This data is accessible from the International Labour Organization (ILO).

Finally, state can be differentiated from market capitalism with differing degrees of rule of law. Consequently, a proxy for the quality of the judicial system is needed. Here, it is most expedient to resort to the Bertelsmann Transformation Index (BTI). In this regard the sub-index of rule of law is selected. This should provide an indication of how far advanced a country is in terms of rule of law.

By now, for all seven constituting principles relevant proxies have been identified. In a next step in the following sub-section these proxies will be applied to upper middle income countries as well as market capitalist US, Germany and Japan.

3.3.2 Applying the Proxies to Upper Middle-Income Countries

In the presented taxonomy a country qualifies as state capitalist, if all seven criteria are fulfilled. Now, this catalogue of criteria will be applied to upper middle-income countries plus Russia and Singapore. Upper middle-income countries are chosen, since they represent typical emerging economies, which are widely believed to be state capitalist in the literature (see Bremmer 2010 and Kurlantzick 2016). Russia is also selected since it ranges only slightly above the income level of upper middle-income countries and is in general seen as a quintessential example of state capitalism. Furthermore, Singapore is also chosen, since in the literature most economists refer to this city-state as being state capitalist as well and it represents one of four case studies below.

As a matter of fact, upper middle-income countries of the World Bank, based on gross national income (GNI) per capita, range from number 64 (Brazil) to number 115 (Paraguay). Since Russia and Singapore do not fall into these income brackets we add them to our list. Russia is insignificantly richer than Brazil at rank 61, whereas Singapore at rank 5 has a significantly higher income. For the analysis of upper middle-income countries, in a number of cases the economic significance as measured in population and GDP, seems to be relatively small. So, the author excludes states with a population below 5 million inhabitants.

In order to test his assumptions, the author compares, whether the industrialized, market-led countries Germany, US and Japan in this taxonomy fall into the category of state capitalism. But at the same time, at this stage it needs to be maintained that in order to identify state capitalist countries in a grounded approach with figures, it is not possible to theoretically justify certain precise thresholds, which indicate, whether a constituting principle is fulfilled. Rather it is argued in this section that the selected proxy numbers present a guideline. It is thus possible to evaluate, whether a country leans more towards state or more towards market capitalism. Therefore, this data cannot be interpreted in a way as to give a razor-thin differentiation between state and market capitalism.

Table 3 shows data of state capitalist constituent state ownership or more general dominance and state capitalist constituent state dominance of the financial sector in the selected countries. The first proxy data is from the Fraser Institute and its Economic Freedom Index. For the second proxy it is analyzed, whether a country has an SWF, a development bank or the state owns vast parts of commercial banks.

Tab. 3 State dominance and State ownership (SO) of financial sector in upper middle-income countries as well as Singapore, Russia, US, Germany and Japan

Country	GNI per capita rank 2014	Sub-index "Government Enterprises and Investment" of "Economic Freedom Index" in points from 0 to 10 2015	SWF, development bank or SO of commercial banks?
Singapore	5	7.00	SWF Temasek and GIC, Development Bank DBS
Russia	61	10.00	SWF National Welfare Fund, Development Bank VEB, SO banks
Brazil	64	4.00	Development Bank BNDES
Kazakhstan	65	6.00.	SWF SamrukKazyna, Development Bank of Kazakhstan
Malaysia	66	4.00	SWF KhazanahNasionalBerhad
Turkey	69	7.00	SWF TSKB, Development Bank of Turkey
Lebanon	70	10.00	No
Mexico	71	8.00	SWF FondoMexicano del Petoleo, Development Bank Nafinsa
Romania	74	8.00	No
Turkmenistan	77	n.a.	SWF Turkmenistan Stabilization Fund
Libya	78	n.a.	SWF LIA
Colombia	81	6.00	Development Bank FDN
Azerbaijan	82	0.00	State Oil Fund
China	84	2.00	CIC, SASAC, CDB, SO Development Bank, SOEs
Belarus	85	n.a.	Development Bank of the Republic of Belarus, SO banks
Iran	90	0.00	SWF National Development Fund of Iran
South Africa	91	4.00	SWF Public Investment Corporation, Development Bank of Southern Africa

Tab. 3 Continued

Country	GNI per capita rank 2014	Sub-index "Government Enterprises and Investment" of "Economic Freedom Index" in points from 0 to 10 2015	SWF, development bank or SO of commercial banks?
Iraq	93	n.a.	SWF Development Fund for Iraq
Peru	94	7.00	SWF FiscalStabilization Fund
Ecuador	95	0.00	No
Dominican Rep.	96	6.00	Development Bank CDB
Cuba	97	n.a.	SO banks
Serbia	100	8.00	No
Thailand	101	6.00	SWF planned, Development Bank SME Bank
Algeria	102	0.00	SWF Revenue Regulation Fund
Angola	103	0.00	SWF FSDEA
Jordan	105	8.00	No
Tunisia	114	7.00	No
Paraguay	115	8.00	No
USA	11	8.00	No
Germany	18	10.00	Development Bank KfW
Japan	25	8.00	Development Bank of Japan

Source: World Bank (2017) Fraser Institute (2017) SWFI (2017)

As can be seen there are only seven countries which have the same score of eight index points as the US and Japan, when looking at the degree of state dominance in the corporate sector. Indeed, the more index points a country has the less the state dominates the corporate sector. In this regard the fact stands out that supposedly the Russian state in this regard dominates its corporate sector less than the US. Possibly this can be explained by the fact that in Russia small and medium size firms are regularly privately owned. Furthermore, the figure for the US can be distorted owing to the fact that after the financial crisis some parts of the industrial and even financial sector had been temporarily nationalized. This had not been done to such an extent in Russia. Nevertheless, the gas monopolist

Gazprom as much as the leading oil company Rosneft are at least partially in possession of the state.

Thus, in general, Russia, Lebanon, Mexico, Romania, Serbia, Jordan and Paraguay tend towards market capitalism, when looking at the proxy for state dominance of the corporate sector. And including the second proxy into the analysis it becomes clear that of these countries only Russia and Mexico either have an SWF, a development bank or an at least partially state-owned commercial banking sector. This serves as a first indication that possibly of upper middle-income countries Lebanon, Romania, Serbia, Jordan and Paraguay tend to be not state capitalist. Therefore, in order to get a clearer picture in differentiating state from market capitalism four other proxies of the constituting principles need to be taken into account (see table 4).

It has been maintained that in a state capitalist system a civil service of a minimum size needs to exist. This can be evaluated by looking at the percentage of civil service employees of the entire employment. All in all, the civil service of state capitalist countries needs to be at least close to as large as those of market capitalist countries. As a comparison therefore again, the US is chosen with 14.6 percent, since it is in the middle of Japan (7.9 percent) and Germany (15.4 percent).

Looking at the relevant data, it becomes clear that Brazil (12.1 percent), Mexico (11.9 percent), Romania (16.2 percent), Columbia (4 percent), Iran (16.9 percent), South Africa (17.4 percent), Ecuador (9.2 percent), Dominican Republic (12.8 percent) are under or closely above the percentage of the US. This is surprising in a sense that Brazil, Mexico, Iran and South Africa are widely assumed to be state capitalist and this has with the exception of Mexico been demonstrated by the fact that the first two proxies do not let them appear as being state capitalist.

In general, it needs to be maintained that upper middle-income countries tend to have for instance less advanced social security systems. This in itself can be an argument that some supposedly state capitalist countries employ relatively fewer civil servants than the US, although the state dominance of the corporate sector and a dominant position in the financial sector should in principle elevate them above the US level. On the upper level Singapore (40 percent), Belarus (40.6 percent) and Cuba (85.2 percent) stick out. This can possibly be explained by the fact that traditionally in Communist states the bureaucracy has been large and institutional change is a slow process. In the case of Singapore it is possible that the large amount of government-linked corporations (GLC) and two

Tab. 4 State Capitalist Proxies

Country	GNI per capita rank 2014	Share of public sector employees of total employment in percent	R&D nominals expenses 2012 as a percent of GDP	Sub-Index "Freedom to trade internationally" of "Economic Freedom Index" 2015 in points from 0 to 10	Sub-Index „Legal System & Property Rights" from 0 to 10 points	Sub-Index "Rule of Law" of the Bertelmann Transformation Index (BTI) 2016 in points from 0 to 10
Singapore	5	40.0 (2011)	2.2 (2014)	9.25	8.29	5.8
Russia	61	n.a.	1.1	6.61	4.85	4.0
Brazil	64	12.1 (2013)	1.2	6.88	4.45	7.8
Kazakhstan	65	23.2 (2012)	0.2	6.38	5.61	2.8
Malaysia	66	16.4 (2014)	1.1	7.51	5.76	4.8
Turkey	69	n.a.	0.9	7.24	4.74	6.3
Lebanon	70	n.a.	n.a.	6.89	4.05	5.3
Mexico	71	11.9 (2014)	0.4	7.52	4.22	5.0
Romania	74	16.2 (2013)	0.5	8.48	5.95	8.3
Turkmenistan	77	n.a.	n.a.	n.a.	n.a.	2.3
Libya	78	n.a	n.a.	4.76	3.21	1.8
Colombia	81	4.0 (2013)	0.2	6.91	3.79	6.5
Azerbaijan	82	25.9 (2013)	0.2	7.10	5.32	3.0
China	84	n.a.	1.9	6.63	5.63	2.3
Belarus	85	40.6 (2013)	0.7	n.a.	n.a.	3.0
Iran	90	16.9 (2014)	0.3 (2010)	4.53	4.54	2.5
South Africa	91	17.4 (2013)	0.7	6.87	5.76	7.3
Iraq	93	n.a.	0.0	n.a.	n.a.	3.5
Peru	94	n.a.	n.a.	8.23	4.80	6.3
Ecuador	95	9.2 (2013)	0.3 (2011)	6.53	3.89	4.5
Dominican Rep.	96	12.8 (2013)	n.a.	8.18	4.07	5.8
Cuba	97	85.2 (2010)	0.4	n.a.	n.a.	3.3
Serbia	100	31.0 (2013)	0.9	7.57	4.89	7.3
Thailand	101	19.4 (2014)	0.4 (Thailand)	6.78	4.77	3.3
Algeria	102	n.a.	n.a.	4.01	4.55	4.3
Angola	103	n.a.	n.a.	5.14	2.96	3.0

(continued)

Tab. 4 Continued

Country	GNI per capita rank 2014	Share of public sector employees of total employ-ment in percent	R&D nominals expenses 2012 as a percent of GDP	Sub-Index "Freedom to trade inter-nationally" of "Economic Freedom Index" 2015 in points from 0 to 10	Sub-Index „Legal System & Property Rights" from 0 to 10 points	Sub-Index "Rule of Law" of the Bertelmann Transformation Index (BTI) 2016 in points from 0 to 10
Jordan	105	33.1 (2004)	n.a.	7.63	4.76	4.5
Tunisia	114	n.a.	0.7	6.81	5.28	5.5
Paraguay	115	0.1	0.1	7.31	3.87	5.8
USA	11	14.6 (2008)	2.8	7.54	7.60	n.a.
Germany	18	15.4 (2009)	2.9	7.92	7.45	n.a.
Japan	25	7.9 (2013)	3.3	7.43	7.23	n.a.

Source: World Bank (2017) ILO (2017), OECD (2017) World Bank (2017) Fraser Institute (2017) Fraser Institute (2017) BTI (2017)

SWFs – i.e. Temasek and the Government of Singapore Investment Corporation (GIC) – provide for a large number of civil servants. Indeed, all three countries in this regard appear to tend towards state capitalism.

Regarding nominal R&D expenses as a percentage of GDP a clear difference of upper middle-income countries including Russia and Singapore compared to Japan, Germany and the US can be identified. None of these countries comes even close to the level of the US of 2.8 percent. This is in accordance with the state capitalist constituting principle of an industrial policy that leads to more imitation than innovation. It should come to no large surprise that Singapore (2.2 percent) and China (1.9 percent) are closest to the level of market capitalist Germany, Japan and the US. Both countries have a successfully operating high-tech sector, where a minimum degree of R&D is essential.

Concerning the degree of "freedom to trade internationally" observers would expect relatively low levels for state capitalist countries, since according to the constituting principles state capitalist countries tend to shield their markets from competition. As a matter of fact Germany, Japan and the US are comfortably above seven index points. This level is also reached by Singapore (9.25), Malaysia

(7.51), Turkey (7.24), Mexico (7.52), Romania (8.48), Azerbaijan (7.10), Peru (8.23), Dominican Republic (8.18), Serbia (7.57), Jordan (7.63) and Paraguay (7.31).

But even these states are with the exception of Singapore not exceedingly above the level of the selected market capitalist countries. In this regard, the small city state of Singapore should serve as an exception, since it opted for a development strategy of attracting large numbers of MNCs. This was only possible by opening up its markets – for exports and imports. Overall, upper middle-income countries including Russia at least appear to tend to protect their markets, and in some cases have a level of "freedom to trade internationally" that is comparable to that of Germany, Japan and the US.

Regarding the potentially most striking difference between state and market capitalism, i.e. a significantly lesser degree of rule of law only Brazil (7.8), South Africa (7.3) and Serbia (7.3) score relatively high index points. All other nations are significantly below seven index points. Unfortunately, it is not possible to compare the data with industrialized nations such as Germany, Japan and the US, since the Bertelsmann Foundation does not give data for these countries.

However, taking into account data from the Fraser Institute about "Legal System and Property Rights" with the notable exception of Singapore (8.29) no country comes even close to Germany (7.45), Japan (7.23) and the US (7.60). Here again Singapore is a special case, since in order to attract foreign direct Investments (FDI) by MNCs it had to guarantee investors a legal system that protects property to the same extent as market capitalist countries do. But as can be seen from the BTI data Singapore's legal system, when bracketing out property rights, does not provide for the same degree of rule of law that industrialized nations do.

Finally, it needs to be turned to the constituent of private property rights. Here only socialist Cuba needs to be scrutinized. The Handbook of Contemporary Cuba reveals that on paper the government does not allow for private property rights for the means of production (Gabriele 2013). Whether this law is still rigorously enforced in practice, is very difficult to assess. While there are a number of middle, small and very small companies, which are managed privately, they operate in a mostly legal vacuum. Investments by foreign companies are difficult and relatively few. A privatization of large SOEs is not to be expected in the near future (Cuba heute, 2016). Therefore, Cuba would possibly constitute a case among upper middle-income countries, which is not state capitalist.

To conclude, an analysis of upper middle-income countries plus Singapore and Russia has demonstrated that in terms of legal system quality with the exception of Singapore no country is on the same level as industrialized nations tend to do. Even though Russia, Lebanon, Mexico, Romania, Serbia, Jordan and Paraguay tend towards market capitalism, when looking at the proxy for state dominance of the corporate sector, other proxy figures show that they cannot be classified market capitalist to the same extent as for instance Germany, Japan and the US. And Singapore, which a number of economists call state capitalist, has a large degree of state dominance of the economy, as for instance evident when looking at the significant role for GLCs. As a matter of fact, Singapore constitutes a case, where state capitalism was very successful though it has been consistently criticized by neo-liberal economists. In the following sub-section, there will be a concise comparison of performances of state versus market capitalist countries.

3.3.3 Competition between State and Market Capitalism

In the literature there is a certain tendency to emphasize the challenges state capitalism poses for market capitalist countries. It seems as if there was a competition between two rival systems with characteristics of a zero-sum game (see for instance Luttwak 1999, p. 129 with regard to former South Korea or Bremmer 2010, p. 4–5 and Bremmer 2014, p. 104). Countries as diverse as not only Russia and China but also Kazakhstan, Brazil or Saudi Arabia are seen more as rivals than potential partners. Therefore, it is little surprising that founders and CEOs of the world's top companies described state capitalism among the ten most important threats to market capitalism (Bower et al. 2011).

While East Asian countries are seen as examples-par-excellence that state capitalism can function, this success is only attributed to technology imports from abroad, open export markets and low labour costs which according to this reasoning allowed for the East Asian miracle. Supposedly, state guidance also just works for a given period of time (Baumol et al. 2007, p. 67). According to Luttwak (1993, p. 299) a key failure of state capitalism is its widespread incompetence of state bureaucracies to effectively administer industrial policy.

Indeed, authors such as Bremmer and Luttwak concede that competition for market capitalism emanates from modern state capitalism. But at the same time this economic order supposedly creates distortions, waste and corruption (Bremmer 2010, p. 151) which would tend to significantly diminish economic performance.

Therefore, it appears to be worthwhile to analyze the economic performance of state capitalist countries over the last 20 years. For this purpose, the author compares growth rates of gross domestic product (GDP) for state capitalist countries – as the prime performance indicator for economies – with those of OECD member nations. The World Bank (2008, p. 26) tends to equate growth with development and also stresses its positive correlation with poverty reduction (World Bank p. 14). In the same vein Bhagwati (2016, p. 19–22) stresses that economic growth is necessary for the fight against poverty and redistribution does not suffice.

But concededly, the growth indicator is not enough to compare state with market capitalism. Countries that start from a lower base in general tend to grow faster than more developed economies. Therefore, the author further down below presents results of poverty rates and the human development indicator (HDI) in order to understand whether there was a tendency to achieve progress in fields such as poverty reduction, health and education as well.[15]

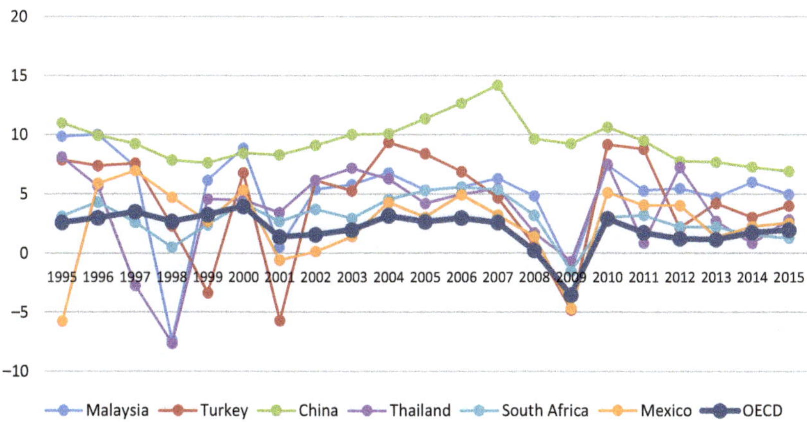

Chart 1: GDP Growth SC Group 1 vs. OECD

15 Jackson (2017, p. 49) even goes so far as to include soft factors such as happiness, family, friendships, fulfilment at work, freedom and a sense of autonomy as desirable dimensions of development. These factors are difficult to measure and though Jackson argues that they are not necessarily positively correlated with higher incomes one could surmise that for instance less poverty indeed increases happiness.

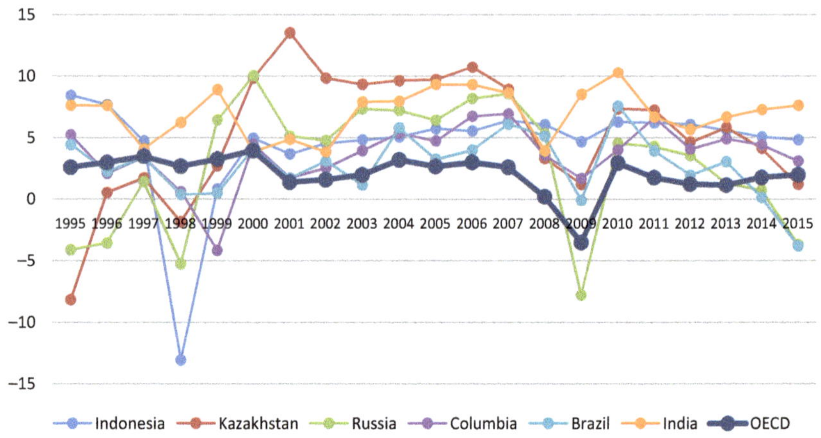

Chart 2: GDP Growth SC Group 2 vs. OECD

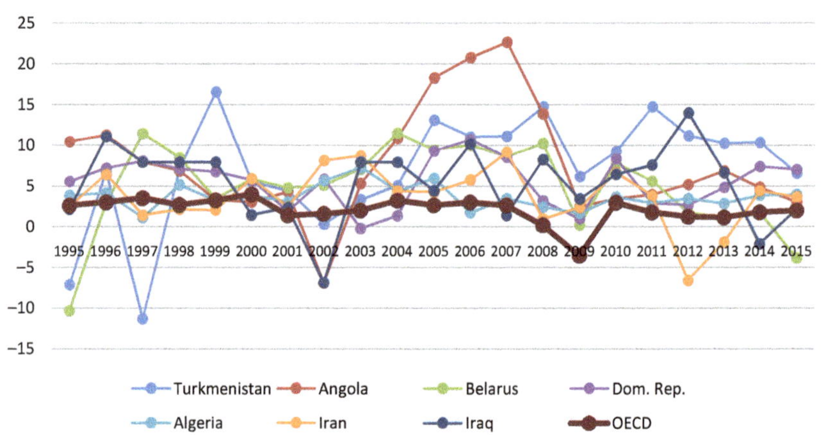

Chart 3: GDP growth SC Group 3 vs. OECD

For the purpose of a clear illustration the author has formed three groups of some supposedly state capitalist countries, i.e. upper middle-income countries. As is clearly obvious countries of all three state capitalist groups fared better than the OECD when it comes to GDP growth. As a matter of fact, GDP growth of state capitalist group one as a simple mean average was 4.6 percent as opposed to 2 percent for the OECD group. For state capitalist group two the figure stands at 4.3 percent and group three even 5.4 percent. Clearly, this is a relatively superficial performance indicator, since in general lower income countries tend to grow faster than higher income countries. Therefore, the author will now look at poverty and development indicators for a more comprehensive evaluation of state capitalist performance.

As a matter of fact, China – as the state capitalist country with the highest GDP – was exceptionally successful in fighting absolute poverty which is defined as a person living with or less than 1.90 US-Dollar in 2011 purchasing power parity. According to World Bank data the percentage of people living in absolute poverty decreased in China from 88 percent in 1981 to just 6.5 percent in 2012. There is a rather similar picture, when looking at the most recent data of state capitalist countries. According to the latest available World Bank data in state capitalist group one on average just 4.39 percent of the population lived in absolute poverty. With 6.56 percent it is rather similar for state capitalist group two and with 14.96 percent considerably higher in state capitalist group three, but still relatively low in historical terms.

Looking at the human development index (HDI), which is based on life expectancy, schooling and gross national income, China achieved rapid progress as well. Thus, from 1980 to 2014 this figure increased from 0.41 to 0.73 points, with 1 point the maximum and 0 points the minimum. Likewise, other state capitalist countries also score relatively high. So, for state capitalist group one the corresponding average 2014 figure stands at 0.74 index points, 0.73 for state capitalist group two and even 0.70 points for group three is still relatively high. Concededly, market capitalist countries Japan, Germany and the USA scored significantly higher in 2014 with 0.89, 0.92 and 0.92 points respectively.

To sum it up, when it comes to growth state capitalist countries are surpassing market capitalist ones. Even with regard to development and the fight against poverty state capitalist countries can point at considerable progress. Critics such as Bremmer, Luttwak and Baumol regularly neglect these achievements when concentrating on shortcomings in governance structures and efficiency.

By now, proxies for the constituting principles of state capitalism have been identified and applied to upper middle-income countries. It has been shown that the constituting principles can serve as a guideline to differentiate state from market capitalism. Finally, it has been demonstrated that especially in catch-up processes state capitalist systems can surpass market capitalist orders as measured by economic growth rates. In the subsequent section differences among state capitalist countries will be highlighted. Therefore, in a grounded fashion again some proxies for state capitalist constituents will be identified.

3.4 Determining State Capitalist Groups

3.4.1 Proxies for the Taxonomy and Application to upper middle-income Countries

As shown above there are four constituting principles for deducing different forms of state capitalism. To repeat, those are divergences concerning quality of the bureaucracy, the degree of protecting domestic markets, the degree of engaging in R&D and the degree to which countries manage to alleviate shortcomings in the rule of law by credibly committing to guaranteeing property rights.

As a matter of fact, a lot of proxy selection has been done and relevant data been selected above, when differentiating state from market capitalism. But for the quality of bureaucracy a new proxy is needed, since above only a proxy for quantity of the civil service was chosen. In this regard, it appears to be fruitful to resort to the dimension government effectiveness of World Bank governance indicators, which has a scale from 0 to 100 percentile points.

There are six dimensions of governance indicators, i.e. voice and accountability, political stability and absence of violence, government effectiveness, regulatory quality, rule of law and control of corruption. In this study it will be concentrated on government effectiveness, since it incorporates the quality of the bureaucracy. Only regulatory quality could also somehow reflect this bureaucratic capability, but is more oriented towards regulations that promote private sector development, which in state capitalism is not of primary importance.

As a matter of fact, definitions concerning governance range from more narrow ones about whether existing rules are indeed enforced to those that are more concerned with the overall justice of the content of laws. In this regard, the indicator of government effectiveness is chosen, since it is relatively narrow and relates to the capability of the government when it comes to formulating and implementing appropriate policies. This yardstick measuring perceptions has the advantage that quality of public service and its relative autonomy vis-à-vis the political sphere are almost impossible to assess with other "harder" and more objective indicators.[16] Consequently, household and firm surveys are utilized as

16 Furthermore, perceptions-based data has other numerous advantages. Overall, agents tend to base their decisions on perceptions and views. Second, in a number of cases no documents exist, which refer to government effectiveness, for instance when it comes

well as expert assessments. In general, the indicator captures the quality of policy formulation and implementation as well as the government's commitment to such policies (Kaufmann et al. 2010, p. 3–4 and p. 18–19).[17]

In table 5 government effectiveness for upper middle-income countries plus Russia, Singapore, Germany, the US and Japan is presented and for a better illustration data for R&D expenses, "freedom to trade internationally" as well as the quality of the legal framework is repeated.

When analyzing the relevant data, three distinctive groups of upper middle-income countries, which lean towards state capitalism emerge. As a matter of fact, most of them have a sufficiently large civil service for conducting an industrial policy and structurally dominating the corporate sector. But regarding the quality of the civil service grave differences emerge. However, this large variety leads to sizable divergences in the other areas of industrial policy and security of property rights.

Therefore, in order to gain an overview of upper middle-income countries and being able to classify them, three distinct groups are formed. In the first group countries are assembled, where government effectiveness is above 60 percentile points. Then, in the second cohort the respective countries' government effectiveness ranges from 40.00 to 59.99 percentile points. Finally, in the least effective group, countries score less than 40 percentile points. Most countries are situated in the middle group. To those in the cohort with the highest score count China, Malaysia and Singapore. In the second group countries such as Russia, Kazakhstan and Brazil are to be found.

---

to corruption. Third, de jure rules often differ tremendously from how these rules de facto work. But concededly, problems remain. For instance, perceptions-based data has the disadvantage of being relatively imprecise. To account for this problem, the World Bank leaves room for a margin of error in its governance indicators. Another problem consists of systematic bias, where for instance a sound economic development distorts the data, so that among others results of business surveys cannot be compared with each other. But according to the World Bank there is only little evidence of such distortions.

17 All dimensions of World Bank governance indicators use percentile ranks. That means on the horizontal axis all more than 200 countries are placed in the order of their performance in government effectiveness with the help of percentiles. The performance ranges from -2.5 to +2.5 and is projected on the vertical axis. Thus, if for instance a country scores a percentile rank of 50 based on its government effectiveness then 50 percent of the selected countries have higher and 50 percent lower scores.

Then in the least government effective group nations such as Iran, Turkmenistan and Angola are situated. It is interesting to note that as a comparison market capitalist US, Germany and Japan score significantly higher than more state capitalist upper middle-income countries. This reflects the fact that those developed countries have reached an excellent level of governance quality, but as a country such as Singapore demonstrates it can even for a state capitalist country be possible to reach or even surpass market capitalist ones.

When looking at the first group, it is striking that they have upgraded their respective economies to such an extent that they engage in R&D expenses of non-negligible dimensions, which nevertheless trail those of developed countries. It furthermore underlines the fact that they engage in industries with a high value-added such as high-tech-sectors. By the same token this does not exclude a tendency of these countries to apply an industrial policy, focusing on imitating products from industrialized nations. This can for instance take the form of seeking to understand products and production processes from industrialized nations and incrementally improving them.

At the same time this group of countries is well integrated into the world economy. They seem to have become a part of the global value chain, which is only possible, if it is not too difficult to trade internationally. Nevertheless, this entails the fact that for instance a country such as China intentionally protects its domestic markets in order to nurture infant industries. Supposedly, the countries of this first group of upper middle-income countries have learned to reap the benefits of globalization by among others increasing currency reserves, partially investing abroad, financing technology imports and likewise being able to uphold certain protections of domestic markets. Naturally, all of this requires a bureaucracy of sufficient size and with a high capability.

Column six in table three hints at the fact that property rights are not as secure as in the industrialized nations Germany, Japan and US, again with the exception of Singapore. Nevertheless, the data simultaneously reveals that this first group with a relatively capable bureaucracy manages to credibly commit to securing property rights and overcoming short-comings regarding rule of law. These countries on average manage to score higher points in legal system quality index of the Fraser Institute than the other two groups with less government effectiveness.

After having categorized group one with the help of four proxies for the relevant constituting principles of state capitalism, it seems to be worthwhile to return to the taxonomy from above. All in all, this group number one displays characteristics of both – developmental state and dual economy state capitalism. The bureaucracy is performing well. It is able to implement an industrial policy

Tab. 5 State Capitalist Groups and government effectiveness as well as other constituting principles proxies

Country	GNI per capita rank 2014	World Bank Governance Indicator Government Effectiveness in percentile points 2014	R&D nominals expenses 2012 as a percent of GDP	Sub-Index "Freedom to trade internationally" of "Economic Freedom Index" 2015 in points from 0 to 10	Sub-Index „Legal System & Property Rights" from 0 to 10 points
Group 1					
Singapore	5	96.15	2.2 (2014)	9.25	8.29
Malaysia	66	83.65	1.1	7.51	5.76
Turkey	69	67.31	0.9	7.24	4.74
Thailand	101	65.87	0.4	6.78	4.77
South Africa	91	65.38	0.7	6.87	5.76
China	84	66.35	1.9	6.63	5.63
Mexico	71	61.06	0.4	7.52	4.22
Group 2					
Jordan	105	59.13	n.a.	7.63	4.76
Serbia	100	58.17	0.9	7.57	4.89
Romania	74	54.81	0.5	8.48	5.95
Kazakhstan	65	54.33	0.2	6.38	5.61
Cuba	97	52.88	0.4	n.a.	n.a.
Russia	61	51.44	1.1	6.61	4.85
Colombia	81	49.52	0.2	6.91	3.79
Tunisia	114	48.08	0.7	6.81	5.28
Brazil	64	47.12	1.2	6.88	4.45
Peru	94	44.23	n.a.	8.23	4.80
Azerbaijan	82	41.83	0.2	7.10	5.32
Mean					
Group 3					
Iran	90	37.98	0.3 (2010)	4.53	4.54
Dominican Rep.	96	37.02	n.a.	8.18	4.07

(*continued*)

Tab. 5 Continued

Country	GNI per capita rank 2014	World Bank Governance Indicator Government Effectiveness in percentile points 2014	R&D nominals expenses 2012 as a percent of GDP	Sub-Index "Freedom to trade internationally" of "Economic Freedom Index" 2015 in points from 0 to 10	Sub-Index „Legal System & Property Rights" from 0 to 10 points
Ecuador	95	35.58	0.3 (2011)	6.53	3.89
Belarus	85	35.10	0.7	n.a.	n.a.
Algeria	102	33.65	n.a.	4.01	4.55
Turkmenistan	77	17.79	n.a.	n.a.	n.a.
Paraguay	115	17.31	0.1	7.31	3.87
Iraq	93	13.94	0.0	n.a.	n.a.
Angola	103	12.98	n.a.	5.14	2.96
Libya	78	2.88	n.a.	4.76	3.21
USA	11	89.90	2.8	7.54	7.60
Germany	18	94.71	2.9	7.92	7.45
Japan	25	89.90	3.3	7.43	7.23

Source: World Bank (2017) World Bank (2017) World Bank (2017) Fraser Institute (2017) Fraser Institute (2017)

upgrading the economy by imitation and integration into world markets, while sufficiently protecting domestic markets. Finally, these countries are in a position to guarantee investors a minimum of property rights security and thereby supporting incentives to engage in productive activities.

Regarding group number two there is a markedly lesser degree of bureaucratic quality to be observed. This structural deficiency reverberates in industrial policy. Here countries have not upgraded their economy to such an extent as to allow for sizable activities in R&D. In general countries concentrate on goods with less value-added than those in group one. As a matter of fact, exports significantly depend on commodities such as oil and gas. Thus, there is only a limited degree of having integrated into the world economy.

Nevertheless, as the column about "freedom to trade internationally" illustrates in general imports tend not to be significantly more inhibited than in group one. This also reflects the fact that for a number of products these countries depend on imports for satisfying the needs of their populations. In a nutshell, countries of group two pursue an industrial policy that is less oriented towards integrating into world markets and gaining market shares by imitating products from developed nations.

Concerning security of property rights there is a slight difference to be observed between group one and two. Nevertheless, countries from group two in a number of instances are capable of securing property rights by credible commitments. This is reflected by a not too significant deviation from group one in column six. As a matter of fact, in group two a large number of countries is represented. It is the largest of all three groups. As a consequence, it reflects a number of state capitalist variants, ranging from dual economy to petro to crony state capitalism.

This heterogeneity is repeated in group three. Countries score just above ten percentile points or comfortably over 35 percentile points in government effectiveness. Nevertheless, these countries have in common that their civil services are weak. In all instances a high degree of corruption and arbitrariness is supposedly involved.

This has direct effects on industrial policy. These countries for instance basically do not engage in R&D. They display grave shortcomings in upgrading their industrial sectors. Thus, the low figures in column four can be interpreted in so far as these nations almost entirely concentrate on exporting primary goods. There are hardly any efforts to improve on industrial structures. A systemically formulated and implemented industrial policy seems to be missing. Most of these countries are only to a small extent integrated into the world economy. This reflects more the fact that countries have a weakness in exporting than being successful in protecting domestic markets. Presumably, markets up to a degree are shielded, but this is more due to rent-seeking by domestic producers than the result of an effective industrial policy aiming to catch-up with developed nations.

The structural weakness of an underperforming bureaucracy and consequently an industrial policy not bent on upgrading the economy has repercussions concerning property rights. As in all state capitalist countries there is less of a degree of rule of law than in market capitalist economies. But whereas in the first group countries manage to nevertheless allow for relatively secure property rights, this is not the case in group number three. Here, economic agents perceive a relatively high risk of having their property rights violated. Admittedly, group number three encompasses a large variety of states. It ranges from crony to petro to predatory state capitalism. As a matter of fact, some factors even hint to Libya being a failed state. But nevertheless, this analysis sought to illustrate the similarities of this group in contrast to the other two groups.

By now with the help of relevant data, three different groups have been identified, which in total are also in line with the qualitative taxonomy created above. Different structures and policies of these respective groups have been elaborated on. In the following subsection, it will be analyzed, whether these differences also translate into different performances regarding development.

3.4.2 Performance Divergences among Varieties of State Capitalism

In the previous sub-section, it has been shown that quality of the civil service, an industrial policy with a successful integration into the world economy, industrial upgrading and security of property rights differed in the respective upper middle-income countries leaning toward state capitalism. Now it will be demonstrated, whether that led to diverging performance outcomes of the respective country groups.

As illustrated above development is a key goal of almost any state capitalist country – with differing results. But how can development success best be captured by relevant data? Traditionally, an economic figure such as real GDP growth has been favoured. It reveals to what extent the size of an economy is growing, showing whether on average incomes of economic and political agents tend to increase.

This tends to give them the opportunity to spend more income and would ceteris paribus result in a higher standard of living with corresponding positive welfare effects. But economic growth in a number of instances leads to more inequality and important development indicators such as poverty rates and life expectancy can even decrease. Therefore, in the following not only real economic growth, but also the percent of population living under 3.10 USD a day, the Human Development Index (HDI), which includes per capita incomes, life expectancies and education, and the Gini-Coefficient as an indicator for income inequality are presented (see table 6). Especially using income distribution as an indicator is in line with North (1981, p. 3), who uses total output, output per capita and income distribution as relevant dimensions of performance.

Strikingly on average countries of group number one have higher incomes than state capitalist countries with less government effectiveness. They rank higher in income levels than both other groups. At the same time, in terms of economic growth no sizable differences seem to be evident, reflecting the fact that countries of group one have already reached relatively high income levels, inhibiting further growth perspectives.

Tab. 6 Performance of State Capitalist Country Groups

Country	GNI per capita rank 2014	World Bank Governance Indicator Government Effectiveness in percentile points 2014	Real GDP growth in per-cent average from 1995 to 2015	Percent of popula-tion living under 3.10 USD a day Respective year listed	Human Develop-ment Index 2014 (est.)	Gini-Coefficient
Group 1						
Singapore	5	96.15		n.a.	0,925	n.a.
Malaysia	66	83.65	5.1	2.71 (2009)	0.779	46.3 (2009)
continued	from	page	123			
Turkey	69	67.31	4.3	3.1 (2012)	0.761	40.2 (2012)
China	84	66.35	9.4	27.24 (2010)	0.727	37.0 (2011)
Thailand	101	65.87	3.5	1.23 (2012)	0.726	39.3 (2012)
South Africa	91	65.38	3.0	34.68 (2011)	0.666	63.4 (2011)
Mexico	71	61.06	2.5	10.32 (2012)	0.756	48.1 (2012)
Group 2						
Jordan	105	59.13		1.99	0.741	35.4
Serbia	100	58.17		1.65	0.776	29.1
Romania	74	54.81		4.08	0.802	27.5
Cuba	97	52.88		n.a.	0.775	n.a.
Kazakhstan	65	54.33	5.3	0.26 (2013)	0.788	26.4 (2013)
Russia	61	51.44	2.9	0.48 (2012)	0.798	41.6 (2012)
Colombia	81	49.52	3.6	13.79 (2013)	0.720	53.3 (2013)
Tunisia	114	48.08		8.4	0.725	35.8
Brazil	64	47.12	2.7	9.06 (2013)	0.755	52.9 (2013)
Peru	94	44.23		9.7	0.740	44.3
Azerbaijan	82	41.83		n.a.	0.759	31.8
Lebanon	70	40.87		n.a.	0.763	n.a.
Group 3						
Iran	90	37.98	3.6	0.66 (2013)	0.766	37.4 (2013)
Dominican Rep.	96	37.02	5.4	9.12 (2013)	0.715	47.1 (2013)
Ecuador	95	35.58		11.64	0.739	46.5

(continued)

Tab. 6 Continued

Country	GNI per capita rank 2014	World Bank Governance Indicator Government Effectiveness in percentile points 2014	Real GDP growth in per-cent average from 1995 to 2015	Percent of popula-tion living under 3.10 USD a day Respective year listed	Human Develop-ment Index 2014 (est.)	Gini-Coefficient
Belarus	85	35.10	4.9	0.03 (2012)	0.798	26.0 (2012)
Algeria	102	33.65	3.6	n.a.	0.736	35.3 (1995)
Turkmeni-stan	77	17.79	7.0	69.14 (1998)	0.688	40.8 (1998)
Paraguay	115	17.31		6.4	0.693	48.0
Iraq	93	13.94	7.9	n.a.	0.654	29.5 (2012)
Angola	103	12.98	7.7	54.25 (2008)	0.532	42.7 (2008)
Libya	78	2.88	2.8	n.a.	0.724	n.a.
USA	11	89.90	2.4	n.a.	0.915	41.1 (2013)
Germany	18	94.71	1.4	n.a.	0.916	30.1 (2011)
Japan	25	89.90	0.8	n.a.	0.891	32.1 (2008)

Source: World Bank (2017) World Bank (2017) World Bank (2017) World Bank (2017) World Bank (2017) World Bank (2017)

Regarding the fight against poverty, fundamental differences within the respective country groups can be observed. Thus, in group one there is Thailand with a poverty rate of just 1.23 percent and on the other hand South Africa with a poverty rate of 34.68 percent. In a certain sense, this heterogeneity limits the explanatory value of this data. But it can be maintained that a country such as China had significant success in the fight against poverty (see sub-section 3.3.3). On the other hand, a country such as Russia had for a sizable amount of time – already during the existence of the Soviet Union – almost eradicated absolute poverty, so that the difference between Russia and China in this regard serves as no indication of the success of their respective forms of a state capitalist system with China leaning more towards dual economy and Russia more towards crony state capitalism.

But overall, the data seems to indicate that countries of group one are superior in terms of development as measured by relatively strong growth, a high HDI and less poverty compared to the other two groups. Likewise, in this regard a superiority of group number two vis-à-vis group number three can be observed. At the same time, it needs to be conceded that success in development does not necessarily translate into a more equal income distribution. Countries such as Malaysia and Mexico with notable progress in development display higher income inequalities than less developed Algeria. It appears as if with more development, income distribution can become less equal and "shared growth" as in the Asian tiger states is not a necessary by-product of a developmental phase.

According to the presented data it is evident that countries leaning towards the state capitalist development model of the developmental state or dual economy were better performing than countries that are closer to crony and petro state capitalism. Likewise, this latter group was more successful than group three, where a number of countries display characteristics of predatory state capitalism.

Thus, by now the research question of why there is such a notable heterogeneity in performances among state capitalist countries has been answered by forming three relevant groups with different forms of state capitalism.[18] As a matter of fact, differences in the structures – as displayed by differences in the quality of the civil service – lead to industrial policies with diverging characteristics. Also, private property rights tend to be more secure in group one than in both other groups and are safer in group two than in group three. This seems to reflect the fact that more successful state capitalist countries were able to credibly commit to securing private property rights and thereby creating incentives for productive economic activities. In principle, this is in accordance with the findings of North (1990 p. 118), who argued that such governance orders stabilize expectations and lower transaction costs thereby enhancing economic development.

In this third chapter a taxonomy has been deduced on a theoretical basis starting from the constituting principles developed in the second chapter. Subsequently, it has been demonstrated, how institutional change is possible from one state capitalist variant to another. Afterwards, there was a grounded analysis with data from upper middle-income countries in order to differentiate state from market capitalism not only on a theoretical basis, but also in terms of hard data. It has been demonstrated that upper middle-income countries are clearly oriented towards state capitalism, whereas countries such as Germany, Japan and the US are strongly leaning towards market capitalism.

---

18 As Witt et al. (2018) point out there could also be other non-institutional drivers of performance. To those they count the presence of external military threats, ethnic homogeneity and the absence of natural resources.

Then, this approach was expanded to include the varieties of state capitalism. As a matter of fact, three groups of state capitalist countries were discerned. All five varieties of state capitalism deduced from the theory could be approximately placed into one or more of the three groups identified with the data-based analysis. As a matter of fact, it was afterwards illustrated that countries close to the economic order of the developmental state or dual economy state capitalism perform the strongest in terms of development indicators such as the HDI and economic growth. The least successful states are those resembling most closely predatory state capitalism.

However, a data and also a theory-based analysis are not sufficient to identify all structural and industrial policy characteristics of the relevant countries. In order to account for a thorough analysis case studies are needed. This will be the task of part number four. There are literature analyses for Singapore and South Korea (the latter from the 1960s to the 1990s), since their development trajectories have been dealt with extensively by prior research. Then there are interviews for the case studies of Russia and Kazakhstan, since there appears to be less literature about the developmental trajectory of those two countries.

4 Case Studies

"If you desire things, many things will seem but a few."

Benjamin Franklin

Abstract

So far in the course of this study it has been left unaccounted for, how diverging performances within state capitalist countries' groups can be explained. In order to achieve this goal four presumably state capitalist countries – Russia, Kazakhstan, South Korea and Singapore – have been selected as case studies. Before leading over to the specific case studies, it is nevertheless needed to introduce case studies as a method of qualitative analysis and to expound on the design of the case studies including justification of case selection. After this introductory chapter the four case studies as such will be dealt with, being concluded by a comparison of all four cases.

Keywords: Russia, Kazakhstan, Singapore, South Korea, Case Studies, Performance Differences

4.1 Case Studies in Theory and as a Method in this Study

4.1.1 Case Studies as a Method of Qualitative Analysis

Over the recent past case studies have gained ground in academia as a scientific analytical method and have even been found out to be the most popular method for qualitative analysis over a 10-year period (Welch et al. 2011, p. 740). Likewise, this method is chosen for a wide array of research questions ranging from health, psychology or consumer studies to social sciences. Potential fields for case studies are group processes, internal organization or strategy. Case studies can as an exception be quantitative, but are overwhelmingly qualitative (Eisenhardt / Graebner 2007, p. 25–30).

When dealing with case studies five stages can be discerned: design, preparation, data collection, analysis and presentation of findings (Yin 2014, p. 2). Along these lines the case study of this monography will be conducted, starting in the next sub-section with describing the design of these specific case studies. Then as the case studies progress the preparation will be dealt with as well as data collected, analyzed and presented. Each single stage is quintessential and errors on any of the five levels can endanger the success of the entire project.

By now, in a certain sense case studies have become a standard procedure of analysis. In general, researchers attribute an important role to qualitative case studies and in a number of instances they are even seen as being superior to a quantitative analysis.[1] Whereas quantitative analysis is population-oriented, concerns effect estimation and deals with statistics, qualitative case studies rely on logic, strive for outcome explanation and are case-oriented (Mahoney / Goertz 2006 p. 245–246). In this regard by now researchers see qualitative case studies as methodologically on an equal footing with quantitative analysis (see Adcock / Collier 2001 and Brady 2004), especially when the relevant research question aims to explain certain phenomena being observed in reality.

Since case studies are conducted in such diverse fields of research, there are numerous distinctions between different forms of case studies. Yin (2014) differentiates between exploratory, explanatory and descriptive case studies. On the other hand, Welch et al. (2011, p. 750) enumerate four different varieties of case studies, i.e. inductive theory-building, natural experiment, interpretive sense-making and contextualized explanation. By the same token, Lee (1989, p. 117) makes a more abstract differentiation between case studies following the subjective or objective school of thought.

Notwithstanding how case studies are classified in the literature they have in common that they deal with contemporary phenomena and are geared towards explaining phenomena, which have come into the focus of science. A standard definition of a case study is that it is "an empirical inquiry that investigates a contemporary phenomenon (the "case") in depth and within its real-world context, especially when the boundaries between phenomenon and context may not be clearly evident" (Yin 2014, p. 16). Key to a case study is the aim to understand the phenomenon and being able to define the boundaries of a case study without in general severing the links to its context.

In essence Yin (2014, p. 9) sees case studies as a method such as also experiments, surveys, archival analysis and history. As a method they do differ from the latter by asking "how" and "why" questions, i.e. concentrating on explaining certain phenomena, and the focus is on contemporary events.[2] Marshall (1999,

---

1 However, as a matter of fact, there are some researchers such as Smelser (1976), who deny the merit of qualitative analysis and stress the advantages of a variable-oriented approach, where correlations between dependent and independent variables tend to be measured mechanistically. This is criticized by qualitative researchers as lacking in explanatory value and not going into depth as can be done by concentrating on a few cases that are selected based on a theoretical background.

2 Case studies are especially promising, when a subject matter is still at the early stages of research (Eisenhardt 1989, p. 549). Therefore, modern state capitalism is especially well suited for case studies, since research is basically deemed not to have started prior to Bremmer's study in 2010.

p. 380) takes a different view. He maintains that case studies are an approach using various methods, such as focused interviews, focus groups, structured interviews or surveys involving questionnaires. This study leans towards the view of Yin, since it appears to be quite logical that case studies can be juxtaposed with and differentiated from experiment, surveys, archival analysis or history (Yin 2014, p. 9).

A crucial part of the process of conducting a case study consists of case selection. Inferior results are to be expected, if random selection is chosen (Seawright 2016, p. 520). Case study analysis cannot be compared with statistical methods, where a researcher strives to find a sample which with a sufficiently high confidence interval represents a larger population. As a matter of fact, in case studies the aim is particularity and generalizability. A case study should concern an idiosyncratic phenomenon observed in reality. The trick is now to choose a case study that is sufficiently particular to come to some specific results, but at the same time being able to generalize the findings in order to build a theory.

Indeed, singularity often carries the risk of not allowing for generalizing case study data, which up to a certain extent can be mitigated by conducting multiple case studies (Stall Meadows / Hyle 2010, p. 412). In this regard then generalizability can only be achieved by resorting to a selection on theoretical grounds. After all the aim of a case study tends not to lie in testing a theory, but to develop one. Building this theory then has a high likelihood of revealing new insights (Eisenhardt / Graebner 2007, p. 27 and Eisenhardt 1989, p. 532).

In recent years case studies tended to rely more on multiple cases. They have increased in frequency and their evidence is often found to be more compelling than those from single-case-studies. Its advantages lie in the fact that they allow for comparison and thereby make replication – either literal or theoretical – possible. On the other hand, single- case studies are deemed to be permissible, for instance if they deal with an extreme or unusual circumstance or a common phenomenon (Yin 2014, p. 56).

By now, cases studies as a method of qualitative analysis have been introduced. They have been defined, their scientific and theoretic value been dealt with as well as the question of case selection been touched on. After this more general introduction in the following sub-section the design of the specific multiple-case study of this study will be concentrated on.

4.1.2 Design of the selected Case Study

Designing the relevant case study entails research questions, propositions, case selection, definition of the cases and methods applied. In this regard, a thoroughly planned design helps to make case studies more systematic, but it should still leave room for contingencies. Thus, it appears to be optimal to strive for a middle of the road approach, which can be termed planned flexibility. Thereby it should be possible to on the one hand ensure a purposeful research, while on the other hand being able to adjust to specific questions (Bazeley 2013, p. 32–33).

Inevitably doing a case study requires formulating the research question and giving some propositions as to where the inquiry is going to lead. In this study the phenomenon of state capitalism is analyzed. As mentioned above a vast number of countries has established a state capitalist economic order. In principle such similar structures and policies should lead to comparable results. But as can be seen from part three, there are significant performance differences. Thus, this case study poses "how" and "why" questions as is typical for case studies. Why are state capitalist countries performing so divergently? How are these differences to be explained?

In order to conduct a purposeful case study, it is not useful to venture into the endeavor without a notion of where the study is going to lead. This is especially important for explanatory case studies as the one conducted here. In this regard, part two and three are important – even partially theoretically grounded building – blocks for formulating propositions as to how these performance differences could possibly be explained.

Propositions of the Case Studies

First of all, in part three by establishing a taxonomy of state capitalism it was likewise hinted at the possibility that from a structural point of view a competent, pragmatic bureaucracy supports performance, such as mirrored in relatively high scores in development indicators, by its capacity and capability allowing for an effective implementation of plans formulated by the political leadership. In cases such as Malaysia and Singapore, which are deemed to be typical examples of the developmental state, such a correlation seems to be evident. Referring to countries being termed as predatory state capitalist such as Angola, in this argumentation bureaucracies are a stumbling block. This relates to the constituting principle of state capitalism about the relevance of bureaucratic capacity and capability.

A second proposition states that structure and policies are interdependent meaning that the quality of the bureaucracy tends to be correlated with a goal-oriented industrial policy. Its existence likewise amplifies the competence of the bureaucracy. This in turn would according to the first proposition increase performance results.

Third, concerning policies in general, a goal-oriented approach with the state as a dominant economic player such as in the developmental states facilitates development by giving the corporate sector a relatively high degree of expectations certainty. This is in line with the theory of Eucken presented in part two. Eucken maintained that the corporate sector most of all needs stability in the form of expectations certainty. Such a proposition might serve as a further explanation for diverging performances of state capitalist regimes, since starting from the developmental state down to predatory state capitalism there is a decreasing reliance on a goal-oriented industrial policy.

Fourth, regarding property rights, various types of state capitalism differ in their ability to overcome a lack of rule of law by the political leadership credibly committing to developmental goals, with the developmental state the most successful and crony as well as predatory state capitalism the least successful. Again, it is possible to resort to Eucken for this proposition, since he postulated secure property rights to be quintessential for a functioning economic system.

A fifth proposition maintains that it appears to be possible that political leaders are able to initiate institutional change, superficial examples provide in rather consensus driven Japan Prime Minister Shinzo Abe and deeply religious India with the uncontested reign of Narendra Modi (see Economist 2019, p. 57 and 59). Despite structural constraints they can in critical junctures establish in-depth changes to the respective economic system, for instance advancing their country from crony state capitalism to a developmental state. Such an endeavor requires a credible commitment, meaning for example that the political leadership will stick to its course – and not be willing to alter its position in the middle of a process – to embark on a developmental path. This proposition is in line with the actor-centered approach presented in part two and three, meaning that in history there is no determination of a country's developmental trajectory based on the respective institutional frameworks. Thus, the credible commitment of a political leader to initiate development-enhancing institutional change can as an independent variable cause the dependent variable of development performance to increase.

By now, five propositions for the success of a state capitalist system have been formulated. The first two propositions are structural. This is taken up by proposition three which argues that structure has significant implications for policy. Proposition four then clearly relates to policy. The last two propositions concern political leadership being able to overcome either certain structural constraints or utilize propitious critical moments in a country's history in order to initiate a sustainable developmental trajectory. Overall, it is argued that different structural and policy factors in the respective cases lead as independent variables to diverging performances as dependent variables. This is in congruence with the research question. In a quantitative analysis the researcher would now seek to find correlations between independent variables – such as secure property rights, a competent bureaucracy, credible commitments by political leaders as well as a goal-oriented industrial policy – and dependent variables such as performance indicators. This approach entails certain problems.

Ragin (2013, p. 171 and 174) points out that such an approach leaves out configurational settings, which lie beneath a comparative analysis. It is thus in a quantitative analysis close to impossible to pursue a holistic approach with these purely statistical means. On the other hand, a qualitative case-oriented approach can analyze single cases more comprehensively and concentrate on how causal factors combine to generate results, in the case of this study the diverging performances of different varieties of state capitalism. As a matter of fact, there is in a number of instances not one cause for leading to a certain outcome. No single variable as such might be responsible for the observed outcome, but it might be due to a combination of factors.

For instance, a competent bureaucracy in itself might not be sufficient to lead to satisfying development results. It could very well be possible that a credible commitment by the political leadership is required that leads to secure property rights and with these positive incentive effects a competent bureaucracy conducts an effective industrial policy. With the help of conducting interviews or surveying the literature and subsequently analyzing these data sources it appears to be possible to gain an insight into multiple cases, which should then in a comparative fashion ideally be able to be generalized to lead to a theory based on the data sources, which were collected guided by the propositions.

Justification of Case Selection

One of the central tasks of conducting case studies is case selection. Cases can be chosen for replication purposes, in order to extend an emergent theory or to fill theoretical categories (Eisenhardt 1989, p. 537). Ultimately, case selection should serve the purpose of being able to answer the research question. Likewise, this selection must under no circumstances be geared towards fulfilling the purpose of simply verifying a theory formulated a priori. It has to leave room for alternative answers and perspectives. In the same vein, it tends to be recommendable to pursue a multi-case study. This opens the opportunity to allow for replication in order to increase the validity of the study.[3]

---

3 Single-case studies have by now become something of an exception. They are said to

Such an approach appears to be all the more promising, since as a matter of fact, in part three five types of state capitalism were established: the developmental state, dual economy state capitalism, crony state capitalism, petro state capitalism and predatory state capitalism. In order to be able to generalize from individual cases to a comprehensive theory it is required not to choose all cases from the same sample, since this variation according to Eisenhardt (1989) can serve the purpose of filling a certain category and improving the explanatory value of the evolving theory.

At the same time, since this study deals with state capitalism, it is expedient to select all cases from state capitalist countries, for instance those identified in part three foremost among upper middle-income countries. By the same token, it is quintessential to keep the focus on the relevance of replication. Results of one case shall be able to be verified by a second case. Thus, first of all the cases should stem from the list of countries established in table 6. Second, all the selected cases ought to come at least from two different variants of state capitalism, since the research question refers to performance differences being epitomized by the countries being grouped in different types of state capitalism.

In order to account for the most successful example of state capitalism the developmental state should be covered. A literature survey reveals that a quintessential example of state capitalism is South Korea from 1961 to 1996 (see Amsden 1989, Kohli 2004). As a matter of fact, starting from 1996 South Korea entered the OECD and was not considered to be a state capitalist developmental state anymore, but leans toward market capitalism. Thus, first of all it is expedient to utilize South Korea as a case study, since this country has closed the chapter of its state capitalist past and progressed into market capitalism. Therefore, South Korea is a particular case, making it especially worthwhile to analyze for theoretical reasons. Second, according to proposition number six political leaders can initiate institutional change and establish a new economic order. This can be especially well analyzed in the case of South Korea, since the start of the developmental state is widely associated with President Park Chung-hee's rise to power in 1961.

Then, it appears to be obligatory to choose a second developmental state for the purpose of replication in order to increase the study's validity. In this regard, the country ought to stem from group number one of table 6, meaning Singapore, Malaysia, Turkey, South Africa, China, Thailand or Mexico. In the literature

be justified in cases, where thick description is needed and an in-depth analysis of one case is required, which leaves no scope for further cases.

among these states Singapore and Malaysia are most often cited as examples of the developmental state. This leaves the residual to a choice between Singapore and Malaysia. In this regard, it is recommendable to come to a decision by considering theoretical reasons, as to which country is most likely to yield the best theoretical explanations.

Here Singapore sticks out. According to the World Bank its development results are outstanding and likewise it has a competent bureaucracy on a globally competitive level. Furthermore, notwithstanding a relatively low degree of rule of law the country manages to secure the property rights of its citizens. Finally, with Lee Kuan-yew there was a political leader, who embarked the country on a developmental path. Selecting Singapore as a case with a time frame from the state's founding in 1965 until today can serve this study to identify, whether the propositions formulated above really suffice building a theory based on the propositions formulated above. In essence, comparing Singapore with South Korea also promises to provide answers to the question of how state capitalist countries progress towards market capitalism, which South Korea has already accomplished and Singapore is possibly currently in the process of achieving.

Thus, so far two cases have been selected. But as stated above, there have to be cases from the other types of state capitalism as well. Therefore, the focus now switches to group two from table 6 with a development performance inferior to that of group one. Possible candidates are Jordan, Serbia, Romania, Cuba, Kazakhstan, Russia, Colombia, Tunisia, Brazil, Peru, Azerbaijan and Lebanon.

Case selection should again keep an eye on the particularity and generalizability of the possible cases. Serbia is a possible EU-member and Romania has gained access to the EU already. Therefore, neither of these countries are typical examples of state capitalism. The same holds true for Cuba, which in a number of ways is more socialist than state capitalist. Brazil on the other hand is often cited as a typical example of state capitalism, but is with its relatively long-lasting democratic tradition and lack of strong authoritarian political leaders more of a deviant case. The same can be said of Colombia and Peru. Lebanon and Tunisia are hardly ever cited as typical examples of state capitalism. Likewise, Lebanon and Tunisia appear to be deviant due to their relative lack of state dominance of the corporate and financial sector, which constitutes a central pillar of state capitalism.

This leaves a choice between Russia, Kazakhstan and Azerbaijan, which are all former states of the Soviet Union. In this regard, Russia should under no circumstances be omitted, since it is in general with its authoritarian political leadership, size, state dominance of the economy and deficiencies in rule of law counted among the classical examples of state capitalism. In Kazakhstan among others the political leadership stands out. Former President Nursultan Nazarbayev embarked his country on a developmental course after the collapse of the Soviet Union. He credibly committed to the goal of becoming one of the 50 most competitive countries of the world by 2030. Its economy has a dual character with strategic industries being state dominated and less strategic industries experiencing fewer state interventions. In this sense Russia and Kazakhstan constitute almost ideal cases number three and four. Since they both belong to group number two and their developmental performances are on a par with each other, they can both replicate each other. But then Russia can be seen as an example of crony state capitalism, whereas Kazakhstan leans more towards dual economy state capitalism. Thus, both fill theoretical holes.

Until now, four cases have been selected. It is not expedient to include more cases to this study, since then the results would become too fuzzy and generalizability as well as comparability would suffer. Therefore – also for reasons of scope of this study – it is not possible to include cases of group number three with the most inferior performances to this analysis.

Case definition and Methods applied

So far, the four countries of South Korea, Singapore, Russia and Kazakhstan have been identified as cases. The logical next step is to define these cases. This entails to define the time frames. Naturally, locations of the cases are evident. In the cases of South Korea and Singapore those are the boundaries of the respective nation state. For Russia and Kazakhstan this could pose a problem, since both countries emerged from the Soviet Union. However, since the time before the collapse of the Soviet Union will not be taken into account, this problem is non-existent.

Regarding the time frames, for South Korea the start of a state capitalist system is regularly equated with the rise to power of President Park in 1961. Thus, this date will be taken as the starting point. By the same token, most observers argue that post-1996 South Korea had advanced to the status of a market capitalist economy, when it became a member of the Organization of Economic Cooperation and Development (OECD) and entered the club of industrialized nation. Therefore, for South Korea the time frame is set from 1961 to 1996.

For Singapore as a starting point the year 1965 should be chosen, meaning the year of its independence. This is expedient, since traces of a state capitalist system were already recognizable and the architect of the developmental state, Prime Minister Lee Kuan-Yew, was immediately in power, reigning until 1990. However, Singapore continued as a developmental state after Lee's resignation until now, so that the relevant time frame for the analysis of Singapore is from 1965 until the present.

Russia experienced a turbulent period of time after the dissolution of the Soviet Union, experimenting with a sort of "wild" market capitalism, as Russians term this phase of their country themselves. This makes it recommendable to leave out Russia's 1990s and start with President Vladimir Putin's rise to power in 1999. Such an approach appears to be all the more justified, since Putin is deemed to have initiated a state capitalist system, for instance by nationalizing vast parts of the corporate sector. Since Russia continues to be state capitalist according to the literature as in the case of Singapore the analysis ends in present times.

Kazakhstan did not experience as severe transformation problems as Russia. After the end of the Soviet Union it embarked on a state capitalist course under its President Nursultan Nazarbayev, who reigned until 2019. Since it is expedient to cover the entire time span of a country's state capitalist phase the relevant time frame is set from 1991 until today. At this point it needs to be noted, however, that in this study there will not be a historical analysis. It is intended to analyze state capitalist systems as they now exist in Singapore, Russia and Kazakhstan and existed in South Korea until 1996, taking into account historical factors, having emerged during the relevant time frames.

Regarding the methods chosen for analyzing the four cases, there is a large variety to choose from, ranging from qualitative approaches, including grounded theory, to quantitative analysis. As a matter of fact, case studies can be designed with a wide array of different methods (Hyett et al. 2014, p. 9). Since this study is foremost concerned with explaining phenomena in four different countries a qualitative-comparative approach appears to be most fruitful. This approach will then be applied to data sources from the respective four countries. In the cases of Russia and Kazakhstan there were interviews conducted with experts and the transcripts of these interviews serve as the data source. This appears to be almost mandatory, since the literature on state capitalist systems in both countries is relatively scant. In general, interviews can be conducted as unstructured, semi-structured and structured interviews. Here semi-structured interviews are selected, since they enable the researcher to maintain some consistency. Furthermore, expert interviews tend to be especially fruitful for phenomena that are – as state capitalism in Russia and Kazakhstan – relatively understudied (Fainshmidt et al. 2018, p. 313). Topics are chosen before beginning the research and the same subjects are covered in every interview. But the advantage is that participants are able to add new input, open and spontaneous questions by the interviewer are possible (Corbin / Strauss 2015, p. 38–39). At the same time, for South Korea and Singapore it is resorted to the relevant literature. Both countries are widely and intensively covered in the literature. Therefore, in this study for the cases of those two countries the relevant literature is chosen as a data source.

So far, the design of the case studies has been illustrated. Preparations for collecting the relevant data for the case studies were taken. Possible data sources of evidence are documentation, interviews, archival records, direct observation, participant observation and physical artefacts (Yin 2014, p. 106), but also survey data (Eisenhardt / Graebner 2007, p. 28). Thus, in preparation questionnaires of the interviews in Russia and Kazakhstan were formulated and relevant experts contacted by e-mail and in the case of a positive reaction in a number of cases also called by phone in order to agree on a time frame for the interview. Experts were selected according to their relevant knowledge of the economic order of their respective countries. Nevertheless, availability also had been a factor, so that in Russia there tended to be a focus on interviewing experts from business while for Kazakhstan it was more from the sphere of academia. A systematic bias owing to the fact that certain experts declined to be interviewed is not to be observed. However, in Russia NGOs were reluctant to be questioned, which could stem from their being classified as foreign agents by the government and that they are in general scrutinized with critical eyes. In most instances experts with one exception were selected from the medium echelons of the hierarchy. This turned out to be advantageous since thus the experts were still familiar with problems on the ground, but nevertheless senior enough for possessing inside knowledge.

For the cases of Singapore and South Korea in preparation the relevant sources in the literature have been screened and one official from the Singaporean pilot agency Economic Development Board (EDB) been interviewed. This leads over to the next stage, i.e. data collection. This process is described prior to each respective case study, followed by analysis and presentation of the data. Therefore, in the following four sub-sections the four selected case studies will be presented.

4.2 Russia

Russia sticks out in the sample of case studies in this sample as being by far the largest and most populous country. There is a constant undercurrent of path dependence involved when dealing with Russia, since the legacy of the Soviet Union is still highly perceivable. Thus, informal institutions are part of the analysis of this case study. However, the focus is on formal institutions evident in structure and policies in the context of the state business nexus and on performance.

4.2.1 Preliminaries

In order to collect data referring to structure, policies and performance of state capitalism in Russia 26 expert interviews were conducted, with most of the experts coming from business and academia. Likewise, prior to a field trip to Moscow in the middle of September 2018 a questionnaire was compiled. This contained ten question blocks with on average three specific single questions. The question blocks related to structure – i.e. quality of the bureaucracy, composition of the corporate sector, degree of lack of rule of law, embeddedness and autonomy of the bureaucracy -, policy – i.e. expectations certainty of the corporate sector, industrial policy, target orientation, and commitment to goals -, performance and actor-centricity of the developmental process.

All the interviews were semi-structured, meaning that in the field the course of the interviews resulted in significantly more questions posed than formulated and it was consequently followed up on certain answers. Only in one case recording was not allowed. The questionnaire is to be found in the annex. By the same token, transcripts of the interviews, which were coded by using MAXQDA software are available on a database. At the same time the code system utilized for the analysis is to be found in the annex. Coding tended on certain occasions to be done utilizing ordinal scales such as high, medium or low. But this was elicited by asking open questions and not constraining experts to give a number on a scale. Utilizing this technique helped to better assess the perception of the experts than a formulation of pure numbers can do.

Overall, the interviews tended to take 45 to 60 minutes and anonymity was generally granted as a precondition. Nevertheless, in order to stick to scientific norms in the transcripts of the interviews – stored on MAXQDA – files such essentials as names or positions are saved. Transcribing was done manually and without the assistance of voice recognition programs. The reason is that this software is until now not advanced enough to convey moods, dialects or gestures (Praxisbuch 2015, p. 31).

For analyzing structure and policies – as well as partially performance – qualitative data from the interview transcripts is used. However, regarding performance it is also resorted to quantitative data from the World Bank in the form of world development indicators and governance indicators as well as for the HDI to data from the UNDP. Although as a time frame de facto rule of President Putin is chosen, this is not a historical analysis. State capitalism as it now exists in Russia is the research focus, but for reasons of contextualization the entire span of Putin's tenures is taken into account. The evolving factors explaining performance differences in state capitalism are not necessarily complete. This study concentrates on an institutional analysis and leaves such more neo-classical variables as factor endowments and total factor productivity aside, which naturally can also be influenced by the institutional setting.

4.2.2 Structure

This study focusses on the quality of the bureaucracy, composition of the corporate sector, the degree, to which there is a lack of rule of law, as well as embeddedness and autonomy of the bureaucracy as key elements of the structure of state business interaction in state capitalism. In coding the transcripts of the interviews with experts on Russia, at least 18 codes emerged that in general relate to the structure of the interplay of state and business in Russia. Since this number of codes is too complex to analyze in detail, in the following the key structural components of state business interplay are dealt with.

Quality of the Bureaucracy

The task of a bureaucracy is to implement policies formulated by policy-makers. This can be accomplished either by meticulously in detail fulfilling each specific requirement. On the other hand, in a number of cases bureaucracy is to implement policies with a sufficiently high degree of autonomy and deciding on a case by case basis. In general, from the point of view of the government, i.e. policy-makers, the bureaucracy displays a high degree of quality, if it facilitates achieving policy goals. From the point of view of the corporate sector the bureaucracy is highly qualified, if it manages to communicate clearly and obligingly, acts in uniform, displays knowledge of business and is not prone to extract bribes. By the same token, the quality of the bureaucracy tends to increase with sufficiently competitive entry tests, high wages compared to the corporate sector, long-term career paths, performance orientation in salaries and promotion as well as a sufficiently subdued fluctuation of staff.

In general, concerning ministries related with the economy the experts identified a high degree of competence in the staff. All in all, only 5 codes denied a performance orientation in those bureaucracies, whereas 19 mentioned for Russia a remarkable competence and performance willingness. "What we are observing – that would now be my personal assessment – that by now especially on ministerial posts there are clever people sitting." (Expert Business 11) "What I can say: over the last years a number of qualified young people came to the ministries. They understand the questions. It appears as if they have a Western education, Western schools, because they exactly understand the questions and the situation about what they are talking." (Expert Business 5). However, apart from Russian ministries by now being able to recruit among the brightest minds of university graduates, there is still old-style bureaucratic procedures basically, inhibiting young career bureaucrats from implementing policies as successfully as they intend to. "They have to be visible and show their energy and act as being responsible, but in questions of detail for the solution of problems it still takes a lot of time… There are still those tedious rounds." (Expert Business 5).

Thus, the pool of ministerial staff appears to come from among graduates of the best Russian and international universities. One reason for this development is attributed to the Russian state enhancing salaries in the course of the last five to ten years. Out of 14 codes relating to the competitiveness of salaries vis-à-vis the corporate sector 11 codes signal rather competitive salaries. Likewise, a sizable proportion (7 out of 16) identify long-term career paths.

At the same time, there is a certain stability in the ministerial staff with relatively low fluctuation. Thus, 13 out of 18 codes mention low fluctuation, only five a medium degree of fluctuation and no expert observed a high fluctuation. This tends to be quintessential for companies, since they have to devote certain expenses to building trust and contacts with ministerial staff. This social capital appears to be rather secure in the context of state business interaction in Russia. Therefore, it appears as if the Russian state was able to staff ministerial positions with highly qualified personnel on a sustainable basis. In this regard, evidently a lack of general entry tests for serving in the ministries does not distort such a tendency.

However, between quality of the staff and quality of the workings of the bureaucracy there is a fundamental difference. Thus, the experts maintain that communication of the ministries is in a lot of respects lacking in quality. As a matter of fact, 9 out of 21 codes point to the fact that information flows are rather not working.

While there clearly is a tendency by the bureaucracy to put all new regulations on the internet first of all, SMEs are put at a disadvantage, since they do not have the capacities to absorb the sheer amount of regulation as well as regulatory changes and secondly, in many cases companies are not being informed prior to the new regulation taking effect. All these factors are seen as rather negative for companies in their business goals of increasing profit and revenue, innovating and venturing into new markets. "There are tons of examples, where I personally have read about, private sector companies getting no information about public sector initiatives. But the government does not have too many incentives to advertise the public sector initiatives. Do not forget: The main objective is to fulfill quantitative criteria" (Expert Academia 1).

This relates to the fact that bureaucrats have no deeper understanding of how important it is for business to know about the regulatory environment they have to operate in. Such a diminished expectations certainty according to Eucken is detrimental for business. Interestingly, the experts likewise voiced the perception that the Russian bureaucracy is very well embedded into the corporate sector, meaning they should be familiar with problems entrepreneurs are facing. 21 out of 24 codes indicated such a setting.

However, it needs to be understood that this can mostly be attributed to the fact that there is to a certain extent what is termed amakudari in Japanese – meaning descent from heaven – where former bureaucrats tend to switch to positions in the corporate sector. "Some of them are actually understand, because some of them came from business. No, of course interests of big businesses" (Expert Think Tank 2). This caveat moderates the finding that bureaucrats are embedded into the corporate sector. It is more of a reminder that contacts to the bureaucracy are very important in the business world and SOEs as well as large private companies are on a regular basis notified a priori about changes in policies as opposed to SMEs.

Finally, business strives for the bureaucracy not to extract bribes. In this regard, none of the experts rule out pervasive corruptive practices. Nine out of twenty-one codes even indicated the perception of a high degree of corruption, with twelve codes mentioning a medium degree. Apparently, for Russian business it is very much a daily affair to have to find the right persons whom to bribe in order for instance to obtain a permit. For companies this increases the costs of doing business and is seen as a burden. Without concretely having been asked for it, four of the twenty-six experts mentioned the strategy of firms to keep a low profile, meaning to arbitrarily decrease visibility by not increasing revenue or profits. There is a constant fear of arousing too much interest for the own company, in case it becomes too successful and then prone for raiding by political leaders, bureaucrats or competitors. This acts as a further drag on the development of the corporate sector, since it forces a number of companies to intentionally stay small, thereby forgoing the opportunity of reaping economies of scale.

All in all, although there is a high degree of competence within the bureaucracy, companies perceive fundamental problems when dealing with the bureaucracy. This short-coming tends to have an effect on performance, i.e. the realization of developmental goals. Consequently, it is worthwhile now to turn to the government in order to assess how from its point of view the quality of bureaucracy is to be seen.

Low autonomy for Russian bureaucracy

From the point of view of the government bureaucratic quality consists of realizing goals that had been formulated by the political leadership. This can on the one hand result in a one-to-one direct implementation of the government's guidelines, principles, standards or requirements with ultimately a complete loss of the bureaucracy's autonomy. On the other hand, the political leadership can communicate goals – or even relatively specific targets – to the bureaucracy and leave the means for goal achievement to the technocrats.

For Russia out of 16 codes not one indicated a high degree of autonomy for the bureaucracy, whereas 10 referred to a low level and six to a medium one. As one of the experts observed: "So, they have very strong incentives not to deviate at all. Even the smallest bit of government instruction has to be conducted... They want to keep bureaucracy in check. If you have very clear criteria to fulfill, you cannot do whatever you want. You have to do, what the government wants to do..." (Expert Academia 1).

The experts allege that the reason for not granting technocrats a modicum of autonomy is to be seen in a lack of trust. One of the defining elements of the Russian politico-economic system is a marked emphasis on loyalty ("loyalty is important", Expert Int. Org. 01). In this regard what counts more than effectiveness of bureaucratic processes, i.e. bureaucratic quality, is for technocrats not to become a threat for the dominance and reigning of the political leadership. Thus, up to a certain extent development is sacrificed in order to prolong the existence of the current regime.

At the same time this phenomenon of a bureaucracy not daring to strive for self-initiatives is exacerbated by a tendency in Russia's state and society to structure interaction in a very top-down manner along the vertical of power. Eight out of twenty-six experts referred to a top-down ordering in relations without in any way being explicitly asked into this direction. "...it is in a lot of ways vertically structured and people are waiting for the exact guidance from above..." (Expert Business 11) This lack of autonomy makes an effective ruling vis-à-vis the government's reigning very complicated. Bureaucrats do not have the leeway to come to creative solutions in order to implement a policy guideline in such a way that for instance the corporate sector increases innovative activity. There is a neglect of flexibility and a lack of bureaucratic capacity to react to ad-hoc changes in general or specifically to changes in the market environment of companies. This is all the more deplorable, since as analyzed above over recent years the quality of staff has increased significantly.

By the same token, to aggravate this entire setting loss of autonomy of the bureaucracy does not entail by far an eradication of corruption. The experts observe a still high to medium degree of corruption in Russia. Not a single expert characterized the interplay of state and business in Russia as being not marked by corruption. This relatively high degree of corruption coupled with a lack of being able to flexibly react to the needs of the corporate sector makes the bureaucracy more of a burden than a boon for business. Out of 20 codes – although 12 indicated a certain ambivalence – eight clearly referred to the bureaucracy inhibiting the corporate sector from achieving commercial goals. Likewise, the interviews revealed a tendency towards red tape in the bureaucracy and interviewees also deplored the ministries acting contradictorily, which is to a certain degree attributed to turf wars and dysfunctional relations between liberal forces and members of the security services. "And I would say there are very rivalling factions within the state, very contradictory factions and the state is not very coherent in its actions." (Expert Academia 2).

For development that poses a major obstacle, since a commitment to developmental goals coupled with a homogenous interaction of the state with the corporate sector – with regard to policy formulation and implementation – strongly facilitates business activity, such as venturing into new markets, imitating products, innovating or realizing economies of scale by merging or organically growing. The reason is that companies have to formulate strategies, devote resources to planning and have to analyze markets. In this regard, non-contradictory actions by the state increase expectations certainty and facilitate forming adequate outlooks.

In this sense, an unequivocal short-coming of the Russian state exists in the lack of a pilot agency. There is in no regard a one-stop or one-window approach, meaning that companies have to deal with multiple ministries, which are occasionally acting contradictorily, and this confusion drives costs for companies upwards, while decreasing efficiency and certainty about future regulatory changes.

This becomes evident by an utter lack of a pilot agency. There is not even a functional equivalent, mirroring functions of such an organization. The experts interviewed identified numerous agencies as taking over coordinating functions, i.e. the finance ministry, the transport ministry, the Presidential administration, the ministry for economic development, the Deputy Prime Minister, the agency for strategic initiatives, the ministry for digitalization and the agency for technological development. However, the experts uniformly observed that there exists no agency to effectively coordinate economic development as it is sketched by the political leadership in the decrees published with each new tenure of the President.

One expert deplored massively: "There is an enormous lack of coordination. Usually, every ministry is doing what it wants and there are people – deputy ministers, they are responsible for coordination, vice prime minister" (Expert Think Tank 3). Another Expert (Business 5) complained that he as an entrepreneur has to approach a multitude of agencies, creating costs and increasing uncertainty. Likewise, this confusion, up to certain extent stemming from the diverging interests of the two most influential power groups, liberals and security forces, in his perception is in violation of the law, which also inhibits development from another perspective, i.e. a markedly pronounced lack of rule of law.

Thus, in many cases the cohesiveness of a pilot agencies' policy formulation and implementation is obstructed by this fragmentation, which emanates from a lock of power for the pilot agencies to enforce rules. In Russia they serve only as coordination device and have hardly any real power. Due to this lack of instruments to effectively implement policies –stemming from a lack of backing from the political leadership – bureaucratic obstructionism comes into force, where ministries actually inhibit initiatives started by the pilot agencies. This setting tends to aggravate the regulatory confusion, when rules of individual agencies compete with one another, making bureaucratic force a weapon against development (Chibber 2002, p. 984).

To sum it up, the Russian state invested significantly in improving the quality of its bureaucracy. Over the last five to ten years salaries were increased remarkably, providing – coupled with a general down-turn of the economy and relative renumeration decreases in the corporate sector – an incentive for highly qualified personnel to enter into the civil service. These investments, however, so far bear no fruits. The reasons for this failure – and consequently low quality of Russia's bureaucracy – are not to be found in a lack of motivation of those cadres. Structural factors are by far more prevalent. First of all, there is an utter lack of coordination due to multiple and overlapping responsibilities of ministries and no agency being in charge of coordination. Second, loyalty is placed before performance and effectiveness. Third, bureaucracy to a high extent mirrors the tendency of Russia's state and society to structure all processes in a top-down fashion, thereby eliminating most initiatives and creative solutions. Fourth, even this lack of autonomy did not succeed in decreasing rampant corruption. Thus, all in all, bureaucracy is not able to effectively implement developmental goals. From a business perspective, entrepreneurs complain about a lack of clear and uniform communications and actions. Therefore, an analysis of the Russian bureaucracy reveals a significant lack of quality. Such a tendency can be mitigated by a corporate sector being structured in a way that embodies a counter-weight to the state, is able to articulate diverging positions and manages to operate with efficiency regardless of a lack of bureaucratic capability. Consequently, it is now turned to the Russian corporate sector.

Structure of the Corporate Sector

Structural factors of the bureaucracy determine a certain quality of the bureaucracy and likewise have an influence on state business interaction. Accordingly, the structure of the corporate sector likewise affects the interplay of state and business. There is no deterministic causation for instance between a very atomistic or oligopolistic corporate sector structure correlating with a facilitated or inhibited exchange between state and business. However, the structure how bureaucracy exists, is a factor in this interplay. Aiming and realizing a high performing corporate sector according to Eucken depends crucially on a level-playing field for economic actors, guaranteeing competition, enticing productive commercial activities, among others by setting low entry barriers.

In this regard, the Russian corporate world is significantly dominated by large companies, either SOEs or huge private companies and with the state acting in almost all the cases as a majority or sole investor. This refers to all industries, where Russia has a relatively strong position by international standards, such as resources, metallurgy, IT, ship-yards, defense, nano-technology, aerospace or automobiles. Building up a successful new-comer in any of those industries, where Russia due to its endowment with natural and labour resources appears to have a competitive advantage, entails disproportionally high costs, in the best case in the form of opportunity costs. "What can happen, if you are really successful is that if you have a niche product that is gigantically successful then Kalashnikov or Rostech can come and then they can come and say, Axel, you have 200 people, what is your revenue, 20 million Euro, you get 100 million Euro – and get lost." (Expert business 9). In very much the same way this phenomenon is reported by Kommersant (5th of February 2019), referring to a de facto acquisition of the highly successful e-commerce company Ozon.ru by the large player Sistema, highlighting that successful SMEs are regularly bought by large actors, often also by SOEs. Thus, a highly concentrated corporate sector is furthermore promoted, which tends to facilitate selective interventions at the cost of broad-based incentives that can assist in forming a level playing-field.

It is also in general, very difficult for SMEs to start doing business and to keep operating in an environment dominated by the large players. 28 codes referred to SOEs or large private companies being favoured vis-à-vis SMEs. Not one single expert pointed out that SMEs are favoured by the state, although officially the Russian government runs a certain number of programs for SME promotion. Thus, the rather oligopolistic structure of Russia's corporate landscape leads to inefficiencies in setting distorted incentives for companies to operate. Size is rewarded and not so much productive and innovative technological activities. This can among others be attributed to large companies being more creditworthy debtors, attracting larger attention by the financial sector, or by employing more people and therefore being for political reasons preferentially treated by the central and local governments, so that job losses are averted or job gains triggered.

The entire visibility of large actors is more pronounced, causing the state – and therefore technocrats – to almost as a habit turn to large actors when the state implements certain programs. This becomes evident when such a program as selecting and forming national champions is taken into account. "So, winners in corporate sector could be picked for several years, even decades ago and picked one more time and one more time. It gets support as brilliant companies and you know now national champions. As far as I know majority of national champions was supported by government or ministries or state foundations for years." (Expert Think Tank 2). Out of sheer ease of comfort technocrats do not make an effort to promote small actors that have large potential, but are so far hardly known. This underlines vividly the proclivity of the corporate sector's oligopolistic structure inhibiting an effective state business interplay.

However, its economic power could pose a lever for the corporate actors to become an effective counter-weight to a state that is quite frequently intervening into the economy. Especially, the business association RSPP, being branded as the oligarchs' club and therefore of large players, wields a certain power and can mitigate planned policy changes that are deemed to be unfriendly towards business.[4] But business associations in the perception of the experts were mostly instruments for the corporate sector to push through particularistic interests. 16 codes indicated a dominance of those interests and experts observe unanimously that the role of business associations is to represent its members' short-term business interests – also of SMEs in the business associations Opora and

4 Indeed, business associations do have a significant influence on government policy. Thus, the association for large companies RSPP managed to in principle avert the introduction of surplus profit taxes on metallurgical and chemical companies, which would presumably have led to less investment in these sectors that compared to other industries of the economy have a relatively high productivity (Kommersant 16th of August 2018).

Delovaya Rossiya – and not to take over a function of assisting in coordinating industries. In this regard they are relatively successful in communicating those interests to members of the state.

But as a matter of fact, not only is there a lack of coordination on the side of the state with no pilot agency or an equivalent existing, but also on the corporate side. Aggravating this development is the fact that there is in general a lack of competition with high entry barriers and large players – such as Gazprom, Rosneft or Rostech – subduing market pressure from rivals, for instance by buying out smaller successful players. In effect, from a structural point of view Russia's corporate sector suffers from a lack of competition while at the same time displaying a lack of coordination. Therefore, it becomes very difficult for the state to build up or modernize industries. Judging from this context the state resorts to promote large – in a number of instances monopolistic – players that face hardly any competition at all on the domestic market and likewise often do not become competitive enough to excel on international markets.

Degree of Rule of Law

As analyzed in part three a lack of rule of a law is a constituting principle of state capitalism. However, there are diverging degrees to which rule of a law is lacking and likewise how strongly it transmits into relatively insecure property rights. The experts unanimously ruled out that in Russia there is a high degree of property rights security. Out of 22 codes eleven referred to a medium degree of property rights security. The rest claimed that in Russia insecure property rights are to be observed.

This is detrimental from a theoretical point of view, since according to Eucken and North secure property rights incentivize productive economic activities. First of all, the reasons for a lack of property rights security can possibly be identified in the court system itself. But this does not fully conform with the evidence. In Russia those, who suffer from property rights violations in a number of cases utilize the courts and also on a number of occasions have success. Out of 21 codes 8 claimed that there is even a low inhibition of going to court. The majority of 12 codes indicated that there is a medium degree of inhibition and only one expert pointed to of a high inhibition of suing in case of property rights violations. "Judicial means are increasingly used. And I believe that also the President is very much intent on further paving this path that the courts are as far as possible independent and make judgments according to the law and not taking into account the interests of certain circles." (Expert Business 8).

By the same token, the experts maintained that there is hardly any point in suing the state in case of property rights violations. The chances of winning in those cases are according to their perception close to zero. Likewise, in case the property rights violations stem from competitors the quality of court decisions increases significantly. But at the same time, it is also relatively futile to sue a company that is large and very well connected in politics. "They make of course, but big businesses have power even in courts. It is not corruption itself. But it is not wise for bodies to contradict interests of big business." (Think Tank 2). There is a clear distinction between commercial and criminal law. If an individual is sued by the state, the judge almost as a rule follows the arguments of the prosecutor. Only in very few exceptions are plaintiffs acquitted. But with commercial law the rules are different and in this regard on many occasions, entrepreneurs are able to protect their property rights. This fact is underlined by twelve out of 21 codes giving the Russian law system at least a medium quality rating. A minority of nine codes rated the Russian law system as having a low quality.

Since undeniably, business in Russia suffers from property rights violations, it needs to be understood, where those are coming from. It has already been pointed out that big companies in a number of instances raid smaller competitors. Also, large companies with acquiescence of the courts can engage in illegal business activities to drive smaller, but successful competitors out of the market.

Apparently, also, a certain degree of property rights violations stems from the state itself. If a company comes into the way of political circles, for instance by leaning towards opposition forces, the management and owners can be sued in a criminal case and the company taken away. In a number of other cases, it was not even for political reasons, but due to bureaucrats striving for taking over a successful business venture by raiding the company. Since Russian regulations are very complicated this can take the form of repeated inspections, thereby disclosing irregularities, or even triggering the company's bankruptcy by suing it on the ground of trumped-up charges. Overall, the web of regulations – which partially even contradict each other – serves as no effective protection mechanism for the companies when it comes to property rights. The same can be observed regarding the quality of the bureaucracy, where quality deficits are evident and have been dealt with above.

In a nutshell, from a structural point of view the interplay of state and business tends to be dysfunctional with short-comings on the side of the state as well as on the corporate side. These deficits are not mitigated through the law system. Although, the quality appears to be higher than widely reported, it does not succeed in protecting property rights. Therefore, state business interaction is at the same time distorted by companies that have relatively low incentives to perform, since they perceive a danger of having their property rights violated. On the other hand, the ubiquitous rents that are accorded to large economic actors likewise disincentivize engaging in productive activities and all the more entice companies to pursue earning rents through aiming for advantages in the face of redistributive state actions. All this mostly refers to structural elements of Russia's state capitalism. To some extent out of structure follow policies and this will be one aspect in the following sub-section.

4.2.3 Policies

In a certain sense in these case studies, structure is the independent variable of analysis and policies are dependent variables. However, a certain degree of interdependency is likewise to be observed. In general, short-comings in quality of the bureaucracy, structure of the corporate sector as well as in the rule of law all affect the quality of policies applied by the bureaucracy. Overall, it is indeed striking that in Russia a clear preference by the state for planning and consequently a target-orientated industrial policy is visible. That results – with the enactment of sanctions as a reaction to international sanctions after the annexation of the Crimea – in a clear emphasis on import substitution and local content requirements.

In the subsequent parts it will be elaborated on how the focus on a target-orientated industrial policy can be traced back to structural and historical reasons. By the same token, the quality of those policies themselves, their attainability and their implementation are analyzed. Ultimately, it is assessed how Russian economic policy alternates – due to the already mentioned structurally and often dysfunctional diverging interests of the power groups of liberals and members from the security forces – between the two extremes of selective industrial policy and strictly market orientated policies.

The Case of a target-orientated Industrial Policy

As a matter of fact, there is a certain tendency of Russian policy-makers and technocrats, observable to strive for imitating the role model of the Newly Industrialized Economies (NIE) of East Asia. Three experts explicitly referred to the East Asian model and emphasized that most of all Russia adopts from that concept its emphasis on target orientation.

However, at the same time, a number of experts pointed to path dependence and informal institutions fostering the proclivity of the Russian state for planning and target setting. They referred to the Soviet legacy and of the super-ministry Gosplan, which had been responsible for setting and implementing targets. To this day, there appears to be an aversion among Russian elites for unexpected phenomena. The elites – and here foremost the political leadership – seek to have as much as possible of politico-economic developments under control. "In Russia it is perceived as a sort of target who should be under the control of the state, should be playing control over appointment of personnel and dismissals and the like." (Expert Academia 5).

Simultaneously, such flexible factors as they emerge on competitive markets are anathema to the majority of Russian elites. Planning is key and reaches back to the 1930s when Gosplan was set up. "since this ludicrous planning that they partly have and is not implementable that somehow does not work. But that exists." (Expert Business 3). However, most of the experts do not in itself see Russian preference for planning as an obstacle to development. In their eyes, it depends on proper formulation and implementation and a willingness to pursue pragmatic solutions.

And here to a certain extent from structure follows a certain policy orientation. Since the Russian state as analyzed above is reluctant to allow for flexible adoptions and prefers a top-down approach, to meticulously control the bureaucrats with hardly any possibility to bend the rules, if needed, in policy formulation goals are set in a very detailed manner and cascaded down to targets for each respective bureaucrat. "That is indeed a very important instrument of policy to set these goals, much more common than we know it from our system. There are really concrete targets for the economy to grow by so much percent. And there are efforts to cascade it down to find out what needs to be done for it." (Expert Think Tank 1).

This leaves little room for adopting to sudden changes or the specifics of individual firms. "when the companies fulfill this requirement then they receive the preferences. What I encountered. There is much small print." (Expert Business 5). Thus, structural short-comings of the Russian state inhibit the effectiveness of policy formulation and implementation. For instance, goals are set in the May decrees with every new presidential tenure and they are set for the entire tenure of six years with no mechanism to accommodate for exogenous changes.

Thus, when the sanctions after the annexation of the Crimea were enacted, the plans of the May decrees of 2012 were still in place and the Russian state struggled to adopt to exogenous changes that occurred afterwards. Another structural factor that affects policy formulation and implementation is corruption in the bureaucracy. In order to counter these additional costs for state, business and society the government becomes all the more rigid in its planning and prescribing how plans are implemented, so that thereby the space for corruptive activities is minimized.

Likewise, the structure of the corporate sector with its emphasis on big business facilitates crony relations, since the number of relevant actors therefore is limited, enabling long-lasting personal connections to evolve, which is even exacerbated by the fact that there is a low fluctuation in the Russian bureaucracy and technocrats stay long enough in their positions for the opportunity to build up a crony network. In this regard such a tendency is obviously not prevented by severe restrictions in bureaucrats' discretionary levers.

Target Setting as Part of Russian Industrial Policy

Among others targets serve the function of setting incentives for agents to perform. Likewise, targets offer a principal the ability to measure performance results and according to these figures of achievement distribute rewards, which then again serve as an incentive to continue performing. To these ends, targets are utilized widely in state capitalism and are applied in a number of ways.

In Russia goals are cascaded down meticulously to very detailed targets, but only sector-wide. With the exception of the instrument specialnij investnij kontrakt (Spik) dealt with below there are no targets for individual private companies as such. There is only on a meta level an indicative planning that does not reach down lower than to sectoral levels.

However, in Russia as mentioned above SOEs do have an over-arching function in realizing goals of the country's industrial policy such as diversification and import substitution. And for those companies the political leadership in conjunction with technocrats indeed formulates and implements targets. These Key Performance Indicators (KPI) are not only applied to the top management, but also to second or third tier levels. Top goals can consist of revenue, profit, market share, employment or product price targets.

However, in many instances, the political leadership pursues non-commercial goals with SOEs. In these cases, SOEs have to bend to political pressure and at the cost of revenue or profit pursue political goals, such as increasing payrolls or employment, lowering prices as in the case of Gazprom or even taking part in non-profitable infrastructure projects. "As I mentioned, sometimes people from the government they prefer to deal directly with the executive power of the company where they have strong state stock. And sometimes it is even a bit informal, you know. So, for instance, they tell them you should just help this region to build a new stadium. Yes, something like that. One cannot say that it is completely out of sense, because somebody has to build stadiums as well. But I am not quite sure this is the best way to ensure the construction of such objects." (Expert Academia 8).

As is evident from this expert's perception, in a number of ways the political leadership does not deal with SOEs in a rule-orientated fashion. It has more characteristics of acting ad-hoc in a discretionary manner, when for opportunistic reasons it appears to be advantageous for the entity to come to a certain decision.

Thus, SOEs are not in a position to solely pursue goals such as maximizing revenue or profit in the long term by innovating or venturing into new markets, since for political reasons double bottom lines come into play. This distorts business strategies and is detrimental for the long-term viability of a company. Such an effect is even exacerbated by the fact that in Russia the boundaries between state and private are blurred. Thus, certain politicians and technocrats might regard an entity as part of their own private business, utilizing for instance its services for private purposes.

For these reasons, Russian SOEs such as Gazprom, Rostech or Rosneft are deemed not to operate efficiently. They are claimed to perform lower than comparable private sector firms. And one of the main reasons is to be found in inadequate target-setting that becomes muddled with non-commercial pursuits. This is a severe drag on Russian industrial policy.

Content of Russian Industrial Policy

Almost right with the start of Putin in his tenures as President and Prime Minister, the political leadership intended to diversify from its reliance on natural resources. By the same token, political leaders strove to increase stability of the country's politico-economic system, increasing the living standards of the population, which had deteriorated dramatically during the first decade of transformation directly after the collapse of the Soviet Union and the transition to capitalism. Russia's policy framework and the general policy orientation can only be understood in front of this background.

Therefore, the current emphasis on import substitution is not only due to the sanctions, but also owing to the political leadership's intention to diversify its economic structure while in the long term maintaining a modicum of improvements in living standards. "Social quietness, yes. Since the leadership is scared that people might stand up and organize the toppling of the government, however that is titled. Help is relatively quickly organized in cases where masses of the population face problems." (Expert Business 7).

Thus, taking into consideration the independent parameter of a minimum of social security and welfare, the state clearly strives to modernize its economy, often as mentioned with the role model of NIEs. In its current strategic focus of import substitution, the country focuses on increasing the degree of local content in sectors such as machinery, automobiles, food, agricultural machines or chemical industry. Furthermore, the state seeks to pick winners and thereby create national champions. By the same token, the political leadership intends to make significant strides towards digitalizing its economy.

Russia's import substitution policy concentrates on increasing local content, aiming for technology transfer and building up domestic industries, since thus far on the home market there exist with a few exceptions no entities that can produce according to international standards. To this end, foreign companies are in order to circumvent tariffs constrained to either become a minority shareholder in a joint venture with a domestic partner or enter into an agreement along the terms of a specialnij investnij kontrakt (Spik).

With this instrument the state grants privileges to companies that commit to a pre-defined level of investments. The advantages or disadvantages of pursuing an industrial policy of import substitution is highly contested and no ultimate judgment can be given here. But overall, the majority of firms interviewed about the content of industrial policies such as Spik, had the fundamental complaint that those are mostly geared towards large players. "The Spik is defined. There are framework requirements which need to be fulfilled. They are separately negotiated: size of production, localization, sort of products, employees. For an SME that is not really interesting only if it is about dimensions which are intended for the Spik. For companies like ours a techno-park with all its possibilities is absolutely sufficient." (Expert Business 7).

But Spik was not only created for foreign companies, intent on avoiding tariffs, localizing and therefore obtaining the status of a domestic producer, but also as a method to stimulate investments of domestic entities. Expert (Think Tank 2) cited as benefits of Spik a stable regulatory environment for those companies that commit to it. Furthermore, they receive tax privileges from the regional level and means from an industrial development foundation, where formally it is only about consulting, but in reality, financial means are flowing. This expert objected that in a number of cases the state constrained companies to pursue projects that were not feasible from a business perspective and therefore politically motivated with a potentially inefficient utilization of funds.

Overall, the key deficiency of the well-intended instrument Spik mirrors short-comings in the overall orientation of Russian economic policy. It does not entail enough flexibility for entities that it concerns. Once more there is a tendency of over-regulation and over-planning to be observed. In cases where companies for commercial reasons – such as a changing market environment – do not manage anymore to fulfill the pre-defined investment levels, there are grave penalties, so that companies in a number of instances had to invest more than any sense of business logic would warrant.

This non-pragmatic, non-discretionary approach fosters market and price distortions, which according to Eucken any state should avoid in order to allow for stimulating an efficient utilization of funds. "I know people with Spik and I am not naming and names or companies, but the majority under four eyes and a glass of red wine said: never again." (Expert Business 9).

Analyzing the interplay of the state with economic actors further, it becomes even more evident that large and especially state companies are preferred. In order to build up or promote industries in the following sectors declared to be strategic – nano-technology, atomic energy, shipyards, aviation, aerospace or defense – especially large state corporations such as Rosnano, Rosatom, Rostech or Rosoberonexport were set up. They were created in order to substitute imports, but also on the other hand to create national champions that can compete on international markets.

This policy in the eyes of an overwhelming number of experts did not bring the desired results. Of 16 codes referring to the existence of a policy of picking the winners, only two assessed this policy to be successful. The cited reasons for this failure are manifold. One explanation are lock-in effects, where bureaucrats stick to favouring one entity for a longer period of time than is feasible, since they are familiar with this company and perceive not to be prone to unexpected problems. Further reasons given are double bottom lines, inefficient management, financial means flowing to companies that are politically well-connected and only to a lesser extent those with potential, an over-emphasis on military purposes, the high degree of concentration in Russia's domestic sector, a tendency to restrict support to proclamation, a blurred line between state and private sector as well as a lack of constraining potential national champions to compete on international markets.

As a matter of fact, problems of Russia's program of picking the winners amount to a general lack of competition and accountability. In many instances there are no hard budget constraints involved when allocating those funds. The majority of codes related to technocrats tending not to be accountable for their actions (16 codes out of 25 codes). And while bureaucrats do not face consequences for a lack of performance, the same appears to apply to selected national champions that are furthermore inhibited by having to pursue double bottom lines.

At the same time, Russia strives to become one of the most modern economies in the world. It intends within a few years to make St. Petersburg to be the first truly digital city in the world. Large funds flow into the project of digitalizing the economy. Even the very controversial raising of the minimum retirement age was justified with a need for these funds in the field of digitalization.

However, experts contend that digitalization will for a significant amount of time be limited to Moscow and St. Petersburg and therefore also the potential to modernize the economy by digitalizing. "You clearly see the goal of the Russian government to modernize the economy through digitalization, to harness the great potential of Russian programmers, the great potential of Russian IT firms and for that you have the program 'digital economy' and also, there you see concrete steps in order to achieve these goals. Therefore, in those two areas import substitution and digitalization those are two very significant examples for such a policy." (Expert Business 10). The digitalization drive clearly has the same characteristics as the overall import substitution policy. In a top-down manner the state strives for fostering innovation in a sector where creativity is the key factor. It is noteworthy that in the field of digitalization Russia excelled with a company that is decidedly unconstrained in its founding, funding and operations from state interventions, the "Russian Google" Yandex.

Attainability of Developmental Goals

A number of experts pointed to the fact that developmental goals are regularly not realized. In case a goal is not accomplished, either in a clandestine fashion goals are adjusted or failure to achieve the goals justified with exogenous factors that inhibited goal attainment. This phenomenon was to be observed regarding the lack of goal attainment in the May decrees of 2012, when the political leadership argued that it was impossible to account for the sanctions imposed after the Crimea annexation while planning for the subsequent six years Presidential tenure.

However, since this reasoning was communicated to economic actors on prior occasions as well, the credibility of developmental goals such as formulated now in the May decrees 2018 suffers significantly. Such a phenomenon can be observed in the qualitative data collected for this study. Of 24 codes about achievement of current goals, only one regards it as likely that those goals are indeed realized. 17 codes straightaway deny such a possibility and only six codes left the answer open and hinted at the chance that goals might or might not be achieved. As one expert (Think Tank 1) put it: "Almost never. You can say that they were reached at the beginning of the 2000s – also due to external factors, oil prices and geography are very important – and then basically the planning was continued. In principle, the GDP should have doubled again since then. But basically, it remained the same then." And another one concurred (Academia 3):

"I would say they are systematically not reached. They are also systematically to highly placed."

So, why does the political leadership then set such unrealistically high developmental goals. One reason is to be found in the political leadership justifying its reign with increasing the living standards of the population. Its legitimacy crucially depends on achieving this goal up to a certain extent. If the political leadership was to not strive for such improvements, the basis of its legitimacy would threaten to become eroded.

Therefore, the state still formulates unrealistic goals in order to create the impression that it really seeks hard to develop the country, but ultimately only fails for exogenous reasons. By the same token, since at the beginning of the 2000s goals were indeed realized, the government perceived that such an ambitious planning had strong motivational effects. This effect however currently wears down, since economic actors do not perceive the developmental goals to be credible anymore.

At the same time, Russia's political leadership has the ambition to in a very short time-frame catch-up to advanced economies. Therefore, developing entire stages in the value chain is skipped. Political leaders are striving for high-tech without having prior excelled in enabling to become competitive in medium-tech. This attitude becomes evident when analyzing the digitalization drive of the country. Obviously, solely by formulating ambitious goals the government intends to skip a number of developmental stages and become one of the most modern economies of the world. Evidence from the interviews, points to the fact that this strategy does not work out. In fact, in a number of cases goals are indeed not realized and therefore goal attainment in the future has to a certain extent become not credible.

Straddling liberal and State Capitalist Policies

The entire orientation towards planning is a hallmark of Russia's inclination towards state capitalism. Doubtlessly, as demonstrated in part three, Russia is state capitalist. However, intrinsically, its economic policy is swaying between more liberal and more state capitalist characteristics. This becomes epitomized in President Putin in his public comments stressing sometimes more liberal and sometimes more state capitalist positions.

Institutionally, this ambivalence becomes evident by the fact that in organizations such as the central bank and the finance ministry liberals clearly do dominate. Indeed, those technocrats and politicians are clearly opposed to any interventionist planning at all. The maximum they would agree to is indicative planning, but not an outright industrial policy.

Thus, industrial policy such as favoured by the ministry of industry or the ministry for economic development is regularly softened by for instance the ministry of finance balking at allowing the necessary funds to flow. Therefore, as already mentioned in the analysis of bureaucratic quality and the lack of a pilot agency, there are dysfunctional inter-ministerial fights inhibiting the development of the country. Five experts without having explicitly being asked about it referred to these conflicting interests of liberals and state capitalist forces.

By the same token, three experts pointed to the widely diverging interests being prevalent within the state. "Yes, or I would say within the state apparatuses the state is not a homogenous actor. This state-capture model would argue that the state is in a certain sense homogenous. And I would say there are very rivalling factions within the state, very contradictory factions and the state is not very coherent in its actions." (Expert Academia 2).

In a certain sense, Russia's political leadership indeed is not really unequivocal in communicating how it intends to achieve its developmental goals. Some decision-makers are clearly opposed to any kind of industrial policy at all, while others see it as a panacea for becoming a modern industrialized nation within a relatively short time-span.

This unclear direction of the country's economic policy tends to undermine expectations certainty, not least of all that of the corporate sector. This is in effect provides for a certain dose of confusion. For economic development on the other hand a certain degree of stability is key. And as analyzed above, Russia's corporate sector has little perception of operating in a stable kind of market environment.

To sum it up, Russia clearly embarked on a target-orientated policy, possibly also for reasons of path dependence and informal institutions reaching back to Soviet times. However, targets are relevant most of all for SOEs, where they serve as more than just indicative functions, but become in a number of instances distorted by politically motivated purposes such as increasing employment. Still, with the means of a targeted-industrial policy the political leadership with the assistance of import substitution and digitalization intends to modernize its economy quickly. However, one of the main obstacles emerges with a lack of credibility. By formulating unrealistic goals, the political leadership risks losing its credibility and therefore the ability to steer the country towards a constant upgrading of its economy. To what extent this loss of credibility has already occurred and how strongly structure and polices – as analyzed above – have an effect on performance is to be presented in the next sub-section.

4.2.4 Performance

In case studies it is not intended to identify correlations and causations in a number-orientated fashion. Nevertheless, case studies deal with why-questions and thus in this sense it is quintessential in this part to answer the question why structures and policies resulted in the performance evident for Russia. In a certain sense above it has already been indicated that Russia to a significant extent failed to reach its developmental goals.

For this sub-section first of all, it is striking that the majority of experts interviewed for this study was relatively critical concerning attainment of the political leadership's own developmental goals. Expert (Business 2) pointed out that "we have a relatively long track record now – 25 years on Kazakhstan, 15 years on Russia – and you do not see success stories. You do not see successful businesses. Or businesses created from scratch becoming competitive internationally." (Expert Business 2).

This perception tends to correspond with data extracted from the World Bank for Russia's developmental performance. To account for the latter data about GDP growth is analyzed. However, in order not to become too focused on quantitative growth measures at the detriment of qualitative development indicators furthermore the HDI of the UNDP is looked at.

But in order to also take into account structural factors Governance indicators of the World Bank (2019a) are also referred to. In this regard, looking at the extent of corruption, meaning in how far it is under control, Russia scores on average from 2000 until 2017 17.4 percentile rank points. And in this time span there is no improvement, but rather a slight deterioration to be observed. However, Russia is performing significantly better when it comes to government effectiveness and regulatory quality, where it scores on average for the same time span 42.1 points and 40.3 points respectively, underlining recent improvements which tend to be mostly due to increasing the quality of the staff of bureaucracy as analyzed above. By the same token, as illustrated above there are shortcomings in rule of law and accountability, where Russia on average for the same time span does only score 22.2 and 24.6 percentile points respectively.

Thus, there indeed appear to be grave structural deficits, which tend to lead to a not very coherent policy framework as mentioned above. Therefore, it would be expected that Russia performs in HDI and GDP growth relatively inferior. And indeed, for GDP growth the World Bank (2019b) identified on average for the time span from 2000 until 2017 3.8 percent, which is significantly below that of other emerging countries. However, it needs to be pointed out that in this time span the financial crisis occurred and the Russian economy suffered from sanctions. By the same token at the beginning of the 2000s GDP growth profited significantly from sharply increasing oil prices on international markets. Furthermore, GDP growth does not account for the quality of economic development, since it is a purely quantitative figure.

And according to the UNDP (2019) Russia from 2000 until 2017 scores 0.77 points in the Human Development Index and this score has increased steadily during those 18 years. Thus, it can be maintained that Russia in terms of such factors as life expectancy and literacy made some significant progress. However, regarding building a dynamic, diversified economy with little corruption the political leadership did not realize its goals.

Therefore, from an economic point of view the years starting with the ascent of President Putin to power were not marked by a steady developmental process such as in the NIE. Economic policy was centered around nationalizing large parts of the economy, foremost in the fields of natural resources, aviation, ship-yards and nano-technology. Currently, efforts intensify to build a domestic industrial base by following an import substitution policy, which up to a certain extent was initiated by the sanctions.

This policy that started in 2014 and is seen by a number of experts of this study as deserving a certain degree of attention and as being promising up to a certain extent. Nine codes stressed that they perceive Russia's import substitution policy as a chance and only two so far observed no results. "The topic of import substitution on the background of the geopolitical situation due to the sanctions of the US and the EU has a lot of momentum" (Expert Government 1). "And there you have to say that a lot has been done. It has been – and we see that in the chemical sector – great efforts taken, yes, and not upstream but also downstream more and more get into the value chain…" (Expert Business 11).

It is too early to assess the success or failure of Russia's import substitution policy. Such an economic policy is indeed controversially discussed in the literature. However, it is mostly conceded that for a large country with a huge domestic market such a policy might in the end succeed. But judging from the time frame under consideration in this study from 2000 until now, there are grave deficits in development performance and those are to a large extent to be attributed to structural deficits resulting in an incoherent economic policy with the impeding deterioration of expectations certainty for the corporate sector and in general the business environment ultimately leading to a situation where Russia tends to lag behind other countries in its developmental process. How far this phenomenon corresponds with actor-centricity in the political leadership of the country and possibly aggravates the problem is a question dealt with in the subsequent section.

4.2.5 Actor Centricity

In a certain sense every political leader is constrained by the institutional framework he is forced to operate in. However, in some cases these constraints appear to be weakened. This can for instance take place at critical junctures of a country when vested interests or particularistic interest groups, but also constitutional safeguards are weakened by the imperiled position this specific country finds itself in. Likewise, in autocratic or even totalitarian regimes in a number of instances the political leader finds himself relatively little constrained by the institutional framework.

In the time frame analyzed for Russia from 2000 until today there appears not to have occurred any critical junctures. The Russian financial crisis of 1998 and the repeated constitutional crises of the entire decade of the 1990s were behind the country and Russia's new political leader Vladimir Putin started from a consolidated power base, where he had to balance the interests of liberals and conservatives. Putin established a vertical of power, i.e.an autocratic regime, but nevertheless was not in a position to liberate himself from having to mediate between both influential power groups.

This empirical finding is backed by the literature and the interviews conducted for this study. Of 26 codes a majority of 13 codes only accorded Putin a medium degree of actor centricity, although as a matter of fact the political leader relatively openly concedes to have installed a quasi-democracy and has repeatedly been voted into office with overwhelming majorities, which should have given him enough electoral support to clearly define a political agenda that is not an at times incoherent mix of liberal and conservative economic policies.

Two codes even granted Putin only a low degree of being able to shape the developmental trajectory of his country. Concededly, 11 codes referred to a high degree of actor centricity, but this appears not to be exorbitant for a country that is ruled in such an authoritarian fashion. "Concerning strategy, it was some people work with him closely like for instance Gref, Kudrin now, which has some kind of vision. At the same time, there is unknown people and invisible and responsible for security agenda. In my opinion they provide stronger influence on Putin and so on and so on. As a result, we can see some form of combination, so." (Expert Academia 7).

Strikingly, even though there is the vertical of power and Russia is ruled and reigned in a top-down manner the experts observed a tendency of an incoherent policy framework, possibly reflecting these turf wars within ministries between the rivalling factions of liberals and members of security services. Russia's politico-economic system is largely dominated by connections and is therefore highly personalized. In a number of instances, in order to realize a certain project, the consent of one single person is required and likewise official procedures sidelined.

In this regard, this grid of inter-connected personal responsibilities and competences seems to limit the dominance of the political leader. A further drag on the political leader's dominance could possibly be his focus on political, economic and social stability. He built his reign on the promise of delivering stability, meaning especially social stability, with a decently high and stable living standard for the population. In order for this commitment to be credible, the political leader had few levers to switch to a more growth-orientated economic policy.

The political leader had to keep inequality at a level that was perceived to be sufficiently moderate by the population. Had Putin in this regard allowed for a higher degree of inequality he would have endangered the legitimacy of his reign. Without a modicum of legitimacy, it is assumed that no political leader can keep himself in office, at least as long as the regime does not resort to outright terror.

This credible commitment from which Putin draws his legitimacy constrained him not to pursue significantly growth-enhancing policies that tend to increase inequality and the political leadership for instance struggles significantly to realize a policy step of raising the minimum retirement age in order to finance the potentially growth enhancing policy goal of digitalization. Likewise, the credible commitment of keeping stable social security did according to the experts interviewed for this study – as analyzed above – not result in relatively secure property rights.

The political leadership did not credibly commit to achieving development. This assumption is backed by the experts, since 20 out of 27 codes denied that there has ever been an emphasis on development as a fully pursued goal. "We see how much how many resources Russia spends in order to fight wars abroad and modernizing its military and having all kinds of goals in mind rather than actually embarking on a comprehensive modernization program and having a real industrialization strategy. So, I do not think they devote all resources to it." (Expert NGO 1).

Russia's political leadership committed to stability and it appears as if such a commitment is not necessarily in contradiction with a certain degree of insecurity of property rights. After all, those violations are zero-sum games, where one's loss is another one's gain. However, a productive economy with constantly high growth rates requires a certain security of property rights, since entrepreneurs have little incentive for productive activities when they perceive that the fruits of their efforts can deliberately be taken away from them. Therefore, a credible commitment to safeguard property rights and economic development appears to be missing in Russia. At the same time, defending the status quo and privileges of particularistic interests appears to have been a credible commitment, incentivizing economic actors to seek to safeguard their property by building the right connections.

Thus, this preference of the political leadership led to a situation where institutional change was hardly sought for. There is a marked stability of the elites to be observed with few rotations at the levers of power in the political as well as the corporate sector. Therefore, no profound institutional change is to be accounted for in the time span from 2000 until 2017, which was nevertheless marked by initial power consolidation and nationalizations, installing a form of state capitalism that partially deviated from the more market liberal institutional framework prevalent under the predecessor of the current political leadership. The political leadership established a vertical of power, guaranteeing autocratic rule, but overall the institutional framework as such persisted. There was up to a certain extent the opportunity of a critical juncture at the outset of the current political leadership. Russia perceived to be threatened in its security by NATO forces at its border. Furthermore, the country had just escaped a severe economic crisis that was mostly due to problems of transformation, but also an inept political leadership. But at this point of time, the political leadership opted for reverting to a system of high stability and decent living-standards. Market liberal institutions and organizations were kept and only complemented by more influence for members from the secret services and the military.

In the concluding final sub-section about the Russia case study it is further analyzed how diverging performances in state capitalism can be explained. It will moreover be dealt with in which variant of state capitalism Russia can be placed and how the country through institutional change can progress to a more productive form of state capitalism or erode to a less productive variant of state capitalism.

4.2.6 Russian State Capitalism

Taking into account the analysis of this case study Russia is to be classified as state capitalist. This becomes evident when referring to the seven constituting principles of state capitalism defined for this study. The state takes the role of an active actor in the economy, as an owner and an entrepreneur. Large parts of the corporate sector are in the hands of the state, mostly through majority stakes or complete ownership. Furthermore, the financial sector is strictly controlled by the state. This becomes evident when looking at the dominant commercial bank Sberbank, where the Russian state owns a stake of more than 50 percent and there are interlocking personal relations between the state and this commercial bank.

At the same time, the Russian economy is not innovative. The state relies on an industrial policy, which borrows partially technology, business models and innovations from abroad, for instance through local content rules that aim for technology transfer. As a matter of fact, one of the goals in the May decrees is to increase the innovativeness of the economy, but whether this can be planned from top-down remains an open question, which is beyond the scope of this study.

Russia explicitly embarked on an industrial policy based on import substitution after sanctions were imposed. Even prior to the sanctions, Russia shielded its markets. Now there is significant tariff protection for domestic companies, so that especially in infant industries the degree of competition is limited. By the same token there is no doubt at all that Russia now and for the foreseeable future allows for a co-existence of public and private property rights. So far, not a single influential political leader of the country has called for a return to socialism.

Much in the same vein the bureaucracy is of a size that is by far significant enough to implement policies, those for instance that are part of industrial policy. There is a sufficient size to guarantee that the state can intervene actively in the economy and be a vital player in the corporate sphere. Regulations are tight and to a large degree also implemented. But that does not equate to Russia becoming a *Rechtsstaat.* In effect there are grave short-comings in judicial quality. This becomes evident when analyzing the interviews conducted for this study and taking data from World Bank governance indicators into account.

To sum it up, according to the seven constituting principles of state capitalism Russia fully qualifies as being state capitalist. Basically, thus, it has been identified what Russia's economic system is, i.e. state capitalist. But furthermore, it needs to be explained why it tends to underperform regarding accomplishing its own developmental goals. Naturally, this question can also be accounted for in a comparison of all the cases, but at this stage it appears to be warranted to list a number of possible reasons based on the analysis conducted in this case study.

Reasons for Russia under-shooting its own Developmental Goals

As a matter of fact, as analyzed above there appear to be profound structural short-comings in Russia. To begin with, there is a lack of a unified policy approach when it comes to interacting with the corporate sector. Diverging interests and overlapping competences on an intra- and inter-ministerial level do distort the functioning of markets for instance by sending contradictory signals to market participants. This aggravates efforts to come to commercially sound strategic and operational decisions, since the business environment is consequently marked by instability. This phenomenon is even exacerbated by the lack of one solely responsible and accountable pilot agency, which could as a one stop agency facilitate business for companies with regard to obtaining permits or applying for subsidies.

In essence the quality of Russia's economic policy and its current emphasis on import substitution is debated in the literature. Some economists reject import substitution outright, whereas others for a transitional period see some benefit in it. But since this policy is implemented poorly, according to the experts interviewed for this study, there is little merit in Russia's economic policy.

Likewise, a high degree of corruption places an additional cost burden on the entities. This becomes among others evident when looking at the extent of property rights insecurity. There prevails a profound lack of rule of law, which is in itself inherent to state capitalism, but becomes especially burdensome in Russia, since the extent of this deficit is so significant. This missing property rights security causes companies to safeguard their property with means of building the right connections in the political sector, meaning resorting to corruptive practices, which is not only an additional cost, but also drains labour resources away from productive activities.

Adding to this problem is the fact that formal distribution of property rights and actual connection between ownership and control in Russia are relatively obscured. In a number of instances property rights only exist on paper. This is among others due to the fact that certain owners occupy significantly influential positions in the management, which offers them a large part of de facto control to the detriment of other owners (Dzarasov 2013, p. 97 and 100).

Moreover, political leaders rather aggravate than mitigate this problem. There is no credible commitment by the political leadership to development – and therefore a minimum degree of property rights security – to be identified. Rather political leaders commit to preserving the status quo, on which they base their legitimacy. Russia appears to fall under the category of crony state capitalism identified in part three.

Russia as a Crony State Capitalist Economic Order

This assumption can be justified when looking at the institutional structure that is very significantly shaped by corruptive activities. The politico-economic order is highly personalized and doing business is mostly only possible with establishing the right connections, which would tend to be crony relations. In this context building trust to important decision-makers can be commercially far more relevant than making sound business decisions, such as venturing into markets with a high potential, developing and marketing products that can compete on product market and utilizing factor markets in a way to attract the most viable human capital and physical capital. Due to this constraint of economic actors having to engage in crony activities, welfare losses are sizable. This becomes evident when taking into account the under-performance of Russia's economy.

Another element of crony state capitalism – i.e. a low quality of the bureaucracy – can also be identified in Russia, as analyzed above. This lack of quality of the bureaucracy is most evident in the low degree of bureaucratic autonomy prevalent. The line between public and private is in a number of ways blurred. In this regard, the wide-spread practice of amakudari allows for SOEs to be on a number of occasions almost be managed as the private property of CEOs. They perceive that due to being in charge of this entity – although having to report to the government about this entity – avenues for insiders for personal enrichment become wide open (Dzarasov 2013, p. 10–12).

Thus, autonomy for the bureaucracy with regard to SOEs is limited regardless of the existence of KPIs for the management of such entities. And in a number of instances the line between public and private property becomes even more blurred by bureaucrats setting up their own companies through proxy representatives. Thus, on numerous occasions public funds are embezzled in order to finance projects of private companies that are de facto owned by a public servant.

Such mingling of public and private interests is ubiquitous in the Russian corporate sector. In this regard, the threat of being raided creates additional distortions in the Russian economy. Instead of engaging in long-term business projects with positive social returns companies concentrate on short-termism resulting among others in asset stripping or extracting wealth by the owners of their companies. This leads to welfare losses for the entire economy and loss of productive capital (Dzarasov 2013, p. 130–140).

This phenomenon is among others caused by the lack of autonomy of the civil service. Moreover, its significant embeddedness into the corporate sector is aggravated due to the fact that the government perceives that there is a high degree of crony relations at the state business nexus, and therefore the vertical of power is rigidly applied to limit discretionary space for the bureaucracy. Consequently, there is not only due to a high degree of corruption and crony relations a low degree of autonomy vis-à-vis the corporate sector, but furthermore regarding the political leadership autonomy is also kept to a minimum, making policy implementation as inflexible as it is and thereby inhibiting possibilities to adopt to changes in market conditions.

By the same token, the political leadership is also in another regard of little assistance when it comes to implementing a development-orientated economic policy. If political leaders achieve to credibly commit to the goal of development and fostering productive economic activities, they thereby manage to alleviate property rights insecurity as a result of lack of rule of law which is inherent in state capitalism.

But in Russia this was not the case. The political leadership committed to defend the status quo, but not to initiate institutional change allowing for an accelerated developmental phase. The problem is not only that the regime bases its legitimacy on stability at all costs[5], it is also that goals themselves are not credible. As analyzed above, repeatedly goals are not achieved and the experts are overwhelmingly skeptical whether current goals can be achieved. When a goal is not reached, political leaders and technocrats, resort to pointing at external factors such as conditions on international markets, for instance the oil price or the sanctions, and fend off being accountable for under-shooting economic performance, among others by formulating new plans that substitute the old ones that were not reached.

The unrealistic and often too ambitious goals have another detrimental effect. Since they have been repeatedly under-shot, political leaders are not credible anymore, and therefore most economic actors also perceive the formulation of plans for the future does not entail a high degree of credibility. Thus, especially taking into account the low quality of the bureaucracy, high corruption and missing credibility of political leaders into account, it appears to be most suitable to place Russia into the category of being crony state capitalist. Since as depicted above no institutional change can be observed so far under the reign of the current political leadership[6], now it appears to be worthwhile to analyze whether Russia can progress into a more efficient state capitalist variant or potentially regress into a less efficient form of state capitalism in the future.

---

5 The political leadership's claim to legitimacy based on stability surfaced and the vulnerability of this commitment became evident when during and right after the financial crisis of 2008 mass protests took place. In that context the high risk eminent in this legitimacy claim became clear. The political leadership acted accordingly and shifted its claim away from this strategy, mostly by resorting to ideology and personalism, i.e. the personality of the political leader Putin, after the crisis (Soest / Grauvogel 2016, p. 27 and 37-38).

6 According to Djankov (2015) there is no real reform effort visible, among others due to few reformers being in the inner circle of power. Thus, there is a continuum of the same stage of state capitalism to be observed under the current long reigning regime.

Avenues for Institutional Change

For Russia to move from crony state capitalism to dual state capitalism would require to first of all improve on structural weaknesses starting with improving the quality of the civil service. To this end, various instruments could be tested. As a matter of fact, Russia has already taken steps to lower bureaucracy's vulnerability for corruption with having increased salaries over the course of recent years. This has shown the effect of having improved the quality of staff. However, structural weaknesses remain. To begin with, the incoherent nature of policy implementation could possibly be tackled by eliminating overlapping responsibilities of ministries or even installing a pilot agency. Such a step could lead to a unified policy implementation, giving the corporate sector more expectations certainty.

It has been observed that when a limited number of technocrats – especially from the Central Bank and the Finance Ministry – are involved in reforms sizable results tend to be achieved, for instance in tax policy and the fight against inflation. In contrast to that, as soon as a vast number of experts from different ministries are involved reforms tend to be watered down to unworkable compromises. In these cases, there tends to be a sclerosis due to overlapping competences and contradictory policy formulation and implementation (Gelman 2018).

Overall, such a measure of a more unified policy approach could be complemented by further increasing the quality of staff, for instance by competitive entry exams, more clearly defined career paths, incentive-based renumeration and promotion as well as more clearly defined targets for bureaucrats. One bureaucrat could be assigned achieving certain goals, concrete KPIs could be set and achievement be measured and the technocrat in the end be held accountable.

Furthermore, low autonomy of the bureaucracy could be dealt with by severing too crony relations between technocrats and the corporate sector. One approach would be to eliminate amakudari for a certain period of time, meaning that no civil servants would for instance be allowed to take an – often lucrative position – in an SOE or even private company for example for five to ten years after departing from a technocratic or political position. In such a way the interplay of state and business could possibly become much less entangled, the line between public and private less blurred by relying on professional managers that have proved to be competent managers in other entities of the corporate sector.

Another means would be for the state to switch from majority stakes to minority stakes in SOEs, allowing for more business orientation and fewer double bottom lines. This could alter the attitude towards entities and make technocrats less embedded into the corporate sector and be increasing their autonomy. If such a step was accomplished and by the same token corruption reduced, the political leadership could venture to grant technocrats more discretion, allowing for a more flexible and efficient interaction mechanism regarding the corporate sector. In such a sense quality of bureaucracy and quality of policy implementation could be improved.

Leading over to credible commitments it would be worthwhile for the political leadership to bring goal formulation closer into the realm of reality. If goals were ambitious while being achievable, this would increase credibility of political leadership and technocrats with potentially positive motivational effects. It could also pose an opportunity to credibly commit to development and switch from the current commitment of upholding the status quo. If the political leadership was to succeed in this regard, it could also up to a degree substitute for a lack of rule of law and make property rights safer, allowing for entities to engage more in productive than in redistributive activities.

Quite likely, to realize such a drastic change a critical juncture is needed. One such critical juncture could have been the start of the imposing of sanctions in 2014. And indeed, the political leadership shifted its policy focus drastically towards import substitution. However, institutional and commitment factors were not tackled. But judging from Russia's tumultuous history a new possible critical juncture could emerge and possibly a new political leader grasp, the chance of instituting a new and more efficient variant of state capitalism, possibly starting with the next step on the ladder of state capitalist efficiency, i.e. dual economy state capitalism.

However, Russia's economic system can also erode to become predatory state capitalist. Such a process would probably start with a reversal of the current grip of the political leadership on the civil service. From hardly any autonomy there would be a shift towards hardly any control anymore over the bureaucracy. This can take place when governance mechanisms are weakened and the government switches to a policy of solely intending the bureaucracy to extract wealth from the corporate sector.

In such a setting the bureaucracy would be granted much more discretion as long as the goal of wealth extraction is reached. This process would possibly occur gradually combined with a deterioration in the staff of ministries. Due to signaling processes ministries would tend to attract staff that is less qualified and more intent on wealth extraction than implementing sound economic policies. Nepotism and outright corruption could become ubiquitous in the ministries.

In such a situation it becomes much more difficult to implement any form of industrial policy, since competent staff is missing. But already in the formulation of policy strategy and policy goals profound short-comings could take place. For instance, the political leadership could for opportunistic reasons such as wealth extractions and generating rents switch to a radical form of import substitution.

In such a way, it would be able to take out most of the competitive pressure of the domestic corporate sector, grant exorbitant rents to corporate leaders and collect bribes in the process. Under such a scenario Russia would become economically even more isolated than today and keep non-competitive industries as well as entities alive with high subsidies. And all this worst-case scenario is even aggravated by a non-competent bureaucracy that is short-term oriented towards extracting wealth instead of long-term supporting a productive, competitive corporate sector that is capable of paying a sizable tax burden.

To summarize, in this sub-section it has been maintained why Russia is state capitalist and falls into the category of being crony state capitalist. In the entire process of this argumentation numerous reasons have been purported as to why Russia tends to underperform in its developmental ambitions. Finally, it has been dealt with how institutional change towards a more or less efficient form of state capitalism – up or down the ladder – could look like. In this regard in the next section now the second case will be analyzed. Kazakhstan according to the case study design has been selected for the purpose of replication, but it is also possible that certain elements of its politico-economic system slightly point towards a different politico-economic system than that of Russia.

4.3 Kazakhstan

Kazakhstan sticks out in this sample of case studies as being very sparsely populated and being in the process of nation-building. It has been selected for this case study for replication purposes as thus offering the opportunity to verify findings of Russia's state capitalism as another example of a post-Soviet country. Both countries went through a partially painful transformation process and the Soviet legacy as an informal institution plays a certain role in both countries' current developmental phase.

However, it is conceivable that differences compared to the Russian form of state capitalism emerge. It is the aim of this case study to understand and explain these similarities and differences in structure, policies and performance. Thus, this case study will also pave the ground for an eventual comparison with Singapore and South Korea, which according to the literature tend or tended to fall into the category of developmental state capitalism

4.3.1 Preliminaries

For this case study the method of semi-structured interviews is selected. As a matter of fact, two field trips were conducted for this purpose – the first one for two weeks in April 2018 to Almaty and the second one in the beginning of June 2018 – also for two weeks – to the capital Astana. In the end – combined with interviews being conducted in Germany – the number of interviews adds up to 32.

These interviews were conducted with the help of a questionnaire that was similar to the one used for the case study on Russia. Except for one interview of a German government official, who objected to being recorded, all interviews were recorded on tape and later on transcribed manually. Since the interviews are semi-structured, spontaneous questions emerged to follow-up on certain aspects that were not clear from the initial answers during the interviews. On a number of occasions triangulation was applied and topics that surfaced unexpectedly in the course of one interview, but not having been answered conclusively, were dealt with during other interviews. Most interviewees stemmed from the profession of academia, followed by experts from NGOs and the government. The transcripts gained from the interviews were later on coded with the help of the software MAXQDA and are available on database.

For the purpose of analysis almost solely this qualitative data is used, but it is also to a small degree supported by evidence from the literature. Numbers from international organizations such as the World Bank and the UNDP are utilized for the sub-section on performance. Overall, the time frame sticks to the period from independence until March 2019, which coincides with the reign of President Nazarbayev, who at that point of time handed over political leadership to the new President Kassym-Zhomart Tokayev, while still up to an extent wielding power behind closed doors (Economist 23rd of March 2019). However, as in the case study of Russia this is no historical analysis. The focus is on state capitalism as it now exists in Kazakhstan. But in this regard the evidence is contextualized by taking into account the time frame from 1991 until today. As in the Russia case study, the analysis is systematized into structure, policies and performance, while another sub-section about actor centricity is added and there is a concluding sub-section.

4.3.2 Structure

Structural components of Kazakhstan's state capitalism are manifold. At the same time, for this study structural elements of the politico-economic order are selected to relate to quality of the bureaucracy, structure of the corporate sector and degree of rule of law. All of these elements are to a high degree interdependent. Thus, for instance a high level of rule of law tends to foster the quality of bureaucracy, since due to the constraints imposed on the bureaucracy by efficient court decisions accountability of technocrats is increased. However, for the purpose of this study all three structural elements of state capitalism are analyzed per se and only partially accounted for their interdependence.

Quality of Civil Service

The quality of the civil service is, as in the case study about Russia, difficult to assess. Different actors have different expectations of technocrats and therefore accord it a high quality for different reasons. In this sense, there can in this analysis be no straightforward answer, but it must be differentiated. First of all, the political leadership intends the bureaucracy to efficiently implement its policy goals. This can take the form of precisely implementing each separate policy framework set by political planners. On the other hand, it can take the form of using discretionary space in order to flexibly react to changing market conditions and take heed of the environment in which entrepreneurs have to operate in. In principle, a development-orientated political leadership is oblivious as to how policy goals are achieved and instead focuses on goal attainment. Developmental goals tend to be realized, if a market environment is created that allows for competition, low entry barriers, innovation and favours productive over redistributive business activities.

In order to assess how civil service fares in this regard, first of all the degree of autonomy of the bureaucracy ought to be analyzed. Naturally, it poses difficulties to find proxies for the degree of autonomy a bureaucracy wields. To approximate towards this rather fuzzy concept of autonomy it was referred to the degree of prestigiousness of serving in the civil sector. It can be deducted that there tends to be a correlation between autonomy and prestigiousness. And thus, it was decided for this study to ask the experts about prestigiousness.

This detour was chosen, since the term autonomy is rather abstract and the experts would not have had a concrete notion of its meaning. When a bureaucrat has a certain degree of autonomy in his actions, he ceteris paribus tends to be held in relatively higher esteem by observers that look at the bureaucracy from the outside. In the case of Russia, the experts were more familiar with the term autonomy and therefore it was directly applied in the interviews.

In the concrete case of Kazakhstan there is evidence for it being prestigious to work in the civil service. Out of 14 codes, ten related to a certain extent of prestigiousness, whereas four declined it. Concededly, two codes attributed prestigiousness to a certain modicum of sufficient salaries in the civil service. "If you are in government position, you have the power, especially working in the ministries in Astana, you working for the President's office, it is like wow. You can call to someone. You can solve your problems" (Expert NGO 2). This expert assessment about the ability of solving problems already accounts for a certain degree of autonomy.

It is also perceived that by being in the ministry it is possible to build contacts and gain power. Furthermore, Kazakhs tend to identify themselves quite strongly with the state and former President Nazarbayev and therefore accord state servants a certain status. Thus, overall, there appears to be rather a certain discretionary space for bureaucrats, which nevertheless tends to be first of all utilized for personal gain and only in a secondary sense in order to improve the performance of the economy.

This room of maneuver does not necessarily induce an exorbitant degree of corruption. Out of 31 codes 22 cited only a medium degree of corruption prevalent in the business state interaction. Concededly, the experts in 9 codes mentioned a rather high degree. But overall, possibly also due to draconian penalties – usually in the form of prison sentences – in case corruptive practices are discovered, corruption tends to be of medium intensity. This does not mean that discretionary space coupled with only medium corruption translates into a generally high degree of bureaucratic quality with technocrats allowing for a competitive and innovative business environment.

Out of 21 codes full 16 observe that information flows towards the corporate sector is rather not working. Only 5 do claim that this essential pillar of the tasks of the state business interface is working. Since there is a high relevance of the SOE sector in Kazakhstan it needs in a certain sense to be differentiated here between SOEs and SMEs. This becomes evident when taking into account the observation of this Expert (Academia 1): "Let the most significant decisions sometimes be made on the information which has been provided through informal channels. It is a pity, but it is a fact. Sometimes the commission which is going through formal channels, is just formalizing the decisions already based on the informal information given." Thus, entities with direct contact – this tend to be foremost well-connected SOEs – to the highest echelons of bureaucracy tend to be favoured in this regard, obtaining the relevant information beforehand. Other entities tend to receive the information when it is a fact and there are no consultation mechanisms anymore available to modify this new regulation and furthermore those entities can only adopt to the new rules later than the favoured companies.

In much the same vein this Expert (NGO 2) relates to the secretiveness of the public sector: "I think the government knows everything. What the government wants to do or what government is making some laws it is always hidden. But what it intends to do is not well known. It depends on an open debate culture. But here it is one person's decision." Information is in many cases only shared, when the law is finally passed. This observation also fits into the prior finding that there is a certain degree of autonomy for the bureaucracy, since one person on his own – with rather low institutional constraints – can come to a certain decision.

Consequently, the information flow is quite significantly inhibited. In order to take one concrete example, it can be referred to the state holding entity Samruk Kazyna that owns large parts of the corporate sector. "I think, they do not see this as a problem. Take Samruk Kazyna for example. The goal was to connect the government more strongly with SOEs. But when ministries contact Samruk Kazyna for instance by e-mail the fund often does not answer and give the information. The process of communication takes so long, the working time." (Expert Think Tank 2). Here it becomes obvious that even for ministries it is tedious to obtain information. Apparently, information flows between the relevant players of the state business sector are quite strongly impaired. Experts do point out that from an organizational point of view there appear to be strong deficits.

In an almost futile fashion in order to mitigate this problem a direct line to President Nazarbayev was erected. But as a matter of fact, he as a person cannot process all the information sent to him, so that it again becomes a bureaucratic issue with all the related problems in information flows that have been mentioned so far. Thus, in a certain sense, from the point of view of the government the implementation of policies appears to be lacking in quality.

Endowed with a certain degree of autonomy – in contrast to that of Russia – the bureaucracy fails to efficiently communicate with the corporate sector. This is also to the detriment of the corporate sector itself. But it deserves a closer look, how far for the corporate sector interaction with the bureaucracy is problematic. Here it first of all is striking that technocrats tend to be seen rather as a burden than as a boon, but at least not overwhelmingly.

Out of 19 codes at least 10 observed that it depends on the concrete circumstances whether the bureaucracy is rather a burden or a boon. At the same time, 8 codes were relating to the bureaucracy being a burden and only one saw it as a boon. One representative of Business (Expert Business 2) pointed out directly: "The same for strategic sectors. I am talking about those that have a very high share in GDP. All these enterprises, they know and they count for the state support. It is one of the principles of the state to help these sectors. There is a distinction between SOEs and SMEs, even for the real sector. The state tries to stimulate, even though he is a burden to the private sector, for instance for SMEs in the agricultural sector."

And here a certain ambivalence of the bureaucracy again comes into play. Strategic sectors can count on being supported, even with financial means, whereas SMEs do suffer from certain burdens, such as for instance repeated inspections. Therefore, from the corporate view it clearly depends on size and the strategic value of a firm – and also especially whether or not an entity is in state hands or not –, whether the bureaucracy takes a rather supportive role.

But up to a certain degree, entities do not even prefer to receive direct – and mostly financial – state support, since it creates dependencies. For them it is rather beneficial when in an Euckian fashion they can operate in a stable market environment with rather few arbitrary regulatory changes. Out of 34 codes fully 15 pointed towards a rather stable system for the entities to operate in. By the same token, 8 codes neglected such a stable framework, whereas 11 remained inconclusive and maintained that the answer depends on concrete circumstances. However, overall the corporate sector tends to be rather benefitting from a certain degree of stability in Kazakh politics, the economy and social affairs. As one expert said: "What concerns the stability of rules of industrial policy they change only maybe every five years, sometimes two to three years. Business knows that. Sudden changes there are not." (Expert Government 5) In this regard, the politico-economic framework is of a rather stable nature. Companies have a certain degree of expectations certainty and are not faced with the prospect of haphazardly having to adapt to sudden changes in the regulatory framework.

To this end it is also beneficial that there tends to be a rather high accountability of the people working in the ministries. 17 out of 26 codes identified a tendency towards high accountability in the ministries. This among others is due to consequent sacking of personnel in case that goals are not reached. On many occasions of mal-performance bonuses are scrapped. "Yes. I think so. And often it are those who are the lowest in hierarchy. But then on the other hand the President also holds responsible ministers or vice-ministers, if economic or social indicators are not good enough they are fired, they are held responsible. To my mind again in the end those get problems and are fired, who do not have the right connections" (Expert NGO 1). This statement also refers to a typical phenomenon in Kazakhstan also indicated above, meaning that without the right connections employees and ministers are at a severe risk of repression in case they display vulnerabilities, such as shortcomings in performance. But overall, it can be maintained that at least there is a certain sense of accountability and technocrats as well as ministers are under pressure to perform.

Therefore, at least in the sense of accountability and stability of business environment, the bureaucracy in conjunction with the political leadership appears to have a rather positive effect on the corporate sector. However, it needs to be taken into account that still companies perceive the bureaucracy as being more of a burden than a boon and that information flows are rather not working.

In general, not all short-comings in the state-business nexus can be brought into conjunction with the bureaucracy, since in a number of instances also the political leadership controls the bureaucracy in a rather arbitrary manner, which makes implementation problematic for the technocrats. The quality of the bureaucracy tends to be increased by the existence of competitive entry tests, to which all of the experts refer. Six experts even evaluate those as being very competitive.[7]

However, this competitive environment regarding entry into the civil service does not translate into the bureaucracy being highly meritocratic during the entire career of technocrats. Salaries and promotion do not unanimously depend on achievements. Thus, out of 20 codes 9 contend that there is no performance-orientation in the bureaucracy when it comes to those two points. Nevertheless, 11 codes observe that salaries and promotion are performance-related.

Another factor dragging the quality of bureaucratic staff down is the fact that salaries are not competitive versus the corporate sector. Out of 25 codes only 3 claimed remuneration of the civil service to be at least in line with what is paid in the corporate sector. On the other hand, 22 codes complained about the bureaucracy being paid meagerly compared to the corporate sector, which naturally tends to invoke the danger of corruption. “The salaries are very, very, very, very meagre. If we are talking about the private economy, you earn much more, if you are successful as an entrepreneur, which is also a challenge, especially in the SME sector. Nevertheless, some of the graduates are pursuing a career in the civil service, because of not only the career, but possibilities to enrich oneself.

7 This contrasts to some extent with other evidence. According to Schiek (2013) there are no unequivocally clearly defined career-paths for bureaucrats. Thus, although there are competitive entry exams, numerous possibilities exist to circumvent this obstacle and gain access to resources of the state. By the same token, the practice of a new office chief bringing his own staff with him is still not abolished. The loyal employees of the old office chief in a number of instances lose their jobs, which is a significant disincentive for graduates to opt for a career in the civil service (Schiek 2013, p. 208 and 212).

That is typical for such economies. If you reach a certain position, you can earn something besides." (Expert NGO 5).

This clearly contrasts with Russia where salaries have recently been increased in order to attract more competent staff. The rather poor salaries in the Kazakh civil service also tend to incorporate signaling problems, since it conveys a message that graduates are not sought for in the public sector that perform highly and earn well those do apply that are more up to accept low salaries and pursue personal gain such as in the form of nepotism and corruption.

In order to counter this risk, the political leadership opted to expose the bureaucracy to a remarkably high degree of fluctuation. In a number of instances, bureaucrats are moved to different positions and often in different regions in a very short time-frame. By shifting bureaucrats in a routine of not keeping technocrats in their positions for more than a maximum of three years, the government intends to prevent crony state business relations from starting to build up.

The negative side-effect of this is first of all that projects can only on few occasions be completed by the person who initiated them and therefore incentives to perform are weakened and there is also a profound loss of knowledge to be complained about. Secondly, in Kazakhstan there is still the unwritten rule in place that a chief always moves with his entire team, so that after his departure the department up to a certain extent has to start from scratch, since a lot of know-how and competence is lost.

Furthermore, the entities have to build completely new contacts, which is all the more deplorable in a country where personal relations are of such primary importance. Expert (Government 2) pointedly underlines this phenomenon: "It is difficult question. Because from one side the policy is crystal clear. But there is so much rotation and instability within the personnel that it is quite often you cannot, one day you are talking to a person and the next day based on certain shifts in the management or in the industry they rotation within the government by itself is quite huge. So, probably due to that the government lacks a bit the continuity and the sustainability if you want."

Overall, the quality of bureaucracy is limited as is evident by its being more of a burden than a boon for the corporate sector and performing rather badly regarding information flows to the corporate sector. Only in terms of a stable regulatory framework for the companies to operate in, a certain positive development is observed. Possible reasons for the overall only mediocre performance can be identified in lack of quality of staff due to low salaries versus the corporate sector. Likewise, the constant risk of being sacked or having the bonus scrapped as well as being forced to rotate on a regular basis give competent university graduates little incentive to apply for positions in the civil service. All of this transmits into a situation where due to signaling effects not the best graduates tend to apply for the civil service, which is rather detrimental for the entire economy since an efficient implementation of policies at the state corporate sector interface improves development performance. But on the positive side, a rather higher degree of autonomy for the bureaucracy compared to Russia makes a more flexible reaction to changes in market environments possible.

Structure of the Corporate Sector

As in the case study of Russia, the composition of the corporate sector has profound implications for state business interaction. It depends on the concrete contingencies of the state business nexus, whether the actual structure of the corporate sector enhances attainment of the goal of achieving development.

Referring to the structure of the corporate sector, first of all, the duality of SOEs and SMEs is striking in Kazakhstan. In the interviews conducted for this study all 15 codes relating to this topic observe a pronounced duality of SOEs versus SMEs in Kazakhstan. "SOEs are usually monopolies are they, there is not much transparency in their procurement practices. So, usually there is no competition among suppliers for SOEs." (Expert NGO 4). "In SMEs it is to be in the mass market mostly. And it is not related to strategic sectors of state importance I should say. Well, SOEs are mostly involved in key sectors such as oil, the extracting industries, infrastructure, or others. When we are talking about redistribution to SOEs the goals are crystal clear for example. To promote experts, to gain foreign currency for the state or to defend national interests." (Expert Government 2).

This concerns the fact that SOEs do concentrate on sectors that the state has declared as being of strategic importance, such as natural resources, infrastructure and transportation. In sectors that are of rather minor strategic importance such as retail and agriculture the state allows for a rather more unimpeded competition among the major players.

Meanwhile, in a sector like banking that is also key to the developmental ambitions of Kazakhstan there is a rather opaque, almost clandestine ownership and governance structure. Officially, most commercial banks are privately held, so that they should in principle be operating without double bottom lines and be maximizing its earnings for the owners.

But de facto the situation differs significantly. Kazakh commercial banks are cozily related to the political leadership with for instance the chief of the Presidential staff de facto owning one of the biggest commercial banks of the country. As a matter of fact, commercial banks are clan-owned – a residue that survived the times of the Soviet Union dating back centuries – and therefore in this regard almost crony relations with the political leadership are in place.

Nevertheless, as mentioned before in sectors such as agriculture and retail the state is hardly meddling in, neither formally nor informally. Here actors have to play according to the rules of competitive markets with low entry barriers, price and quality competition, pressures due to imitation of foreign technology as well as proprietary innovation and a constantly high entry and exit rates.

The situation is markedly different for the SOE sector, where monopolistic structures are partially imposed such as those the largest uranium producer Kazatomprom is operating in or to a lesser extent the oil and gas producer Kazmunaigaz. Concededly, these companies do have to compete on international markets, where they tend to be a price taker and not a price setter. However, they are domestically in a monopoly-like position and can skim off rents. For them doing business is to a large extent determined by building or grooming connections to influential political leaders. In a certain sense they do engage more in redistributive than in productive activities.

For them the pressure to perform, increasing the satisfaction of its customers, innovating or venturing into new markets, is alleviated by having crony relations with the political leadership. That said, it needs to be maintained that most SOEs are controlled by the state holding Samruk Kazyna, which is very intent on operating according to standard business principles, such as maximizing shareholder value. Furthermore, representatives of the holding ardently argue that they operate with complete transparency. For their companies they formulate and rigorously enforce KPIs in order to guarantee maximum performance, stresses the management of Samruk Kazyna.

But according to the experts interviewed for this study and the literature in practice the situation varies widely. First of all, there is informally the policy of double bottom lines, meaning that besides commercial goals also other interests have to be heeded, such as increasing payrolls and offering products such as gas and oil below market prices to large parts of the population. This becomes obvious when looking to the phenomenon of mono-towns that have de facto only one employer, in most cases a large plant. Here these SOEs are guided to keep the plants in operation, even if they are commercially not viable any longer, since the political leadership is afraid of inducing political protests.

To conclude, SOEs do enjoy preferential treatment by the state[8], such as upholding monopolistic structures, but that comes at the cost of having to accept

8 A typical patronage group was formed by Timur Kulibajev. He started as vice-president

double bottom lines. This point of view is confirmed by the perception of the experts interviewed for this study. 18 out of 21 codes refer to the overarching and dominating role of SOEs in the corporate sector as well as to the preference the state accords to them. Only in three codes there was a perception palpable that there is such a thing as a level playing-field for SOEs and SMEs. Likewise, in two codes it was mentioned that SOEs actually do support SMEs, mostly in the field of procurement.

Overall, a situation persists in Kazakhstan where the corporate sector is divided into two parts with the government by now actually perceiving the advantages of SMEs in terms of fast adaption to changes in the market environment, being able to quickly absorb excess demand and a certain tendency to be open for process and products innovations. "I think that as there is not much of a division between SOEs and state structures I think they are favoured. However, I think you have to say that the government recently said that it wants to promote SMEs. What the situation right now is, I am not so sure. I mean publicly the government is very much in favour of SMEs. Now they have to develop them for the diversification of the economy. But I think they still face difficulties with bureaucratic decisions, the SMEs." (Expert NGO 1)

There was a clear tendency of the experts to identify a very significant cleavage between SOEs and SMEs. However, on the effects and dimensions of this phenomenon the experts brought differing, though not contradicting elements into play. One very striking effect of SOEs is a certain reduced competition as Expert (Academia 10) observed: "An SOE in a sector is a disincentive for newcomers, even though the government might not be trying to favour them. If it slimmed down, this would create competition." This statement needs at the same time be taken with a grain of salt, since it tends to relate to strategic sectors.

---

of Kazmunaigaz. By selling his shares he supposedly earned 1 billion Dollar. He owns large parts of the HalykBank and has direct connections to the Kazkommertsbank. He profits from direct connections to President Nazarbayev and offers a so-called krisha for other entrepreneurs as well. Supposedly he is a multi-billionaire. After 2011 he became once again President of Samruk Kazyna. Other well-connected leaders of patronage groups are – to name just a few – Bulat Utemuratov and Marat Taschin. The former was among others member of the security council and external consultant of the President. He reportedly owns an empire of companies, among others the TV channel 31, and is also a billionaire. The latter's career is tightly connected to President Nazarbayev. He used to be foreign minister and was consultant to the President for security topics and by now oversees a business empire (Schiek 2013, p. 144–145).

There a market environment with a subdued intensity of competition is clearly discernible.

At the same time, it needs to be affirmed that in sectors typical for SMEs SOEs do overwhelmingly not participate and thus those sectors are in a certain sense unaffected by the dominance of SOEs. By the same token that does not transmit into a situation where SMEs can competitively engage in activities in their sectors without any negative external effects from the overarching role of SOEs in the wider economy. "The problem here and at other places of entrepreneurs is lack of finance, access to finance. And some of this for them would be tax incentives, simplify regulations. I think they are doing that. They are getting better, but still…entrepreneurship has to come from the bottom and not from the top. I mean, I do not exclude that Samruk Kazyna should get into SME development. But there are all these companies that are under their control that they need to find way for them." (Expert Academia 10).

This statement demonstrates that in Kazakhstan a potential means to support SME formation is seen in more interventions by the state holding Samruk Kazyna, which could in a certain sense enlarge state dominance from the strategic sectors also to non-strategic sectors.

The status quo and the main problems also become evident. There is a lack of financing for SMEs first of all due to a relatively small size generally being perceived as incorporating larger default risks and secondly due to a lack of state-backed guarantees which are implicitly implied in loans to SOEs.

At the same time those crony relations tend to induce commercial, privately held, but strongly state-connected banks to concentrate credits on SOEs. Thus, one major set-back of the tentatively identified dual economy state capitalism in Kazakhstan is a credit drain for SMEs, even for those with large potential.

But market distortions are not contained to this dimension. Concerning communication of economic policies there also tend to be distortions that favour the best-connected entities – in almost all instances SOEs – by giving them a certain voice in policy formulation as well as being at a relatively early stage in the policy-making process informed about final policy changes and therefore gaining an advantage by being able to adapt to those modified or new rules earlier than less well-connected entities.

"But I easily assess the situation when SOEs are favoured more to the detriment and cost of SMEs. Just the fact that SMEs do not get enough information from the government compared with the SOEs and SOEs have this advantage of getting this information first. And usually they might be getting it faster and in larger scope than with the formal channels of information." (Expert Academia 1). In this regard it needs to be analyzed how the SOE-SME duality emerged and there the experts rather uniformly point to the high embeddedness of bureaucracy and even political leadership with the corporate sector.

Out of 30 codes only 2 codes point to a rather low degree of embeddedness. The majority of 28 codes attests a high degree of embeddedness of the bureaucracy into the corporate sector with at the same time 12 of those referring without being explicitly asked for in this regard to the significant role of SOEs as a reason for this phenomenon. "The public sector is very much incorporated into the state economy, because the huge oil and gas companies that belong to the state they are to my mind there is no division between these economic structures and the public service structures." (Expert NGO 1). And Expert (NGO 2) agrees: "Herr Wölk, it is for example a government structure, where we have Samruk Kazyna and the national companies. It's sometimes, we have a blurred lined, what is private and what is the government."

Embeddedness is largely a consequence of strong links between state and SOEs structures. There is a much lower degree of embeddedness to be observed of the bureaucracy and the SME sector. In this regard, the civil service is up to a certain extent almost oblivious of SMEs and the interaction is rather contained to the implementation of policies in a top-down fashion for instance by repeated and very unpopular inspections. To this end, the duality nature of the corporate sector in this sense directly translates into a special form of state business interaction, where the bureaucracy is cooperating with SOEs – consulting with them on policy proposals, informing a priori about coming policy modifications, influencing the setting of KPIs and informally guiding changes in the management.

Here Samruk Kazyna as a transmission device between the state and the corporate sector is of crucial importance. Officially, Samruk Kazyna controls the bulk of SOEs in a transparent and profit-orientated fashion. But according to the experts, the ministries wield a significant influence on Samruk Kazyna. The state is not intent on limiting its role to nominating corporate leaders according to their having a successful management track record and subsequently refraining from interventions into the SOEs sector. There are clear phenomena discernible, where especially the President's office is actively involved in strategic decision-making by SOEs.

For such a focus of the state on SOEs while rather neglecting any attention it might bestow on SMEs certain reasons can be given. As mentioned earlier SOEs are operating in strategic industries, where the state reserves for itself the prerogative of active intervention. And furthermore, SOEs are by far the largest tax-payers as well as employers in Kazakhstan. So, for the political reason of avoiding lay-offs that can potentially destabilize the country as well as its political leadership and the dependence of the state on their tax revenues, the state keeps quite a tight control on SOEs and incentivizes them to be loyal to and useful for the political leadership, granting them favours versus smaller players or potential new private entrants into their markets.

The state as the owner of SOEs is de jure in control of them. But de facto the situation could conceivably be different. To guarantee its tight control the state utilizes certain levers. First of all, it formed Samruk Kazyna as a vehicle to better control and monitor SOEs. This comes at the cost of having created a behemoth that is difficult to maneuver and reacts with significant time lags to changes in market environments. This is cited as one the main reasons why the state officially intents to privatize significant portions of Samruk Kazyna, but during the time of this study this project has only very inconclusive results.

The second main lever of the state maintaining de facto control of SOEs as a majority investor is what is called amakudari – "or descent from heaven" – in Japanese and means that officials from ministries – political leaders as much as senior bureaucrats – do change positions into management functions of SOEs. This phenomenon is fostered due to the state being a majority investor and therefore has the privilege of appointing the management of SOEs.

Full 25 codes referred to widespread amakudari in Kazakhstan. For former political leaders or senior technocrats, the incentive to switch is clearly pecuniary, since they earn far higher salaries at their new employer. For the efficiency of SOEs this has on a number of occasions detrimental effects, since those former members of the ministries tend to lack business savvy. "Yes. I mentioned before for example the exchange between the high levels of bureaucracy and Samruk Kazyna, the state holding, there is definitely change of personnel" (Expert Int. Org. 1) "The other way around. A lot of people from the ministries serve in the corporate sector…" (Expert Government 5). And Expert (Academia 6) is even more specific: "… There are many. And who used to be former bureaucrats for example current head of the Samruk Kazyna, which is the main sovereign wealth fund of the country is led by a former governor of the regions. And the same with the main development institute the head is the former vice minister of the national economy. And KazakhAgro is also a former vice minister."

This strong embeddedness of the ministries into the SOE sector has effects on the management of those entities. Three codes indicated that those companies have double bottom lines and cannot solely pursue commercial goals. This leads to inefficiencies, being evident in the over-staffing of those companies. And these non-commercial interests of the state cause frictions within state structures. Thus, Expert (Academia 10) points out: "Absolutely. The goals are not aligned. And Samruk Kazyna wants them to run like a professional company. But the ministry sets rather other goals, social goal. Samruk Kazyna wants to run it like a private enterprise that is focused on profits and things like that. Of course, the ministries have other goals, like social goals. I am not saying that these goals are wrong. I am just saying that these goals should be aligned sometimes." In a certain sense, these contradictory signals and interests within the state make it even still harder for SOEs to operate according to business standards such as serving markets in an efficient manner with smoothly running production and management processes.

In a nut-shell, in Kazakhstan there is a profound duality between SOEs and SMEs to be identified. SOEs concentrate on strategic sectors, whereas SMEs focus on non-strategic ones. This duality has profound effects on the interplay of state and business. There tends to be preferential treatment for SOEs to the detriment of SMEs, especially concerning finance, but also in information. The state has an incentive to uphold this duality, since SOEs stand for the bulk of employment and taxes in Kazakhstan. Furthermore, for political leaders and senior bureaucrats it offers the opportunity to switch to lucrative management positions in SOEs. But in the end, this leads to a situation, where in strategic sectors a relatively high degree of inefficiencies is to be observed and only on competitive non-strategic markets do entities operate rather more efficiently. After now having dealt with the structure of the corporate sector extensively, subsequently the final structural component – i.e. the degree of rule of law – will be tackled.

Degree of Rule of Law

The extent to which there is rule of law has among others relatively significant consequences for the composition of the corporate sector and therefore the state business nexus. For instance, a highly efficient judicial system will remarkably reduce entry barriers into industries even in strategic sectors. By the same token, it would allow for companies to reach the size the management strives for and assumes to be the optimal scale from a business perspective.

This is decidedly not the case in Kazakhstan. Without explicitly being asked for it eight experts referred to companies intentionally keeping a low profile in order not to risk being in the worst case raided or in the most propitious case having their profits skimmed. Not one single expert doubted the prevalent strategy of most managements of SMEs not to arouse the interest of the authorities. Expert (NGO 3) pointed out: "If you are in business there is an unwritten rule. It is good to be not big enough. If you are not big enough you are not seen for the top business-man or officials. You are a kind of you are doing your job in the shadow, but it is o.k. But government is saying expand your business, expand your business, but at the same time if you are expanding you are attracting attention it might lead you to some problems, some challenges with the local or national authorities."

This assessment refers to an institutional framework in Kazakhstan, where property rights are only relatively safe. It demonstrates that business leaders have to resort to non-commercial efforts to secure their property. To the detriment of efficiently operating their company thus managers engage in building connections in order to avert having the entity being raided. "But in Kazakhstan, if your company becomes bigger and more and more successful it's a case where you want to secure your position. You should find some kind of safety net. Otherwise your company will be taken from you." (Expert NGO 2).

This creates distortions in the economy and has negative signaling effects concerning the overall quality of the judicial system. But here it is striking that 15 out of 26 codes accord the law system a medium quality with only eleven assessing it as being of poor quality. Thus, it appears as if efforts to improve on the courts' independence and the quality of their rulings bear fruits. Nevertheless, the experts pointed out that the impartiality of a ruling critically depends on who the parties concerned are. In case for instance that the government is sued the chances of success before the court are minimal. The same tends to be true, if highly connected persons commit a property rights violation and are sued by the person bearing this property rights violation.

Overall though, the state in Kazakhstan seeks strongly to overcome a lack of rule of law. One element of this effort is to introduce common law for its international financial center in Astana. Here the judges are coming from Great Britain in order to rule out any form of corruptive activities. But it relates only to commercial activities in this specific jurisdiction. In general, regarding litigation of commercial court cases, there tends to be a relatively high degree of rule of law as opposed to criminal court cases, where in the overwhelming majority of cases the state prosecutor wins the case.

At the same time, the efforts concerning common law in the international financial center of Astana are intended to have a lighthouse effect and eventually through this beacon Kazakhstan's judicial system is supposed to reach international standards, in essence guaranteeing rule of law. But for the time frame relevant for this study – as is constitutive of state capitalism – there is no rule of law.

However, Kazakhstan is making certain progress in this regard. For instance, the degree of property rights safety is in in line with or above the average for a state capitalist country. Out of 31 codes 25 rate the degree of property rights safety in Kazakhstan as to be medium and only in three cases it is deemed to be low, while in three more cases it is even assumed to be high. Therefore, in this regard – owing to a relative safety of property rights – up to a certain extent, productive commercial activities are supported. "They are relatively safer than in all other Asian countries, but not as safe as it should be." (Expert Int. Org. 2).

At the same time, the experts stress the fact that while for ordinary citizens judicial protection appears to be working relatively well, for companies of a certain size severe property rights risks emerge. Nevertheless, on paper in those instances the plaintiffs have the means to challenge property rights violations before court. 19 out of 25 codes hinted to the fact that there is only a medium inhibition of going to court, whereas five saw a low inhibition and only one a high inhibition.

But, as mentioned before, the success rates of suing are always a matter of who is being sued. This is underlined by Expert (Academia 11): "I do not any person who said that government stole him money, went to court and got things back, apart from some small things when you have a dispute with your neighbor and you are both unconnected. Then of course the courts work here. I would not say that it is completely raiding here. But I think the more political it gets the less likely it is that the court will make an independent judgment."

All in all, Kazakhstan seeks to improve its judicial system in order to increase investment and attract more FDI. Structurally, however, there is still a lack of rule of law to be observed. Equality before the court is by far not guaranteed and corporate actors need to take precautions and utilize financial and manpower resources in order to protect themselves from property rights violations.

To summarize, from a structural point of view, there appear to be rather profound weaknesses in Kazakhstan's politico-economic system. The interaction of the bureaucracy – endowed with at best a medium quality – with the corporate sector is inhibited by a largely preferential treatment of big players. And although there tends to be in low profile cases rather a remarkable degree of quality of court rulings, in cases where political levels are implicated equal treatment before the law is hardly to be expected. Consequently, structurally, there tend to be significant short-comings and it remains to be seen in the next sub-section how this affects policies.

4.3.3 Policies

The Kazakh political leadership sets itself traditionally ambitious goals. According to the experts, this serves to emulate the successful East Asian model of state capitalism and is intended to motivate economic actors. From a policy point of view, Kazakhstan tended to pursue a hybrid approach, incorporating some elements of market capitalism and other from East Asian state capitalism.

Ultimately, Kazakhstan then applied a mixture of policies, allowing partially for import substitution, export orientation, technology transfer and an emphasis on attracting FDI. Likewise, while being firmly state capitalist, the country also sought to reduce state dominance of the economy, foremost by privatizing companies that are under the umbrella of Samruk Kazyna.

However, this effort becomes diluted by the fact that in cases of privatization those entities are regularly transferred into the control of persons with sufficient financial means, mostly stemming from influential families, i.e. the notorious clans of Kazakhstan.[9] This is in so far, an encumbrance for the goal of introducing market capitalist elements by privatizing, since the line between private and public is significantly blurred.

Traditionally, clans are strongly linked with the state and therefore one of the main characteristics of the Kazakh economic system is a lack of clearly differentiating between resources belonging to the state and those belonging to private economic actors for the utilization of channeling those means into the most productive investment purposes and projects, thereby maximizing profits of the entrepreneur.

Consequently, under this premise of a policy framework that is generally marked by a blurred line between public and private, Kazakh economic policy is analyzed. This is done by looking into the target-orientated selective industrial policy approach, the policy of picking winners, the contents of policies themselves, the role of business associations and in general idiosyncratic characteristics of planning in Kazakhstan.

Target-orientated Industrial Policy of Kazakhstan

As a matter of fact, Kazakhstan strongly pursues a target-orientated approach concerning industrial policy. Out of 26 codes only 2 denied the existence of such a policy approach with the rest confirming it unaminously. Strikingly, first of

9 Undoubtedly judging from the qualitative data from the interviews, clans are playing a significant role in the economy and development of Kazakhstan. Nevertheless, it can lead astray and distort evidence, if the existence and dominance of clan structures are overemphasized as tended to occur with regard to analyses of African economic structures. Thus, the relevance of clan structures needs to be taken into account but is not to be seen as determining the developmental trajectory of Kazakhstan. Such a point of view would be in violation of available evidence about Kazakhstan (Schiek 2013, p. 25–26).

all Kazakhstan's economic policy approach entails indicative planning over long time horizons.

There are plans for 2025, 2030 and even 2050. For instance, until 2030 Kazakhstan intends to become one of the thirty economically most competitive countries of the world according to the World Economic Forum (WEF) of Switzerland. These plans reach far into the future and are for instance indicating which industries are set to be primarily supported. According to Expert (Government 2) those are currently transport, logistics, metallurgy, mining and agriculture.

Subsequently – and likewise overall basing their calculations on those broad indicative plans – the technocrats are cascading down those goals to lower levels. This for instance concerns the ministries, where Government officials 4 and 5 named volume of investments, volume of construction, also industrial construction, number of investment projects, the total amount of business, number of international corporations, who participate in local projects as well as growth of productivity, growth of transport, attracting investments, growth of exports as being respectively relevant as targets for their specific ministries.

However, in case a goal is not achieved the person responsible is not automatically sanctioned, but the circumstances are being looked at. As Expert (Government 5) puts it: "Well, then you need to see. Then there be exogeneous factors such as a fall in the prices oil. Or another factor could be the enactment of sanctions. There are circumstances which the ministry has not influence about. In this regard it needs to be explained why it happened." This already hints to the fact that rationales for failing to reach goals are relatively easy to be found and thus the stringency of implementing a carrot and stick approach to target-orientated economic policy is diluted.

Nevertheless, those goals are existing and they become especially relevant for SOEs while SMEs are not guided or controlled by targets that were set by the bureaucracy and the political leadership. "Yes, sure. We have a cascading of our strategic goals and KPIs. The strategic goals cascade to goals for portfolio companies and these goals cascade to KPIs for top managers and then employees, a performance management system." This is what Expert (Business 3) is pointing out, who is in an executive function in the leading holding company of Kazakhstan and herself being subject to a KPI.

Thus, especially for SOEs there is a strict planning by setting targets and here on the corporate level there is also a relatively high performance-orientation meaning that when targets are missed penalties do follow, such as lowered or eliminated bonuses and in some cases even lay-offs. But then again, Expert (Think Tank 1) argues that there are for example no specific targets demanding of companies to reach certain export quotas.

Overwhelmingly, Samruk Kazyna controls SOEs by setting profitability and revenue targets and having as a double bottom line to follow such factors of keeping a certain level of payrolls. This is indirectly conceded by Expert Business 3: "All companies have special KPIs. Different from company to company. But for most companies the goal is to make profit." This means that there are also factors such as employment and low prices as being part of Samruk Kazyna's policy in terms of controlling its SOEs.

Picking the Winners

In guiding the corporate sector Kazakh political leadership and bureaucracy apply a second instrument in the form of the policy of picking the winners. This program is part of an industrial policy that intervenes into the corporate sector and favours companies, which the state assesses to have a high potential. 16 out of 23 codes report about such a policy taking place in the Kazakh politico-economic system. In the year 2016 there was even a contest within the program of picking the winners. "I was once even a witness of such a big event. The President himself was present and it was about SOEs and SMEs, altogether. And the best companies received awards." (Expert NGO 5).

Although this contest was later on said to be scrapped as a new minister for the economy entered into office, the policy of picking companies that are expected to have a high potential, be able to outperform others and be able to compete on world markets is applied. According to Expert (Business 2) special emphasis is in this regard placed on companies that perform as export champions. "We have these kinds of institutional instruments. Exporters can become part of this program. The state supports those export champions."

The decisive question in this regard is, whether the policy of picking the winner actually works in Kazakhstan or not. Overall, there are profound doubts about the effectiveness of this program. Thus, from those 16 codes reporting about the existence of a program of picking the winners fully 12 codes considered it as having been a failure. Most experts refer to too much state interference into companies' business plans as one reason. But it is even more strongly emphasized that this program is about national champions, meaning large SOEs, which are once again favoured as mentioned above. "There is a program about national champions. But then there are those companies chosen that help the government to solve problems. In most cases national champions are SOEs like KazAtomprom." (Expert Think Tank 2).

Expert (Government 2) openly concedes that national champions are supposed to stem from strategic sectors. Consequently, SMEs that are only operating on non-strategic markets are therefore in effect excluded. In this regard, the program of picking the winners can be placed into an overall structural context where technocrats favour SOEs as was mentioned above.

The effectiveness of this program is consequently inhibited by not allowing for sufficient competition. It appears as if picking the winners as part of a selective industrial policy is not bearing the intended fruits and places an emphasis on those already large SOEs from the mining sector that can compete on international markets anyway, but are an obstacle in the path intended by the political leadership and the bureaucracy to diversify the economy.

Policy Mix relies on various Role Models

In this regard, overall, as in the case of Russia the state intends to diversify away from its large dependence on natural resources. This goal of diversification, industrialization and development has been tantamount for the entire time span that is analyzed in this study. To that end content-wise the state pursued a pragmatic policy approach.

Despite ever ongoing power struggles of the clans behind the scenes Kazakhstan tended to pursue a consistent, although varied policy framework as such. Clashes of interests such as in the case of Russia between the power groups of liberals versus members of the security services are not evident.

Economic policy rather tended to borrow approaches from foreign advisers and role models, sometimes referring to Kazakhstan as the "snow leopard" with reference to East Asian "tiger states". Thus, the policy of picking the winners was borrowed from East Asian role models, but as explained above with only very modest success. Preferential treatment in the form of tax subsidies, preferential credits and direct subsidies were given as incentives in order to selectively support entities from preferred industries.

But Kazakhstan – being situated in central Asia and always in the focus of the interests of the great powers Russia, China and the Western states – in this regard chose a middle path as it pursues in diplomacy. While the policy of picking the winner clearly emulated East Asian experiences, it embarked on privatization programs heeding calls from international organizations and Western advisors.

Incentives were introduced to support the creation of start-ups. Likewise, a number of programs were implemented so that de jure SMEs are now even preferred versus SOEs. But as much as the policy content in privatization can at best be termed half-hearted, so it is for SME promotion programs. Until the end of the time horizon selected for this study, the state remained the majority investor, sometimes even with 100 percent of sizable parts of the corporate sector.

State dominance of the corporate sector was hardly reduced, so that in effect Kazakh economic policy did not commit to a certain economic model as well as its instruments and implemented it then effectively. Rather a mix of Chinese, East Asian, Russian and Western economic models was applied and continuously adapted, in a number of instances also affected by changing winds in domestic and external power struggles. Therefore, it can be maintained that the overarching goal of diversification, industrialization and development was pursued with constantly and pragmatically adapting the implementation of the relevant targets that were cascaded down from the long-term economic plans.

Strong Emphasis on Planning

All in all, Kazakh reliance on planning can be interpreted as a remnant of Soviet times, displaying sizable elements of path dependence in the informal institutions, i.e. foremost the belief systems of elites, and the formal institutions as evident in rules and regulations allowing for such a pervasive planning. The commitment to a plan that reaches as far as the year 2050 can probably best be understood in this context.

From the point of view of the efficiency of such a reliance on planning it can be maintained that planning tends to have the advantage of strengthening the commitment and motivation of economic actors to achieve a certain goal. Resources tend ceteris paribus theoretically to be able to be allocated according to this plan in an efficient manner.

But this belief system does not account for uncertainty. The developmental trajectory of any economic system is subject to changing conditions, in the case of state capitalism economically, foremost changes in market environments – domestically and internationally –, and politically, in power struggles within the elites, among the population as well as between the elites and the population.

Thus, planning is a two-edged sword and the political leadership has to consider this trade-off. In the case of Kazakhstan this becomes exacerbated owing to the fact that planning itself does not follow one economic model but rather is a mix of different power groups wielding their influence on the Kazakh political leadership.

And then in Kazakhstan there is a tendency to be observed to be rather negligent on strictly implementing plans, such as when – owing to the structural characteristic of high ministerial fluctuation – a new head of ministry discretionarily scraps old plans and introduces new ones. In this regard the consistency of planning and implementing – being supported by the non-existence of struggles between power groups with diverging belief systems – is significantly impaired by a constant rotation in the ministries.

Relevance of Business Organization

One instrument of the state to alleviate this negative impact on the business environment – for instance a higher uncertainty about future rules and regulations due to ministerial reshuffling – is by having created the powerful business association Atameken. From 29 codes 21 codes refer to Atameken as being a highly effective means for improving on the quality of policy implementation.

Only two codes deny a supportive role of Atameken for the policy making and implementation process. Six are divided on this issue and call its effect rather mixed. Enhancing the standing of Atameken in the political and corporate sphere is the fact that the son-in-law of President Nazarbayev is head of Atameken, sending a strong signal in a politico-economic system – based strongly on personalization – that the highest echelons of power do support Atameken. "They are very involved in this circle of industrial policy. The government listens to them. It is an effective instrument." (Expert Business 2).

In this sense Atameken opens an important avenue for communication between the corporate sector and the state. In a number of instances rules and regulations that potentially would have had detrimental effects on the economy were scrapped or modified. It serves as a quintessentially important instrument of the state to be able to obtain signals from below. This is all the more important in a country where owing to path dependence stemming from the times of the Soviet Union there is so much reliance on ruling top-down at the state corporate sector nexus.

At the same time the information gathered with assistance of Atameken significantly helps the state to be able to adapt its planning by receiving signals about changes in market environments which the state as such would not be able to obtain due to not being proximate enough to those processes. Expert (Academia 6) even points out that to some degree potential laws have to be accepted by Atameken before they can pass, with the intention of ensuring that no law initiative can end up severely harming the economy.

However, Atameken nevertheless mirrors an emphasis of Kazakh elites on planning and also the blurred line between public and private interests. There prevails a top-down approach when it comes to the state private sector nexus. Thus, the chairman of the business association Atameken has to report to the President about the performance of the chamber (Kazakhstanskaya Pravda 2017). This perception also echoes from statements of the experts. "And then, if there is again some son-in-law, who wants a share. They always put attention to it that it is in the hands of a few. Private interests in this country are still far too much interwoven with political interests. Just one example is the Tsesna-bank. Whom does it belong? The chief of the presidential administration. In such a way state are linked with private interests." (Expert NGO 6).

This assessment already mirrors one significant short-coming of the creation of Atameken. Reflecting the ever present, structural pillar of the Kazakh economy of being divided between SOEs and SMEs, the experts tend to object that they doubt Atameken properly defends the interests of SMEs.

Furthermore, they tend to see the problem that in the policy making and implementation process positions of SMEs are not sufficiently considered. "But some say, it is a formal organization that just – one guy called it a racket – they extort membership fee. And basically, because I think it became obligatory for all entrepreneurs to belong to Atameken." (Expert Academia 11). This statement already points to the risk of Atameken becoming only a formal mechanism without a profound grounding in the real economy.

Nevertheless, in principle the erection is assumed to be a change to the positive with regard to information gathering, lobbying or even a minimum of coordination. "They are quite important, basically they have an alternative view to the government of what should be developed, which areas and of course they try to lobby in certain areas to attract more funding for industrial policy." (Expert NGO 4). And Expert (Academia 8) sees a further advantage of Atameken for the corporate sector: "Entrepreneurs can get advice, also in terms of exploring international markets. So, to stimulate export behaviour, export statistics is still dominated by resources, oil, steel, minerals. And there is a huge potential in exploring export markets for young firms."

At the same time, one potential opportunity of Atameken for the state could consist in the assistance in forming business clusters that allow for firms to be able to compete on international markets. In this regard argues Expert (Government 3): "It assists in solidarity decision from enterprises, because we have many enterprises. And they have many interests and Atameken hears all enterprises. It integrates and analyzes of all situations in the market and gives decisions from business to government." But so far in Kazakhstan there are no sizable clusters in businesses with a high value added visible. But in the overall goal of the government to industrialize Atameken could potentially play a role in coordinating a number of entities with the goal of overcoming coordination failures that in developmental processes often exist when seeking to establish new domestic sectors.

All in all, Kazakhstan follows a targeted industrial policy approach with comprehensive planning efforts. Here the state takes a pragmatic stance, experimenting with a number of policies that have proved to be successful elsewhere. However, for the program of picking the winners that has been copied from East Asian role models this seems not to be the case, having in a certain sense failed due to too much preferences for SOEs. In this regard structure tends to wield sizable effects on policies. Short-comings – such as at best only a medium degree of bureaucratic capabilities – inhibit an effective policy formulation and implementation, for instance by decreasing expectations certainty in the business environment. In order to among others alleviate these problems, Atameken was formed. Indeed, it is of some assistance in improving the information channels between bureaucracy and the corporate sectors. However, some experts perceive that Atameken is part of Kazakh elites' general tendency to plan entire economic processes and does not effectively account for voice of SMEs.

4.3.4 Performance

It is beyond the scope of this study to account for a statistically verified correlation or even causation between structural as well as policy factors as independent variables to the dependent variable performance. But as a matter of fact, there is sufficiently valid data and there are perceptions available as to how the Kazakh politico-economic system performed overall.

First of all, there are eleven codes generated for this study, which show a decidedly mixed picture. Eight of these codes perceive that only some of the intended goals of the political leadership were realized. Two perceive an utter failure in this regard, whereas one evaluated economic policy to have achieved its goals.

The experts were relatively reticent about giving explanations for such partial success. However, they were not hinting at deficiencies in policy and goal formulation. Rather the reasons tended to be perceived in a lack of institutional capacity to implement policies that had been formulated a priori. "From the other side it is much easier to declare than to implement." (Expert Government 2).

These assessments reflect structural deficiencies analyzed above in the course of this case study. In this regard, up to a certain extent this phenomenon is mirrored in the World Bank Governance Indicators (World Bank 2019a). For instance, Kazakhstan scores relatively poorly in control of corruption and there has been no real improvement in the available data ranging from 1996 until 2017. The mean average for this period of time is 16.42, meaning that from all countries of this sample only 16.42 have less control of corruption than Kazakhstan.

Referring to government effectiveness a different picture emerges. Forming the mean average for the years from 1996 to 2017 Kazakhstan scores 36.34 percentile rank points. In the course of this time span government effectiveness has considerably improved in Kazakhstan with even 53.85 percentile rank points for 2017. This is in line with government effectiveness in Russia and underlines efforts by the government to embark on a developmental path. However, this is still considerably below scores of industrialized countries or developmental states, which Kazakhstan seeks to emulate in terms of living standards and economic development.

Regarding rule of law in Kazakhstan there are significant short-comings evident in the data as well. On average for the relevant span of time Kazakhstan reaches only 25.02 percentile rank points, meaning that as depicted above and is typical for a state capitalist system the country can hardly be termed as allowing for the rule of law. Some improvement is evident with the most recent tally being 38.46 percentile rank points. But overall, there tends to be below average quality of the judicial system in Kazakhstan, reflecting a certain structural weakness of its economic system.

In terms of accountability, the situation in Kazakhstan has even deteriorated. The mean average for the relevant period of time is 16.81 and for the last available data for 2017 it is even only 13.79. In sum, Kazakhstan is from a structural point of view – meaning overall institutional capacity such as is evident in technocratic performance – behind the majority of other countries covered by the World Governance Indicators. This does not in itself translate into a lack of policy quality. Evidently, the political leadership is remarkably intent on adopting lessons and advice given from other countries with their respective experiences in development.

But as demonstrated above and in this sub-section structural weaknesses exacerbate the capacity of the state to implement its ambitious goals. In order to give an assessment of how Kazakhstan performed in development – as in the case study for Russia – it is looked at economic growth and HDI. For the available data within the relevant time span – covering a time series from 1992 until 2018 – Kazakhstan has achieved a GDP growth of 2.91 percent (World Bank 2019b), which ranges significantly below levels prevalent in other emerging economies.

As a matter of fact, there had been a transformational crisis that is reflected in the data, but even for the most recent available data for 2017 and 2018 GDP growth stands at 1.1 and 4.1 percent respectively. Kazakhstan has indeed achieved continuous economic growth over the relevant time span. It has transformed its economy from a command economy with plan bureaucratic decision-making to a state capitalist system with a partially vibrant dual economy.

But for a country comparing itself with the tiger states of East Asia economic growth is lagging behind. The experts interviewed for this study perceived that thus far the goal of diversifying away from natural resources has at best been only partially achieved. Economic growth and revenues collected by the state are still decisively contingent on oil prices on world markets, which for Kazakhstan as such is an exogenous factor. However, when accounting for the HDI (UNDP 2019) it becomes evident that with this even relatively modest economic growth Kazakhstan managed to achieve considerable success in development.

From 1990 until 2017 the HDI averaged 0.72 points while having started in 1990 with 0.69. This improvement in terms of development is even more evident when taking into account in the two last years for which data is available – 2016 and 2017 – Kazakhstan had a score of 0,79 and 0.8 respectively. This reflects the fact that since 1990 perspectives for the population have increased markedly.

Consequently, for Kazakhstan a mixed picture emerges when accounting for its developmental success or failure. The political leadership in tandem with the bureaucracy managed to embark the economy on a constant growth and developmental trajectory. This in itself is an accomplishment which allowed the regime to rule with relatively little political pressure calling for change coming from the broader population. Whether this relatively calm and stable political environment could have been utilized in order to provide for a more dynamic economy with a more impressive developmental performance remains an open question. Judging from the evaluations of the experts interviewed for this study, however, it appears as if deficiencies in institutional capacity dragged developmental performance down to some extent. In this regard, it is relevant to understand, whether or not the political leadership was able to rule relatively autonomous and a certain degree of actor centricity was observable. Therefore, the next sub-section considers whether significant constraints on the political leadership existed, potentially limiting its scope for coming to plan-rational choices.

4.3.5 Actor Centricity

A high degree of actor centricity is a two-edged sword regarding the probability of being able to successfully initiate economic development. Political leaders that are only to a limited degree constrained by the institutional framework, interest groups or political factions are in a position to face less resistance when formulating goals and economic policies, which are ideally first-best plans and measures.

However, in reality, unconstrained political leaders in a number of instances established economic systems that were plagued by corruptive activities, nepotism and in general a high degree of cronyism. Thus, it is the sole intention here to point out how far the political leadership for the relevant time span was constrained and to subsequently hint at certain consequences of the existing setting.

In this regard the interviewed experts are in the case of Kazakhstan unanimous concerning the ability of former President Nazarbayev to decisively shape the developmental trajectory of his country. There is not a single code relating to a low dominance of the political leader, whereas 38 codes emerged referring to a high degree of dominance. Only one code points to Nazarbayev having ruled with a medium degree of dominance. "It is not just political propaganda. He is a real leader and very very respected. And that is why political power is associated with Nazarbayev. So, if you are in the civil service you serve President Nazarbayev." (Expert Business 2). "For over 20 years the man is now in power and means stability for the people, a key word. And sometimes the society is deterred from occasions in the Ukraine, Kirgistan or Tajikistan. And so, people they: I do not want that. That Presidents are constantly changing. My President for me means stability." (Expert NGO 5). "Yes, he did so much for our country, developed the infrastructure, the law system. We have some problems, but he also developed our economy." (Expert Think Tank 1).

Judging from the statements about Nazarbayev – even the capital has now been renamed into Nursultan, paying tribute to the former President, whose first name is Nursultan – there is a high degree of confidence – almost faith – in this person. Governments under his rule came and went, but he acted as an anchor of stability and expectations certainty. This complete orientation of the political system towards one single person became evident at the beginning of 2019, when once again the government resigned.

The prime minister, who had been installed, but also been dismissed by Nazarbayev, took responsibility for certain underperformances concerning the development of the country and at the same time deflected any blame from the person of the President. This phenomenon might also be a symptom of the continuous rotation in ministries and the government. However, the almost faith-like loyalty to the political leader became evident in dismissed Prime Minister's Bakythhan Sagintayev departure statement: "The government has resigned. Elbasy (i.e. Nazarbayev, A.W.) – the founding father of our state always makes decisions issuing from the interests of the state and the people, prioritizing the well-being of all the country's citizens. Creating a state is hard work, and creating such a state as our country in such a historically short time without internal upheavals and conflicts deserves respect and admiration throughout the world.

Our President is a great creator of our time. Kazakhstan people connect their present and future with Elbasy alone. I want to thank Elbasy, (…), for the high confidence given me all these two and a half years of work as Prime Minister of the country." (Kazakhstanskaya Pravda 2019).

Evidently, state and nation are associated with Nazarbayev and vice versa. As suggested in the code by Expert (NGO 5) this allegiance served the very specific function of trusting a stabilizing anchor in the time of transition from communism to state capitalism and the building of an independent state after the break-up of the Soviet Union. For a country that is to such a high extent dominated by the existence of rivalling clans and their economic as well as political interests, Nazarbayev as "father of the nation" served as an identification figure, guaranteeing unity of the country.

Owing to this reliance of elites and population on him, the President had a considerable amount of discretion in steering the country on its developmental trajectory. Institutional constraints were at the same time furthermore largely missing due to the remarkable degree of personalization of Kazakh politics and the economy. The experts tended to perceive a prevalence of personal relations versus knowledge of how to utilize the institutional framework. Out of 33 codes pertaining to the degree of personalization in the politico-economic system of Kazakhstan only 7 considered it to be of medium intensity. Likewise, 26 referred to personal relations being of high relevance. "No, genetically it is more personal. It is not so much institutions. The people grew up in this environment for ages." (Expert Business 1).

Therefore, from the outset of its developmental path Kazakhstan was geared towards relying on a strong political leader. In this case besides facilitating political stability for the population, it also served to underline the commitment by the political leadership to achieving developmental goals, which it had formulated. Out of 40 codes 25 codes mentioned straight away development as a fully pursued goal. 13 codes pointed out that there is a sizable difference between the de facto situation and de jure proclamations by the Presidency. Only two codes denied that there exists a strong commitment by the political leadership to its own developmental goals.

"Yes, absolutely. Because for every single minister there is a KPI. And it is very important for the government that these KPI are reached. It is the most important task for the government and also the diversification of the economy. Those are very difficult tasks." (Expert Government 5). "Yes. They are really focused on that. The message comes regularly from the top that it is really important. So, these goals are regularly communicated through various media on different occasions." (Expert Academia 10).

Such a strong commitment by the political leadership tends to have beneficial consequences. It appears to be the most probable explanation for Kazakhstan's remarkably high reputation among the experts interviewed for this study in terms of property rights (see 4.3.2) that a credible commitment helped to increase the security of property rights even in the face of a pervasively low quality of the judicial system. Thus, in this regard a high degree of actor centricity fostered credible commitments – also owing to a high degree of stability even for relatively long time-horizons –, which in turn ceteris paribus increased property rights security and thereby entrepreneurial activity and ultimately economic development.

In contrast to Russia the Kazakh political leadership in this regard relied on setting realistic economic goals for development, with potentially beneficial effects on the incentive structure. As a matter of fact, out of 28 codes a majority of 15 codes assessed goals of industrial policy to be achievable and three attributed it to certain contingencies, which is in stark contrast with Russia's developmental path. Although ten codes perceived goals of industrial policy as not being achievable, overall a picture of the politico-economic system emerges, where goals are not far away from the real world.

Opposed to Russia this means that the Kazakh political leadership is not in a position of having repeatedly to justify performance failures with detrimental external factors that could not have been accounted for while planning. "They are realistic. They are realistic. The programs are actually very simple. They are not complicated. And everything is managed with integrity and appropriately, professionally these goals are very much achievable." (Expert Int. Org. 2).

This sense of reality while planning and taking into account potentially negative effects on credibility and the incentive structure in the case of underperformance becomes apparent when analyzing goal realization. Out of eleven codes eight perceived at least a considerable extent of goal realization with two denying it and one observing a complete fulfillment of formulated plans. In this sense, the political leadership that was dominated strongly by the person of former President Nazarbayev acted economically prudential.

Naturally, a more constrained Presidency could have also formulated prudential plans with positive incentive effects. But as a matter of fact, in Kazakhstan this dominance of one person on economic decision-making existed and here it did not result in the formulation of high-flying goals that were not grounded in reality. To sum it up, actor centricity was significantly in place in Kazakhstan. It resulted in a focus on and guarantee of stability as well as it tended to serve as a functional equivalent in order to support and promote property rights safety in a politico-economic system with a pronounced lack of rule of law. Detrimental effects on goal formulation are not evident and the political and corporate leadership tended to deliver on developmental promises given to the broader population. All this occurred in a system where the political leader was only to a small degree constrained by the institutional framework or elitist groups. Whether this relative political leeway can result in significant institutional change will be dealt with in the final sub-section of this case study, where Kazakh state capitalism on the whole is analyzed.

4.3.6 Kazakh State Capitalism

According to the taxonomy developed for this study Kazakhstan is to be subsumed under the economic system of state capitalism. Kazakhstan qualifies in all constituting principles of state capitalism as belonging to this economic order. Most of all, there is a significant tendency towards state dominance of the economic sphere evident in this country. The state acts as a majority investor – sometimes even with a share of 100 percent – in strategic industries such as mining, metallurgy and machinery.

State dominance of the economy furthermore extends to the financial sector, where commercial banks for instance are strongly linked to the state. At the same time Kazakhstan tends to shield its markets, mostly by employing the policy instrument of imposing tariffs. By the same token technology is imported from abroad with the economy thus far trailing industrialized nations in terms of innovativeness. One intention of the government is to attract FDI, which shall subsequently allow for a sizable technology transfer.

Concurrently, Kazakhstan firmly sticks to the co-existence of private and public property rights. There is no single statement by any leading official recognizable in the media that Kazakhstan shall embark on eliminating private property rights and also no expert interviewed for this study pointed to any such endeavor.

At the same time, Kazakh state bureaucracy is of a large enough size to conduct state capitalist policies such as trade policy. Its capacity is sufficiently high that rules enacted by the political leadership can at least to a certain extent be implemented. This does not necessarily translate into a very high degree of capability, with certain deficiencies in the quality of the civil service being evident. Finally, in Kazakhstan judging from the testimony of the experts there are profound deficiencies in the rule of law. It can thus far be determined that Kazakhstan does not qualify as being a *Rechtsstaat*. Owing to the factors analyzed above this does not prevent the country from allowing for a relatively high degree of property rights safety. All in all, Kazakhstan fulfills all seven constituting factors and thus has to be classified as state capitalist.

Reasons for a Mixed Picture in Performance

As explained above regarding development Kazakhstan displays a mixed performance. From an institutional economics point of view the political leadership has created a stable system with an institutional framework that does not change abruptly. This in itself can provide for expectations certainty and therefore support productive economic activities. But the stability of the politico-economic system does not transmit into a fully stable and growth-enhancing business environment.

Rather factors such as a high degree of personalization of the politico-economic system undermine the effectiveness of the institutional framework. Adding to that for economic actors being dependent on stable connections to officials from the bureaucracy the constant rotation in the ministries entails high costs such as repeatedly having to build new connections to the ministries from scratch. Thus, structurally, there are factors inhibiting developmental performance as is evident when the experts are rather critical about the quality and quantity of information flows to and from the ministries. In this regard, the structure of the corporate sector matches the rather mixed performance picture.

While the state engages strongly in strategic industries and here SOEs do dominate, in non-strategic sectors there is a relatively high degree of competition and the existence of a large number of SMEs to be seen. Entrepreneurs tend to engage in such fields as agriculture, retail and IT. Therefore, it cannot be maintained that Kazakhstan's corporate sector in general lacks dynamism.

In non-strategic sectors the state tends rather not to intervene. By the same token, this translates into a preference of the state for SOEs, since they dominate in the strategic sectors, where Kazakhstan seeks a leading position on world markets. Regarding financing, involvement in the decision-making process and access to information SOEs are in a better position. This is also evident regarding court decisions, where in a number of instances for SMEs to sue SOEs tends to be futile. The lack of rule of law has a number of detrimental effects on the incentive structure of private economic actors. Likewise, owing to a certain functional equivalent for the lack of rule of law to support property rights security by issuing credible commitments to development this effect is diminished.

All in all, structurally, there are factors supporting productive economic activities and some inhibiting it. But certain weaknesses in implementing industrial policy are evident. From a policy point of view Kazakhstan intends to substitute reliance on natural resources with building up a sizable industrial and service sector. The policies as such are based on experiences of other nations and the political leadership is willing to allow for a certain degree of experimentation.

In this regard, it is beneficial that political elites do not fall into two groups as in Russia, but there is rather a unified and pragmatic position prevalent with regard to industrial policy. This relative unanimity in formulating industrial policy continues in implementation in comparison to Russia with a relatively low degree of inter- and intra-ministerial strife. Although as in Russia there is no pilot agency, Kazakhstan as a functional equivalent relies on the Office of the President where a significant amount of coordination work is conducted. Consequently, taking into account that structurally and policy-wise there are short-comings and strengths within the politico-economic system it relatively reasonably follows that there are mixed results in development performance.

Kazakhstan as a Dual Economy State Capitalist System

For a number of reasons Kazakhstan is to be subsumed into the group of dual economy state capitalism countries within the taxonomy created above. There are also some overlaps with crony state capitalism, so that in general the justification in case selection of allowing for replication through choosing Russia and Kazakhstan remains uninfringed.

First of all, the corporate sector of Kazakhstan can as analyzed above be divided into a strategic and a non-strategic part. SOEs tend thus to be preferred, which adding to the factors mentioned above consists in controlling entry and exit to markets defined as being strategic. The state therefore significantly regulates competition in strategic sectors. This has the advantage of allowing entities to gain in size and be ceteris paribus able to reap economies of scale. But likewise, there is the risk of slack and inefficient operational activities, as is to a certain extent visible in the continued movement of top technocrats into better paid management positions in SOEs.

In Kazakhstan, SOEs are assembled under the umbrella of the holding company Samruk Kazyna that directly reports to the President's office. Having created such a large organization as Samruk Kazyna entails sizable risks as to its management losing control and oversight of company processes such as daily operations and even strategic decisions. Furthermore, the ability to adopt promptly to changing market conditions tends to erode and therefore flexibility be diminished.

This is different in non-strategic sectors with numerous SMEs competing for market share. Here entry and exit are rather not regulated by the state and markets are so contested that pressure on prices tends to be significant with positive welfare effects for consumers. This cannot be equated with high innovative activities of those entities. Rather they tend not to reap any economic rents, which could subsequently be channeled into research and development efforts.

Such opportunities are more in the realm of possibility for SOEs with being able to collect rents and afford a relatively high degree of innovative activities. Such efforts could theoretically be supported by a competent bureaucracy with sufficient technical knowledge. But this is rather not the case. Although in Kazakhstan there are competitive entry exams for the civil service in place, there is a lack of quality perceived by the experts, which might among others be attributed to a significant salaries gap versus the SOE sector. There is a perceptible degree of corruption, cronyism and nepotism evident within the civil service, inhibiting efficient policy implementation.

Although the bureaucracy is of a sufficient size for upholding a state capitalist system and implementing industrial policy, its capabilities for instance in assisting companies to venture into new markets, create business clusters or increase innovativeness are lacking. By the same token, there is a pronounced target-orientation evident in Kazakhstan – for the technocrats themselves as well as for SOEs. This clearly has the advantage of giving performance incentives as well as a certain degree of expectations certainty. And KPIs are indeed quite rigorously enforced with for instance cuts in bonuses occurring in case of underperformance.

As is typical for dual economy state capitalism a certain amount of "systemic vulnerability" exists, which results in legitimacy problems for the political leadership. The political leadership of Kazakhstan countered this risk by committing to the goal of development and also having been able to deliver on some of its goals. This credible commitment had among others the effect of working as a functional equivalent for a lack of rule of a law in providing a relatively high degree of property rights security. It tended to be the person of the President who managed to issue this credible commitment in the context of his having a sizable degree of actor centricity.

From a policy point of view Kazakhstan as a typical dual economy state capitalist country intends to reap advantages of integrating into world markets. In this sense, the most competitive sectors of its economy are those that the political leadership has defined as being strategic. In areas such as uranium and oil as well as gas production Kazakhstan is among the world market leaders

Its respective SOEs Kazatomprom and Kazmunaigaz are geared to compete internationally, although there are double bottom lines in place, at least informally. By the same token, it is striking that those entities that are competitive on world markets tend overwhelmingly to stem from the natural resources sector.

There is no Kazakh national champion active in the production of finished or half-finished goods with a competitive edge on world markets. Therefore, as is typical of dual economy state capitalist countries there is a considerable integration into international markets, but its leading entities are not part of the international division of labour and supply chains, since they are focused on extracting the mineral wealth of the vast territory of Kazakhstan.

Avenues for institutional Change

After having achieved the transformation from a communist to a state capitalist economic system, the political leadership perceived the risks of a too significant reliance on capital flows stemming from mineral wealth extraction. This reliance is one element of the country's position as being dual economy state capitalist with such a pronounced emphasis on strategic sectors.

The political leadership seeks to progress from the state capitalist variant of dual economy to the more efficient form of developmental state. Judging from the fact that for a time span of more than ten years the political leadership is intent on diversification and establishing a system, where strategic natural resource sectors are not as dominant anymore, it is hard to give a reasonably realistically grounded outlook that the current system can out of itself progress from one state capitalist variant to the next.

One essential indicator of this inhibition is evidently the drive for privatization having repeatedly stalled. As it appears right now based on the evidence of the qualitative data Kazakhstan has institutionally reached a steady state with dual economy state capitalism. There are hardly any political or economic initiatives discernible hinting at the outlook of a move forward to the developmental state.

Elites and the broader population place among the highest of priorities on stability. Thus, at this stage of Kazakhstan's developmental trajectory it appears ceteris paribus to be highly unlikely that the country can become a developmental state. However, developmental states are usually formed at critical junctures of a country's history. And here there exist a number of external and internal vulnerabilities, which could potentially surface.

Externally, Kazakhstan is wedged between Russia and China and could face hostile aggressions from either side. Moreover, Western states and organizations pursue their interests in Kazakhstan, which the political leadership has to take into account. Thus, the interplay of pressure from all three sides could induce a situation of crisis, which opens the door for a critical juncture offering the opportunity to progress to a developmental state economic model.

In such a situation with strongly reduced rigidities and resilience stemming from meaningful actors of the politico-economic system, foremost the clans, the political leader could pursue a reform path to modernize the bureaucracy.[10] Potential efforts in this regard could be reductions in headcount, which opens up opportunities for raising salaries in order to attract the brightest minds among university graduates, which tends to improve bureaucratic quality.

By the same token, the pervasive and by the interviewed experts harshly criticized policy of comprehensive inter- and intra-ministerial rotations could be eliminated with potentially fewer costs at the state business nexus, since companies are not constrained to constantly have to adapt to new contacts.

The most striking element of the developmental state is bureaucratic capacity and capability. And consequently, any reform towards this direction would have to start with improving the quality of the civil service. Subsequently, policy-wise measures would have to be formulated and implemented to integrate supply chains effectively into the international division of labour. But to that end first of all an internationally competitive industrial and service sector would have to be formed. For such an endeavor there are no foolproof blueprints and is no panacea available.

The developmental state relies on a policy of picking the winners, meaning to select companies from the industrial and service sector with a high potential and support it financially, organizationally and with technical expertise. However, as is evident from the interviews this policy failed in Kazakhstan potentially for structural reasons that technocrats were not qualified enough and also a certain degree of cronyism was involved. Consequently, any drive for becoming a developmental state would have to begin with the creation of a qualified bureaucracy and subsequently improvements in policy could be aimed for.

Probably, in this regard experimentation and pragmatism are recommendable. In the former sub-section, it has been indicated that under President Nazarbayev a sizable degree of actor centricity existed – such as the Presidency being able to move the capital from Almaty to what was formerly called Astana

10 Kazakhstan is a classic example of power structures being divided between legal-rationalistic versus neo-patrimonial rule. Both forms of governing can be extensively observed in Kazakhstan with consequences for lower levels and economic agents that have to adapt to both forms of being ruled. In this regard in order to modernize bureaucratic procedures were standardized, but this did not overcome neo-patrimonial structures, so that members of the bureaucracy as well as the corporate sector still had to adapt to both forms of rule, since indeed only a partial modernization occurred so far (Schiek 2013, p. 28–30 and 40).

against significant resistance. But even during this long tenure meaningful structural changes in the civil service – aiming at formal as well as informal institutions – were either not possible or not intended by the President himself. At the critical juncture straight after independence decisive steps into this direction could have possibly been taken, but afterwards resilience of intra- and inter-ministerial forces stemming from among others the clans would have anyway been too strong to energetically pursue decisive institutional changes.

Thus, for progressing to a developmental state it would take a critical juncture. Towards the other direction of crony state capitalism neglect and constant erosion do suffice. Again, potentially the process of institutional change would start structurally with a deterioration of bureaucratic quality.

Possibly, the political leadership loosens its control over the civil service, intensifying principal agent problems. Technocrats could perceive that there are fewer incentives to perform, for instance when KPIs become mere cosmetics and failure to perform in this regard carries no sanctions with it. This loss of bureaucratic quality would affect the state business nexus directly with potentially more skimming of profits of the corporate sector by the bureaucracy. Costs for the corporate sector would consequently increase due to higher pecuniary and non-pecuniary means having to be transferred to the bureaucracy.

Among others for instance, the phenomenon of ministerial staff switching into considerably higher paid positions in the corporate sector could increase which tends in Kazakhstan to carry with it a lowering of managerial skills, since the technocrats usually had acquired no business background a priori. Thus, for the entire interplay of state and business negative effects are to be expected and gradually also the entire fabric of the dual economy state capitalist system could fray.

Thus far, non-strategic sectors are in a position to be relatively unconstrained from state interventions and a number of SMEs do profit from this benign neglect, even seeking not to become too visible for the state. A deterioration of bureaucratic quality could lead to a situation where the civil service intends to extend its reach on non-strategic sectors, taking away liberties from SMEs and also burdening them with heightened control and regulation, but without the rewards enjoyed by SOEs regarding informational advantages and certain means to participate in the law- and regulation-making process.

Such a development would intensify the sort of crony relations typical for crony state capitalism. Companies would receive significantly increased incentives to engage in redistributive rather than in productive activities. Investments into crony relations would result in higher pay-offs than maintaining productive commercial activities. Thus, ultimately especially at the state business nexus a heightened degree of cronyism would prevail.

In the rationale and argumentation presented here the starting point are losses in bureaucratic quality due to neglect. But possibly the process could start more markedly with the political leadership. Here reductions in the commitment to development are possible, for instance for reasons of altered belief systems of political leaders or a loss of skills to credibly communicate goals. This would not only in itself affect bureaucratic quality due to reduced incentives for technocrats, but also influence property rights security. As mentioned above the political leadership in the relevant time span managed to – owing to the functional equivalent of a credible commitment to development – provide for a relatively high degree of property rights safety. In the process of a degradation towards a crony state capitalist system this functional equivalent could erode as well with the abounding negative consequences for productive economic activities amplifying the emergence of more crony relations at the state business nexus analyzed above.

However, currently the dual economy state capitalist system appears to be firmly in place in Kazakhstan. There is no evidence of institutional change in either direction discernible. This could change with the new political leadership, but apparently the relevant elites taking part in this process of changes at the political top, have no interests and even no evident incentives to transform the system through institutional change.

All in all, in this case study, Kazakh state capitalism has been analyzed. Structural, policy and performance elements were taken into account. Weaknesses and strengths of Kazakh dual economy state capitalism were analyzed and enunciated. This served to better understand the nature of the current economic system of Kazakhstan and also to be able to venture an outlook for the future institutional development of the country. After having by now dealt with Russia and Kazakhstan based on the expert interviews it is turned to the case study of Singapore for which there will be a comprehensive literature survey conducted.

4.4 Singapore

Singapore stands out in the selection of the four case studies as with a population of around 5 million people and being a city-state the smallest of selected countries. It profited significantly from the rise of globalization post World War II, when with a certain time lag the country entered into world markets, and one of the main factors for the unexpected and ad-hoc success of Singapore's export orientation was that the US needed an export base in Asia while Hongkong's political situation had become less secure (Rodan 1989, p. 102 and Haggard 1986, p. 363 and 367). Singapore was part of the four little dragons – to which also Taiwan, South Korea as well as Hong Kong belong – and a late industrializer behind Japan, emulating Japanese developmental processes (Vogel 1991, p. 4–5).

Later on, at around the turn of the millennium Singapore's elites perceived the city-state to be at the epi-center of an upcoming Asian century.[11] The city-state epitomizes multi-racialism and an inclination of state and society towards multiculturalism. Likewise, Singapore incorporates what is sometimes referred to as being based on a framework of informal institutions, which became known as Asian values. This emphasis on neo-confucianism serves as a focal point in the quest of the country for its identity and future development (see Yew 2014, p. 1).

Intriguingly, fundamental elements of its formal institutional framework and its national language reside in its British legacy, which up to a certain extent provided a significant degree of path dependence referring to elite formation and resilience of elitist rule (King 2008, p. 127–128).[12] Such an ambivalence is also to be found in Singapore's economic order. Judging from the literature, by now Singapore can be neither classified as market nor as state capitalist. The city-state is seen as a rather archetypical developmental state that however is on the brink of progressing from being state capitalist to becoming market capitalist as South Korea has already done.[13] The constant factor in Singapore's ongoing metamorphoses during its perennial developmental course is its entrepreneurial orientation. Therefore, it appears highly adequate that Huat (2017, p. 7) terms the state in Singapore as being an "entrepreneur in global capitalism".

Especially, owing to this significantly amorphous economic order from a theoretical point of view it appears to be fruitful to strive for also analyzing the developmental phase of a country, as it still currently unfolds. Its economic system has been categorized by some observers even as a neoliberal developmental state (Liow 2011, p. 241), which in itself resembles an oxymoron, since neoliberalism

---

11 Singapore achieved such a significant development performance that for China the Singapore variant of state capitalism advanced to a role model for its proprietary developmental process (Ortmann, S. / Thompson, M. R. (2018).

12 There is a large degree of path dependence also relevant in the fact that the city-state looks back on centuries acting as a commercial center and on this basis the modern state of Singapore could build up (Regnier 2000).

13 Some observers while calling it developmental also refer to it as a virtual state, meaning that it operates in essence like a brain center, being streamlined and intellectual, managing activities such as design and research or also financing, networking and marketing (see Low 2006, p. 4–8).

is associated with hardly any state interventions. All these phenomena are taken into account in the following analysis of Singapore's economic system as it evolved during its developmental process.

4.4.1 Preliminaries

After having dealt with Russia and Kazakhstan – which have been classified as crony and dual economy state capitalist respectively – now the focus is shifted on a country that tended to be perceived in the literature to a certain extent to be state capitalist in the form of developmental state. It is among others selected as a case in this study's sample, since Russia, Kazakhstan and South Korea constitute a type of corporate structure, which favours and is dominated by large enterprises. In order to include a deviant case, it was necessary to include Singapore, whose corporate sector is qualified as being atomistic as opposed to South Korea (see Low 2006).

By some accounts in recent years Singapore shifted to become more market capitalist. This aspect is dealt with below. However, during the majority of its developmental path starting with creation of the city-state in 1965 Singapore was firmly classified as being state capitalist according to the literature. This economic system of a developmental state carries some problems with it concerning an analysis. Some authors perceive the state with its high capacity and capability to be an independent variable and development performance as a dependent variable (Boyd / Ngo 2005, p. 9). This approach is to a certain extent taken up for this study by dealing with structure and policies on the one hand and performance on the other hand. But admittedly, the state cannot be unequivocally be seen as a monolithic entity. Rather it consists of a political leadership and the bureaucracy, where in the latter numerous technocrats tend also to pursue self-orientated goals. Subsequently, as has been done before in this study the state will be divided into the political leadership as well as the bureaucracy and as far as conceptually possible divergent interests of technocrats will be taken into account.

As a matter of fact, this entire case study is not a historic analysis, but an institutional one, where institutional change is also considered. Thus, it will at times be referred to the emergence of the current economic system of Singapore and partially be referred to today's institutional framework.

A comprehensive survey and analysis of the literature has been accomplished for this case study. Likewise, it needs to be cautioned that due to the sheer size of the literature on Singapore it is possible that certain works in the literature about the economic system of Singapore have been unintendedly omitted. But the most often cited and most relevant literature on the developmental state of Singapore shall be accounted for in this case study. Moreover, for this case study an interview with an official from the pilot agency Economic Development Board (EDB) has been conducted. The transcript is to be found in the documentation and the information extracted from this source is indicated at the relevant passages of the case study.

Overall, as with Russia and Kazakhstan there will be a focus on structure – with a view towards bureaucracy, structure of the corporate sector and the judicial system –, policy – regarding content and implementation as well as performance. Afterwards there will be a sub-section on actor centricity and in the final sub-section the findings about the economic system of Singapore will be summarized and an outlook on potential institutional change presented.

4.4.2 Structure

Singapore has a reputation in the literature for being ruled by competent and capable technocrats. Bureaucratic and more general institutional capacity as well as capability are seen to have scale and scope comparable to the most competitive countries world-wide. Consequently, this element of Singapore's state capitalism – in a broader politico-economic setting being characterized by the Economist (2015) as "ruthless pragmatism" – is dealt with comprehensively in this sub-section about the structure underlying Singapore's developmental trajectory.

Likewise, this element must be contextualized and will therefore subsequently be analyzed in connection with the structure of Singapore's corporate sector as well as the constituting institutional principle of state capitalism, i.e. a degree of rule of law which deviates from a complete institutionalization of the legal system of a *Rechtsstaat*.

Quality of the Civil service

Overall, Singapore's developmental path was characterized by elitist rule and that was based on the conviction that pursuing an almost scientific, rational and logical approach to policy implementation is economically superior to other approaches of regulating the economy, such as those allowing for a higher degree of voice and participation (Chong 2015). Barr (2014) refers to a policy approach of "scientism" in formulation and implementation, widely free from political considerations and ideology. Consequently, there was an emphasis on the best possible arguments in inner-organizational discourses, meritocracy and in general plan-rationality prevalent in Singapore's bureaucracy.

In general, there are a number of factors driving this high degree of bureaucratic capacity in Singapore. First of all, renumeration is seen as a decisive factor in attracting and retaining talented university graduates (see Barr 2016). As a matter of fact, in this regard salaries are at least kept in line with those paid in the corporate sector. To some extent these salaries are based on performance (Carney 2014, p. 4, also see Vennewald 1994, p. 52, Schein 1996, p. 9). But in certain instances, excesses in renumeration for technocrats are evident, when for instance broader segments of the population are angered by the fact that very senior bureaucrats occasionally were income millionaires. Thus, it can occur that salaries of technocrats in Singapore supersede those in other industrialized countries significantly (Barr 2016, p. 4–7, Huff 1995a, p. 748–749, Huff 1995b, p. 1433–1434, Barr 2016) with in some extreme cases technocrats earning more than one million Dollar in a year (Thio 2012, p. 285). This high remuneration in conjunction with severe fines consequently contributes to a bureaucratic tradition, where corruptive activities by technocrats are significantly limited due to a decisively adverse trade-off between accepting bribes and the ensuing penalties in case such occurrences are uncovered. But the reasoning behind relatively high wages was most of all that those civil servants are superior in virtue, meaning almost on moral grounds and therefore per se incorruptible and this in itself deserved a high salary (Barr 2016).

Secondly, it tends to increase bureaucratic quality if those relatively high salaries are linked to performance criteria. Here there is relatively broad evidence available for such a linkage. Similar to executive remuneration with an allotment of shares in public companies according to the shareholder value model, civil servants are awarded a bonus based on the overall performance of the economy, implying that an expanding economy with economic growth is among others also an achievement of civil servants. It is widely perceived that this performance-based remuneration for bureaucrats serves as an incentive for civil servants to uphold or even expand individual performance (Straits Times 2017). It serves as a typical example for this performance orientation in pay that in 1985 the pilot agency Economic Development Board (EDB) was able to implement an across-the-board pay cut of 12 percent due to lost competitiveness (Schein 1996, p. 50).

A third essential pillar allowing for bureaucratic quality is a limited access to technocratic positions. Selection among a pool of applicants is conducted based on successful candidates having superior competences. In this regard, the literature perceives that requirements for being allowed to serve in the public sector are relatively high (Carney, 2014 p. 4). Such a limitation of access to technocratic positions is secured by relying on and requiring recruitment to accept only entrants from renowned universities, where they graduated with sufficiently high grades. In order to have a pool of potentially overperforming graduates the state enacted a scholarship program for students to go abroad (Schein 1996, p. 171 and 185). Technocrats were recruited with a preference for employing engineers, since they had superior technical knowledge when it came to implementing industrial policy (Tsui-Auch 2004b). In a number of instances those specialists – generalists were not in high regard – were trained in South Korea (Huff 1995b, p. 1433–1434). Instances of nepotism are very rare, where top officials managed to allocate positions to family members or friends. Intriguingly, judging from the literature a lack of competitive entry exams did not result in adverse signaling effects, where less qualified graduates were attracted. Rather due to high requirements of academic performance Singapore tended to recruit competent technocrats.

Fourth, this setting led to a situation where a kind of elitist self-esteem ensued with some sense of a mission and an esprit de corps. This is mirrored in the following observation about technocrats in the pilot agency Economic Development Board (EDB): "The EDB is a proud…organization" (Schein 1996, p. 3) and it presents itself as acting in the spirit of having 30 years of accomplishment, which serves as a motivation and a positive kind of path dependence (Schein 1996 p. 15–17), providing for a self-perception of being exceptional, but most of all in its ability to outperform the broader population (Barr 2016). Lim (1983, p. 762) perceives that state servants are motivated by the "glory of the very success". This third-party and self-perception – with an ensuing high degree of cohesiveness – was one contributing factor in endowing the bureaucracy with a relatively high degree of autonomy, evident among others in the low incidence rate of corruption.[14] Evidently, straight from the start the state insisted on an "intellectual elite", not only on the political level, but also in endowing its technocrats with first of all a high degree of discretion and secondly promoting a perception of their elitist superiority among broader segments of the population (Wilson / Peebles 2002, p. 7).

Fifth, these effects were supported by the state of Singapore offering members of the bureaucracy long-term career paths, so that they have an incentive to perform and as a result steadily climb up the career ladder. Overall, those bureaucrats tend to stay with a single agency for a long duration of on average more than

14 This potentially positively influenced those technocrats in the meantime to disregard recommended steps in the post Asian crisis era due to the EDB's personal experience, varying circumstances of regulated firms as well as formal and informal information channels of the EDB (Lai / Yeung 2003, p. 483).

ten years (Tsui-Auch 2004a, Von Alten 1994, p. 181–194, see Barr 2014). And at the same time, gifted and industrious young entrants can in certain instances progress to the very top in relatively short time spans (Schein 1996, p. 100).

Sixth, furthermore, bureaucratic quality profits in general from a remarkable degree of autonomy versus corporate players or social groups from society as well as the political leadership (Huff 1995a, p. 748). Singapore's bureaucracy is able to impose even unpopular decisions on the population due to its credibility, autonomy and a social contract centered on the conviction that in the medium term the economic situation will provide for constantly improving living standards (Yeung 2005) and in the course of the developmental phase the EDB even gained in relevance through its remarkable cohesion and strong links to the ruling party PAP (Yeung 2017 p. 93–94). To contribute to technocrats' autonomy, there is only a limited amount of rotations between bureaucracy and the corporate side. For instance, relatively few top technocrats hold director positions in government-linked corporations (GLCs) (Vennewald, 1994, p. 52, see Huff 1999a). However, Low (2006) diverges to a certain extent from this perception. According to her Amakudari is a widely applied practice in Singapore, relating especially to officials for instance from the EDB moving to positions within newly privatized GLCs or other entities of the corporate sector. In the same vein Carney / Zheng (2009, p. 301) perceive a significant porousness between the state and GLCs. To some extent this leads to a situation, where the traditional dichotomy between state and private is impaired, meaning that there are up to a point, blurred lines (Henke / Boxill 2000, Yeung 2000, p. 138). But according to some other accounts this embeddedness promotes a clarity of rules and a commitment to solve problems, since technocrats understand business and have business acumen (Schein 1996, p. 21–22).

Often former officials from ministries serve in those state-linked companies and on the other hand managers move from GLCs to the ministries. Although this setting enables an exchange of tacit knowledge by increasing the connectedness of the state and the GLCs, grave problems as to a potential emergence of crony relations emerge. But surprisingly, nepotism as it is prevalent throughout South East Asia was never a topic of high concern within the corporate sector of Singapore. This enigma will be sought to explain below. However, in a certain sense it augments autonomy versus the political sphere that agencies tend to be completely apolitical organizations, where there is little interference from politicians into bureaucratic processes (see Schein 1996, p. 33).

Seventh, by the same token also in its organization of internal processes Singapore's bureaucracy tends to provide for a relatively high quality. Thus, for instance the EDB concentrates on the multi-tasking of several projects for individual members at the same time, which due to job rotation tends to increase staff motivation as well as flat hierarchies and in general no top-down attitude. Usually ideas for new plans originate below, are taken up further above in the hierarchy and widely communicated (Schein 1996 p. 11–15). Another indication of a well-managed bureaucracy is the fact that in 1968 the EDB perceived itself to have grown too large to be able to be continued to be effectively managed. Therefore, the Development Bank of Singapore (DBS) was separated, providing one of only few examples where an agency actually sought to slim down (Schein 1996, p. 61). There is an emphasis on a can-do-atmosphere, which is strengthened through tight networks by meetings and also mutual recreative activities (Schein 1996, p. 15–17).

Ultimately, bureaucratic quality in Singapore is according to the literature profiting significantly from the existence of a pilot agency in the form of the EDB which moreover was in its business-friendly policies highly credible in never rescinding on any promises made to investors (see Huff 1999a). In general, the EDB tends to be placed as a node in the web, being situated into an entire network of policy-making (Tsui-Auch 2004b). The role of those bureaucrats in Singapore is "pervasive" (Rodan 1989 p. XIV). As a matter of fact, those technocrats serve as a one-stop agency, which in the course of Singapore's developmental process was facilitated by the EDB chairman being a trusted friend and confidante of Prime Minister and Minister of Finance. Nine agencies were for instance involved in continuing on a developmental path in the 1990s and the EDB sat right in the middle as the coordinating instance assisted by a constant exchange with other agencies, also in personnel (Schein 1996, p. 168). Such an organization that coordinates tends to increase the uniformity in content and implementation of policies. Diverging interests within the political and technocratic sphere were thus pooled and a consistent approach to policy formulation and implementation was made possible.

To conclude, most factors relating to the quality of bureaucratic processes point to high capabilities in Singapore, which will be underlined with some numerical data below. It has been consecutively formed through the application of an eclectic approach, meaning regarding informal institutions as the framework in which the bureaucracy is embedded and according to which it acts itself there are certain elements as described in the Western tradition as Weberian and evident in its belief in scientism and on the other hand neo-confucianism. What emerged were technocrats that mostly acted rationally and dutifully, while at the same time accepting to take risks (Chew 2012, p. 4–6). Singapore's bureaucracy was to this end marked by a high degree of autonomy versus the political sphere with a certain degree of embeddedness into the corporate sector. Technocrats tend to perceive themselves as an elite, having graduated from among the most renowned universities. This significant propensity towards meritocratic principles is mirrored by the fact that salaries of technocrats are highly performance-based. This overall guaranteed a high degree of cohesion and integration of the bureaucracy (Barr 2014). The quality of the bureaucratic system reverberates in the corporate sector, since both spheres are highly interdependent, and therefore now the structure of the corporate sector is dealt with.

Structure of the Corporate Sector

Singapore's political leadership starting from inception of the nation in 1965 sought to in parallel to a highly meritocratic bureaucracy also form a corporate sector that is competitively as well as efficiently structured and where corporations strive for profit-maximization. There tended to be a significant caveat of the political leadership regarding traditional Chinese and Malay forms of doing business, which to a large extent relied on a personalized form of commercial exchange.

Due to a perception of being confronted with a crony domestic corporate sector, the political leadership in conjunction with technocrats orchestrated to a large extent the entry of multi-national companies (MNCs) into Singapore. With the means of industrial policy – also supported by a comprehensive liberalization of its domestic markets – Singapore managed to attract subsidiaries – sometimes even Asian headquarters – of MNCs by a large scale.

Thus, added to existing domestic corporations there are especially MNCs as dominant players in Singapore's corporate sector. Since Singapore still tends to be state capitalist, it is of little surprise that there is also a large role accorded to state-led companies, the government-linked corporations (GLCs).

All in all, entities from those three spheres of the corporate world appear to rather have a level playing-field with no formal privileges for any of those players, but a certain degree of formal preferences for GLCs (some special licenses, concessions, special procurement contracts and even reduced rents (von Alten 1994, p. 213)) and informal preferences for MNCs.[15] Consequently, the composition

---

15 Some observers see traces of a dual economy in this regard. The first part of the economy is outward-orientated, MNC-dominated and successfully integrates into world markets. It is bent on continuously increasing efficiency and can compete with advanced nations. During the majority of Singapore's history this part of the economy has been favoured. On the other hand, there is the domestic sector, which has up to a certain degree been squeezed, with pressure to lower wages and rein in consumption (Chua 2007).

of the corporate sector with those three branches was at no point in Singapore's history put in question, neither as a result of market outcomes nor due to state interference. However, in the course of Singapore's developmental phase this composition of the corporate sector underwent a certain evolution. At the beginning of Singapore's statehood domestic entrepreneurs dominated the corporate world. Those domestic private companies were by a vast majority controlled by ethnic Chinese families (Tsui-Auch 2004a).

In this regard, Singapore pursued shortly after state-inception a policy of marginalizing those Chinese domestic entrepreneurs, thereby increasing autonomy of the bureaucracy (Huff 1995b, p. 1431) and put an emphasis on attracting MNCs, which only gradually changed post 1990. Thus, a significant part of top jobs in the Singaporean economy were until the 1990s filled with foreigners (Huff 1994, p. 35–36). As illustrated above this preference for the presence of internationally operating companies was due to the perception that thus efficiency and competition could be increased.[16] To this end, the labour force in Singapore was trained by the government to serve MNCs establishing production facilities in the city-state. In this regard to a certain extent, domestic entrepreneurs were marginalized and did not play the key role in the developmental phase of Singapore.

State founder Lee mistrusted ethnic Chinese business-men as being unproductive and making profits as typical rentiers. Only in the course of the city-state's developmental trajectory did a meaningful domestic business community gradually emerge (Tsui-Auch 2004a, p. 26). This neglect of private domestic corporations furthermore becomes evident when accounting for the fact that when at the turn of the century Singapore embarked on building up a biotechnology sector, the state again relied on attracting MNCs. In a certain sense, with this approach regarding the structure of the corporate sector the state again preferred growth of establishing a domestic industrial base (Pereira 2008, p. 1195).

As mentioned above domestic corporations to a significant extent operate with an Asian framework of informal institutions, following a neo-confucian approach with an emphasis on family and respect for seniority. Traditionally, those

16 In general, due to economic policies such as attracting MNCs those cleavages emerged in Singapore's politico-economic system: between foreigners and inlanders, between GLCs and domestic private companies, between the Chinese-speaking population and more cosmopolitan orientated people. This is at the same time not all too surprising, since this heterogenous composition reflects a largely inhomogenous society (Peebles / Wilson 2002).

family businesses relied on managers from the family so that the family was not only controlling the group and setting the strategy, but also ruling operational activities. This created the problem that career paths up to a certain extent were more based on ancestry than on merit, with all the ensuing problems for business growth and profitability due to a lack of expertise and business acumen. Only recently did those domestic corporations lay management increasingly into the hands of well-educated and highly trained family members. Therefore, trust is still very highly valued by family groups. Such a tendency of personalized relations is less evident among MNCs and GLCs and most dominant in private domestic corporations (Tsui-Auch 2004a, p. 22–23).

The key characteristic of those domestic corporations are hierarchical and highly personalized forms of management, which at the same time conflict with the organization culture of the bureaucracy, which relies on flat hierarchies and transparency. There is only a limited degree of delegation incorporated into those corporate structures and thus centralization tends to be significant (Wee / Chua 2013). This gap in informal institutions prevailing between domestic corporations and state agencies reverberated in the way those companies were regulated by the state. There tended to be a discrepancy in belief systems between both spheres, which led to a situation, where policies were more geared towards the advantage of MNCs and GLCs. However, as an advantage for the nexus between the state and domestic corporations emerged the fact that due to those companies being paternally structured speedy internal corporate decisions were common. (Carney 2014, p. 14). This setting facilitated guidance of domestic corporate players for state regulators, among others also due to those patriarchs in most cases tending to commit to the long-term goals and projects of the state. In a certain sense a relatively high degree of accountability of those entities towards technocrats was to be observed. Thus, in the course of Singapore's developmental phase the political leadership also started to include private domestic entrepreneurs into its policy formulation and implementation calculus, since those entities tend to have longer time horizons than MNCs, which are more prone to exist when the business environment – foremost in the form of revenue and profit prospects – deteriorates (see Tsui-Auch 2004a, p. 26).

At the same time, while granting private domestic players a more significant role, the government kept strictly controlling the developmental process and relied extensively on the economic order of state capitalism, as evident for instance by the essential role of GLCs. Here the state imposed a relatively strong position of state structures in GLCs, although overall utmost importance was placed on an efficient and profit-orientated corporate governance. In this regard, while retaining a focus on profitability the heads of GLCs were routinely members of the ruling PAP and in a number of cases also members of parliament. This tendency was even fostered through widespread inter-locking directorships, so that a select number of individuals basically controlled the SOE corporate sector of Singapore (Huff 1995a, Pereira 2008, p. 1192–1193).[17]

Such a focus on staffing director positions in GLCs with loyal members extends even further. Thus, as directors of GLCs often civil servants do serve, which are occasionally drawn from the military. By the same token, those directors on the boards tend not to interfere with day-to-day operations and primarily deal with nominating managers, so that efficiency of the GLCs is not imperiled. As is the case with the EDB in general the state takes significant efforts to keep the operation of GLCs free of politics, for instance by effectively preventing politicians from switching into well-paid executive functions in GLCs and strictly binding itself to a hands-off approach towards day-to-day operations of the management (Rodan 1989 p. 152).[18] A managerial instead of a political view concerning GLCs prevails. In the literature there is comprehensive evidence that a significant portion of GLCs' efficiency is to be attributed to strict corporate governance with clear target setting and only a minimum degree of political interference (Sim 2011, p. 75–77).[19]

17 This was to a certain extent criticized. Thus, in GLCs in a number of instances even generals became CEOs, which led to discomfort by international investors, being doubtful of the military leaders' business acumen (Low 2001, p. 420–429).

18 Nevertheless, this strict separation of politics and business did not extend to the highest echelons of the political leadership. Tellingly, there are dominating to a certain extent networks in the politico-economic system of Singapore. The GLC sector is not unaffected by these traces of crony state capitalism, as is evident by the fact that at the beginning of the 2000s for instance while Lee Kuan Yew served as President his son was deputy prime minister, his brother CEO of Singapore Telecommunications (Singtel) and his wife CEO of Temasek (see Low 2006). But the political leadership in this regard had managed to perceive the risk of ensuing efficiency and incentive losses and allowed for an effective counter-weight by attracting MNCs and integrating comprehensively into the world economy, which served as a means to constrain GLCs to keep on focusing on operating efficiently for the sheer purpose of not having to exit the market due to a too severe lack of competitiveness.

19 The fact that GLCs are up to a certain extent internally structured like family-owned corporations with relatively little transparency and inter-locking ownerships, being exacerbated by the fact that the state is only a minority investor, does not infringe on operating efficiently (Carney (2014). Again, this relatively unexpected outcome is due to GLCs at least partially having to compete with MNCs and private domestic companies on a level playing-field domestically and on international markets.

GLCs are subject to the same regulatory framework as MNCs and domestic corporations and as a further decisive factor in order to allow for hard budget constraints as well as a limit on building up slack is the setting that they have to compete on contested markets. According to the literature those companies – owned by the SWF Temasek – consistently managed to earn above average returns by international standards and thus do not trail behind privately owned companies in terms of efficiency.

They are to the same degree as subsidiaries of MNCs and domestic corporations subject to commercial failure, if too severe losses are accrued. GLCs are in a position to operate independently and issue new equity as well as bonds, if the majority of the board backs such plans and the state can act as a veto player in this regard only by utilizing its minority investor stake.

The management is able to enter into partnerships and venture into new businesses and is controlled in this regard to the same extent as it occurs according to internationally approved corporate governance standards. Regarding recruiting new staff GLCs compete for talents with MNCs and domestic corporations. They appear to have a reputation of being attractive employers to begin a career, since salaries are competitive and there tend to be business dynamics as in privately held companies that also operate on competitive and innovative markets. (Sim 2011, p. 71–73).

This setting helps in explaining an essential quandary encountered above, meaning that although there is a relatively constant exchange of staff between tenures at the state and board positions in GLCs, those entities are managed without accounting for double bottom lines or other political considerations. Such potential structures of crony state capitalism are avoided foremost due to Singapore being a small economy that is very well integrated into world markets. There prevails a competitive environment – best reflected by the continuing dominance of MNCs in the corporate sphere – and the country constantly having to adapt to global conditions on factor and product markets. Due to this effective counter-weight there is no discretion for engaging in the pursuit of corrupt practices (see Low 2006).

In a nut-shell, the structure of Singapore's corporate structure consists largely of GLCs, MNCs and privately held domestic corporations. In contrast to dual economy state capitalism there are no strategic sectors, meaning that entities from all three corporate spheres do compete on overlapping markets. This fosters a competition setting, where in principle relatively low entry barriers were in place (Peebles / Wilson 2002, p. 12).

As a further factor driving efficiency of the corporate sector serves the comprehensive integration of Singapore's economy into world markets. The bureaucracy fosters such a corporate structure, since it effectively mirrors its own belief systems of meritocracy, transparency and competition. Since the state did not perceive these values to be upheld by private domestic corporations its policy approach was more dented towards MNCs and GLCs. All in all, the tendency of Singapore's economic order to function efficiently – as already illustrated for the bureaucracy above – is therefore repeated in the corporate sector. It remains to be seen how this efficiently organized city-state fares with regard to rule of law, where certain discrepancies are a constituting principle of state capitalism, but it is seen as essential for the security of property rights.

Degree of Rule of Law

To a large extent Singapore fulfills decisive structural elements at the state-business nexus for a high degree of efficiency. The overall framework of this interaction tended to be business-friendly. But those factors would be of little effect in terms of economic development in case of a significant lack of property rights safety. Those are usually secured through a comprehensive system of rule of law emanating from the judiciary. But how does Singapore score in this regard?

First of all, there is no independent judiciary in Singapore. A clear separation in terms of judges being at least to a certain extent invulnerable to political pressure and a constitution guaranteeing basic rights do not exist.

By some accounts Singapore's legal system is seen as being significantly manipulated by the executive power. Supposedly, the judiciary does not decide autonomously, but is severely influenced by the political leadership. It is even claimed that in the developmental phase of Singapore the judiciary served only as a kind of instrument at the disposal of the political leadership (Thio 2012, p. 269 and Thio / Tan 2009). It is widely seen as one of a number of variables facilitating economic development (Rajah 2012, p. 14–15 and 21). A mitigating counter-weight to decisions of the executive was according to this account not to be observed. Furthermore, an effective control of utilization of funds, implementation of policies and granting of political rights by the executive power through the legal system does not take place (see Seow 2006).

Thus, it appears to be contradictory that Singapore's judicial system, which is based on common law, is able to effectively defend property rights. Nevertheless, most observers rate the judicial system with high marks concerning commercial law, while being broadly critical of the city-state's dealing with criminal law. As a matter of fact, the state is put above the law and there is a plethora of instances with unjust detentions and efforts to subdue the right of the citizens for freedom of speech (Thio 2012, p. 269–270).

Effective and efficient government is in general given preference over the principles of rule of law. While Singapore scores high on international indices of rule of law, at the same time it limits to a considerable degree the freedom of its citizens, i.e. civil rights (Rajah 2012, p. 3–6). This means that civil and political rights tend to be curtailed, especially when the working of the machinery of Singapore's politico-economic system warrants such a move. Singapore's judicial system in its "Asian value" orientation is supposed to follow moral principles instead of sticking to the letter of codified rules. (Thio 2012, p. 272–273).

By the same token, the legal system relies on the politics of virtue, meaning that the government and bureaucracy are supposed to rule with a large degree of wisdom and superior moral values. This insistence on a superior moral integrity of technocrats and politicians helps to explain, why for instance technocrats are well-paid and there is a conjunction between the generally high level of reputation of state agencies and a relatively high remuneration.

This results in a significant degree of legitimacy bestowed on the political leadership and technocrats, but this is not mirrored in the judiciary. The city-state allows for no constraints on the state through law.[20] It incorporates what can be termed as being an oxymoronic "authoritarian legitimacy" that can best be understood in the context of Singapore combining the British common law tradition with an Asian approach to law (Rajah 2012, p. 8–9).

Whereas in crony and dual economy state capitalism it appears to be futile, to challenge certain influential vested interests in court, in Singapore this relates to issues where the state perceives societal harmony – as is the case with certain political rights – or bureaucratic homogeneity at risk (Rajah 2012, p. 30–35).

In commercial law, however, Singapore allows for a significantly higher degree of investor protection. Here as in the overall politico-economic system a paternal attitude of the political leadership towards the corporate sector prevails (Thio 2012, p. 283–284). And as a matter of fact, some researchers attribute Singapore's legal system the same degree of investor protection as it persists in New York or London (see Rajah 2012, p. 24). On the other hand, constitutional safeguards for a legal hedging of those paternalistically protected property rights are virtually non-existent in Singapore. It tends to be possible for the PAP dominated legislature to modify the constitution almost arbitrarily (Barr 2011, p. 367–368). The

20 Such a potential constraining function fulfilled by the judiciary in combination with a vigilant public, among others a critical press, is significantly inhibited by the practice of defamation suits by state servants in case of public criticism as well as relatively common internal security detentions (Rajah 2012, p. 20).

country subordinates its relevance and its principles to the overarching belief system of pragmatism by political leaders and technocrats, Asian values as well as a focus on development. In this regard constitutional topics were sidelined and in a number of instances the constitution was de facto violated (Thio / Tan 2009).[21]

Paradoxically, it has been pointed out that Singapore's legal system allows for security of property rights, while in principle violating civil rights such as freedom of expression, being in very high regard domestically and internationally and seen as one of the contributing factors for Singapore' economic success (von Alten 1994, p. 68–71). This ambivalence cannot as such be explained by the judiciary's lack of independence from the executive power, since state officials would have an incentive to violate property rights in order to in a short-term orientation skim off assets from entrepreneurs. In this regard the judiciary is in no sense an effective counter-weight.

However, the political leadership manages to overcome those potentially negative incentive effects for the corporate sector through credible commitments to protect property rights by basing its legitimacy on development performance and therefore productive activities of corporations. Such a commitment serves as a functional equivalent for the lack of a high degree of rule of law and thus nevertheless allows for the perception of property rights safety. There tends to be a sort of "performance legitimacy", where credible commitments also extend from the political leadership to technocrats.

By now structural elements of Singapore's state capitalism have been analyzed. Bureaucratic quality and a competitively organized corporate structure in conjunction with the functional equivalent for a certain degree of lack of rule of law are all linked in order to allow for an effective interplay of state and business. The quality of the bureaucracy facilitates strong competition in the corporate sector by allowing for a relatively level playing-field for GLCs, MNCs and

21 A leading minister once referred to Singapore's constitution as being the untidiest and most confusing constitution at the outset of the creation of any country. Curiously, first there was the Parliament that passed the constitution. In this sense the power relationship between the constitution in particular and the judicial system in general is determined. A number of court decisions refrained from constraining the executive at the cost of not sticking to principles laid out in the constitution. In this regard, freedom is a privilege granted and withheld by the government and not a right defended by a strong constitution with the help of a robust court system. Individual cases abound, where for instance citizens are detained without being convicted with any crime for years (Barr 2011, p. 367–368).

private domestic companies. By the same token this mutually complementary interaction is even supported by the legal system, although it is in principle not independent of the executive power. By credible commitments the bureaucracy has likewise enacted a self-constraint as to not favouring certain sectors of the corporate world over others and at the same time refraining from property rights violations.

4.4.3 Policies

Until relatively recently Singapore was considered to be a standard example of a neo-liberal politico-economic system. As has already been maintained with regard to the structure of the city-state's politico-economic order such a proposition cannot reasonably be upheld. At the same time, also when looking at policies a supposedly clear commitment to a liberal regime needs to be taken with more than a grain of salt.

While the city-state indeed integrated into world markets and instituted one of the most liberal trade regimes in the world, still Singapore pursued a remarkably stringent industrial policy, focusing on integrating into world markets, foremost due to the limited size of the domestic market and thereby realizing economies of scale through internationalization.

In this regard it did not ideologically stick to localization incentives, but also fostered global procurement, while in the course of development putting more of an emphasis on producing locally (see Haggard 1986, p. 363 and 367, Low 2006, p. 4–8).[22] But backed by an efficiently working bureaucracy, it formulated and implemented a mix of policies – market and state capitalist –, which were geared towards the politically defined overarching goal of development and retained

22 Intriguingly, initially in 1959, Singapore opted for an import-substitution policy, since it was part of the much larger market of Malaysia. After this arrangement with Malaysia failed, Singapore instead opted to aggressively internationalize, formed for this effort a specific export promotion agency called Intraco and promoted this drive further by the pilot agency EDB operating numerous offices worldwide, which was advantageous for contacts in the business world and the organization thus served as the business card of Singapore (Schein 1996, p. 18–20, Huff 1987, p. 309–310).
Thus, overseas offices of the EDB assisted in venturing into new markets, such as when the office in Taiwan reported early on about success of the electronics industry in that country and that effort was emulated in Singapore (Huff 1995, p. 748–749). Eventually, all of those efforts paid off and the city-state attracted a significant number of MNCs with its initial comparative advantages such as low wages and low taxes (Von Alten 1994, p. 32–38, see Rodan 1989, p. 64 and 94, Kuo / Low 2001, p. 283–285).

control over the economy not least of all due to state ownership as a minority investor of large parts of the corporate sector (see Low 2001, p. 414–416 and Bercuson 1995, p. 1). And in this guidance of the corporate sector the state business nexus according to the literature tended to rely mostly on formal institutional procedures. This is echoed by Expert (Government): "I think, definitely, it is the institutional framework. But I would be lying if I was saying there is no personal connections anymore."

Overall, technocrats tended to in the course of development concentrate on certain sectors and also switched the focus repeatedly, when this appeared to be economically feasible. The state defined and even created sectors, where it had comparative advantages (Rodan 1989, p. 6 and Low 2006, p. 47–53). The EDB in this regard served as a command bridge overviewing and controlling the emergence of each respective new industry with its strong political backing and remarkable cohesiveness. To this end, the EDB screens long-term orientated investors from those with short-term goals. In this regard only one person is responsible, and thus a one-stop-approach is made possible. Consequently, the bureaucracy has a clear focus and orientation on certain sectors and does not indulge in vying for opportunistic bargains (Schein 1996, p. 23).

This on the other hand, does not conflict with the overarching approach of the state to be pragmatic and apply policies that do work, reflected in what King (2008, p. 240) called an "ideology of pragmatism". As such the state does not rule out any policies on ideological grounds (see How 2007). As a result, Singapore as mentioned above pursued a mixture of different policies.

Long-term orientation of the state

To begin with, concerning policy formulation and implementation the long-term orientation of Singapore is striking, succeeding in attracting mostly capital from abroad in the form of foreign direct investments going for instance into new plants by MNCs.

Deyo (1987, p. 16) specifically introduces the term "strategy-directed development". There was a commitment to development and a coherent economic planning fostered by the fact that the political leadership perceived to be in power for long time horizons, which countered the risk of pursuing short-term orientated economic policies or outright rent-seeking (Deyo 1987, p. 16).

This long-term orientation was fostered by five- or ten-year plans, although those did not play as pronounced a role as in other developmental states, underlining pragmatism as Singapore's state doctrine, so that formulated plans were not rigidly implemented and served more as guidelines for policy-makers and bureaucrats, allowing for a large degree of continuity in economic policy and therefore fostering expectations certainty for the corporate sector (von Alten 1994, p. 117–136, Mirza 1986, p. 2, Low 2001 p. 433–435, see Wilson 2011, p. 2).

However, this does not mean that Singapore resorted to purely indicative planning, but rather acted as an occasionally interventionist entrepreneurial state. "It is clear, however, that planning for manufacturing development in Singapore never involved detailed blueprints, because of the priority accorded to reaction to the international market" (Huff 1995a, p. 748). In this regard, policy-making and implementing were to a large extent constrained by international markets, so that a reckless and strict realization of plans was straight from the outset not feasible (Huff 1995b, p. 1433).

This pragmatism was as has already been analyzed enabled through a large degree of state capacity, which transmits into the ability to flexibly adapt while still sticking to core strategies with a long time-horizon. (Yeung 2005).[23] This long-term orientation surfaces when considering how actively the state in the course of Singapore's history pursued a policy of industrial upgrading (Koh / Koh 2002), where the policy of attracting MNCs and offering them reservoirs of low-cost labour and a central location in Southeast Asia, took center stage. But while the elites reacted remarkably flexibly and pragmatically to changes on world markets, such as price modifications or technological upheavals such as progress in gene sequencing and the inception of the internet, structurally the politico-economic system stayed largely unaffected (Wilson / Peebles 2002, p. 19–20).

Changing policy focuses in the course of development

Singapore's ignition of the developmental process dates back to its inception as a nation at the middle of the 1960s, when it concentrated on labour-intensive products such as garments, textiles, toys and wood products (see Deyo 1987, p. 16). This approach profited significantly from simultaneously going through a demographic phase with one of the highest birth-rates in the world (Vasil 2000, p. 5–6). Subsequently, in the 1970s the focus shifted to the production of electronics and IT related products: computer parts, silicon wafers and software. In

23 The propensity towards such a policy approach was largely promoted due to Singapore's lack of size and having to adapt to market situations instead of being able to shape them, effectively being a price taker. This served as a very effective constraint on politico-economic elites to continuously adapt the domestic economic structure and not to engage in such activities as rent-seeking (Wilson / Peebles 2002, Li 2002).

the 1980s Singapore opted for a diversification of its industries and moved into more capital-intensive manufacturing, such as oil refining.

Afterwards, in the 1990s Singapore focused on knowledge intensive technologies, venturing into biomedical manufacturing and doing more research and development. This policy shift was accompanied by becoming at the end of the 1990s an investor in emerging markets in the region, thereby securing essential supply chains and imports of components from subsidiaries of Singaporean corporations. In this regard, those components were then assembled domestically and to a large degree again exported while to a certain extent venturing into new markets (Sim 2011, p. 56, Low 2006, p. 47–53, Vu 2011, p. 5 and 20).

In the meantime, industrial upgrading and adapting the economic structure to price changes on world markets as well as rising wages on the domestic market continued. Starting with the beginning of the 2000s the government decided to move into sectors with a still higher value-added than even high-tech manufacturing and ventured into research intensive industries such as bio technology, but also the commercially lucrative industry of luxury tourism (How 2007). In a certain sense the perception of increasing competition from abroad, not least of all from other East Asian nations led the state to switch from being "developmental" to becoming "entrepreneurial" (Pereira 2004 p. 131–132).[24]

In this regard the government acted up to a degree as a property developer when it created industrial regional parks, among others in Indonesia, Vietnam and China. Profits were only partially reaped from these projects and flowed directly into the state budget. After having acted as an entrepreneur itself the government ceded control to private enterprises or GLCs. The program helped to increase regionalization of the Singaporean economy, but significant financial

---

24 Opposed to other emerging nations the SWFs of Singapore – Temasek a1nd GIC – were not only strategic instruments of Singapore's state in order to foster economic development by maintaining dominance of the state as an economic actor and enhancing Singaporean economic diplomacy and thereby supporting Singapore's relevance in the world economy, but also were successfully constrained to operate profitably (Yeung 2011). At the same time, initially, Singapore concentrated its activities of investing abroad on the US and Europe in an effort to become a high-quality producer. Then in 1993 it shifted its focus from globalization to regionalization in order to grasp the opportunity of reaping the advantage of low labour costs. In this regard the state pursues what can be called "political entrepreneurship", meaning that it paves the way for SOEs and the private corporate sector to do business (Yeung 2000, p. 143–144). During the Asian crisis the state orchestrated significant merger activity among GLCs in order to form more viable entities (Yeung 2000, p. 148–149).

means had to be channeled into this project, which did not pay off from a commercial perspective. Such entrepreneurial activities by the state focused on new technologies such as bio tech, but as pointed out also on regionalization, with the aim of securing access to lower-qualified labour (Yeung 2017).

Regionalization was intended to reduce dependence on foreign capital and vulnerability to international markets. In this regard the state acted as an entrepreneur, substituting for the lack of domestic private entrepreneurship. (Yeung 1998, p. 390–391). All in all, there was lack of entrepreneurs to be found in Singapore to pursue projects, which would serve to fulfill the interests of the EDB to allow for guaranteeing such supply chains. Consequently, GLCs were at the forefront of the regionalization drive as private corporations also tended to lack sufficient scale. One rationale behind regionalization is furthermore feasibly the fact that MNCs with their dominating role in Singapore's economy enter and exit in a rapid manner according to the respective situation on world markets and market conditions in the domestic economy (Yeung 1998, p. 399–400 and 402–403). Therefore, once again the strong institutional capabilities of Singapore's bureaucracy become evident.

At the same time, starting with the 2000s other incremental and pragmatic policy shifts set in to partially move away from investments by large companies to the economic activities of SMEs, among others also through promoting the creation of start-ups geared for the technological upheaval of the internet age (Tsui-Auch 2004). The state fostered SME creation and also its more vital role in Singapore's regionalization strategy through numerous promotion schemes, such as for instance in the area of tax incentives. (Yeung 1998, p. 410–412).

In this regard the state even orchestrated building up of a venture capital industry for financing those endeavours. Government-linked venture firms continue to play a major role and are dominating this industry in Singapore, foremost in bio technology and in electronics (Koh/Koh 2002). This policy shift in the direction of focusing more on SMEs bears the fruits that those engage strongly in the provision of parts and components for international markets and even transfer this expertise to MNCs, in effect creating a "reverse transfer". Local SMEs being explicitly supported by the EDB have comparative advantages in areas such as local knowledge – i.e. local technical specifications, standards and management styles – and are becoming increasingly essential for product designs of customers (see Chew / Yeung 2001).

Thus, in the course of its development Singapore experienced an impressive upgrading of its economic structure from low-cost manufacturing into high-tech production and services and from solely being a destination of capital-flows to investing itself abroad. As pointed out, one factor in recent years has been promoting regionalization of Singaporean firms. All of this amounts to the state in Singapore reacting pragmatically and plan-rationally to contingencies in the evolution of domestic as well as international factors affecting Singapore's economy (Yeung 1999)[25]. But which policy instruments did the state apply in the pursuit of this approach?

Policy content

First of all, one instrument of its selective industrial policy consisted of programs to de facto pick winners, on an industry level as well as on the level of a single company. In this regard this did not per se result in discrimination against certain segments of the corporate sector – meaning GLCs, MNCs or private domestic entities – and thus occasionally foreign firms were favoured as winners.

However, officially, the state never conceded to pick winners and highlighted the de jure setting that the bureaucracy received market signals from the private sector and as a reaction selected certain sectors for a thorough and assiduous promotion (Low 2006, p. 47, Tsui-Auch 2004b). But the practice of picking the winners was abandoned towards the end of the 1990s (Low 2001, p. 420–429).

This perception is echoed by Huff (1995a). State business interaction according to this account functioned largely through incentives in the form of tax concessions, which were pragmatically finetuned according to changes in the country's developmental strategy and therefore it was up to a certain extent refrained from an outright policy of picking the winners (Huff 1995a, p. 748–749, see Yeung 2017).

As a second more intensively utilized policy instrument the technocrats applied labour policies, which were constantly adapted to external and domestic factors (see Rigg 1988, p. 340–352), relatively recently becoming evident in Singapore's reaction to the Asian crisis, which consisted mainly in lowering costs for international capital by reducing wages through informal guiding by the National Wages Council (Chong 2007). Due to political support and the prospect of in the medium term again rising living standards even drastic wage cuts by the NWC – initiated by the EDB – were accepted by the labour force in a city-state where a strong co-optation between the state, business and labour prevails.[26]

25 Typical of Singapore's pragmatic, non-ideological approach is the fact that political leaders partially considered themselves as being democrats and socialists, demonstrating that an a priori orientation towards one economic model was not pursued (Tan 2012, p. 85).

26 This even refers to compulsory arbitration procedures in case of labour disputes (Lim 1983, p. 754–755).

Tellingly, the state intervened in this regard into industrial relations right at the outset of state inception – and therefore also the developmental trajectory – by creating official government-sponsored trade unions (Huat 2017, p. 37).

Especially subsidies for the state's industrial policy program to foster development were financed through such widely suppressed wages (Huff 1999a, p. 30–33). In this regard, labour laws were part of industrial policy with an in general relatively liberal labour market regulation, as epitomized by a limited degree of employee protection.

By the same token, the government strove very decidedly to train and educate the city-state's population, allocating sizable funds for instance in order to support vocational training (Mirza 1986, p 65–66, Yeung 2005, see How 2007, Schein 1996, p. 165, Carney 2009). Owing to this state support MNCs shifted part of their research and development activities to Singapore taking advantage of relatively low costs for a significantly highly technically educated work force. This among others helped Singapore to become the globally leading place for hard-disk drive business (Yeung 2007, p. 18).

At the same time, wage policy was not utilized in a one-way direction. When at the end of the 1970s the state perceived the need to move into production with a higher value-added the state increased wages in order to exert pressure on companies to upgrade production and allow for a higher productivity (Von Alten 1994, p. 34–38, Huff 1987, p. 311–314). In order to incentivize such strategic management decisions, the EDB supported foreign companies among others with grants based on their having to increase local content in production chains (Schein 1996, p. 150) and counted on the potential of technology transfers to local producers (Pereira 2008, p. 1195).[27]

Third, tax policy also served as an instrument in the city-state's developmental strategy with relatively high personal income taxes. Thus, state expenditures throughout Singapore's developmental phase were remarkably high, with certain funds being especially earmarked as a separate budget for developmental purposes. In certain cases, those expenses reached almost one half of the city-state's GDP (Chua 2007, p. 6 and Mirza p. 50–51).[28]

---

27 For fostering those ambitions, it also selectively and aggressively cut taxes and decided to liberalize immigrations policy paying tribute to the fact that the global race for talents intensifies and without the attraction of talents Singapore would not be able to advance into new industries (How 2007).

28 To a significant degree to finance those developmental activities the city-state's revenues from dividends of GLCs were used, where the state acted as a minority investor (Von Alten 1994, p. 104).

Nevertheless, for instance tax breaks were applied for high-tech firms from abroad to relocate to science parks in the city-state's premises. This policy approach was in so far of heightened relevance, since it enabled lighthouse projects to be realized, which fostered the building up of clusters and domestic hubs for delivering products to world markets in activities such as electronics and bio technology. Therefore, in both industries Singapore managed to create clusters, taking advantage of its deep integration into world-markets and also its small size, which facilitates cooperation of cluster firms. (Koh et al. 2003, Low 2006, p. 4–8, Kuo / Low 2001, p. 283–285).[29]

Tax policy in Singapore worked in two directions. Relatively immobile production factors such as the domestic work force were taxed quite intensively, so that enough funds were collected for instance to finance infrastructure such as port facilities, which were indispensable for economic development. Likewise, for more mobile production factors such as international capital Singapore's technocrats granted significant tax incentives. Never in Singapore's history were corporate tax rates raised to an extent that would have imperiled business activities (Low 2006, p. 167, see Huff 1999a).

This indeed attracted a number of internationally operating MNCs and fostered integration into global supply chains and thereby a continuous internationalization of the economy. This policy focus is underlined by the fact that during the city-state's developmental phase MNCs settling in Singapore tended to export more than 50 percent of their output produced in the city-state (Mirza 1986, p. 101).

Fourth, even the liberal trade regime of Singapore can be seen as one form of industrial policy, allowing for a large extent of a free flow of goods and services (von Alten 1994, p. 153). Considering the composition of the corporate sector analyzed above with a strong role for GLCs and also relatively connection-orientated domestic corporations it constrained those segments of the corporate sector to constantly increase competitiveness, since there were hardly any protectionist policies applied in order to nurture those domestic players. Thus, in addition to attracting MNCs liberalized markets also helped to guarantee competitive pressures on the domestic market.

---

29 Intriguingly, even the widely unknown strong performance of Singapore's chemical industry in recent years is attributed to the industrial policies – such as tax policy – implemented by the EDB. Especially in the chemical industry companies realized cluster-based advantages to enhance their capabilities and thus contributed to overall industrial upgrading and economic development (see Wang / Yeung 2000).

Fifth, Singapore did not actively enter into a target-orientated industrial policy rewarding fulfillment of targets with direct subsidies. But on a horizontal basis, incentives were given to the corporations in order to develop commercially into directions desired by the state. Thus, the policy instrument of subsidies was widely applied, occasionally resulting in two thirds of manufactured output paying no taxes. These incentives were among others linked to companies having garnered pioneer status as perceived by the bureaucrats with the intention of allowing for technology transfer (see Huff 1999a, p. 28).

This instrument was not based on operating with direct targets for corporations, but functioned with incentivizing corporations, although at numerous junctures of the developmental course certain sectors were preferred, which the state had singled out as a potential industry of the future (von Alten 1994, p. 170–180). In this regard the state committed overall to development as such, but only gradually went into the offensive of propagating such ambitions as a drive towards higher productivity (Rodan 1989, p. 162). However, it needs to be stressed that at the same time, ambitious goals such as reaching a certain rank internationally, for instance in GDP per capita, or achieving an a priori defined economic growth number were not formulated.

Sixth, the state acted in its industrial policy as an active participant in research and development. It promoted innovations, participating to a large degree in research efforts and did not leave this field to the markets. Thus, special incubators were created, innovation funds set up and financial incentives for companies given. This policy of the government was in its core selective and did not solely work by giving companies horizontal incentives.

There is a constant planning in innovation policy with revolving multi-year plans. Singapore specializes in its innovation activities on electronics, but has recently increased its efforts in bio technology. Specially favoured local companies indeed managed to reduce the innovation gap to more developed economies, but a lot of innovation still comes from GLCs. In effect, one of the core problems of state promotion of innovation is a tendency to foster concentration, which conflicts with the goal of fostering SMEs and creation of start-ups (Wang 2018, p. 400–407).

This innovation policy was significantly promoted through what is called institutional thickness in the literature meaning that developments of and in the tech-sector were surrounded by a dense network of institutions. This furthermore helped industrial upgrading in a city-state, where due to rising wages comparative advantages of being a low-cost producer gradually eroded (Phillips / Yeung 2003, p. 723).

Seventh, opposed to typical state capitalist countries the state had only few levers to implement its industrial policy – with constant industrial upgrading through adoption as the core goal – by controlling the financial means of entities.[30] Although the city-state had a bank-dominated financial sector, under a liberal trade and investment regime foreign actors dominated. Only a few domestic players existed. However, in the course of development starting from the 1980s the state perceived the opportunity to deepen development by forming a financial center for the region in Singapore among others through a certain – though half-hearted – privatization of GLCs through IPOs (Mirza 1986, p. 126 and 158 and Low 2006, p. 222).[31]

In this sense, technocrats could not effectively steer entities with a carrot and stick strategy founded on financial control and instead had to rely on instruments such as those analyzed above, but also supported for instance by the EDB being authorized to grant loans or permit investments (von Alten 1994, p. 170–180). The structure of the financial system gave corporations either the means to finance themselves through international banks, eventually through financial markets or the state. The latter was indeed a significant source of credit for the corporate sector (Tsui-Auch 2004).

Overall, an analysis of policy content and implementation in Singapore has highlighted how the state displayed a significant capability to adapt to changing external and internal conditions with consistently modifying its policies in order to keep its comparative advantages through numerous historical phases such as increasing domestic salaries towards the end of the 1970s and the emergence of an internet economy starting around the turn of the millennium.

This state interventionism from a policy content perspective relied largely on regulating wage growth as well as tax policy (Huff 1995b, p. 1431). Moreover, navigating through these changing internal and external conditions of the business environment was accomplished without relying on the coordinating functions of business associations. The state dealt directly with entities and did not

30 In general, such a structure of the financial sector was not to the detriment of the city-state. Singapore's financial sector in the course of the city-state's developmental trajectory was resilient enough to cope with numerous crises. Mostly in such situations Singapore was affected through the trade channel, since the economies of major Asian trade partners contracted or stagnated (Bhaskaran / Wilson 2011, p. 22).

31 To some extent this policy decision was also due to a perception of the state – meaning political leadership and technocrats alike – of weakening competitiveness with one cause being wage cuts, but the policy response also consisted in a further liberalization of the financial sector (Bhaskaran 2003).

rely on such organizations to bundle interests of the business community (Low 2001, p. 418–422).

Entrepreneurial state

Most of all Singapore's bureaucrats and policy makers reacted by identifying new priority sectors with large potential through dealing with corporations on an individual basis, and thus concentrated on industries where sizable future returns were to be expected. In this regard the overarching policy approach of the bureaucracy was not only pragmatic, but especially entrepreneurial.[32] Investments by the state tended to be market orientated, since instead of crowding out private investments they usually crowded in those investments by being complementary to those of private business (Huff 1995a, p. 746–747).

The city-state does rely at critical junctures of its developmental phase on bureaucrats and policy makers acting in concert with the corporate sector – but not through business organizations – however, also including labour representatives. In general, the policies, which could for reasons of scope only briefly be dealt with in this study, were of a complex nature. The prerequisite for assessing effects of those highly complex instruments while at the same time balancing the interests of numerous players in the corporate sector from abroad and the home market, is a highly qualified task. Since for reasons of flexibility technocrats need to be granted a certain degree of discretion instruments such as innovation and tax policy could only be applied through a bureaucracy of high quality as it has been identified above for Singapore. This decidedly strong institutional capacity – as evident in structure and policies of the politico-economic order – needs subsequently be scrutinized from the perspective of performance. Therefore, in the next sub-section this aspect of the case study is dealt with.

32 As an example, serves Singapore' entry into the IT industry with a comprehensive and coordinated effort of multiple agencies. High cohesiveness clearly worked to the advantage of this endeavor. Members of the corporate sector served in the decision-making board, taking account of business needs and marketability (Wong 1992, p. 1817-1819). A further example is the reorganization of former telecommunications monopoly Singtel as a joint effort of the EDB and the National Computer Board, basically enabling the company to expand into export markets and also concentrating on services. This state effort was not to the detriment of the entity, since the SOE kept on operating profitably, reducing the urgency of privatizing the corporation (Heng / Low 1990, p. 307 and 311).

4.4.4 Performance

As has been the case with Russia and Kazakhstan no scientifically grounded causation between structure and policies of the politico-economic system as independent variables on the one hand and performance as a dependent variable can be verified here. This is beyond the scope of this study. However, some indications of how the politico-economic system of Singapore performed can be given at this point. It will be analyzed how Singapore performed with regard to the overall economy, in governance indicators, economic growth as well as in indicators of development.

First of all, in the literature there are numerous accounts of how superior Singapore's politico-economic system did perform compared to other late-industrializing and developing nations. For instance, Huff (1995b, p. 1431) points out that Singapore's policy approach proved to be extraordinarily successful in terms of developmental indicators and competitiveness of the domestic industry. This is echoed by Yeung (1998, p. 395), who identifies a remarkable economic growth in the city-state.

Such assessments are repeated in virtually every account about Singapore's developmental course and for reasons of scope are not reiterated here. Rather it is referred to relevant figures, such as first those of the Governance Indicators of the World Bank (2019a). First of all, it is striking that regarding control of corruption Singapore scores from 1996 – this is the first year for which data is available – until 2017 on average 97.58 percentile points which means that the city-state is even among industrialized nations one of the least corrupt.

This remarkable performance in lack of corruption is accompanied by Singapore being in a number of years the country with the highest of all analyzed nations in the World Bank's sample for Governance Indicators regarding government effectiveness with a score of 100. For the relevant time frame this transmits into an average value of 99.1 percentile points in government effectiveness. This corresponds strongly with the results already identified by the literature survey conducted above. And in regulatory quality the average score is with 99.08 almost in line with government effectiveness. This serves as quantitative evidence for the results derived from the literature survey above. Evidently, the state business nexus of Singapore is functioning very effectively.

Considering the degree of rule of law, however, there are fewer percentile points for the relevant time frame. On average the country scores in this regard 92.25 percentile points, which is still one of the best results of the sample, but as a matter of fact significantly less than what Singapore scores in the other governance dimensions presented above. Here such factors as cases of arbitrary arrests and the minor role of the constitution in the legal framework of Singapore – as has been argued above – come into play.

However, it needs to be maintained that the degree of rule of law has significantly improved in Singapore over the relevant time frame. The city-state started out in 1996 with 87.94 percentile points, which gradually improved to 96.63 for the most recent data available, meaning for 2017. This remarkably high score – as analyzed above – mirrors the fact that in Singapore the state is able to protect property rights and in commercial law operates one of the most effective legal systems of the World Bank sample.

However, the suppression of political rights reverberates in Singapore's notoriously low scores regarding voice and accountability. Here the country reaches only 45.89 percentile points and for 2017 it was even only 41,38 percentile points. Obviously, there is no civil society in place to provide for effective accountability of the political leadership and the bureaucracy to the public. The state tends to utilize the concept of civil society only as a means to induce citizens to be acquiescent and consequently refrain from voicing opposition (Tan 2007, p. 8 and 30).[33]

But as has been analyzed above there are numerous mechanisms in Singapore in place that even with a lack of political competition and regard for civil rights the state business machinery of Singapore works significantly well. This is not least of all due to the fact that formal and informal institutions in the country are geared towards meritocracy and in the corporate sector as such a high intensity of competition prevailed.

This highly effectively working politico-economic system translated into strong economic growth rates in the course of development. Thus, from state inception in 1965 until the most recent available data from the World Bank (2019b) for the year 2017 Singapore achieved on average an annual real economic growth rate of 7.54 percent. In the course of its development in numerous years – especially in the 1980s – the city-state's GDP even grew with consistently more than 10 percent.

33 Checks and balances in the political realm are also not to be identified. There existed only a fragmented opposition that mainly consisted of individual charismatic leaders who utilized a party to promote their own agenda. Efficient opposition party structures nearing the cohesiveness and degree of unity of the party apparatus of the ruling PAP are not to be found in the developmental process of Singapore (Barr 2004). Thus, action of the opposition was largely ineffective.

And economic growth rates tend even today to range higher than those of other developed nations. Thus, for 2017 the city-state realized a real GDP growth rate of 3.62 percent. From this perspective, the economic performance of Singapore's politico-economic order is striking. But overall, it was the goal of the elites – meaning political and technocratic leaders – to provide for increasing living standards of the population, which can best be captured by looking at development indicators.

Here data from the UNDP (2019) reveal that in the Human Development Index (HDI) Singapore is by now on a par with other developed nations, since the city-state scores 0.932 points out of 100 points in the HDI for 2017. Unfortunately, there is HDI data from the UNDP available only starting from 1990 and therefore long after the country embarked on its developmental course. However, for this time frame from 1990 until 2017 the city-state achieved on average 0.842 points with a discernible upward trend. Thus, in 1990 Singapore scored 0.718 points and in 2000 0.819 points, so that a clear upward movement is observable. This is a clear indication that significant results in economic growth also transmitted into overall development and therefore improved living standards for the population.

In a nutshell, this quantitatively orientated sub-section has illustrated that Singapore's politico-economic system – as it has been presented regarding its structure and policies – managed to realize significant performance results not only in economic growth, but also development. Since it is the purpose of a case study to answer why questions, it has been with the help of a literature survey been verified that the structure and policies of Singapore's state business order did at least largely contribute to this performance. However, a developmental effort tends to be initiated by the political leadership. And the characteristics of Singapore's political leadership with an eye on actor centricity will be illustrated in the next sub-section.

4.4.5 Actor-centricity

As illustrated above there are profound advantages and disadvantages of actor-centricity being in the hands of a political leader. As a matter of fact, especially at critical junctures actor-centricity facilitates enforcing policy steps that in the short-run carry significant social costs and tend to diminish the living-standards of broader parts of the population. Long-term these measures can pay-off for the country in the form of – owing to higher competitiveness on world markets – more exports, sustainable economic growth and eventually higher living-standards.

In case of a reduced or even non-existing actor-centricity there is a risk of the state – meaning government and bureaucracy – giving in to vested interests that tend to be short-term orientated. However, on the other hand such a constraint of being embedded into a network of formal and informal institutional frameworks diminishes the risk of the political leader acting arbitrarily, potentially transforming the country into a predatory state, and thus seeking short-term gains.

In the case of Singapore, state founder and political leader for the majority of the developmental course, Lee Kuan-Yew, was only relatively unconstrained in his decision-making. There existed numerous checks and balances. As a matter of fact, Singapore during its developmental phase tended to be much more formed by the ruling party PAP[34] and the ensuing formal and informal rules than by the political leader Lee.

Low (2001) formulates this phenomenon with referring to the widespread theme in Singapore "in PAP we trust". Thus, up to a certain extent Singapore relied more on processes than on persons (Low 2001, p. 420–429). The developmental path was therefore significantly shaped by PAP rule and there was more of a one-party than a one-man rule (Mauzy / Milne 2002, p. 144). PAP dominance was at the same time fostered by the PAP having independent resources and it did therefore not hinge on donations by companies, which would have potentially intensified state business relations to an extent bordering on crony state capitalism. In this sense, the PAP kept relatively strict boundaries between the state and business even in the process of creation of GLCs and consequently upheld a high degree of autonomy (Gomez 2003, p. 25, Chong 2015).

In a certain sense, in Singapore there was a distinction between the person of Lee and the belief system of the PAP, meaning pragmatism, and what can be termed as perpetual revisionism so that there are constant incremental changes. Whereas the former was considered to be of minor importance, the latter was a quintessential factor for the state of Singapore to define itself. In this regard only incremental criticism against the PAP is allowed and the opposition is in a certain sense organized under the umbrella of the state. The red line that the opposition is not allowed to cross is open confrontation while being allowed to voice

---

34 The initially social democrat PAP was also in so far synonymous with the state of Singapore, since it organized the transition of the city-state into independence (Vasil 2000, p. 5–6).

criticism behind closed doors (Barr 2003, p. 78–79). Consequently, as such Lee was an integral part of a larger mission that by far transcended his own person.[35]

Development as the Basis for Legitimacy

However, this reign hinged on the performance regarding development. In this sense, the legitimacy of Singapore's government is based on economic prosperity (Barr 2003, p. 93, Peebles / Wilson 2002, p. 5, Vasil 2000, p. 18), but this did not mean that elites and broader parts of the population insisted on short-term increases in living-standards. Rather they expected to in the medium term reap the fruits of a pragmatic industrial policy being efficiently implemented. This acquiescence of broader parts of the population was likewise increased by the political leadership taking an active role in the provision of cheap housing, meaning below market prices (Huff 1995a p. 753, Hill / Lian 1995).[36]

Such a strategy by the political leadership resulted in a highly inclusive social policy, so that large parts of the population participated in and profited from the developmental process of the city-state (Goodman et al. 1998, p. XV). However, overall, primarily economic growth was the fully and credibly pursued goal of the government. All other potential goals – such as an equitable development – were subordinated under this key goal and supposed to be subsequently reached (Wilson / Peebles 2002, p. 17).

It meant that due to credible commitments and a social contract – i.e. that in the medium-term living standards will improve – the political leadership in concert with the EDB was able to impose even unpopular decisions on elites and broader parts of the population (Yeung 2005). Here the political leadership demonstrated a significant degree of political skills and acumen by setting itself realistic and credible goals, while still being ambitious and in most instances the

35 Vennewald (1994, p. 52) takes a slightly different view. He refers to a highly personalized system based on the loyalty to the prime minister, i.e. for many years Lee. In this system power and control supposedly are highly centralized. And in this significantly personalized system according to this account endemic corruption is prevented by a complex rotation system, high salaries and harsh punishments for accepting bribes. Barr / Skrbis rather share a similar perception that there were some traces of a personality cult around Lee discernible, but on the whole, they point out that Lee acted within the mechanisms of the ruling party PAP, which served as a certain constraint on his powers (Barr / Skrbis 2008, p. 59–60).

36 As a matter of fact, the state traditionally enlarged its land holdings and tends to own between 70 to 80 percent of all available land (Von Alten 1994, p. 153).

state delivered on these commitments (see Low 2001 p. 433–435). Incentives to indeed realize developmental goals and accountability were at the same time significantly increased by the PAP regularly having to compete in at least partially democratic elections (Huff 1999b p. 1431).

Overall, the technocratic approach of policy formulation and implementation again comes to the fore. This primacy of bureaucratic rationality was only possible owing to the backing of the political leadership, so that within the institutional constraints the political leadership had discretion to credibly commit to support the EDB and its policy approach. In this sense, the explicit statement that Singapore is a meritocracy[37] and relies on strategic pragmatism in political as well as bureaucratic leadership increased the room of maneuver for the EDB and other economic agencies (Yeung 2005, p. 170–171 and 185). This reverberates in the perception of Expert (Government): "We (i.e. the EDB, A.W.) believe in meritocracy in the Singapore government. Of course, for us whoever is the strongest is the best is best doing the job, we are going with that."

This created a virtuous circle and a positive reputational equilibrium, where through a credible commitment to subordinate all other political objectives to developmental goals and eventually indeed a convincing economic performance was delivered, the political leadership gained legitimacy in the population, thereby increasing political stability.[38] This in turn increased investor confidence, since foreign and domestic companies regard political stability highly in their investment decisions and that by the same token likewise increased developmental performance (Huff 1999b, see Li 2002).

Vulnerability of Singapore

One decisive factor facilitating credible commitments and a modicum of actor centricity within institutional bounds was Singapore's perceived high degree of

37 In a certain sense the principle of meritocracy was even applied in order to counter tendencies within the electorate of demanding more political participation and an orientation towards Western consumer patterns (Hill / Lian 1995). Other overarching belief systems as the foundation stones of the informal institutional framework were multi-racialism, multi-culturalism, patriotism and an emphasis on political stability (King 2008, p. 151, Tan 2007, p. 4).

38 Concededly, also due to idiosyncrasies of informal institutions in Singapore – among others a strong Confucian tradition – no political protests erupted, since the technocratic response to economic challenges was perceived as being wise and for the best of the city-state (Chong 2007).

vulnerability, as is typical of a developmental state. On the one hand the city-state was from the outside imperiled by the military might of much larger neighbour-countries and domestically it had to cope with the challenges of a multi-ethnic population (Low 2006, p. 96, see Regnier 2000, p. 59).[39]

The political leadership in this regard explicitly stresses vulnerability of the city-state as a means of upholding PAP rule, which also tended to increase inner party cohesiveness, but also of the polity as such, and this perceived vulnerability extended also to fears about assimilating to Western decadence as well as to Muslim extremism (Peebles / Wilson 2002, Hill / Lian 1995, Vasil 2000, p. 17).

Such a sense of vulnerability is furthermore reinforced by the state stressing the strong dependence of Singapore on the vagaries of international markets (Huat 2017, p. 2 and 34). And in accordance with the concept of the developmental state this vulnerability was utilized by the political leadership to align interests of elites with those of the broader population in order to by realizing developmental goals reduce effectively the city-state's vulnerability.

To conclude, the political leadership of Singapore tended to be embedded into structures of the ruling party PAP. However, within these constraints a certain degree of actor centricity still prevailed such as is evident by the fact that state founder Lee personally mistrusted ethnic Chinese entrepreneurialism and therefore marginalized these business-men. Overall, the reduced actor-centricity in an otherwise autocratic regime helped significantly to create the politico-economic order of Singapore with its emphasis on rationality, meritocracy and pragmatism while at the same time the relevance of personal connections was effectively subdued.

After having analyzed structure, policies, performance and actor-centricity in Singapore in the following sub-section in a concise fashion the characteristics of Singapore's economic order are presented. Tentatively reasons for the outstanding development of the city-state are given.

4.4.6 Singapore's Hybrid Form of Capitalism

As has been pointed out above Singapore displays a hybrid form of capitalism. Consequently, it can be neither classified as being state nor market capitalist. Taking into account the constituting principles of state capitalism first of all there undoubtedly prevails a high degree of state dominance in the economy, being

39 So, it comes as little surprise that historically close to half of the government operating expenditures were designated for security purposes (Low 2006, p. 96).

first of all demonstrated in the form of minority state holdings in GLCs and secondly in the overarching role of the EDB concerning activities of the corporate sector.[40] This transmitted into a situation, where the state actively formulated and implemented industrial policies, and consequently acted in a state capitalistic fashion. Furthermore, as has been pointed out above, the bureaucracy of Singapore displayed a sufficient capacity to be able to implement and assist in the formulation of industrial policy.

However, the limits of the state's powers are already evident when looking at the financial sector and therefore the second constituting principle of state capitalism. Here MNCs do dominate and thus there are hardly any levers for the state to steer the financial sector into desired directions or utilize it for the purposes of its industrial policy. And correspondingly, regarding shielding its domestic markets Singapore cannot in any form be considered as being state capitalist, since in trade as well as the foreign investment regime Singapore established a very liberal system with only few barriers for actors from abroad. Obviously, by the same token Singapore did not erect a communist system, although initially within the PAP there were traces of socialist activities.

And regarding rule of law as the final constituting principle of state capitalism the entire degree of the hybrid character of Singapore's politico-economic order comes to the fore, when taking into account that regarding civil rights and criminal law there are short-comings in the quality of the legal system, whereas the extent of property rights protection is among the best world-wide. The legal system of Singapore has its roots in the British law system and thereby common law. It is in high regard domestically as well as internationally and its existence is widely seen as one of the contributing factors for Singapore' economic success (von Alten 1994, p. 68–71). Thus, also in this regard, Singapore constitutes no immaculate case of a state capitalist country.

Overall, four out of seven constituting principles of state capitalism are fulfilled by Singapore. However, the reliance on a liberalized trade and investment regime as well as the degree to which the state refrained from dominating the financial sector reveals that Singapore after all is not state capitalist, but due to state dominance of the corporate sector also not market capitalist.[41]

---

40 As a matter of fact, in Singapore even venture funds were dominated by the state financing projects and by the EDB attracting large technology-orientated corporations from abroad. (Tsui-Auch 2004b).

41 Wilson / Peebles take a slightly different view. Starting from the mid-1990s according to their perception Singapore is to be considered a developed nation, but nevertheless kept in principle being state capitalist (Wilson / Peebles 2002 p.10)

Reasons for Singapore's strong developmental Performance

Clearly, as has been illustrated above Singapore achieved a remarkable progress in terms of development. However, the developmental path of the city-state is not without critics. Thus, for instance Krugman (1994) compares Singapore to the Soviet Union and highlights the low productivity of Singapore's economy. He argues that the economy was marked by little creativity and relied on massive inputs of the production factors capital and labour.

Having come to a rather similar conclusion as Krugman political leadership and bureaucracy of Singapore reacted and therefore in the 1990s Singapore became the only country in the world to formulate a total factor productivity (TFP) growth target, i.e. of 2 percent. Policy changes were made to venture into industries, which require higher qualified and more creative labour, such as in biotech. (see Huff 1999b).

This development all the more demonstrates how the state in Singapore, although consisting of self-confident politicians and technocrats is not deceitful and has the capacity to adapt, in order to tackle weaknesses in its structure and policies. Consequently, most striking about Singapore's economic order are the belief systems of meritocracy and pragmatism as well as strong institutional capabilities.

This flexibility can be illustrated by taking into account how after the Asian crisis a rethinking set in to partially move away from investments by large companies to economic activities of SMEs, among others also through creation of start-ups. The government fostered entrepreneurship in the bio-tech-sector, attracted top researchers from abroad and funded research institutions (Tsui-Auch 2004b). Correspondingly, a large element of paternalism by the state remained in order to reduce political discontent to a minimum. Consequently, this authoritarian developmental state played a dominant role on housing markets, ensuring that accommodation for its citizens is virtually guaranteed, which especially favours households with low incomes (see Low 2006). Therefore, Singapore is a case, where in a very paternalistic fashion owing to a rationally and pragmatically acting state a remarkable performance was achieved, while at the same time holding inequality to acceptable levels.

Singapore as a hybrid form of State Capitalism

All in all, Singapore displays a number of elements of a typical developmental state, for instance strong bureaucratic capabilities. However, there is as explained above such a significant deviation from state capitalism in some regards that it is a hybrid form. First of all, in Singapore it is striking that the state acted in its function as an investor with minority holdings. Therefore, in the classification of Musacchio / Lazzarini presented above Singapore presents a case of minority investor capitalism.

Through its role as a junior partner in GLCs, however, the state is among others able to complementarily to its overall industrial policy steer the corporate sector. In this regard, it managed to avoid the trap of a classical market state dichotomy. Its success significantly hinged on combining market principles and state interventions with each other (Huff 1995 p. 754 and p. 748–749, see Wilson / Peebles 2002, p. 13).

One additional striking element of Singapore's politico-economic order is its export orientation[42] and the overall liberal trade and investment regime served as an effective constraint to counter a potential evolution of the state business nexus into crony relations. The remarkable developmental success can therefore to a large extent be attributed to large inflows of foreign labour and capital. Factor accumulation consequently played an overarching role during the developmental process of Singapore. (Pang / Lim 2015).

At the same time Singaporean capitalism never took the form of neoliberalism. The economic model during the entire developmental phase reminds Huff even of "socialism".[43] He points to the fact that the government drastically intervened into savings and investment decisions, for instance by wage repression and deep taxation of immobile production factors, facilitating in the face of an occasionally alleged over-investment a traditionally low growth of productivity, as has also been criticized by Krugman. However, Huff evaluates Singaporean industrial policy as "growth-maximizing" (Huff 1995 p. 749–750).

In this sense, Singapore is a classic example of a late industrializing country, getting the prices wrong. The state did distort the price mechanism, especially of factor prices, but such a move as keeping wages below market prices improved the competitive advantage of the city-state as a manufacturing hub. At the same time, therefore adjustments being triggered by market forces were postponed. Such adaptations in the course of development tended to be rather state- than

42 Overall, Singapore demonstrates that in order to opt for export orientation it is not obligatory to have prior for a relatively long time-frame focused on import substitution. However, this is an important lesson for small countries. Large countries tend to be in a better position to initially rely on substituting imports (Huff 1987, p. 305–326).

43 That perception is echoed by Wilson / Peebles referring to state interventions and a de facto one-party rule over large passages of Singapore's developmental courses earning the city-state a reputation as pursuing a form of socialism that works and the state acting pragmatically to an upmost extent (Peebles / Wilson 2002, p.16–17 and 20).

market-led. Therefore, change tended to be rather incremental. But which patterns in institutional change can be accounted for during the developmental process and which one could possibly be expected for the future?

Avenues for Institutional Change

Overall, there were only gradual institutional changes in the course of Singapore's development. The most drastic alteration consisted of the fact that the PAP at the start of Singapore's independence adhered to a belief system of socialism shaped by British Fabians and this inclination gradually evolved to a belief system based on an US thinking about free markets combined with neo-confucianism, state activism and economic pragmatism (Lee 2008, p. XII and 68).

Indeed, the state – strongly dominated by the ruling party PAP – committed credibly to growth and a tightly knit society. By the same token, in staffing decisions preference was given to technocrats and not to politically well-connected charismatic persons. This promoted an institutional framework, where state and society all interacted in order to mutually achieve the national ambition of development, meaning that unions, corporate and political leaders, the financial sector and technocrats all cooperated to achieve this end. There were not as in other emerging countries rivalling factions fighting for influence and power. There was a high degree of cohesiveness in the pursuit of developmental goals as well as in the means to achieve this goal (see Chong 2007, p. 953–955).[44]

In this sense, structurally, there were few changes in Singapore's developmental phase regarding the state-business nexus, composition of the corporate sector as well as the legal system. There were also few privatization efforts of the state and the relative dominance of ministries and GLCs persisted. At the same time policy-wise the state reacted flexibly and ad-hoc. Therefore, modifications

---

44 For this remarkable cohesiveness there are a number of explanations. In the eyes of Singapore's political leadership and broad segments of the population virtue and competence are closely linked. Elite formation and selection are at the same time driven forward by generous financing of elitist schools and universities, later on being continued by scholarships for prestigious international universities. Elites are mostly recruited from similar ethnic groups, universities and even families. Among others through this formation process a high degree of cohesion and esprit de corps are fostered among the class of technocrats in the ministries and GLCs. These elites are supposed to constantly replenish themselves, staying sharp and nimble. It is intended to keep elites basing their rule on merits and not heritage, countering the risk of elites transforming themselves into mere power groups that extract wealth from the population (Barr 2014 and Barr 2016, p. 4–7).

were mainly caused by technological changes on an international level, such as advances in ICT (Wilson / Peebles 2002, p. 19–20).

There was hardly anything organic or natural in the process of this evolution of Singapore's politico-economic system. It was based on micro-management by the state and ownership of all developmental processes was claimed by the PAP government, which based its legitimacy on eventual success of its efforts (Barr / Skrbis 2008, p. 6). The overarching belief systems and guiding principles of an elitist meritocracy were the driving factor behind the few institutional changes taking place in Singapore in the form of intensifying for instance state dominance of the corporate sector by formation of GLCs as well as SWFs. Correspondingly, the dominating role of the pilot agency EDB and primacy of technocratic rule had never been questioned or quintessentially been diminished.

However, within this established order certain tendencies toward the evolution of a family system are discernible. Obviously, ethnic Chinese with rather similar background coalesce into one cohesive elitist group with limited access for outsiders even with means of merits and this could potentially in the course of time usher in an institutional change towards a more crony economic order (Barr 2014).

This potential deterioration of Singapore's economic order into more of a system of crony relations is reflected by an erosion of self-confidence of the political leadership and technocrats starting with the 2000s. In a number of official speeches mistakes were conceded by leading politicians and this modicum of an unusual self-critical assessment was induced by the PAP losing ground in elections (Barr 2016, p. 9).

This is reminiscent of a gradual institutional change, since even the political opposition mostly demands small modifications and at the utmost there is a tendency to perceive the elites increasingly as ordinary and not exceptional, which appears to indicate an inclination towards transformation in the direction of a market capitalist system. Constituents are demanding competence and view technocrats and the PAP increasingly as not anymore intrinsically superior in virtue and achievement (Barr 2016).

Consequently, there is overall a prudent deviation from the hybrid form of capitalism towards more market-based element. One reason is that for the state it has become more difficult to steer industrial transformation. A contributing factor is that national firms operate more internationally and thus decouple from developments in Singapore, making interventions more difficult. These companies increasingly disembed from the politico-economic system of Singapore and integrate much more into global supply chains.

The latter are governed by inter-firm dynamics and shaped by the necessity to compete on international markets. In this regard, the state is not entirely steering domestic firms and industrial transformation anymore. Therefore, the developmental trajectory hinges much more than before on domestic firms acting successfully on their own as entities operating purely market capitalistic (Yeung 2014).

In this regard, such a gradual transformation of Singapore into a market economy results in the fraying of the state's exceptionalism as well as its superiority and therefore the broader population doubts the unrivalled knowledge of technocrats. Correspondingly, PAP rule and the ensuing performance legitimacy are not taken as given anymore by the electorate (Barr 2016, p. 1–2).

Thus, there appears to be a transformation of the politico-economic system of Singapore from two sides. On the one hand, in the corporate sphere there tend to be fewer interventions by the state and also in GLCs the state appears to pull back its influence. And in the political sphere technocrats and the PAP are not perceived as being per se exceptional anymore and therefore a tendency towards a competitive authoritarianism is increasingly in evidence in Singapore (see Barr 2016).

Economically, the erosion of state dominance needs to be orchestrated prudentially. It is quintessential to consolidate the institutional capacities when transforming from a state capitalist to a more market capitalist economic system. The solution is to not in the wake of rigorous liberalization allow for a weak state, but to uphold the institutional framework while permitting more private sector initiatives and thereby less state intervention (Yeung 2000).

On the one hand, whereas an institutional transformation towards a more market capitalist system appears to be likely with more privatization and deregulation, there is on the other hand the risk of the city-state eroding into more crony relations and practices. When the state dilutes the extent to which it acts with a strong hand, initially East Asian style relations-orientated forms of doing business can in the informal institutional framework be reinvigorated.

Such a situation can deteriorate to a degree that those more crony informal institutions spill over into the formal institutional framework. Incrementally, the legislature in conjunction with the government can adopt such laws as to allow for less transparency, accountability and hard budget constraints. In this sense, it is not a merely theoretical conjecture that Singapore erodes from its hybrid economic order into a crony state capitalist system.

However, as Singapore's politico-economic order exists today, it displays strong institutional capabilities with the structural and policy strengths illustrated above which translate into a remarkable performance in terms of development. Its economic order is seen as a role model by a vast range of countries among emerging nations, for instance also Russia and Kazakhstan. But it needs to be taken into account that this hybrid system of capitalism emerged in a process based on numerous feedback mechanisms, gradually determining the city state's politico-economic structure and its policies.

Therefore, this relatively unique politico-economic system, which now apparently incrementally transforms into a form of market capitalism is the outcome of evolutionary processes and cannot deterministically serve as a blueprint for a one-by-one re-implementation in other countries (see Chong 2015). In order to better illustrate how unique Singapore is even among East Asian developmental states subsequently it is turned to the last case study, where the politico-economic order of South Korea during its developmental course is analyzed.

4.5 South Korea

Most of all Singapore and South Korea were selected for the purpose of replication in covering the developmental state in an analysis of state capitalism and how profound performance differences can be accounted for. However, there are also some fundamental differences and this deviance from a theoretical point allows for a number of fruitful results concerning the analysis. South Korea already started its developmental phase in 1961 with the coup of general Park Chung-hee, which is about the same point of time of Singapore's embarking on a developmental course with state inception in 1965.

On the other hand, Russia and Kazakhstan followed with their developmental ambitions significantly later in 1999 and 1991 respectively. As a matter of fact, South Korea sticks out of the sample of selected countries by its ethnically homogenous population. With a population of roughly 50 million it is significantly smaller than Russia, but much larger than Singapore and Kazakhstan. Of relevance is also the fact that opposed to Russia and Kazakhstan South Korea has no mentionable natural resources to allow for some income. In this regard, a similarity to Singapore emerges, which to the same extent depended on the import of natural resources, but correspondingly never risked to fall into the trap of the resource curse, for instance Dutch disease or the pitfalls of a rentier economy.

As is the case with Singapore and Kazakhstan, the politico-economic order of the country was to a highly significant degree formed by another country. As a colonial power from 1910 until 1945 Japan with brutal force industrialized certain parts of the country and integrated the economy of its colony into the own supply chain of production, thereby increasing Korea's dependence on the militarily and economically superior colonizer. Whether for South Korea's economy

(North Korea as a special case of probably the only remaining Stalinist country of the world shall be left out at this point) this colonization through Japan had more development-enhancing or development-inhibiting consequences is a highly debated topic in the literature. Since in the form of path dependence the Japanese legacy had profound effects on South Korea's developmental course, it is at certain points of the analysis referred to this.

South Korea has especially been selected, since it is deemed to have been state capitalist in the form of the developmental state. Since Singapore represents a hybrid case of the developmental state, it appears especially fruitful to analyze this economic order with its reliance on technology transfers, the large companies or chaebols and an aversion to allow MNCs into the country.

4.5.1 Preliminaries

For the subsequent analysis as in the case of Singapore a thorough literature survey is conducted. This entails some problems, since the relevant time span for this analysis is from 1961 until South Korea's inclusion into the group of industrialized nations in the OECD in 1996, and recent literature tends to deal with the current economic order of South Korea. Nevertheless, observations regarding the current politico-economic framework of South Korea are mostly excluded from the analysis and only dealt with towards the end of the case study when relating to institutional change of the state capitalist order of the developmental state.

There is a vast collection of data from the literature included in conducting the subsequent analysis. However, since there has been such a vast amount of research been conducted about the developmental state of South Korea and this topic tends to in itself entail enough complexity for deserving a dissertation project while here its scope is limited to a case study, there will only be the most relevant literature about the developmental state and the reasons for its surprising performance results covered. As has been the goal with all case studies of this dissertation project, the focus is on dealing with why South Korea achieved a certain degree of developmental success. Since this study is qualitatively grounded again no straightforward quantitatively verified correlation between on the one hand independent variables such as structure and policies and on the other hand the dependent variable of performance will be established.

Rather this study endeavours to with a high plausibility – based on expert perceptions – verify whether the study propositions formulated above can be upheld for South Korea. This effort has already been undertaken for Russia, Kazakhstan and Singapore and its results will in a comparative fashion with the inclusion of South Korea be presented in section 4.6. But for now, it is turned to the case study of South Korea as being considered to having been a state capitalist system of a developmental state variant during its developmental phase.

4.5.2 Structure

In this sub-section first of all, as a variable allowing for a certain performance in development, the structure of South Korea's economic order is analyzed. To this end, it is differentiated between quality of the bureaucracy, structure of the corporate sector and the degree of rule of law. This tends to be a fruitful approach, since according to Mason et al. (1980, p. 6) and other sources all three factors are interdependent and in sum allow for an assessment as to whether the structure did rather enhance or rather inhibit development. This analysis serves as the backbone in order to determine whether the state had the capacity and capability to formulate and implement an effective industrial policy in order to industrialize and develop the country.

Quality of the Bureaucracy

To begin with, it is striking that in South Korea the pilot agency Economic Planning Board (EPB) was erected, where the state tended to assemble the most competent bureaucrats in a centralized fashion (Chibber 2002, p. 975–977, Han / Kim 2017, p. 57 and p. 69). In general, the EPB served more in the form of a commanding height in a vertically administered system that was dominated by top-down commercial, political and technocratic relations (Tsui-Auch 2004b).

Entry into this organization was very competitive and limited to the best graduates – often coming from foreign universities – who moreover had to pass through entry tests. Between 1949 and 1980 only about 2 percent of applicants for the civil service as a whole were accepted, coming mostly from elite universities or to a lesser extent the military academy (Evans 2012, p. 51–52, see Lim 2010b p. 192). Moreover, it tended to be nearly as prestigious to serve in the bureaucracy than in prior times of Confucianism (Mason et al. 1980, p. 49). This created positive signaling effects for graduates so that among the most competent university graduates did apply especially for the EPB.[45] By the same token,

45 In this respect the government doubtlessly profited from informal institutions. In Korean culture education was always held in very high esteem with university professors occupying the highest valued of all professions. Clearly this informal institution helped in acquiring capable personnel for staffing the echelons of bureaucracy. Likewise, Confucianism is seen by some observers as one of the driving forces behind the relatively

it allowed for the EPB to build up a reputation as consisting of an extremely competent pool of technocrats. This served as a tool to increase autonomy and discretion vis-à-vis the political leadership as well as the corporate sector.

Recruitment of new cadres tended in general to be intelligent and conducive to developmental goals. Thus, owing to the decidedly international background of its technocrats South Korea's integration into global supply chains was fostered, since those architects and masons of industrial policy therefore were inclined towards international markets. This in turn facilitated export promotion. And recruitment adapted to changing contingencies. Thus, especially with technological changes in the 1980s a switch in recruitment policy was conducted away from generalists – often with a law background – to more technically educated experts that tended to be needed to understand and design the new technologies (Larson / Park 2014, p. 357).

Secondly, not only was recruitment conducted on a competitive and meritocratic basis, but also promotions were decided upon based on those principles (Han / Kim 2017, p. 57 and p. 69). A sense of an esprit de corps was created, supported by technocrats having overwhelmingly graduated from the so-called SKY, meaning Seoul National, Korea and Yonsei universities. These connections tend to last the entire career span of members of the political leadership, the bureaucracy or business and increase cohesiveness (Schwak 2019, p. 109–110).

For technocrats the approach of giving graduates long-term career perspectives in the bureaucracy increased meritocratic orientation, since technocrats could plan for long time horizons and see that with significant efforts it is possible to climb up the career ladder. At the same time, this long-term orientation regarding recruitment resulted also in the bureaucracy rather planning for long time horizons with a series of five-year plans.

Third, bureaucrats tended to be endowed with a relatively high degree of discretion, enabling them to decide on a case-by-case basis and up to a certain extent even entrepreneurially (Hellmann 2018, p. 72). This provided for the capacity to modify plans and to flexibly react to unforeseen challenges (Kang 2008, p. 6, Larson / Park 2014, 357–358, Mason et al. 1980, p. 16–17). In a rather meritocratic environment technocrats were supposed to perform self-responsibly in order to promote economic development of the country. Technocrats of the EPB in this regard even initiated legislation themselves, therefore also promoting

smoothly functioning of the civil service in South Korea in particular and development in general (Kim 1997, p. 10). It can be seen as a functional equivalent to Protestant ethics in Weberian terms (Song 1997, p. 3 and 31).

policy changes. By the same token, individual technocrats were to a large extent rewarded with promotion or salary increases for successful policy implementation (see Lim 2010b, p. 192).

Fourth, a certain degree of embeddedness into the corporate sector with a modicum of *amakudari* – and therefore a familiarity with entrepreneurial thinking – was clearly perceptible. Thus, for instance towards the end of the 1980s technocrats perceived a need to venture more decisively into electronics and IT and coordinated efforts of the chaebols to become viable players in these industries. This worked for instance through setting up joint committees, where a state-business exchange took place and certain elements of informal guiding were in evidence (Lim 2010b, p. 198–199)

In this sense a deep embeddedness of the bureaucracy within the corporate sector was observable. There were close-knit networks between chaebols and the state with leaders from both sides often having attended the same universities and often there was behind the scenes maneuvering in informal settings and an opaque way of interacting at the state business nexus. Thus, private interests were to a large extent included in the political decision-making process. Therefore, in the course of development an adaptive partnership emerged and structurally chaebols were included into the political as well as technocratic processes (Schwak 2019, p. 114–115 and 119–121). However, this was accompanied by the state achieving to uphold a certain degree of keeping business at arm's length, which did not decisively abate over the course of the developmental phase, even in the 1980s (Chung et al. 1997, p. 16–17 and 35).

Over the entire time span of South Korea's developmental path, the bureaucracy's embeddedness into the corporate sector continued with an increasing focus of manager recruitment from the corporate side, where candidates were encouraged to apply or even poached in order to increase embeddedness (Larson / Park 2014, p. 357). This never ceasing embeddedness – mirrored as a trademark in a high relevance for state business interaction (Cho / Yoon 1991a, p. XXIV) – became especially evident at important junctures in the evolution of the corporate sector, such as in the 1980s when technological innovation in ICT required policy responses. Technocrats perceived their lack of technical expertise as well as the superior adaptation of chaebols to the new technologies and therefore technocrats cooperated even more strongly than before with corporate leaders. In this regard in a give and take fashion concessions were made to business leaders and the newly founded Korea Telecom was for instance privatized by allowing the chaebol SK Telecom to obtain a controlling stake (Larson / Park 2014, p. 349–350).

At the same time, South Korea's bureaucracy successfully defended its capacity to uphold what Evans (1995) calls "embedded autonomy". On the one hand, this was achieved through deterrence in the form of draconian penalties in case of corruption as a stick while at the same time applying a carrot with competitive salaries compared to the corporate sector. On the other hand, technocrats were also rather well insulated from political pressures and interference of competing agencies.

Not even the Ministry of Finance was able to obstruct plans formulated by the EPB, thus strongly increasing cohesiveness of the pilot bureaucracy. The EPB had the power to push through policies and did not have to cumbersomely negotiate with other agencies and ministries. It had the means to advance and retard expenditures according to the emergent course of industrial policy and it was also in charge of budgets of public corporations (Cooper 1994, p. 116 and 118). In this way a credible industrial policy could be pursued that was discretionary and technocrats for instance ruled over access to cheap credits for companies on a case-by-case basis. Most of all, this setting was possible due to the EPB reporting directly to Park and thereby decision-making processes were not encumbered by continuous negotiations with other policy-makers (Chibber 2002, p. 975–977).

Fifth, however, in the course of development relevance of technocrats tended to be diluted. Thus, although as a matter of fact still a significant degree of state activism existed, towards the beginning of the 1990s industrial policy in the form of coordinating industries and planning was abandoned and the EPB in 1994 merged with the Ministry of Finance. In this late stage of South Korea's state capitalism, the efficiency as well as discretionary powers of technocrats were severely curtailed, most visible with the merging of the EPB into the MOF (Lim 2010b, p. 201–202 and 204). Coincidentally, almost exactly with the phasing out of state capitalism and the gradual transformation to a mostly market capitalist order, the EPB ceased to exist and therefore, arguably the EPB had been a symbol of South Korea's state capitalist developmental phase (see Larson / Park 2014, p. 352).

Sixth, regarding information flows the EPB due to a high degree of embedded autonomy functioned efficiently as a bridge for the exchange of information between the corporate sector on the one hand and the political leadership on the other hand. In this function the EPB also acted through informal channels to while gathering and disseminating the relevant information align all ministries behind the long-term goals of industrial policy formulated by itself in conjunction with the political leadership (Chibber 2002, p. 958).

Seventh, the bureaucracy in the South Korean developmental state was at the early and middle stages of development not overly politicized, a technocratic approach was pursued. Thus, questions of loyalty and trust were of minor importance as opposed to the priority goal of successfully implementing developmental policies (Chibber 2002, p. 982). This strict emphasis and orientation towards development was a fully pursued goal of the government and successfully transmitted as a key motivation to technocrats. Here the professional composition of the bureaucracy was of significant assistance. While the political leadership was dominated by individuals with a military background, as technocrats in the ministries mostly served until the 1980s civilian experts with a strong knowledge of law, which facilitated a generalist and flexible approach of the bureaucracy in dealing with the corporate sector (see Chung et al. 1997, p. 9–11).

Eighth, the South Korean approach of installing in its developmental phase a pilot agency had its short-comings. The EPB gradually became large to an extent that an effective governance was inhibited. Instead of opting for organizational reform in order to streamline procedures and keep the interactions of technocrats with the business side efficient, the EPB kept on growing and eventually ceased to exist. Its existence was to a large degree coupled to the person of Park, who guaranteed its autonomy.

In this sense, the EPB was no purely rationally acting organization, but profited from the personality of Park and could thereby not risk to stray from political guidelines. This became evident in the 1970s when Park opted for the drive into Heavy and Chemical Industries (HCI) and although the EPB initially objected due to the large amount of investment needed for this creation of entire industries, finally the technocrats relented to political pressure and had to implement this policy.

Here consultation processes between political and technocratic leaders were not on an equal basis, which led to a situation where less emphasis was placed on rationally and incrementally upgrading the economy and more on pushing through political interests in an ad-hoc manner, where efficiency was only of secondary importance. In this regard the autonomy of the bureaucracy was to a certain extent infringed upon. But it needs to be taken into account that decision-making is the prerogative of the political sphere and implementation is the task of the bureaucracy. Especially, starting with the death of Park in 1979 within the EPB and overall technocratic organizations divisions in the belief systems of its members escalated increasingly.

There tended to erupt turf wars between liberals and proponents of state activism, which mirrored the disunity of the entire country as to whether the economic model of the developmental state was viable for the future (Hundt 2009).

Although among South Korean top bureaucrats there had been simmering a constant dispute about whether to follow a dirigiste industrial policy or to subscribe to a more liberal approach the South Korean pilot agency EPB acted in a largely consistent manner (Haggard 1994a). However, the decreasing extent of cohesion surfacing with the start of the 1980s resulted in a gradual approach to reforms with the core of the developmental state staying intact until the middle of the 1990s (see Larson / Park 2014, p. 348).

Overall, with an emphasis on a competent and capable pilot agency South Korea was able to mostly cohesively pursue its developmental ambitions and operate with a high bureaucratic quality (see Hellmann 2018, p. 68, Naseemullah / Arnold 2015, p. 124–125). But by the same token this setting was organizationally geared to achieve a rather speedy industrialization of the country. When this goal tended to be close to realization, cohesiveness suffered and long lingering disputes between liberals and state proponents surfaced. Therefore, the bureaucratic focus on the EPB served developmental goals and was eventually discarded when the end of the developmental state was on the horizon and the bureaucratic framework not flexible enough to adapt to new contingencies within the existing structures.

Structure of the Corporate Sector

While the structure of the technocratic sphere centered around the EPB on the corporate side likewise large entities dominated (Hellmann 2018, p. 70). However, initially, at the beginning of the 1960s South Korea's corporate sector due to the Japanese legacy of the country was structured on the Kairetsu model with large numbers of small firms acting as suppliers for larger actors. This model was initially after 1961 at the outset of South Korea's developmental course upheld.

However, starting with the HCI drive at the beginning of the 1970 the archetypical composition of South Korea's business sector with an overarching role for the chaebols – conglomerates mostly controlled by families with a wide scope of dealings ranging occasionally from hotels and ship-building to electronics (Kim 2013, p. 185) – finally emerged (Choi / Glassman 2018, p. 406). This dominance of family business and the ensuing long-term orientation with relatively little pressure on chaebols to professionalize management persisted during the entire developmental process and even beyond, also with continuation of relatively intransparent corporate governance structures (Tsui-Auch 2004a p. 26). Resources tended to be concentrated within family entities. This governance structure despite all its diminished transparency facilitated decision-making within short time-frames due to overall rather simplified internal governance procedures (Jung 2015, p. 49).

In order to allow for a speedy industrialization, the EPB for reasons of scale concentrated on those large players to effectively manage and utilize the sizable investments needed for the erection of advanced industries. There was a sort of pact between the state and the business sector, but this did not amount to a dictate by the government. The state did not orchestrate development in an outright top-down manner, but managed the developmental phase in a cooperative fashion (Chibber 1999).

This effort was from the technocrats' point of view reflected by the high degree of concentration in the business sector, since coordinating and controlling fewer entities meant fewer transaction costs. The bureaucracy had the opportunity to become well embedded into how those relatively few chaebols functioned and were thereby able to gain trust and credibility, which facilitated interaction. A clear indication for such a rationale of the state in dealing with the corporate side is to be seen in the promotion of business associations.

Political leadership and technocrats urged companies to join business associations. This assembling of entities under the umbrella of business associations facilitated an interaction between state and business, where in a rather top-down manner business decisions could be made and implemented (Kohli 2004, p. 97). Such a top-down approach was facilitated by the dominant informal institution of patrimonialism, which induced chaebols to function very hierarchically, abetting the streamlining of procedures by being able to implement changes relatively smoothly, allowing for mass production and realization of economies of scale. In very much the same sense, the South Korean state had a perception of how the economy should be run that was very top-down with the government formulating policy goals, the bureaucracy implementing them and the corporate sector in a position to be coerced to follow the directives of bureaucrats in strategic decisions and even up to a certain extent in operations (Biggart / Guillen 1999, p. 731–733).

Hundt (2015, p. 470 and 477–478) echoes this perception and observes that moreover in South Korea associations traditionally had played an important role and were utilized by state actors to pursue policy goals. This focus on business associations in turn again favoured a high concentration in the corporate sector with chaebols dominating associations and being accorded privileges in this setting.[46]

---

46 South Korean chaebols were to a large degree governed by the personality of its

Thus, in being able to concentrate on a limited number of actors, technocrats gained more comprehensive corporate insights in order to better understand operations and thereby accumulated business acumen. By the same token, the most urgent rationale for technocrats to rely on promoting the formation of large entities was the economic constraint that scale was needed in order to compete on international markets.

In this sense, a large number of relatively small domestic players on a competitive market at home would have due to lack of scale potentially resulted in competitive disadvantages on global markets. Therefore, relatively early in the developmental phase of South Korea the country opted for internationalization – foremost in the form of export promotion – and adapted the structure of its corporate sector towards this end regardless of potential negative trade-offs with regard to trust policy. However, since chaebols were constrained to compete with rivalling companies on international markets, negative effects on the degree of competition intensity on the domestic market were successfully contained.

In pursuit of such a "big is beautiful" approach by the state towards composition of the corporate sector, SMEs were clearly discriminated against. First of all, entry into markets was severely inhibited, since chaebols with their superior scale were in terms of product price and quality hard to compete with. In this sense, markets tended not to be contestable. Second, SMEs were to a large extent locked out from preferential credits and had to resort to the curb market with significantly higher financing costs. This was the result of a tight control of the number of credits, inducing a compartmentalization of the financial sector in an official one and a curb market. The Bank of Korea had the right to set ceilings for commercial state-owned banks for granting credits to companies. Ultimately, that led to a situation where SMEs had to borrow on the curb market, whereas chaebols were favoured by being able to tap into the official financial sector (Ro 1994).

This discrimination and promotion of a highly concentrated business sector entailed the entire process of interaction. For instance, in the ICT reforms of the 1980s chaebols were clearly favoured, such as when during this time period

founders with some extent of professionalism. Although the high concentration of the corporate sector mitigated collective action problems, state activities were still in need, since by the same token, there existed a lack of cooperation among chaebols. There tended to be very few linkages between them with hardly any mutual activities in procurement, export promotion or research, enlarging the need for state interventions in order to coordinate industrial upgrading. (Biggart 1998).

the chaebol SK group was allowed to acquire a controlling stake of Korea Telecom. At the same time, sizable funds were allocated to the chaebols for ICT activities. In return the technocrats and political leaders insisted on chaebols to effectively progress in forming a globally competitive ICT sector (Larson / Park 2014, p. 349–350). Indeed, for obtaining privileges chaebols had in return to deliver sizable progress in the build-up of industries that had been prioritized by the state. In certain instances, the state preferred to act itself as an entrepreneur through formation of SOEs, as in the steel sector. In this regard, in some instances, markets were not left to be shaped by private actors, but in essence dominated by the state. However, the key difference to an outright socialist setting was that SOEs in South Korea nevertheless had to compete with rivals from the private sector, either domestically or globally (Kohli 2004, p. 104–105).

Certainly, the evolution of a corporate sector with dominance of typically two to three large entities on each respective market (Kim 2013, p. 185) occurred in parallel to the economic development of the country. For the state chaebols were an effective means to realize the national goal of development. In this regard, the interaction between state and business is to a large extent influenced by the degree of rule of law the state applies in dealing with the corporate sector, which will be taken into account next.

Degree of Rule of Law

In general, during the developmental phase from beginning of the 1960s until the 1990s administrative guidance was widespread in South Korea and tended to conflict with principles of rule of law. In this sense, though for chaebols or also other business entities state guidelines were legally not binding, they nevertheless followed the policy goals and policy focusses of the state.

One factor behind this compliance can possibly be attributed to the general public intending for the state to constrain chaebols through such administrative guiding. And as a result, chaebols placed less emphasis on efficiency and more on business strategies that served the national goal of export promotion and development. Towards achieving those goals, the state did nimbly and regularly amend the statutes that legally underpinned South Korea's industrial policy. For these constant changes, even a separate ministry was created that nevertheless did not challenge the superiority of the EPB (Lee 2018, p. 438–439 and p. 450). In this sense the institutional framework was clearly flexible and also allowed for a sufficient degree of discretion for technocrats in dealing with corporate entities.

Efficient as it was, the legal system doubtlessly, did not follow a textbook case for the primacy of rule of law. A clear indication of short-comings with regard to rule of law during South Korea's developmental path is the fact that prior to the 1990s hardly any lawsuits were filed against the discretionary practice of administrative guiding. However, with the transition to a market capitalist system and more elements of rule of law in the end of the 1980s the number of law suits increased significantly (see Lee 2018, p. 439).

Therefore, a turning point in the evolution of South Korea's politico-economic order is to be seen in the comprehensive constitutional amendment of 1987 (see Ahn 2007). Following those constitutional amendments basic rights such as freedom of speech and civil rights in general were guaranteed, which reverberated through the entire politico-economic order and did also improve property rights and the safety of investments. In general, in terms of the degree of rule of law with the constitutional reform a path was embarked on to stray from state and to seek to erect a market capitalist system (see Park 2009).

However, during the developmental phase as such while in commercial legal aspects rule of law was not strictly applied, the regime did significantly more suppress civil liberties and freedom of speech. Although property rights were granted and up to a certain extent guaranteed, repeatedly under states of emergency civil rights were suspended (Lee 2018, p. 453). In this regard the political leadership and technocrats held the decisive levers in hands that the judiciary was de facto under administrative control of the executive branch of power and thus developmental goals gained priority versus allowing for rule of law (see Lee 2018, p. 442—443 and p. 453).

Accordingly, up to a certain extent a trade-off between civil rights and rule of law on the one hand and developmental goals on the other hand is discernible. Initially at least, the country reaped competitive advantages through an affluence of cheap labour. This supply of labour by the same token was secured through repressing unions in particular and the labour movement in general. Courts did in this phase not rule according to the principles of rule of law, but relented to political pressure.

Concededly, by the same token, those laws and regulations – thus formal institutions – tended to be crafted complementary to informal institutions, such as the Confucian heritage of the country (Lee 2018, p. 453). Overall, the prevailing and instrumentally utilized lack of rule of law per se had in South Korea during its developmental phase in some regards been complemented by Confucianism with its emphasis on harmony and the avoidance of confrontation (see Lee 2009). Elites and also broader segments of the population tended to be reluctant to solve clashes of interest before courts. Therefore, deficiencies of rule of law were initially accepted, at least until conflicts in industrial relations repeatedly escalated starting from the beginning of the 1970s (Heo / Hahm 2014, p. 938).

But not only labour was adversely affected by a lack of rule of law. Likewise, a number of commercial entities were de facto barred from obtaining preferential credits. In this sense, the implementation of industrial policy through the bureaucracy with a set of policies was broadly discriminative. And commercial entities had no realistic opportunity to challenge these discriminations before independent courts. In this context within the existing system of state capitalism, the practice of favouring chaebols and discriminating against SMEs hinged legally on a plethora of mere statutes and not fully passed legislation (Lee 2018, p. 445).

All in all, priority for the safety of property rights in South Korea was per se a blurred line, since technocrats in pursuit of industrial policy – based on a very flexible and adaptable set of laws, statutes and regulations – could ad-hoc sever credit lines and thereby de facto arbitrarily drive an entity into bankruptcy and for instance merge the remnants with another entity. This was an effective means to constrain chaebols into economic and political acquiescence, but it signifies all the more the prevailing lack of rule of law.

This phenomenon once again underlines the dominance of chaebols and technocrats in South Korea's state capitalist phase. There existed fundamental deficiencies in rule of law, which the state utilized in order to shape the corporate sector according to its plans, i.e. a high degree of concentration. From a technocratic point of view likewise a highly centralized approach with a large pilot agency dominating implementation of industrial policy. How these policies were implemented and what their content was is analyzed in the next sub-section.

4.5.3 Policies

Overall, the overarching goal of industrial policy in South Korea was economic growth, industrialization and ending absolute poverty (Lee 2018, p. 447). In this regard, from the point of view of goal orientation the political leadership was largely inflexible. Those goals were national ambitions and accordingly cascaded down to the technocratic level for realization. On a technocratic level by the same token a thorough inclination towards pragmatism is not observable. Rather technocrats formulated specific goals based on guidelines set by the political leadership and in a carrot and stick strategy with a limited degree of flexibility constrained economic actors to deliver a priori agreed upon targets such as export or production quotas.

A clear indication of such a strategy with rather limited room for maneuver for contingencies is the fact that South Korea took sizable efforts to formulate five-year plans which in their rigidity up to a certain extent resembled socialist planning and where "prices were intentionally gotten wrong" (see Amsden 1992) with policy makers intervening heavily into the price setting mechanism, repeatedly applying price controls (Haggard 1994a).[47] Content-wise the entire developmental phase with its emphasis on industrial policy was structured in timing and sequencing by the political leadership in tandem with the EPB through a series of six five-years plans with the first one being initiated in 1962, shortly after the military coup of Park.

Especially in the 1960s and 1970s planning tended to be very much micro-orientated with very concrete targets. With the gradual transformation towards market capitalism these plans concentrated more on macro-economic figures and were not going into detail to such an extent anymore. In implementation of plans vis-à-vis the corporate sector occasionally very rigid measures were applied in order to guarantee plan fulfillment. Thus, there were systematic and detailed investigations of tax returns to discipline companies that were not co-operating with the government (Song 1997, p. 140–144).

As a matter of fact, in guiding the economy in the 1960s the political leadership and EPB were confronted with high unemployment and a huge degree of poverty. Cheap labour accordingly was in ample supply. In this setting the state initially unsuccessfully experimented with import substitution (Hellmann 2018)[48], which was in 1964 replaced by a transition to export orientation. In formulating its second five-year plan for a time frame from 1967 until 1971 the state perceived to depend in the realization of its developmental goals on applying the competitive advantage of an abundant supply of low qualified labour. Therefore, export bases which focused on light industries such as textiles, toys and food processing were with huge efforts created (Mason et al. 1980, p. 6, Hellmann 2018, p. 72), largely by strictly guiding privately owned chaebols. Owing to favourable

47 However, the EPB did retain a minimum of adaptiveness and did not implement five-year plans in a linear fashion, but reacted flexibly to such contingencies as labour shortages or rising inflation (Hellmann 2018, p. 72–74).

48 However, this policy was discarded after three years. First of all, the country had to succumb to US pressure as being one of the main donours of the South Korean government. Secondly, the government realized that its industrialization could not to be financed with domestic financial means and therefore needed foreign exchange. This could most easily be earned by relying on an outward orientation and export promotion (Cho / Joon 1991b, p. 20).

geopolitical conditions (Kohli 2004, p. 110–112, Glassmann / Choi 2014, Choi / Glassman 2018, p. 418, Chung et al. 1997, p. 1–3 and 9, Deyo 1987, p. 19) – with large support from the US and Japan due to South Korea being perceived as an outpost in the cold war fight against communism – export markets were successfully expanded into (Suh / Kwon 2014, p. 678, Chibber 1999). Skillfully the state enabled interaction with the corporate sector chaebols to successfully integrate into global supply chains (Yeung 2007, Kim 1997, p. 8–9). Likewise, this outward orientation also allowed for technology transfer, including reverse engineering.

At the beginning of the 1970s the political leadership around Park perceived a need to venture into heavy and chemical industries. This resulted in massive investments with occasionally only low to medium potential or even negative returns. At this point a cleavage between the EPB and the political leadership emerged with technocrats opposing the ambitious HCI drive, since they apprehended the creation of white elephants. Although during the entire developmental phase being mostly unpopular among larger segments of the population – as evident in repeated mass protests (Clark 2015, p. 41–42, Kim 1997, p. 2–3, Hellmann 2018, p. 68–70) –, the executive branch pushed this effort through. As a policy tool served once again the financial sector as evident by the fact that between 1972 and 1982 43 percent of credits in South Korea went into projects related to forming an HCI sector. During this phase South Korea came to depend more on capital inflows than on the availability of cheap labour as before (Lim 2010b, p. 195–196).

Technocrats were constrained to implement the new policy focus on an HCI drive and in a rather Weberian fashion the EPB relented to this reduction of autonomy and effectively implemented the plans laid out by the political leadership under Park. This drive, which allowed for the sustainable creation of domestic steel, automobile, and shipyard industries, was initiated in the third plan, but reiterated in the fourth one which was formulated for the years from 1977 until 1981. In the time span of the latter plan the state also opted to become an entrepreneur on a large scale itself by setting up the steel mill Posco as an SOE (see Lee 2018, p. 441, Clark 2015, p. 44).

With the assassination of Park in 1979 a re-thinking in terms of industrial policy set in. Thus, in the fifth plan – valid until 1986 – promotion of quality and precision in products was emphasized. During this time frame efforts were made to steer away from a focus on growth to more efficiency and therefore the financial sector was completely reformed with financial entities being largely privatized and constrained to pursue sufficient returns when allocating capital for projects they intended to finance (see Heo 2014). During these time frames technocrats perceived a need to venture into electronics and IT and coordinated efforts of the chaebols to become viable players in these industries. This worked for instance through setting up joint committees, where a state-business exchange took place and certain elements of informal guidance were in evidence (Lim 2010b, p. 198–199).

In this sense, regarding policy content the first prudential measures were taken to shift from state to market capitalism. In the final and sixth five-year plan the state set the target of South Korean industries to attain world-class quality in their products, becoming in sectors such as electronics leading actors on global markets, and even the attempt was formulated to risk an entry into the aviation industry (see Lee 2018, p. 441).

Before Park's assassination the state controlled the financial sector with ownership, nominating managers and the allocation of policy loans as well as subsidized credits. Then the financial sector was liberalized and banks were privatized. This resulted in lower entry barriers and from 1985 until 1992 the number of commercial banks nearly doubled. Eventually, industrial policy in the form of coordinating industries and planning was abandoned and inflows of foreign capital to domestic entities significantly liberalized (Lim 2010b, p. 201–202).

How did in the period before cautious liberalization the political leadership in conjunction with the EPB orchestrate this constant upgrading of the industrial base? All in all, technocrats and political leaders applied instruments ranging from financial, fiscal, export, competition, tariff, currency and investment to research policy as well as labour policy and even publicity campaigns.

However, the primary instrument for the state in conducting its industrial policy consisted of control of the financial sector (Lee 2018, p. 447, Frieden 1981, p. 428, Clark 2015, p. 33, Heo 2014, p. 693).[49] Accordingly, at the outset of the developmental phase banks in South Korea were nationalized (Suh / Kwon 2014, p. 681). Likewise, the evolution of financial markets was suppressed and

49 The government had almost complete control on finances, owning commercial banks and being legally entitled to permit through the EPB every foreign lending conducted by the corporate sector (Mason et al. 1980, p. 20–21). This instrument was also utilized in order to allow foreign borrowings to provide for technology imports and therefore technology transfers without FDI. This had a certain direct advantage, since the political leadership perceived a risk of losing control over the developmental process when allowing foreigners to directly invest on the domestic market (Fischer 2018, p. 3359–3360).

consequently continuation of a bank-centered financial system guaranteed.[50] Through control of access to finance for commercial entities the state secured its position of constraining the corporate sector to follow industrial policy plans. This resulted in the provision of specially designed policy loans granted to entities that fulfilled previously set export goals (Lee 2018, p. 446).

This tool of providing financial means for the corporate sector – access to international banks and capital markets was inhibited through certain capital account controls – was the decisive lever for the EPB to enforce industrial policy targets. Even though the corporate sector mostly consisted of private actors thus strategic and operational decisions by the management could effectively be guided, since the sanction mechanism of severing credit lines carried such risks for company survival that compliance of boardrooms presented until the 1980s no barrier for policy implementation.

Chaebols owing to their reliance on massive investments were highly leveraged (Jung 2015, p. 49) and this meant that they depended on prolongations of credits, which was contingent on approval by the EPB. The only resort to survive in case of non-compliance or falling out of favour of technocrats was the curb market. But interest rates there tended to be so high as to be in many instances prohibitive for continuing to operate profitably.

Draconian as this policy instrument seems, the EPB was highly transparent in formulating and implementing targets. Thus, businesses could count on continued bureaucratic support by achieving target fulfillment and although in cases of failure sanctions tended to be enforced, the interaction in such instances was nevertheless to such an extent pragmatic as that only projects were cancelled that apparently did not succeed and offered no potential for the future.

In such a manner this transparent and credible sanction mechanism created expectations certainty among corporate players (see Lee 2018, p. 447–448). Instances, where failed projects were carried on for political, i.e. for example crony state capitalist reasons, are rare during South Korea's developmental course. Thus, when the drive into the chemical industry did not bear fruits in the 1970s it was without protracted discussions abandoned. Similarly, the expansion into aviation was cancelled at a certain point.

With its high-quality bureaucratic capacity South Korea relied on a plethora of other policy instruments. One was fiscal policy, where tax exemptions and

50 At the same time, financial supervision tended to be weak and subordinated to economic growth with a focus on guaranteeing state control of the financial sector (Heo 2014, p. 693).

subsidies were granted to corporate players that either promised to gain export markets or had already fulfilled export targets. In this regard, for a relatively transparent provision of such incentives the state erected export promotion councils, where only chaebols were represented. This resulted in a systematic neglect and even discrimination against SMEs (Larson / Park 2014, p. 348, Kim 2013, p. 185) through a widely selective industrial policy with a comprehensive set of instruments (Haggard 1994a, Chung et al. 1997, p. 9–11), ranging as far as being at a disadvantage regarding procurement (Schwak 2019, p. 105). However, in those councils, practical problems of chaebols were discussed and binding goals agreed upon (Lee 2018, p. 457–458). Export promotion councils were installed at the highest organizational level with Park and chaebol CEOs participating.

Here it was among others agreed upon which subsidies and tax exemptions were offered for companies that excelled in the national pursuit of promoting exports. In this sense, also non-monetary incentives were applied by honouring especially successful exporters and naming national champions. Consequently, South Korea's industrialization program also entailed a policy of picking the winners where technocrats had to identify corporate players with high potential and support them (Clark 2015, p. 37–38). In pursuit of export goals by the same token an export agency with numerous affiliations abroad was founded. This served as a business card to potential partners, customers and suppliers on industrialized markets.

In competition policy the EPB did allow for oligopolistic and sometimes even monopolistic domestic markets to evolve. This high concentration was even fostered through supporting national champions financially, technically and organizationally. Entry barriers that were due to effects of scale already significantly high were thus even increased.[51] However, the EPB guaranteed that this lack of competition domestically was compensated for by competitive pressures on international markets and constrained chaebols to export and not simply reap rents domestically to the detriment of consumers.

---

51 In South Korea in its developmental phase post 1961 only few new companies emerged. This is especially evident when looking at the fact that in 1970 one had to obtain 312 signatures from the state in order to found a company. According to the Federation of Korean Industries it took more than 350 days to collect all of these signatures. For the creation of SMEs that is an overarching burden and corresponds to the fact that tedious procedures were in place for obtaining preferential credits, which again favoured chaebols since they tended to have more resources available for mastering all of this red tape (Song 1997, p. 63, 73 and 111).

Consequently, competition policy was accompanied by tariff policy to protect infant industries, but also domestic industries which yet had to advance to maturity. This protectionism to a certain extent favoured the build-up of excess capacities (Suh /Kwon 2014, p. 684, Jung 2015, p. 46), but through the stick of having to compete internationally negative incentive effects were subdued.

Moreover, this protectionism was even intensified by an accommodating currency and investment regime. Thus, foreign currency was allocated to preferred entities, so that they could import technology. Here again, the EPB held the decisive levers, since domestic corporations depended on foreign technology, but had no foreign currency to finance those imports. The EPB granted those licenses and thereby allowed for technology imports and transfer. Regarding investment policy once again the entire extent of protectionism surfaces, since foreign actors were barred from obtaining majority stakes in domestic corporations (Clark 2015, p. 37–38) and for national champions there were even investment guarantees granted (Hundt 2009). This practically shielded South Korea's markets from foreign players to seize shares and domestic commercial entities had only to compete internationally with corporations from abroad.

At the same time, chaebols depended on research and education, which also entailed infrastructural support (see Kohli 2004, p. 119). The state fostered educational programs so that companies had capable graduates for staffing positions. And in research the state promoted universities in order to facilitate the technological advancement of the country (Larson / Park 2014, p. 349–350). The state formed institutes in order to promote innovation and research (Yeung 2007). However, in the initial phases of development the country tended to rely on emulation of foreign, especially Japanese, technology and not proprietary research efforts.

Moreover, strong cooperation of state and business led to suppression of the labour force and in so far can be counted as one part of industrial policy. South Korean labour, however, did not accept being suppressed and union leaders were at the forefront of changing the politico-economic system struggling against state capitalism in the form of the developmental state (Kim 1997, p. 4, Pirie 2018, p. 133–135). Furthermore, the EPB launched publicity campaigns on TV and the radio in order to create an inclination towards development among broader segments of the population, but also elites, such as corporate leaders (Lee 2018, p. 446).

Overall, economic policies were conducted in a mostly pragmatic and flexible fashion based on the five-year plans, for instance during the first oil crisis resorting to a number of supports for exporters. This included tax deferments to troubled export industries. Furthermore, cuts in interest rates on local currency export finances were instituted as well as prolongations on the maturing of loans for importing raw materials (Haggard 1994a).

Technocratic and corporate structures – such as dominance of the EPB and chaebols – as well as the multitude of policy instruments applied and sketched out in this sub-section were no ends in themselves. Rather they were means to reach national goals. As pointed out in the beginning of this sub-section those were economic growth, industrialization and ending absolute poverty. Whether the independent variables of structure and policies did positively affect the dependent variable of performance will in a concise manner be analyzed in the next sub-section.

4.5.4 Performance

South Korea's developmental success is well documented in the literature with an astounding rise from an economically backward country technologically on a par with average African nations to an industrialized nation with national champions that compete with the most advanced technologies on world markets (see for instance Amsden 1992, Kohli 2004, Evans 2012, Hundt 2014, Haggard 1986, Chang 2007, Chang 2006, Jones / Sakong 1980, Wade 1990, Clark 2015). Above structural and policy factors were analyzed serving as independent variables that the state tended to apply in order to achieve its national goals. Subsequently, it will be illustrated whether in utilizing those instruments the goals of economic growth, industrialization and ending poverty were indeed accomplished.

This is in so far, a promising approach, since world governance indicators are only available starting from 1996. Consequently, the extent of bureaucratic quality cannot be accounted for with statistical data, but the literature analysis conducted above has already provided for such broad evidence as to illustrate strengths and weaknesses of South Korea's bureaucracy during the developmental course. In terms of overall developmental goals data for the HDI is only available starting from 1990. Therefore, in this sub-section about performance of South Korea's developmental state it will be related to World Bank data about development (World Bank 2019), which dates back to the 1960s, in order to assess whether the national goals formulated at the outset of the developmental phase were indeed realized.

In this regard, only in the case of economic growth an average is formed for the developmental phase in order to analyze, whether overall this goal was reached. For the other two dimensions – ending poverty and industrializing – the trend, meaning constant improvements, is the most relevant evidence and therefore the course of events is taken into account for this study.

To begin with, the state did realize its goal of economic growth. On an annual average basis South Korea managed to achieve from 1961 until 1996 a real economic GDP growth rate of 9.37 percent. This is all the more impressive as that during this time span of the developmental course there was only one single year with negative growth, in 1980 with minus 1.7 percent. In 1973 South Korea's real GDP even grew with 14.83 percent. Consequently, the state did in this regard perform according to its commitments made to broader segments of the population and elites, forming a sizable contrast to the years of President Rhee prior to 1961.

However, Park did commit on not only achieving growth, but also to industrialize and providing for a higher value-added stemming from the industrial sector. The political leadership intended to alter the structure of the economy with a more prominent role for industry and less of an emphasis on agriculture, on which South Korea had been largely dependent on prior to 1961.

Here again constant improvements are evident. As a matter of fact, in 1961 the country started with a share of the industrial sector of GDP value-added of mere 17.62 percent. During the 1960s with a focus on mass production with cheap labour of low value-added goods this share increased until 1970 to 24.5 percent. The state then did plan for even more industrialization in the form of the HCI drive and until 1980 increased this share to 31.5 percent. Starting with 1980 there was a remarkable policy shift away from state capitalism of the developmental state variant and towards more market capitalist elements.

But still the share of the industrial sector of GDP value-added increased to 35.77 percent. In this regard the country had reached a plafond and the economic structure evolved towards a higher weighted role for the tertiary sector. Thus, until 1996 – the last year that is counted as South Korea being state capitalist – the share of industry staid roughly constant at 34.81 percent.

Overall, the country did indeed successfully industrialize away from the agricultural sector (Deyo 1987) and created a large number of jobs in the secondary sector, thereby taking pressure from the labour market, when at the beginning of the 1960s an abundance of labour had caused high unemployment. However, for the population the most pressing need was a successful fight against poverty, which prior to 1961 had devastated the standards of living of large segments of the population. Unfortunately, for South Korea there is no comprehensive data series regarding poverty available. Therefore, it is resorted to proxies, i.e. life expectancy, infant mortality and school enrollment.

When analyzing the data about life expectancy a sustainable and constant improvement is observable. In 1961 it stood at 53.74 years, accelerating to 62.15 years in 1970. In 1980 it reached 66.05 years and then in 1990 with 71.6 years

South Korea already tended to be on a par with industrialized nations. At the last year of the relevant time span – in 1996 – the population had a life expectancy of 74.15 years, meaning that in this sense poverty had successfully been conquered, since only with a drastic reduction in poverty such progress can be explained.

This tendency is also reflected in data about infant mortality. From 1961 until 1996 this figure continuously decreased, starting with 75.8 deaths per 1.000 life-births, to 47.1 in 1970 to 29.5 in 1980 and in 1990 as well as 1996 it stood only at 13.3 and 8.3 deaths respectively, meaning regarding provision of medical services the country had reached industrialized nation status. But mere survival does not automatically translate into improved life perspectives for broad segments of the population. Mostly through education people tend to be able to sustainably improve their economic perspectives and job opportunities in their lives. Therefore, it will now be turned to tertiary school enrollment as a percent of gross total.

Here unfortunately the data series only reaches back until 1971, when mere 6.79 percent of gross total were enrolled. This figure improved to 12.44 in the year 1980. With the gradual transformation towards market capitalism this data significantly improved further. In 1990 already 36.51 percent were enrolled in tertiary education. And for the last relevant data point in 1996 53.74 of gross total were enrolled in tertiary education. This underlines the fact that also regarding the most pressing demand of the population of ending poverty and increasing living standards indeed the political leadership and technocrats did deliver. They effectively managed to largely extinguish poverty, selecting as an instrument the creation of jobs, initially in industries that required labour with low quality such as textiles and later on with creation of higher qualified jobs (Kwon / Yi 2009, p. 779–781).

As a matter of fact, all three national aspirations – economic growth, industrialization and ending poverty – were thus fulfilled. In a relatively short time-span the country did progress to the status of an industrialized nation being on the same level as its former colonial mother country Japan or even Western nations. Whereas at the outset of its developmental course the economic structure was dominated by agricultural production with a slowly growing share of the textile industry, the country did energetically progress into producing steel, automobiles and ships.

Nowadays, South Korean chaebols are among the most valuable brands in the world, being among global leaders in high technology such as soft- and hardware. Corporations such as Samsung, Hyundai, SK Hynix or LG are as national champions widely known on a global scale. As the analysis of this and the preceding sub-sections has shown this success can mostly be explained through a rather well working interaction between state and business, meaning that structural and policy factors significantly contributed to this performance. Those factors were partially intentionally created and formed to achieve those results, but in other regards fortunate contingencies drove performance results. They also tended to favour conditions, where structure and policies did successfully and interdependently contribute to the outcome of one of the most impressive developmental courses in the history of mankind. How far political leaders did shape this developmental trajectory or whether it was the mere outcome of a favourable institutional framework is the topic of the next sub-section.

4.5.5 Actor Centricity

During the developmental phase of South Korea party structures played a minor role in state business interaction, meaning on the structure and policies of this exchange as well as policy formulation and implementation. Having gained power through a military coup Park's belief system regarding coordination of the economy largely preferred a top-down approach, as evident by the fact that initially chaebol leaders were incarcerated for collaboration with and corruptive activities under the Rhee regime.

As a matter of fact, Park skillfully utilized a critical juncture in the history of his country, when discontent with the corrupt government of Rhee, the threat of North Korean communism and the hardly healed scars of the Korean as well as the second World War in conjunction with atrocities during Japanese colonialism all converged to give broader segments of the population and elites a perception of deeply ingrained vulnerability (see Lim 2010a). This critical juncture Park seized by imposing an at best semi-democratic military rule on the country with himself as the undisputed ultimate decision-maker.

Overall, Park and his political allies were highly educated and had a long-term vision for the country. Having been as a young man a convicted socialist, who now turned towards nationalism (see Lai 2018) Park had a penchant for planning and thus forged his vision for the economic future of South Korea into five-year plans, which served as relatively rigorous guidelines for policy formulation and implementation. However, Park acted in a plan-pragmatic manner and thus allowed for experimentation, amending plans in the case of unexpected contingencies. As a rule, when it became evident that a policy did not work it was discarded and not for reasons of principle kept in force (see Gemici 2013, p. 178–179, Lee 1991, p. 463–468).

In this sense, the politico-economic order erected by Park tended to be relatively personalized (Low 2001, p. 414–416) and significantly orientated towards his person (Haggard 1994a). This nationalist and authoritarian leadership style with repression of labour becomes most evident, when looking at the two key pillars of his rule, the EPB and the military (see Kohli 2004, p. 119). Here both entities directly reported to Park and were thus under perennial control of the political leader. The EPB as such had always to a certain extent been politicized and been a symbol as well as a signal for the strength and viability of state capitalism in the developmental state variant (Jung 2011).

No significant party structures – or other elements of a formal as well as informal institutional framework – were allowed to emerge. Accordingly, Park in this regard acted largely unconstrained (see Gemici 2013, p. 180). This became especially obvious with the push for the Heavy and Chemical Industry, which was strongly supported in the 1970s by Park and where he displayed a large degree of stewardship (Haggard 1994a).

But there were limits to the actor centricity of Park.[52] During the entire time span of development governments tended to be unpopular and regular outbreaks of political mass protests as well as the absence of regular free elections (see Lee 2018, p, 457–459, Clark 2015, p. 33) constrained Park to seek for ways to justify his rule, i.e. legitimacy of his regime, for instance by installing a sizable pension program (Goodman et al. 1998).[53] But overall, he placed top priority on achieving development and when his own decisions were in conflict with this ambition, he changed his perception, becoming most obvious with drastic modifications to the HCI drive towards the end of the 1970s, which he originally had personally propagated and pushed through (Haggard 1994b, p. 64).

This induced Park all the more to give absolute priority to achieving the national goals of economic growth, industrialization and ending poverty and credibly committed to those ambitions (Mason et al. 1980, p. 16–17, see Lai 2018, Gomez 2003, p. 8–9, Hundt 2009). However, as such a mere proclamation

---

52 Thus, Park early on during the developmental phase had in 1967 to give in to pressure from within, at one point even having to offer his resignation and having his time in office limited to three tenures. Subsequently, in 1972 he freed himself from these constraints, usurping quasi-dictatorial powers and repeatedly ruling by emergency decree, justifying this foremost with South Korea's vulnerability in the face of a communist threat as evident by the developments in Vietnam (Mason et al. 1980, p. 52–54).

53 To this end, the political leadership widely used propaganda means to promote support for the government and thereby more legitimacy among the population (Kohli 2004, p. 119). Furthermore, he underlined his resolve for the population to make sacrifices for the national ambition of development by limiting himself personally to humble living standards.

carries little if any credibility. Park demonstrated his resolve to promote economic growth, exports and industrialization by signaling in a binding manner to protect property rights of business owners. He could not possibly renege on this promise, since he would have devastatingly tarnished his own credibility in case of repeated property rights violations.

In practice he instituted export promotion councils as his instrument on the highest political and corporate echelons to in a carrot and stick approach interact with business and likewise signaling the highest possible political support. Here he discretionarily made decisions to the advantage of certain industries and firm. In this sense, the President micro-managed the export-driven developmental path of his country with the policy instruments illustrated above (Song 1997). The councils made relatively rapid decisions on the highest political level possible. For chaebols this furthermore facilitated contact to the highest echelons of political power mitigating information asymmetries on both sides. Furthermore, Park's direct involvement also helped the EPB to more effectively lead the policy coordination and implementation efforts (Kang 2008, p. 10).

In these meetings decisions such as venturing into new industries were discussed. The formal inclusion of business leaders into the decision process assisted in facilitating acceptance of administrative interventions. By following a strictly transparent route of coordinating the corporate sector, the state managed to create a relatively level playing field for chaebols, which after all competed against each other for state resources and on domestic as well as foreign product markets.

But protecting property rights cannot be equated with guaranteeing rents to entrepreneurs regardless of such factors as efficiency and innovativeness. Rather Park indeed did distribute rents among chaebols with leaving domestic markets in most instances from two to three dominant players. He shielded those rents by erecting high entry barriers for potential domestic and international rivals.

This functioned domestically through limiting access to credits as well as allowing chaebols to grow to such a size as giving them an insurmountable comparable advantage in terms of economies of scale. Regarding foreign competition as explained above Park utilized tariff and investment policy instruments to deter rivals from abroad to enter into domestic markets. And market outcomes in the form of revenues and profits were credibly left to corporate entities.

No prohibitively high taxation, no confiscations or arbitrary inspections were realized. In this sense, for entrepreneurs the business environment was very friendly. However, as such Park also did not institute a crony state capitalist economic order. He perceived a need for his country to constrain chaebols to compete on international markets and realize export revenues.

For two reasons this stick was indispensable. First of all, domestically chaebols were under little competitive pressure and allowed to reap rents. Those were among others distributed through state-owned commercial banks and took the form of licenses, state-controlled concessions, state funding, contracts and preferential treatment in the course of privatizations (Gomez 2003, p. 4–5). But secondly, it was ensured that those rents were not unproductively utilized for purposes such as lavish headquarters or excessive managerial renumeration, but reinvested with the goal of promoting exports.

Thus, Park skillfully perceived and utilized a powerful lever to intervene into corporate strategies. Since chaebols tended to be highly leveraged mere threatening of non-extension of credits was an effective means to coerce companies into cooperating with the industrial policy of the state. Another means of the state to make companies compliant was the threat of disconnection of infrastructure services. In this regard, South Korean companies learned that in order to survive and prosper it was advisable to heed directives of Park and his government as well as the EPB (Song 1997, p. 140–144).

And for Park's developmental plan of constant economic upgrading exports were essential in a sense that they guaranteed the foreign currency needed to finance technology imports for reverse engineering and constant learning. Although South Korea as a cold war outpost received generous aid by the US, the extent did not suffice for sizable technology imports and was also conditioned on certain political bargains, leading for instance to reductions during the Nixon years. Thus, Park did rely on private property and guaranteed those rights with his personal credibility, but simultaneously he adroitly managed to avoid the trap of too crony relations.

4.5.6 State Capitalism in South Korea

Overall, the phenomenal success story of South Korea cannot be explained by one variable alone. There were a number of exogenous and endogenous variables influencing the developmental trajectory of this nation state, foremost stemming from the seven constituting principles of state capitalism. Thus, for instance South Korea's success cannot solely be attributed to comparative advantages owing to suppressing workers to accept low wages. What is needed is an in-depth analysis of key building blocks for development, a multi-factorial approach (Kohli 2004, p. 102).

South Korea as State Capitalist

As illustrated above state involvement in the economy was rather severe. Unions were sought to be marginalized, being even persecuted. Although the leading companies, the partially oversized chaebols, were mostly in private hands, the fact as such that commercial banks were state-owned and through the powerful instrument of granting or withholding preferential loans, the state could effectively control corporate decision-making and thereby to a large extent the developmental course of the country.

Furthermore, there also existed in South Korea an SWF, although of minor size compared to those in the Middle East, Singapore or Norway. In shielding domestic markets, the government was very apt. Tariffs tended to deter imports of goods the country itself produced and thereby the state protected among others infant industries. But in a rather opportunistic fashion, for technological goods that the country so far had not the capacity to produce locally, tariffs were enticingly low or even non-existent. This as such promoted technology imports, especially from Japan.

In a certain sense, those policy measures were part of an elaborate industrial policy plan. As such the state never ceased to intervene into the economy, clearly pursuing for instance a policy of picking the winners. As a matter of fact, this policy meant that prices were intentionally gotten wrong (Amsden 1992) and it was also naturally accepted that there were in the rights of means of production clear distinctions made between public and private. That meant that private property rights were respected even directly after Park come to power in South Korea in 1961 and business leaders on grounds of having engaged in corruption with the former Rhee-regime were incarcerated.

As comes to the fore in this regard, the standards of rule of law in South Korea during its developmental course were low. Without due process those business leaders were imprisoned in a rather arbitrary manner. To illustrate how deeply the government disregarded rule of law it can be referred to the fact that there were state orchestrated attempts to kill opposition and labour leader and later President Kim dae-jung. No independent judiciary existed at all. All in all, relatively severe constraints in South Korea on civil liberties and freedom of speech were applied and only starting from the 1990s did the judiciary become independent of administrative control by the executive branch of power (Lee 2018, p. 442–443).

Overall, in the 1960s and 1970s, in general, the business climate was conducive. Park was seen as delivering on promises and this increased business confidence as well as an inclination to invest. The personality of Park served as a functional equivalent to protecting property rights. Likewise, political leaders formed the pilot agency EPB with its impressive capacity as well as capability and this ensured a cohesive policy approach, since the competence for implementation of policies was to a large extent concentrated in this organization. This analysis of state capitalism during South Korea's developmental course stresses that the country was an almost arch-typical form of state capitalism.

South Korea as state capitalist of the developmental state variant

But was South Korea a state capitalist developmental state? With few doubts it is at this stage possible to classify South Korea to be state capitalist in the form of the developmental state. For instance, at the outset the Southern part of this divided country was in permanent peril of being invaded by the Communist north.

But not only were there military threats from North Korea – backed by the huge Chinese state –, there was also the threat that economically communism in the North could prove to work better than the state capitalist system in the South. In this state of vulnerability Park clearly had to deliver and be able to eventually raise the standards of living of large segments of the population.

This pressure from below was one factor in keeping corruption at bay – at least up to a certain point. A relatively homogenous society also helped to rally the population behind the aim of achieving developmental goals, which with inclusion into the OECD in 1996 indeed occurred. Clearly, the government committed itself to the goal of development, which meant a sizable degree of property rights safety for business-men. This was especially important for domestic economic agents and less foreigners, since the state virtually crowded out most FDI right from the start.

By the same token, concededly, South Korea profited enormously from Japan's tremendous economic success. Operating at the limits of its production factors capacity, Japan chose to outsource significant portions of its production of lower value-added goods to the neighbour state, while Park meticulously ensured that control of the entities producing goods for Japan, for instance semi-finished ones, remained in South Korea.

Institutional Change

Although South Korea's developmental path appears to be straightforward, clearly at the same time a high degree of institutional change took place, though. For most of his reign, especially shortly after the coup, the entire politico-economic system centered on the personality of Park. Top-politicians even after Park's assassination tended to have military backgrounds during most of the time horizon relevant for this study (Minns 2001, p. 1025 and 1036). Consequently, a sense of militaristic loyalty was prevalent in the political apparatus. In this regard Park created the EPB, from which he not only expected technological and economic expertise, but also strong loyalty. This was not least of all demonstrated by the EPB chiefs constantly being confidantes of Park.

Therefore, through all the institutional change South Korea pursued its developmental course utilizing to a large degree technocratic support, central decision making and a rather top-down approach. Thus, until it became an industrialized nation, efforts were made to uphold structures allowing for pilot agencies to coordinate industrial policies (Larsen / Park 2014, p 357–358). This setting helped to further strengthen Park's position in initiating a developmental trajectory.

Overall, Park transformed a rather corruptive economic system of his predecessor Rhee, which had elements of state as well as market capitalism, into the state capitalist form of a developmental state. To this end, he structure-wise placed most economic clout into the loyal EPB. But not only did he change the formal institutions, such as also instituting export promotion councils, but also ventured to alter informal institutions prevalent in the population. Using means of propaganda – such as placards or TV spots – he enticed his fellow countrymen to seek the same goals as he, i.e. economic growth, national wealth, being competitive on world markets and overall entering into modernity. The means for realizing those goals, mostly through the formulation and implementation of an ambitious industrial policy plan, were extensively dealt with above.

As a matter of fact, in South Korea starting from the beginning of the 1980s a strong inclination among elites emerged to move beyond the developmental state towards a market capitalist system. This reform drive was to a large extent due to the increasingly large legitimacy problems of the chaebols, stemming from a certain deeply ingrained unpopularity towards those conglomerates among elites and broader parts of the population (see Lim / Jang 2006). Public opinion tended to sway away from support of chaebols.

On the other hand, the traditionally loyal EPB started in the 1970s to criticize the government's economic plans, especially the HCI drive, which the technocrats tended to detest for squandering valuable resources. This led to the gradual erosion of power of the EPB and was seen as a symbol for the transformation to market capitalism (Jung 2011). The EPB eventually was in 1994 merged with the Ministry of Finance. Likewise, within the power balance at the state business nexus, chaebols grew even more powerful and were supposedly in a position to wield enormous politico-economic power in the country.

Combination of Market and State Capitalism

Technically speaking, starting from the 1980s a process set in that transformed South Korea's state capitalism into an idiosyncratic form of market capitalism (Suh / Kwon 2014, Hundt 2014). The country underwent liberalization, deregulation and privatization.[54] In this sense, the policy of preferential credits was streamlined and more emphasis placed on policies such as training and giving tax incentives, in a number of instances phasing out policy loans. Overall, the policy of preferential credits has for a rather long time been criticized significantly. Repeatedly, preferential credits tended to be used more widely for real estate and speculation on the curb market instead of financing investments and promoting exports.

In a rather undisguised fashion, the Federation of Korean Industries (FKI) intervened significantly in order to turn down the policy changes, such as abolishing policy loans, from which most of all the chaebols had profited. As a matter of fact, the South Korean government starting with the 1980s strove to promote SMEs as well. But this policy change was successfully attacked by chaebol business associations, so that the political struggle of the political sphere seems to have been a rather futile feat (Haggard / Collins 1994, p. 80–84 and 91). Thus, the Federation of Korean Industries as the chamber of chaebols demonstrated its relatively large power (Lim p. 197b).

All in all, Park tended to be in a position to justify his legitimacy and linked it to the country's breath-taking economic performance with increasingly improving living conditions for broad segments of the population. After Park's death broader parts of the population demanded changes. Much of the furor of broad segments of the population was directed against the chaebols themselves, causing a situation where the government was constrained to make reforms, especially after the Kwangju massacre in 1980 (Hellmann 2018). Those reform efforts lasted until at least 1996 with OECD inclusion and were accompanied

---

54 The ultimate transformation from a state to a market capitalist system post 1997 entailed a large degree of experimentation with no clear strategy as to which economic system shall in the end be established. Rather contradictory policy moves were taken with occasionally more welfare, at other times more neo-liberal and at certain times even state-focused content. Thus, a hybrid form of a market capitalist order emerged that can neither be classified as an LME or an CME (Suh / Kwon 2014, p. 677). It appears to be fruitful to analyze this transformation in depth, but since market capitalism as such is utilized here only as a form of reference model no deeper attention is paid to this transformation process.

with the population demanding concessions in terms of democratic reforms and a more market capitalist economic order.

Generally speaking, in this politico-economic environment, there occurred a pronounced shift in the state corporate sector interaction in South Korea. While at the outset of the developmental phase the state dominated this interplay, in the course of time the corporate sector became more autonomous and gained significantly in bargaining power. Some observers attribute this change in bargaining power to increasing complexities and uncertainties on world markets. And even domestically the state in East Asia was not able to effectively control the path of the economy anymore (Yeung 2017).

End of the EPB

Arguably, the single most prominent symbol for moving away from economic planning and placing more emphasis on the coordination mechanisms of the market occurred in 1994 by merging the EPB with the Ministry of Finance. Rather in parallel the central bank was granted independence and not being subject anymore to directives from the government.

What ensued was a certain fragmentation of planning and of financial supervision, while the chaebols became increasingly outsized almost to the extent of hypertrophy, expanding in ever more businesses, establishing numerous subsidiaries and therefore becoming so complex as to hardly be able to be supervised and controlled by an economic bureaucracy that was streamlined (Yeung 2017, p. 88–89).

Quite naturally that allowed chaebols even more advantages on the domestic playing-field, which could even less be termed as equal. Purportedly, the chaebols enforced a relatively high degree of financial deregulation resulting in large sums of foreign capital flowing into the country. At the brink of the Asian crisis, chaebols were among the most highly leveraged business entities in the world due to reception of credits from abroad.

The increasingly lopsided playing- field in negotiations – strong chaebols on the one side and a weakened bureaucracy on the other – regarding the state business nexus amplified in some cases not adequately considered and evaluated policy measures. For instance, the government especially hastened as mentioned above, to open access to foreign capital (Heo 2014) and this hot money is now seen as a main cause for the severity of the Asian crisis in South Korea. The situation was in general aggravated, since there existed continuing state involvement in South Korea due to path dependence stemming from its history of being state capitalist in the form of the developmental state (Jeong 2015). Thus, doors were opened up for the inflow of foreign capital, but no checks and balances and especially corporate governance such as they are applied as standards in other industrialized nations were installed.

This systemic mismatch was one of South Korea' policy blunders. In most regards in the 1980s the state had reached goals that were defined at the outset of the developmental course and now an emphasis placed on more efficiently utilizing resources. Of overarching importance, it is to note here that transformation into a market capitalist system did rather not have an impact on the corporate structure, foremost meaning concerning concentration. A coherent plan as to transformation was missing, at least beyond orchestrating some cosmetic corporate merging.

While technocrats moved from its role of controlling the corporate sector to merely coordinating it, the economic might of chaebols simultaneously increased. Mostly, this transformation was not due to the technocrats and the political leadership perceiving a need for less draconian interventions into the corporate sector, but more owing to chaebols with their increased economic power leading to their improved bargaining position at the state business nexus (see Kim 2016). In this sense a sort of oligopolistic market capitalism emerged that rather does not have a counterpart or an antecedent in the world.

After having by now illustrated the institutional changes taking place in South Korea from 1961 until becoming an industrialized nation, it appears to be worthwhile to enlarge on this analysis, how South Korea could in a negative scenario revert back to less efficient economic systems such as crony state capitalism. But so far, no explicit case seems to exist, where a country relapsed back from market capitalism into more inefficient economic orders. Therefore, such analysis would rather tend to be speculative, but could nevertheless as a conjecture possibly be the subject of further research.

Here at this point it shall suffice to having scrutinized the institutional changes having taken place in parallel to South Korea's developmental trajectory. While there were frequent power-shifts nevertheless foremost under Park the interplay between State and business worked impressively smooth. Now, after having presented all the four selected case studies – Russia, Kazakhstan, Singapore and South Korea – it is now time to venture a comparative analysis of all four cases while not neglecting the theoretical parts and the taxonomy elaborated upon in the first two parts.

5 Conclusion: Comparative Analysis of Case Studies

"There is hardly anything more stupid than talking about lessons of history. From history we only find out something about the historians, whether they have style or spirit etc. And about those, who take themselves too serious we have to laugh."

Paul Valery

Abstract

In this final chapter conclusions are drawn as to how the four state capitalist countries performed under its respective structural and policy approach. It becomes clear that the developmental state with a huge degree of cohesiveness was superior to that of crony capitalism and even dual economy state capitalism. As main factors for diverging economic and social performances qualities of the bureaucracy as well as the degree of credibility of political leaders' commitment to development emerge.

Keywords: Structure, Policy, Performances, Developmental State, Crony State Capitalism, Credibility of Commitment to Development, Quality of the Bureaucracy

Thus far, the entire approach to tackling the research question of what is state capitalism and how its profound performance differences can be accounted for was positive. Value judgments for instance were missing. By now this perspective will be shifted up to a certain extent. First of all, it is postulated that development with all its advantages and disadvantages is a goal that ought to be aimed for. In this regard as illustrated throughout this study of all state capitalist variants the developmental state has proven to be the most efficient and best performing in terms of economic development.

In order not to get lost in the complexities of comparing four case studies to seven in this study extensively applied constituting principles, the focus will be on the propositions formulated at the beginning of the case studies. Those were to begin with the proposition that a viable, competent and capable bureaucracy is a key factor for economic orders to excel, i.e. to develop.

Furthermore, there is a certain interdependence between bureaucratic capability on the one hand and content as well as policy framework on the other hand to be observed. This has numerous reasons: for instance, the bureaucracy plays a central role in formulating policies and the more capable the bureaucracy the more stringent and achievable will be content and framework of policies. To give another explanation: When policies are illusory and constantly not reached this reverberates into the motivation of bureaucrats. Clearly, credibility of the bureaucracy suffers and by the same account the pride to serve this organization. Ceteris paribus this should lead to a situation, where the brightest, most talented and most motivated tend to start seeking for job positions outside of the bureaucracy. This creates a vicious circle that sets in due to negative signaling effects.

The next study proposition is that goal orientation regarding policies with clear commitments by a strong state serve to facilitate attainment of developmental goals. It will be part of the ensuing, partly normative analysis whether goal orientation should rather stress flexibility or be so rigid as to not allowing for unexpected contingencies. The penultimate proposition for the case studies is that when – as is the case in most state capitalist countries – there is a lack of rule of law putting property rights at risk, there can be significantly powerful functional equivalents at work. Mostly the political leadership can credibly commit to the safety of property rights and thereby increase in an Euckian sense expectations certainty for economic actors.

Finally, one proposition stated that despite tightly knit institutional frameworks political leaders are in a position to initiate institutional change and are not merely figures that have to act according to the laws of history. One political leader as such can overcome the maze of numerous institutions and make a difference in the developmental trajectory of his country. In the following, for reasons of keeping the argumentation simple Russia and Kazakhstan as low or medium performers are juxtaposed with Singapore and South Korea as high performers. This also follows the justification of the case selection, when Russia and Kazakhstan were seen as replicates and the same with Singapore and South Korea. Nevertheless, enough space is left to put an emphasis on the peculiarities of each single case itself.

Relevance of a capable Bureaucracy

In the course of this study it has been repeatedly demonstrated how essential the creation of a capable bureaucracy is. Beginning with Russia and Kazakhstan it is striking how ardently both countries endeavor to build up capable bureaucracies. In Russia salaries were raised to an extent that is by now almost as high as that for comparable positions in the corporate sector. Furthermore, efforts in recruitment policy were taken to attract the most talented staff from universities, among others by providing for job security and long-term career paths. The overarching key factor, however, keeps being loyal to President Putin.

In Kazakhstan the political leadership places the utmost importance on preventing crony relations from starting to be built up and has therefore enacted a system of constant rotation among bureaucrats. However, regarding corruption this did not really bear fruits, since it is still wide-spread. Another possible factor might be that former President Nazarbayev intended to quell any form of dissent right at the roots and it might have been of help that as soon as groups of resistance might emerge, those are automatically again dissolved by rotating dissenters away.

The result, however, is a bureaucracy that is hardly accessible and in a number of instances even engages in confiscation of economic property by means of trumped-up charges. How in turn function the bureaucracies of Singapore and South Korea? Especially in Singapore a bottom-up approach is to be observed, where new innovation, ideas or policy proposals originate on low levels of the pilot agency EDB and are effectively taken up by higher echelons. Emphasis is placed on efficiency and pragmatism as a sort of rallying hymn for the entire nation.

It would tend to overstrain the bureaucracies of Russia and Kazakhstan and their respective informal institutions to emulate the civil service of a country like Singapore with a history as a British colony, long legal traditions, pragmatism and rather flat hierarchies. It seems to be far more promising to look for South Korea with its hierarchical setting in politics, corporate sphere and society.

Park in a fast manner opted for creating the pilot agency EPB, which did coordinate all developmental efforts under one roof, thereby strengthening accountability, since blame for blunders could not be passed from one ministry to the other anymore. Furthermore, there is an enviable degree of cohesiveness visible in South Korea's developmental trajectory, especially in the gradual industrial upgrading. This stringent approach – almost according to a master plan – would probably not have been conceivable without the EPB and its strong political backing through Park.

In contrast, in Russia – although state and society are very hierarchically structured – there is a pilot agency conspicuously missing. It seems as if the relevant ministries were at times fighting with each other rather than cooperating. This is endogenous to Russia's politico-economic situation with turf wars between liberals and members of the security apparatus. Even if path dependence is taken into account, it should be worth the effort to set aside ideological battles and let in a pragmatic fashion do technocrats in a concerted effort aided by a pilot agency reform the country. In principle, Russia has taken a first step into this direction by making the civil service more attractive. With this talented staff it should be able to forge a pilot agency where the threads are held together for developing the country in a way that its ships, jets, computers or smartphones could be sold on world markets and not have a quality that is sufficient just for the domestic market.

In a way Kazakhstan's structural problems resemble those of Russia. However, here there are no turf wars between two groups with differing ideologies, but clans that tend to come to pragmatic solutions behind the scenes. Currently, there is only the functional equivalent for a pilot agency – the Presidential Cabinet – in place. However, economic policy would be far more cohesive, if there was more coordination.

The clans could agree on a clear-cut economic agenda for development and create a pilot agency that is responsible for implementing it. Nevertheless, it should be mentioned that the Soviet Union has rather disappointing experiences with the super-structure of Gosplan. A pilot agency risks to become like a large tanker that can hardly be navigated anymore. In this regard Russia and Kazakhstan should carefully weigh the advantages and disadvantages of such a super-ministry, in case of growing too unwieldy smartly streamlining the organization and paying heed to South Korea's EPB as an opportune timing and sequencing for abandoning such a pilot agency in the process of transforming to market capitalism.

Interdependence of Policies and Structural Components

Structure and policies are evidently linked in an interdependent fashion. This becomes especially notable when relating Russia's civil service with the economic policies the country applies. There are myriads of ministries and other agencies responsible for economic policy. This leads to a situation where there is a decisive lack in the coherence of the policy framework.

Decisions are often taken on an ad-hoc basis without really committing on long time horizons. Though the political leadership is almost obsessed with planning those plans have little credibility, since in case of non-achievement certain external factors are blamed and quite regularly the plan simply scratched and formulated anew. What remains is that despite all the propaganda for long-term visions such as diversifying the economic structure away from the dependence on natural resources, Russia only tends to react to changes in exogenous factors. The classical example is import substitution. For a long time, Russia relied on imports, ranging from technology to food. Then came the sanctions as a reaction to the annexation of Crimea and now instead of focusing on export orientation, the country looks inwards and seeks to become as autarch as by any means possible.

Possibly, the lack of an agency that coordinates all efforts supported a tendency to react ad-hoc to certain new contingencies without really placing enough significance to fulfilling goals such as President Putin and former President Medvedev declare and declared during their “state of the union” addresses. This rather incohesive industrial policy also has to do with the self-image of Putin as the “good tsar”, who might right out of nowhere direct corporations to employ people, even if there is no need for them. In other instances, companies are outright constrained to finance infrastructure projects.

Had Russia a pilot agency those problems could be mitigated simply through the credibility of an organization that is perceived to be an impartial arbiter between the interests of liberals and members of the security services and is also up to the task of withstanding political pressure from the very top.

The same kind of negligence for really implementing plans is observable in Kazakhstan. Plans are ubiquitous, but when a plan is not fulfilled it is simply rewritten and in the worst case a minister has to go – sometimes even to prison. But this does not change the fact that a real commitment to plans is not perceivable among broader segments of the population. A lack of a pilot agency – with the Presidential Cabinet as just some form of functional equivalent – might help to explain why in Russia and Kazakhstan such an outspoken rupture exists between words and deeds and developmental goals are not systematically pursued.

In this regard, both countries could profit from analyzing the developmental phases of Singapore and South Korea. Overall, in both cases structures of the bureaucracy were interdependently with regard to corporate structures formed. Thus, Singapore with a diverse corporate structure that partly had flat hierarchies did establish a nodal agency that acted more as a part of a network, whereas in South Korea the EPB functioned as a commanding height due to the corporate sector being dominated by hierarchically organized family businesses.

Singapore all in all acted relatively pragmatic concerning the realization of plans. They were modified and adjusted to new contingencies. But what the EDB signaled to all parts of the population is that there would be no stepping back from the developmental effort even when this meant for the population having for a certain time to forego consumption, for instance having to accept suppressed wages.

The EDB was able to control the developmental process and was even able to during the developmental phase streamline its organization. Admittedly, Singapore is a city-state and especially Russia, but also Kazakhstan are significantly larger. However, at least the example of South Korea as a relatively large country with a complex economy could be helpful for Russia and Kazakhstan.

Thus, in the South Korean case the EPB operated with five-year-plans, which were up to a certain extent even reminiscent of the ones in the Soviet Union. The organization accompanied and controlled the economy on its way through the industrial upgrading and concentrated its efforts on big business, meaning the chaebols. All of this was possible due to the explicit and repeated backing by the political leadership during most of the existence of the EPB.

Russia and Kazakhstan could try to emulate this element of South Korea's developmental path, among others since South Korea dealt with a highly concentrated corporate structure such as is prevalent in Russia and Kazakhstan. It would have to entail that the political leaders subordinate themselves repeatedly under the guidance of technocrats. Ad-hoc interferences and interventions into corporate strategies or in general the developmental path of the country should stop or at least be negotiated with the "wardens of development", i.e. the pilot agencies.

Goal orientation during Developmental Phases

As has been already pointed out in all four case studies industrial policy entails a significant number of goals and a certain effort is put behind goal attainment. However, in Russia and Kazakhstan the goals are traditionally placed too high with the justification that a goal level that is too low would demotivate economic agents. This again bears two risks in itself. When the goal setting is almost as habitually illusory high economic agents tend to not perceive them as realistic anymore. They stray from ambitiously striving for a goal. Secondly, an atmosphere tends to emerge where a disconnect tends to rupture between elites and broader segments of the population. On lower level scorn could erupt with a perception "that those at the top have no knowledge about what is going on on the ground".

To aggravate the situation in many cases pretexts are construed why a particular goal could not have been achieved, and in many instances, this relates to exogenous factors that the state had no control over. Thus, due to this questionable reasoning the credibility is deeply impaired and likewise the credibility of the entire state. Clearly, there is nothing wrong with formulating ambitious plans. A problem arises, when those by all possible means are hardly to be realized. Furthermore, in the instances of Russia and Kazakhstan there is also no clear road map presented as to how to achieve those goals. In both case studies a neat cascading down of goals to lower levels with a transparent timing and sequencing of policy moves is not observable.

Although Singapore and South Korea are not in all regards, perfect role models, there are some elements, where both developmental states in goal formulation and implementation successfully swayed from those in Russia and Kazakhstan. Singapore and South Korea at first tended to rely on technocrats in goal formulation in order to see what is conceivably possible to reach. Especially the EDB with its grass roots approach was very familiar with how the situation was on lower levels.

Thus, instead of acting from some kind of ivory tower, EDB-bureaucrats planned according to what can feasibly be accomplished in a limited amount of time. There were clear steps laid out in order for instance to build up new industries such as electronics or later on a bio-tech industry. This was all conducted gradually with a step by step approach and not one overarching large design that might turn out to be unrealistic.

Overall, there clearly was a focus on efficiency. This was up to a certain point different in South Korea. Here large investments with little or even negative returns were conducted. Nevertheless, the country did not create white elephants, but industries that successfully compete on world markets.

And in this effort for the most part the experts from the EPB were decisively involved – for the most parts even writing the five-year plans. However, at a critical juncture the political leadership clashed with the EPB. In the 1970s Park perceived that for South Korea to economically keep on progressing a heavy and chemical industry push was needed.

Consequently, large sums were invested and technology imported from abroad to build the steel mill of Posco, which at the same time aided in building up a car industry. Here Park overcame resistance from the technocrats of the EPB. But at the same time had the HCI drive early on demonstrated signs of not working in all likelihood it would have been discarded.

The political leadership and the bureaucracy were very pragmatic in not sticking to unsuccessful projects, just because they were pet projects of influential political leaders or technocrats. All this entails valuable lessons for Russia and Kazakhstan. First of all, it appears to be advantageous in policy formulation to gather information as much as possible on the ground. This can prevent the formulation of de-motivating high economic goals. The second factor is that – as long as there is the readiness to scrap a project in case of failure – it is worthwhile to risk venturing into new industries, when there is a credible rationale behind it. Up to a certain extent Russia already demonstrated such risk taking by the state, when building up a nano-technology industry. Overall, it is worth to emulate Singapore's and South Korea's propensity to in a trial and error fashion kickstart certain endeavours and give them a chance. The only prerequisite is not to throw good money after bad, meaning squandering resources for a project that has obviously failed.

Credible Commitments as a Functional Equivalent for a limited Degree of Rule of Law

As has been pointed out above in the case studies, in Russia and Kazakhstan economic agents perceive a lack of property rights safety. In the case of Russia that has severe consequences with capital flight, commercial entities intentionally staying below a certain threshold not to become too big and visible, so that raiding might occur. In general, the flowing of resources into the most productive commercial activities seems to be impaired.

Rather congruous – even if not as devastating – is the situation in Kazakhstan. A traditional legal system with a high reputation and credibility to judge impartially takes generations to build up. So, clearly it is difficult to expect Russia and Kazakhstan to in a short time-frame create a highly regarded judicial system.

In principle South Korea and to a lesser extent Singapore were confronted with the same kind of dilemma. In order to develop economically a credible legal system is needed, but on the other hand the judicial system can only become resilient and not bending to pressures in the course of development with the passage of long time horizons. Singapore clearly had an advantage here of having been a British colony and therefore having the legacy of common law. Thus, here property rights – as opposed to civil rights – were held in high regard.

However, Russia and Kazakhstan can seek to emulate the solution of South Korea during its developmental phase. Initially, business leaders were even afraid to be incarcerated, which in certain cases was even put into reality by the state. At this point, where the cooperation of the private corporate sector was at stake, Park reacted in a way to entirely commit his own political future on developmental goals, which is only possible through implicit guarantees for private property rights.

Possibly, Russia and Kazakhstan can aim into the same direction. But in Russia President Putin scolded oligarchs and – with almost only the exception of Mikhail Khodorkovsky – guaranteed them their wealth accumulated from dubious sources during the time of transformation. In a way Putin kept to his promise, although from time to time constraining oligarchs to engage in what he deems to be service for the entire society, such as building infrastructure. Restraining from so drastically interfering straight into corporate affairs should be one means of improving private property rights.

Nevertheless, it needs to be taken into account that regarding property rights also informal institutions are of high importance and those cannot be changed overnight, but it usually takes the course of the lifetimes of a generation. It is intriguing to see how under Park the functional equivalent worked, under PAP reign in Singapore obviously, too, with limited success in Kazakhstan and a virtual failure in Russia.

Of high significance is here the personality and the personal integrity of the political leader himself. If as in the case of Putin sizable personal wealth is skimmed and apparently goes straight into the coffers of political leaders themselves, the political commitment to development and making sacrifices for a better future sounds hollow. The degree to which in the form of actor-centricity political leaders could liberate themselves from institutional constraints will be dealt with by giving answers to the fifth and thereby last study proposition.

Actor Centricity

To differing degrees the political leaders being of key importance in this study did overcome partial resistance through the formal and informal framework of their respective countries. In two cases – Russia and Singapore – the political leaders were to a relatively high degree constrained in their decision-making, creating a situation of certain path dependencies. With Kazakhstan under Nazarbayev and South Korea under Park it was different.

Presidents Nazarbayev and Park were in such a strong position to push through decisions almost on their own. This refers as much to Nazarbayev's decision to move the capital from Almaty to what is now called Nursultan. And such widely unconstrained decision-making power is also demonstrated by Park realizing the HCI push against the majority of his most trusted technocrats.

Up to a certain extent a different picture emerges when taking a look at Russia and Singapore. Shortly after the inception of Singapore as a city-state, the political leadership imposed a trade-off on the broader population. On the one hand, a state apparatus with a significant institutional capacity of government and bureaucracy – with virtually no corruption and strict adherence to meritocratic principles and these being the decisive source of the government's legitimacy – provided for stable economic development, while it demanded acceptance of political repression in return (Huat 2017, p. 1–3 and 8). This is reminiscent of Russia, where there is a trade-off between stable standards of living and political repression. But this does not translate to an overly large degree of actor centricity.

In Russia after the breakup of the Soviet Union the country's leadership tended to be divided between two rivalling factions, the liberals and the members of the security services. Putin himself is not in a position to enter into one of both camps. As President he is constrained to straddle the interests of both power groups. Admittedly, he has enough leeway for instance to coercing oligarchs to make contributions to society such as building new roads.

But was he for instance to introduce an immaculate liberal politico-economic system, resistance of the group of security service members would be so strong that in the end the plan in all probability had to be discarded. Thus, the informal and formal institutional framework in Russia compels the political leader to be constantly looking for compromises. This limited discretionary power entails certain problems.

First, economic policy tends to be incohesive, occasionally swaying from one direction to another. An example was the tax on imported Japanese vehicles in the Far East that was later on abandoned. Second, this unpredictability of decision-making regarding the regulatory framework hinders expectations certainty that is so vital for businesses to thrive. Virtually overnight the regulation can change and a company needs to make sudden adjustments.

In a completely different fashion Singapore's long-term President Lee Kuan-yew was confronted with obstacles when seeking to come to lonely decisions. Here the ruling party PAP played a decisive role and decision-making occurred within the established procedures prevalent in the PAP. This strong role of the party however did facilitate a cohesive economic policy, since the PAP in terms of leading personnel and its belief system was very stable. Rationality was the mantra of Lee and the PAP.

Thus, it becomes obvious that the degree of actor centricity does not as such determine over the economic perspectives of a country. Most important of all is the ability of the political leadership to not contradict itself while communicating and having the bureaucracy implement those plans without significant alterations.

Out of clear visions, plans and concrete measures economic success stories are born. Here Russia and Singapore vary wildly, although in terms of being constrained from domestic political forces, both are rather similar. But while in Russia this takes the form of two opposing factions, stymying to a certain extent the developmental trajectory of the country, in Singapore there has always been a rather constant and long enduring consensus as to progress with state capitalism in the form of the developmental state through step after step in industrial upgrading.

Not even the fact that up to a certain extent the state in Singapore took over a role as an entrepreneur did not fracture this approach which was with little resistance put into reality. Possibly it can be deducted here that uniformity of economic policy and unity among political and corporate leaders fosters economic development. Constant bickering and turf wars about the fundamental economic direction of the country entails costs in the form of using resources in order to quell opposition instead of concentrating on developing products for instance for the world market.

The situation differs in Kazakhstan and South Korea. Here both political leaders could almost unfettered come to certain decisions. While in Kazakhstan this led to the building of certain prestige projects in the former capital Almaty and the new capital Nursultan with large parts of the country still suffering from widespread poverty, resources in South Korea tended to be used productively, gradually building up new industries with a higher value added. It is close to impossible to explain why one political leader puts all his nation's resources behind achieving development with the means of committing utterly on export orientation, the other uses the income generated from exploiting natural resources to a certain extent on favoured pet projects.

Possibly cultural factors can account for this cleavage in decision-making of two political leaders being mostly free from the constraints of a burdensome institutional framework. Since such cultural considerations go beyond the scope of this economic analysis, at this point it shall suffice just to conjecture that Park in his personal lifestyle tended to keep on living with medium standards, being humble and had according to certain sources accumulated hardly any private wealth during his tenure. This belief system of Park could possibly stem from in essence following the principles of Confucianism.

On the other hand, Nazarbayev was geared in an environment where clans played a vital role and therefore to demonstrate his superiority the chief of the clans had to build monuments in order to underline his power. For the analysis of how the economic system of state capitalism can yield such widely differing performances, this could pose one conjecture: to a certain extent, informal institutions determine success or failure of a state capitalist system with its relatively high degree of actor centricity, where often contacts are more important than the formal procedures.

A demonstratively humble style of living of the political leader can possibly cause broader segments of the population to accept some sacrifices in living-standards themselves, when therefore in the future there is a realistically high chance of living in a developed country with all the amenities existing there. To conclude, in South Korea a high degree of actor centricity worked, whereas in Kazakhstan rather not. In Russia the fact that President Putin has to balance between two power groups and is therefore relatively constrained was rather not development-enhancing. Quite the opposite is true for Singapore, where the strong role of the party constrained Lee quite significantly and this did not stymie development.

Reasons for Performance Differences

By now – with the aid of seven constituting principles of state capitalism – it has in part two been illustrated what state capitalism is. In a further analysis five variants of state capitalism were identified. Subsequently, four case studies of state capitalist countries were conducted in order to more precisely find out what accounts for those varying performance differences. While each case is unique and no panacea that works deterministically towards the goal of positive developmental performances exists, this study has identified certain elements of state capitalism which tend to be development-enhancing.

It would be for instance a mistake to bluntly utilize the recipes of the developmental state as a "one size fits all" and blueprint for other countries. Meanwhile there obviously is a considerable amount of evidence discernible of how late developers can profit from the experience of the countries with a developmental state past, especially African from Asian nations (see Ayelazuno/ Mawuko-Yevugah 2019). When giving advice to countries intending to embark on a developmental course such as South Korea pursued, it needs to be taken into account, though, that informal institutions and the entire institutional framework evolve only with a considerable amount of time. Some form of continuity is a key characteristic of institutions (Kohli 2004, p. 16). Therefore, it is impossible to imitate the institutional setting of a developmental state overnight and observe rapid advances in development.

Nevertheless, there are numerous avenues in terms of structure for adapting developmental state recipes and the most important are summarized here. First of all, it has proven to be conducive to growth and development to create a pilot agency with a flexible agenda that can pragmatically react to unexpected contingencies.

In this regard a highly qualified staff is needed and the state should take the opportunity to use signaling effects. As soon as the first highly talented graduates start working for the pilot agency and it gains a certain positive reputation, other highly qualified graduates tend to want to follow. Such a recruitment policy can take the form of purely pecuniary incentives, but also non-monetary incentives are conceivable, for instance by allowing the technocrats discretion in their work projects or airing commercials in the media to underline how attractive an employer this pilot agency is.

What can ensue quite naturally is as in Singapore with the EDB and in South Korea with the EPB that an esprit de corps emerges, where members are so proud of serving their organization that they have an incentive to perform even more than is expected from them. It could be of considerable help, if talented new-comers were offered a long-term perspective to serve the organization as a career technocrat for long time horizons.

That by itself also increases identification with the pilot agency. Not least of all, the pilot agency is in urgent need of political backing. It helps when the leaders of the pilot agency and the political leader have established a trustful atmosphere between themselves that on the other hand does not border on a crony relationship.

Secondly, it is of great advantage to rally the nation behind the goal of development. This can again be done through the media. In South Korea, Singapore and Kazakhstan such communication was widely applied. It would, however, have been of far less effectiveness when the political leadership was not ready to embrace those goals for itself as well.

Thirdly, bureaucracies always carry the risks with them of becoming too bloated and keep on existing long after its original purpose has vanished. Therefore, it is of utmost importance to smartsize a lead agency in case the processes become too complex and the entire organization is unwieldy.

Then it would be recommendable to form baby agencies of the mother agency, so that accountability and responsibility do not suffer. What has proven a considerable boon in Singapore is the concept of the one stop agency. Thus, instead of – as in Russia – having to deal with numerous agencies and bureaucrats at the same time, it facilitates business enormously to just need one agency and in the best of cases one contact person to be dealing with. It creates transactions costs to establish a relationship with each single technocrat and thus limiting the contacts to the bureaucracy to one stop appears to be of significant help for businesses, but also the effectiveness of technocrats.

Fourth, in some regards, pragmatism can be of considerable help for business. Thus, if corruption as such cannot be eradicated, it would be development-enhancing to at least endow technocrats with exact competences, so that in case of for instance the need for a permit, the economic agent knows at what level who is to be bribed. Russia serves here as a deterring example, where it often takes months to identify who in the bloated bureaucracy is to be bribed and then in certain instances even numerous technocrats open their hands.

Kazakhstan provides for another development-inhibiting example. The policy of constantly rotating technocrats and politicians has shown little positive effects, since corruption has definitely not nearly been eradicated. Instead it increases costs for the state and business when – in a country that relies more on personal relations than formal procedures – contacts have to be built at least every three years anew. Trust is a valuable commodity and it tends to be connected with high costs when the economic agent needs to build it up again. Furthermore, in a number of instances one bureaucrat starts a project and still in the phase of duration the responsible bureaucrat is rotated somewhere else, which creates incentive problems. When the technocrat knows that he will not earn the praise or bonus for a project he initiates, he will have fewer incentives to perform.

For recommendations concerning policies the same caveat needs to be formulated as for structural aspects. Those are merely elements to gradually improve the quality – meaning the performance – of an economic system. It seems as if a grand approach where an entire system can be in a shock-wise manner introduced into a country is futile at best and creates a severe economic and possibly political crisis at worst. History matters and path dependence always needs to be taken into account.

Judging from the four case studies conducted here, it appears most fruitful to opt for export orientation and not import substitution. By entering into ever new markets abroad – utilizing their respective comparative advantages – Singapore and South Korea built their wealth. Russia inadvertently now strays from this policy approach, since it has to cope with the sanctions because of being excluded from a number of markets and their products. So far, however, the results of the switch to import substitution are mixed at best with an economy that does not really reach growth rates typical for an emerging nation. There are some lighthouse projects in the metropolises of Moscow and St. Petersburg, especially in terms of digitalization, but a country-wide push to development remains relatively far away. Kazakhstan seeks to orient its policy towards export promotion, but thus far the export mix consists overwhelmingly of those from natural resources.

As a whole, there ought to be one policy measure utilized in order to improve on one target figure. When coming to some normative implications, a number of problems ensues. For instance, isolating a few independent variables that have an effect on dependent variables is extremely difficult, especially given the fact that societies are not be analyzed under test conditions (Kohli 2004, p 421).

If one policy measure is used for a plethora of goals the side effects might turn out to be unexpectedly devastating. In order to avoid such negative side effects, it is always best to cautiously operate in a trial and error method with one policy measure at the time. In such a setting also a carrot-and-stick approach is possible, where initiators of the successful implementation of a certain tool are rewarded.

Accountability is in such a manner to a huge extent possible with all the ensuing incentive advantages. By the same token a pilot agency should ensure that the industrial policy does not become entirely fragmented. The policy steps should be carefully finetuned to each other. This requires skillful economic planning as having been accomplished in Singapore and South Korea. Ad-hoc measures were rather seldom applied in both developmental states, so that the business side overall had a significant degree of expectations certainty.

In this manner both developmental states created a rather stable regulatory framework to the benefit of business, while in the interviews the perception reverberated that there is too little regulatory stability and formal institutional changes come too soon and unexpectedly in Russia and Kazakhstan.

In the course of development only due to unexpected contingencies profound changes in policies are warranted. In general, the principles of industrial policy as a means for achieving development shall only in severe cases, such as a deep economic crisis owing to endogenous or exogenous factors be touched upon. Such a steadfastness while sticking to a certain pragmatism provides for a development-enhancing structural and policy background. Finally, the most important policy prescription is for political leaders to stick to their promises. Credible commitments take years to build up and are destroyed within a few days or even virtually overnight. Therefore, the credible commitment to development shall be something of a holy cow for all state capitalist political leaders who embark their countries on a developmental path. It is the backbone through which investor trust is built and therefore regarding domestic as well as foreign economic actors a golden rule not to renege on promises.

By now a point is rather reached, where the fuzzy concept of state capitalism has been given a sharper form and it seems to be possible to for future research rely on defining state capitalism through the seven constituting principles. By the same token with establishing five variants of state capitalism there are now hints as to how state capitalism – as theoretically rather a second best to the economic order of market capitalism – should be structured in a country in order to during developmental phases lift countries to the level of industrialized nation.

In this regard South Korea and Singapore are worthy role models to follow. It has been listed above what elements of state capitalism deserve to be tried in other countries. A guarantee for success cannot be given, but at least the likelihood that it will work is relatively high.

In this study significant developmental progress was analyzed, especially for Singapore and South Korea and to a markedly lower extent for Russia and Kazakhstan. For reasons of scope the external effects – on pollution, but also income and wealth inequalities – of these developmental processes were not dealt with. From an economic point of view, these external effects should be internalized and it might be possible to better account for such external effects in future research.

Referring to positive external effects, it might be argued that countries can take a rather similar path to wealth along the lines of the developmental state and this is probably one of the most effective ways to prevent migration streams from threatening the social fabric of industrialized nations by lessening the incentives to seek for a better life in industrialized nations. In this sense development can also help to mitigate the burden of overpopulation in the world. Currently we observe one of the largest phases of species extinction ever and that has to do with overpopulation of the human species. Wealth creation has shown to be an effective means to limit a constantly higher birth rate and thereby could facilitate a more cautious approach to protect our nature.

Future research can tackle in more depth the question of how to progress from state to market capitalism and at what stage it is ideal to go into this direction. It has only been superficially analyzed how South Korea managed to transform itself into a market economy. Also, it is probably worthwhile to look deeper into the question of how structure and policies in state capitalist, but also especially industrialized nations, interact to provide for performance results. And research could be done whether under certain circumstances it might for a late developer even be better to transform straight into a market capitalist system.

Likewise, it remains an open research question whether elements of state capitalism are promising within the context of developed nations. A number of economists hedge fundamental doubts about a wide-spread and permanent adoption of such instruments in industrialized states. In this study state and market capitalism were sharply separated as two distinct phenomena. However, in general, a distinction could also be drawn between state-led and state-induced. This could open the door for a theoretical approach dealing with hybrid forms of state and market capitalist systems. Future research can put more of an emphasis on opportunities to induce economic development rather than control the process as is common in state capitalism.

Thus far, in history late industrializers tended to be rather state capitalist with a lot of state interference and protection for domestic markets. It would be worthwhile to find a country that in its developmental trajectory opted straight at the start for the market capitalist way. At this stage with a rather optimistic undertone that late developers can profit from the experience of state capitalist successes by developmental states it needs to be cautioned that especially Singapore and South Korea profited tremendously from open markets into which they could export their goods. And during this phase for geopolitical reasons South Korea did not even have to open its own markets. Thus, it was a very specific time in the course of history post WWII, when Singapore and South Korea grasped their chance to become prosperous. But history has shown that other nations might also perform surprisingly well, especially when it is looked to China. In this regard history remains an open process, where actor centricity drives forward the nations to always new stages.

6 Annex

6.1 Questionnaire for Field Trips to Russia and Kazakhstan

Four Hypotheses:

1. From a structural point of view a competent, pragmatic bureaucracy supports performance, such as relatively high scores in development indicators.
2. Concerning policies, a goal-oriented approach facilitates development by giving the corporate sector a relatively high degree of expectations certainty.
3. Structure and policies are interdependent meaning that for instance a competent bureaucracy tends to pursue a goal-oriented industrial policy and the existence of such an industrial policy amplifies the competence of the bureaucracy.
4. Regarding property rights, various types of state capitalism differ in their ability to overcome a lack of rule of law by credibly committing to developmental goals, with the developmental state the most successful and crony as well as predatory state capitalism the least successful.

Are there competitive entry exams and are there performance-based career paths for civil servants? Is remuneration at least partially performance-based? How does remuneration in the civil service relate to salaries in the private sector?

Would you consider the civil service to be more aloof from the corporate sector, directly connected to it or somewhere in between? Do you observe a number of instances, where companies managed to undermine the industrial policy formulated by the government by buying influence regarding bureaucrats? Do former bureaucrats regularly serve as managers in companies?

Do companies perceive the bureaucracy as more of a burden or a boon in achieving business goals such as increasing revenue and profit or venturing into new markets? Are SOEs favoured to the detriment of private sector companies? Are civil servants in your country capable of picking winners and upgrading the industrial base? Are there short-comings in information flows from the bureaucracy to the private sector and vice versa?

Do bureaucrats use a steady hand, when dealing with the corporate sector? Are there sudden policy changes, for instance after the government or ministers change? Are goals of industrial policy credible and viable regardless of the political leadership?

Does the bureaucracy apply any goals, when dealing with the corporate sector in order to conduct an industrial policy? Are industrial upgrading and development explicit goals of the government? Can anyone be held accountable for achieving goals?

Does the government commit to developmental goals, for instance economic growth or diversification? If yes, are these goals credible? Can anyone be held accountable in case goals are not reached?

Do you observe a tendency in your country that goals by the political leadership are indeed realized? Is measurement of goal attainment objective?

Are property rights relatively safe in your country? Do citizens have the means to challenge property rights violations in court? How do you rate the quality of the judicial system in your country?

Is the politico-economic system more based on creating win-win-situations or is there more of a tendency of pursuing narrow self-interests with all the resulting welfare losses? Does the political leadership give in to special interest groups or does is it more bent on maximizing benefits of the entire population?

How would you classify your country? Is there more of an emphasis on crony or developmental activities or somewhere in between? Can you observe that institutions have changed since the 1990s? If yes, in which form?

6.2 Codesystem for Russia

Codes	Frequency
1. High entry barriers	1
2. Social peace at all costs	3
3. Top-down approach	8
4. Inflexibility of the labour market	2
5. Importance of the Industrial Military Complex	3
6. Relevance of loyalty	1
7. Double bottom line	3
8. Specialnij investnij kontrakti (SPIK)	10
9. Special Economic Zones	1
10. Import substitution	1
10.1 With no real results	2
10.2 As a chance	9
11. Keeping a low profile	4
12. Liberals vs. siloviki	5
13. State acts contradictorily	3
14. Short-term orientation of Russian business	1
15. Dominance of political leader	

Codes	Frequency
15.1 Middle	13
15.2 Low	2
15.3 High	11
16. Degree of Personalization	
16.1 Middle	16
16.2 Low	0
16.3 High	12
17. Corruption	
17.1 Middle	12
17.2 Low	0
17.3 High	9
18. Relevance of business associations	
18.1 Middle	9
18.2 Low	6
18.3 High	8
19. Dominance of particularistic interests	16
19.1 Has its boundaries	1
20. Quality of the judicial system	
20.1 Middle	12
20.2 Low	9
20.3 High	0
21. Inhibition of going to court	
21.1 Middle	12
21.2 Low	8
21.3 High	1
22. Property Rights	
22.1 Secure	
22.2 Insecure	11
22.3 Relatively Secure	11
23. Data	
23.1 Valid	15
23.2 Not valid	3
24. Decision-makers	
24.1 To some extent accountable	2
24.2 Accountable	7
24.3 Not accountable	16
25. Development as a fully pursued goal	

Codes	Frequency
25.1 No	20
25.2 Yes	7
26. Developmental goals	
26.1 It depends	6
26.2 Not achievable	17
26.3 Achievable	1
27. Target-orientated policy	
27.1 No	0
27.2 Yes	28
28. Fluctuation in ministries	
28.1 High	0
28.2 Middle	5
28.3 Low	13
29. Business environment	
29.1 Stable	5
29.2 Instable	24
30. Information flows	
30.1 Rather Working	12
30.2 Rather not Working	9
31. Picking the winners	
31.1 Is conducted	17
31.2 Is not conducted	4
32. SOEs and SMEs	2
32.1 SOEs support SMEs	1
32.2 Large actors favoured over SMEs	5
32.3 SOEs favoured over SMEs	23
33. Bureaucracy	
33.1 Boon and Burden	12
33.2 Rather a boon	0
33.3 Rather a burden	8
34. Amakudari and vice versa	22
35. No industrial policy	3
36. Embeddedness of civil service	
36.1 Not embedded	3
36.2 Embedded	28
37. Salaries compared to the corporate sector	
37.1 Not competitive	3

Codes	Frequency
37.2 Rather competitive	11
38. Autonomy of bureaucracy	
38.1 High	0
38.2 Middle	6
38.3 Low	10
39. Salaries and promotion performance-based	
39.1 No	5
39.2 Yes	19
40. Long-term career paths	
40.1 No	9
40.2 Yes	7
41. Lack of entry tests	6
41.1 As an exception	3
42. Pilot Agency	14
43. NIE and Russia	3

6.3 Codesystem for Kazakhstan

Codes	Frequency
1. State as a majority investor	1
2. Interference of Samruk Kazyna into SOEs	1
3. Pilot Agency	1
4. Issue of career perspectives	5
5. Entrepreneurialism	1
6. Double bottom line for SOEs	3
7. Keeping a low profile	8
8. Salaries and promotion	
8.1 Not performance-based	9
8.2 Performance-based	11
9. Lack of autonomy of bureaucracy	1
10. SOE SME duality	15
11. Urban rural divide	3
12. Lack of information obstacle for entrepreneurship	1
13. Dominance of political leader	
13.1 Middle	1

Codes	Frequency
13.2 Low	0
13.3 High	38
14. Dominance of particularistic interests	14
15. Relevance of clans	12
16. Relevance of business associations	
16.1 Middle	6
16.2 Low	2
16.3 High	21
17. Degree of personalization	
17.1 Middle	7
17.2 Low	0
17.3 High	26
18. Quality of the judicial system	
18.1 Middle	15
18.2 Low	11
18.3 High	0
19. Inhibition of going to court	
19.1 Middle	19
19.2 Low	5
19.3 High	1
20. Property rights	
20.1 Relatively safe	25
20.2 Not safe	3
20.3 Safe	3
21. Validity of data	
21.1 Not valid	12
21.2 Valid	9
22. Realization of goals	
22.1 Some	8
22.2 No	2
22.3 Yes	1
23. Accountability of technocrats and ministers	
23.1 Not accountable	9
23.2 Accountable	17
24. Development as a fully pursued explicit goal	
24.1 There is a de jure and de facto difference	13
24.2 No	2

Codes	Frequency
24.3 Yes	25
25. Target-oriented industrial policy	
25.1 No	2
25.2 Yes	24
26. Goals of industrial policy	
26. 1 It depends	3
26.2 Not achievable	10
26.3 Achievable	15
27. Fluctuation in Ministries	
27.1	0
27.2	23
28. Information flows	
28.1 Rather working	5
28.2 Rather not working	16
29. Picking winners	
29. 1 Is not conducted	7
29.2 Is conducted	3
29.2.1 Unsuccessfully	12
29.2.2 Successfully	1
30. Burden of bureaucracy	
30.1 It depends	10
30.2 Boon	1
30.3 Burden	8
31. Porousness between SMEs and public sector	3
32. Amakudari and vice versa	25
33. Corruption	2
33.1 Middle	22
33.2 Low	0
33.3 High	9
34. Overarching role of SOEs	3
34.1 Level playing-field	3
34.2 SOEs preferred over SMEs	15
34.3 SOEs support SMEs	2
35. Embeddedness of civil service	
35.1 Not embedded	2
35.2 Embedded	16
35.2.1 Due to role of SOEs	12

Codes	Frequency
36. Prestigiousness of civil service	
36.1 Civil service not prestigious	4
36.2 Civil service prestigious	8
36.2.1 Prestigiousness related to salaries	2
37. Salaries in comparison	3
37.1 Salaries not competitive versus corporate sector	22
37.1 Salaries competitive versus corporate sector	3
38. Entry tests exist	21
38.1 Very competitive	6
38.2 Easy application	3

7 Literature

Adcock, R. / Collier, D. (2001): Measurement Validity: A shared Standard for Qualitative and Quantitative Research, in: *American Political Science Review*, Vol. 95.

Ahn, K.-W. (2007): The Rule of Law in South Korea: Insights into the Social Evolution during the Two Decades with the New Constitution (1987–2007), Seoul National University, accessed 2nd of July 2019 under: *www.law.wisc.edu/gls/documents/ahn_paper.doc*

Ahrens, J. (1994): Der russische Systemwandel: Reform und Transformation des (post)sowjetischen Wirtschaftssystems, Frankfurt.

Ahrens, J. (2002): Governance and Economic Development: A Comparative Institutional Approach. New Thinking in Political Economy, Cheltenham.

Ahrens, J. / Hoen, H. / Spechler, M. (2016): State Capitalism in Eurasia: A Dual-Economy Approach to Central Asia, in: Brusis, M. et. al (eds.): Politics and Legitimacy in Post-Soviet Eurasia, Houndmills.

Ahrens, J. / Stark, M. (2012): Unabhängige Organisationen in autoritären Regimes: Widerspruch in sich oder effektives Instrument von Developmental States?, Research Paper, No. 9, PFH Private Hochschule Göttingen.

Aiko, M. (1994): Monitoring Characteristics of the Main Bank System: An Analytical and Developmental View, in: Aoki, M. / Patrick, H.: The Japanese Main Bank System: Its Relevance for Developing and Transforming Economies, Oxford.

Aligica, P. D. / Tarko, V. (2012): State Capitalism and the Rent-Seeking Conjecture, in: *Constitutional Political Economy*, Vol. 23.

Aligica, P. D. / Tarko, V. (2014): Crony Capitalism: Rent Seeking, Institutions and Ideology, in: Kyklos, Vol. 67.

Amable, B. (2003): The Diversity of Modern Capitalism, Oxford.

Amsden, A. H. (1989): Asia's Next Giant. South Korea and Late Industrialization, New York.

Amsden, A. H. (1992): Asia's Next Giant: South Korea and Late Industrialization, Oxford.

Amsden, A. H. (2001): The Rise of "The Rest". Challenges to the West from Late-Industrializing Economies, Oxford.

Aoki, M. (1996): Towards a Comparative Institutional Analysis: Motivations and Some Tentative Theorizing, in: *Japanese Economic Review*, Vol. 47.

Aoki, M. (2003): Information, Corporate Governance and Institutional Diversity, Oxford.

Aoki, M. (2007): Endogenizing Institutions and Institutional Change, in: *Journal of Institutional Economics*, Vol. 3.

Aoki, M. (2013): Comparative Institutional Analysis. Theory, Corporations and East Asia. Selected Papers of Masahiko Aoki, Cheltenham.

Aslund, A. (2013): How Capitalism was built: the Transormation of Central and Eastern Europe, Russia, the Caucasus and Central Asia, New York.

Ayelazuno, J. A. / Mawuko-Yevugah, L. (2019): Development Failures in Ghana, Development Micracles in Asia: Whither the African Rising, in: African and Asian Studies, Vol. 18.

Barr, M. D. (2003): Perpetual Revisionism in Singapore: the Limits of Change, in: *Pacific Review*, Vol. 16.

Barr, M. D. (2004): Parties and Politics: A Study of Opposition Parties and the PAP in Singapore, in: *Pacific Affairs*, Vol. 77.

Barr, M. D. (2011): Evolution of a Revolution: Forty Years of the Singapore Constitution, in: *Journal of Southeast Asian Studies*, Vol. 42.

Barr, M. D. (2014): The Ruling Elite of Singapore. Networks of Power and Influence, New York.

Barr, M. D. (2016): Ordinary Singapore: The Decline of Singapore Exceptionalism, in: *Journal of Contemporary Asia*, Vol. 46.

Barr, M. D. / Skrbiš, Z. (2008): Constructing Singapore: Elitism, Ethnicity and the Nation-building Process, Copenhagen.

Barthes, R. (2010): Die Sprache der Mode, Berlin.

Barzel, Y. (2015): What are Property Rights and why do they Matter? A Comment on Hodgson's Article, in: *Journal of Institutional Economics*, Vol. 11.

Baumol, W. J / Litan, R. E. / Schramm, C. J. (2007): Good Capitalism, Bad Capitalism, and the Economics of Growth and Prosperity; New Haven.

Bazeley, P. (2013): Qualitative Data Analysis. Practical Strategies, London.

Beck, U. (2015): Risikogesellschaft. Auf dem Weg in eine neue Moderne, München.

Beetham, D. (1991): The Legitimation of Power, Houndmills.

Behuria, P. (2015): Between Party Capitalism and Market Reforms – Understanding Sector Differenced in Rwanda, in: *Journal of Modern African Studies*, Vol. 53.

Bercuson, K. (1995): Singapore: a Case Study in Rapid Development: A Case of Rapid Development, IMF Occasional Paper, Washington.

Bhagwati, J. / Panagariya, A. (2014): Why Growth Matters. How Economic Growth in India reduced Poverty and the Lessons for other Developing Countries, New York.

Bhaskaran, M. (2003): Reinventing the Asian Model. The Case of Singapore, Institute of Policy Studies, Singapore.

Bhaskaran, M / Wilson, P. (2011): The Post-Crisis Era: Challenges for the Singapore Economy, in: Wilson, P. (ed.): Challenges for the Singapore Economy After the Global Financial Crisis, Singapore.

Biggart, N.W. (1998): Deep Finance. Organizational Bases of South Korea's Financial Collapse, in: *Journal of Management Inquiry*, Vol. 7.

Biggart, N.W. / Guillen, M.F. (1999): Developing Difference: Social Organization and the Rise of the Auto Industries of South Korea, Taiwan, Spain, and Argentina, in: *American Sociological Review*, Vol. 64.

Bjorvatn, K. / Naghavi, A. (2011): Rent seeking and Regime Stability in Rentier states, in: *European Journal of Political Economy*, Vol. 27.

Bower, J. L. / Leonard, H. B. / Paine, L. S. (2011): Capitalism at Risk: Rethinking the Role of Business, *Harvard Business Review*, Vol. 89.

Boyd, R. / Ngo, T.-W. (2005): Emancipating the Political Economy of Asia from the Growth Paradigm, in: Boyd, R. / Ngo, T.-W. (eds.): Asian States: Beyond the Developmental Perspective, New York.

Brady, H. E. (2004): Data-set Observations versus Causal-Process Observations: The 2000 U.S. Presidential Election, in Brady, H. E. / Collier, D.: Rethinking Social Inquiry: Diverse Tools, Shared Standards, Lanham.

Bremmer, I. (2010): The End of the Free Market. Who Wins the War between States and Corporations, New York.

Bremmer, I. (2014): The New Rules of Globalization, in: Harvard Business Review.

BTI (2017): Bertelsmann Stiftung Transformation Index, available under https://www.bti-project.org/en/home/, accessed 30th of November 2017.

Carney, R. W. / Zheng, L. Y. (2009): An Explanation for Singapore's Innovation Gap, in *Journal of East Asian Studies*, Vol. 9.

Carney, R. W. (2014): Singapore: Open, State-Led Capitalism, accessed on the28th of November 2018 under file:///C:/Users/woelka/Downloads/CarneySingaporeopenstate-ledcapitalism2014.pdf

Carney, R. W. (2015): The Stabilizing State: State Capitalism as a Response to Financial Globalization in One-Party Regimes, in: *Review of International Political Economy*, Vol. 22.

Chang, H.-J. (1995): The Transformation of the Communist Economies: against the Mainstream, Basingstoke.

Chang, H.-J. (ed.) (1995): The Role of the State in Economic Change, Oxford.

Chang, H.-J. (2003): Kicking away the Ladder: Infant Industry Promotion in Historical Perspective, Oxford.

Chang, H.-J. (2006): The East Asian Development Experience: the Miracle, the Crisis and the Future, London.

Chang, H.-J. (2007): Institutional Change and Economic Development, New York.

Chang, H.-J. (2011): Institutions and Economic Development: Theory, Policy and History, in: *Journal of Institutional Economics*, Vol. 7.

Chang, H.-J. / Rowthorn, R. (1995): The Role of the State in Economic Change, London.

Chew, E. (2012): Introduction: Heroic Public Servant and History-Maker of modern Singapore, in: Chew, E. / Kwa, C. G. (eds.): Goh Keng Swee: A Legacy of Public Service, Singapore.

Chew, Y. T. / Yeung, H. W.-C. (2001): The SME advantage: Adding local Touch to Foreign Transnational Corporations in Singapore, in: *Regional Studies*, Vol. 35.

Chibber, V. (1999): Building a Developmental State: The Korean Case Reconsidered, in: *Politics & Society*, Vol. 27.

Chibber, V. (2002): Bureaucratic Rationality and the Developmental State, in: *American Journal of Sociology*, Vol. 107.

Cho, L.-J. / Yoon, H. K. (1991a): Economic Development in the Republic of Korea. A Policy Perspective, Honolulu.

Cho, L.-J. / Yoon, H. K (1991b): Major Economic Policies of the Park Administration, in: Cho, L.-J. / Yoon, K. (eds.): Economic Development in the Republic of Korea. A Policy Perspective, Honolulu.

Choi, Y-J. / Glassman (2018): A Geopolitical Economy of Heavy Industrialization and Second Tier City Growth in South Korea: Evidence from the "Four Core Plants Plan", in: Critical Sociology, Vol 44.

Chong, A. (2007): Singapore's Political Economy, 1997–2007, in: *Asian Survey*, Vol. 47.

Chong, A. (2015): The Ruling Elite of Singapore: Networks of Power and Influence, in: *Journal of Southeast Asian Studies*, Vol. 46.

Chua, H. B. (2007): Asia Macro Views. Singapore Economy: The New and The Dual, Citigroup Note, accessed on the 12th of November 2018 under: https://

furrybrowndog.files.wordpress.com/2010/07/asia-macro-views-singapore-economy-the-new-and-the-dual.pdf

Chung, K.H. / Lee, H.C. / Jung, K.H. (1997): Korean Management: Global Strategy and Cultural Transformation, Berlin.

Cimoli, M. / Dosi, G. / Stiglitz, J. E. (2009): The Political Economy of Capabilities Accumulation: The Past and Future of Policies for Industrial Development, in: Cimoli, M. / Dosi, G. / Stiglitz, J. E.: Industrial Policy and Development. The Political Economy of Capabilities Accumulation.

Cimoli, M. et al. (2009): Institutions an Policies Shaping Industrial Development: An Introductory Note, in: Cimoli, M. / Dosi, G. / Stiglitz, J. E.: Industrial Policy and Development. The Political Economy of Capabilities Accumulation.

Clark, C. (2008): Preußen. Aufstieg und Niedergang 1600–1947, London.

Clark, C. (2015): The Paradoxes in Globalization's Economic Empowerment of South Korea, in: *Korea Journal*, Vol. 55.

Clo, S. / Fiorio, C. V. / Florio, M. (2017): The Targets of State Capitalism: Evidence from M&A deals, in: *European Journal of Political Economy*, Vol. 47.

Coase, R. (1937): The Nature of the Firm, in: *Economica*, Vol. 4.

Cooper, R.N. (1994): Fiscal Policy in Korea, in: Haggard, S. / Cooper, R. N./ Collins, S./ Kim, C./Ro, S.-T.: Macroeconomic Policy and Adjustment in Korea, 1970–1990, Harvard.

Cuba heute (2016): Der VII. Parteitag der PCC – eine Analyse (Teil I), available under: https://cubaheute.wordpress.com/tag/selbststandige/; accessed on the 15th of February 2017.

Cummings, S. N. (2012): Understanding Central Asia. Politics and Contested Transformations, New York.

Deyo, F. C. (1987): Introduction, in Deyo, F. C. (ed.) (1987): The Political Economy of the New Asian Industrialism, Ithaca.

Diamond, J. (2018): Arm und Reich. Die Schicksale menschlicher Gesellschaften, Frankfurt.

Diamond, L. (2008): The Democratic Rollback: The Resurgence of the Predatory State, in: Foreign Affairs, Vol. 87.

Di Iorio, F. (2016): World 3 and Methodological Individualism in Popper's Thought, in: *Philosophy of the Social Sciences*, Vol. 46.

Djankov, S. (2015): Russia's Economy under Putin: From Crony to state Capitalism, PIIE, accessed on the 24th of August 2018 under https://piie.com/sites/default/files/publications/pb/pb15-18.pdf.

Doner, R. F. / Hicken, A. / Ritchie, B. K. (2009): Political Challenges of Innovation in the Developing World, in: *Review of Policy Research*, Vol. 26.

Dow Jones (28th of June 2019): Hintergrund/US-Chipkonzern AMD gab China "Schlüssel zum Königreich".

Dzarasov, R. (2013): Conundrum of Russian Capitalism. The Post-Soviet Economy in the World System, London.

Economist (18th of July 2015): The Singapore exception. Special Report, accessed on the 27th of November 2018 under: https://www.economist.com/special-report/2015/07/18/the-singapore-exception.

Economist (23rd of March 2019): A Showman exits.

Economist (2019): The World in 2020.

Eisenhardt, K. M. (1989): Building Theories from Case Stuy Research, in: *Academy of Management Review*, Vol. 14

Eisenhardt, K. M. / Graebner, M. E. (2007): Theory Building from Cases: Opportunities and Challenges, in: *The Academy of Management Journal*, Vol. 50.

Estrin, S. / Zhixiang, L. / Shapiro, D. (2019): State Capitalism, Economic Systems and the Performance of State-owned Firms, in: *Acta Oeconomica*, Vol. 69.

Eucken, W. (1990): Grundsätze der Wirtschaftspolitik, Tübingen.

Evans, P. (2012): Embedded Autonomy. States and Industrial Transformation, Princeton.

Fainshmidt, S. / Judge, W. Q. / Aguilera, R. V. / Smith, A. (2018): Varieties of Institutional Systems: A contextual Taxonomy of understudied Countries, in: *Journal of World Business*, Vol. 53.

FAZ (28th of October 2017): "Wir brauchen kein europäisches Google".

Feldmann, M. (2019): Global Varieties of Capitalism, in: *World Politics*, Vol. 71.

Ferguson, N. (2011): Wir sind alle Staatskapitalisten, in: *Die Zeit*, Nr.47.

Ferris, J. S. / Gawande, K. (1998). Coordination Failures and Government Policy: Evidence from Emerging Countries, Carleton Economic Papers, Nr. 3.

Fine, B. (2013): Beyond the Developmental State: An Introduction, in: Fine, B. / Saraswati, J. / Tavasci, D.: Beyond the Developmental State. Industrial Policy into the Twenty-First Century.

Fischer, A. M. (2018): Debt and Development in historical Perspective: The external Constraints of late Industrialization revisited through South Korea and Brazil, in: *World Economy*, Vol. 41.

Fraser Institute (2017): Economic Freedom, available under: https://www.fraserinstitute.org/economic-freedom/dataset?page=dataset&min-year=2&-

max-year=0&filter=0&most-free=1&quartile2=1&quartile3=1&least-free=1, accessed on 30th of November 2017.

Frieden, J. (1981): Third World indebted Industrialization: International Finance and State Capitalism in Mexico, Brazil, Algeria and South Korea, in: *International Organization*, Vol. 35.

Fukuyama, F. (1992): The End of History and the last Man, London.

Gainsborough, M. (2009): The (Neglected) Statist Bias and the Developmental State: the Case of Singapore and Vietnam, in *Third World Quarterly*, Vol. 30.

Gell-Mann, M. (1996): Das Quark und der Jaguar. Vom Einfachen zum Komplexen – die Suche nach einer neuen Erklärung der Welt, München.

Gelman, V. (2018): Technocratic Traps of Policy Reforms, in: YaleGlobal Online, accessed under https://yaleglobal.yale.edu/content/technocratic-traps-policy-reforms on the 22nd of August 2018.

Gemici, K. (2013): South Korea during the Park Chung Hee Era: Explaining Korea's Developmental Decades, in: *Asian Journal of Social Science*, Vol. 41

Gilley, B. (2008): Legitimacy and Institutional Change. The Case of China, in: *Comparative Political Studies*, Vol. 41.

Glassman, J. / Choi, Y.-J. (2014): The Chaebol and the US Military Industrial Complex: Cold War Geopolitical Economy and South Korean Industrialization, in: *Environment and Planning A-Economy and Space*, Vol. 46.

Gomez, E. (2003): Introduction: Political Business in East Asia, in: Gomez, E. (ed.): Political Business in Asia, London.

Goodman, R. / White, G. / Kwon, H.-J. (1998): The East Asian Welfare Model: Welfare Orientalism and the State, London.

Greif, A. (2008): Institutions and the Path to the Modern Economy. Lessons from Medieval Trade, Cambridge.

Greif. A. / Iyigun, M. (2013): Social Organizations, Violence & Modern Growth,Institute for the Study of Labour (IZA), Bonn, Discussion Paper 7377.

Guriev, S. (2018): Soft Budget Constraints and State Capitalism, in: *Acta Oeconomica*, Vol. 68.

Guriev, S. / Kolotilin, A. / Sonin, K. (2009): Determinants of Nationalization in the Oil Sector: A Theory and Evidence from Panel Data, in: *The Journal of Law, Economics & Organization*, Vol. 27.

Haggard, S. (1986): The Newly Industrializing Countries in the International System, in: *World Politics*, Vol. 38.

Haggard, S. (1994a): Macroeconomic Policy through the First Oil Shock, 1970–1975, in: Haggard, S./ Cooper, R. N./ Collins, S./ Kim, C./Ro, S.-T.: Macroeconomic Policy and Adjustment in Korea, 1970–1990, Harvard.

Haggard, S. (1994b): From the Heavy Industry Plan to Stabilization: Macroeconomic Policy 1976–1980, in: Haggard, S. / Cooper, R. N./ Collins, S./ Kim, C./Ro, S.-T.: Macroeconomic Policy and Adjustment in Korea, 1970–1990, Harvard.

Haggard, S. / Collins, S. (1994): The Political Economy of Adjustment in the 1980s, in Haggard, S.: The Political Economy of Adjustment in the 1980s, Harvard.

Haggard, S. / Thiede, L. (2011): The Rule of Law and Economic Growth: Where are We?, in: *World Development*, Vol. 39.

Hall, P. / Soskice, D. (eds.) (2001): Varieties of Capitalism: The Institutional Foundations of Comparative Advantage, Oxford.

Han / Kim (2017): The Changing Modes of Administrative Reform in South Korea, in: *Transsylvanian Review of Administrative Sciences*, Vol. 50

Haveman, H. A. / Jia, N. / Shi, J. / Wang, Y. (2017): The Dynamics of Political Embeddedness in China, in: *Administrative Science Quarterly*, Vol. 62.

Haynes, M. J. (2011): Labor, Exploitation and Capitalism in Russia before and after 1991, in: Pollard, V. K. (ed.): State Capitalism, Contentious Politics and Large-Scale Social Change, Leiden.

Heilmann, S. (1999): Verbände und Interessenvermittlung in der VR China. Die marktinduzierte Transformation eines leninistischen Staates, in: Merkel, W. / Sandschneider, E.: Die Rolle von Verbänden im Transformationsprozess.

Heilmann, S. (2011): Policy-Making through Experimentation: The formation of a Distinctive Policy Process, in: Heilmann, S. / Perry, E. J.: Mao's Invisible Hand. The Political Foundations of Adaptive Governance.

Hellmann, O. (2018): High Capacity, low Resilience: The "Developmental" State and Military-Bureaucratic Authoritarianism in South Korea, in: *International Political Science Review*, Vol. 39.

Heng, T. M. / Low, L. (1990): Towards greater competition in Singapore's telecommunications, in: *Telecommunications Policy*, Vol. 14.

Henke, H. / Boxill, I. (2000): Introduction, in: Henke, H. / Boxill I. (eds.): The End of the 'Asian Model'?, Amsterdam.

Heo, I. (2014): The Political Economy of Reforming Financial Supervision in South Korea, in: *Journal of Asian and African Studies*, Vol. 49.

Heo, U. / Hahm, S. D. (2014): Political Culture and Democratic Consolidation in South Korea, in: *Asian Survey*, Vol. 54.

Hertog, S. (2010): Defying the Resource Curse: Explaining Successful State-Owned Enterprises in Rentier States, in *World Politics*, Vol. 62.

Hill, M. H. / Lian, K. F. (1995): The Politics of Nation Building and Citizenship in Singapore, London.

Hodgson, G. M. (2015): Conceptualizing Capitalism. Institutions, Evolution, Future, Chicago.

Hoen, H. W. (1998): The Transformation of Economic Systems in Central Europe, Cheltenham.

Holmes, L. (2016): Comparative Conclusions: Legitimacy and Legitimation in Eurasian Post-Communist States, in: Brusis, M. et. al (eds.): Politics and Legitimacy in Post-Soviet Eurasia, Houndmills.

How, T. T. (2007): Singapore Perspectives 2007. A new Singapore, Singapore.

Huat, C. B. (2016): State-owned Enterprises, State Capitalism and Social Distribution in Singapore, in: *The Pacific Review*, Vol. 29.

Huat, B. C. (2017): Liberalism Disavowed: Communitarianism and State Capitalism in Singapore, Singapore.

Huff, W. G. (1987): Patterns in the Economic Development of Singapore, in: *The Journal of Developing Areas*, Vol. 21.

Huff, W. G. (1994): The Economic Growth of Singapore: Trade and Development in the Twentieth Century, New York.

Huff, W. G. (1995a): What is the Singapore model of economic Development?, in: *Cambridge Journal of Economics*, Vol. 19.

Huff, W. G. (1995b): The Developmental State, Government and Singapore's Economic Development since 1960, in: *World Development*, Vol. 23.

Huff, W. G. (1999a): Hypergrowth in an East Asian NIC: Public Policy and Capital Accumulation in Singapore, in: *Word Development*, Vol. 27.

Huff, W. G. (1999b): Turning the Corner in Singapore's Developmental State?, in: *Asian Survey*, Vol. 39.

Huizinga, J. (2004): Homo Ludens: Vom Ursprung der Kultur im Spiel, Reinbek.

Hundt, D. (2009): Korea's Developmental Alliance: State, Capital and the Politics of Rapid Development, New York.

Hundt, D. (2014): Economic Crisis in Korea and the Degraded Developmental State, in: *Australian Journal of International Affairs*, Vol. 68.

Hundt, D. (2015): Neoliberalism, the Developmental State and Civil Society in Korea, in: *Asian Studies Review*, Vol. 39.

Hvidt, M. (2011): Economic and Institutional Reforms in the Arab Gulf Countries, in: *Middle East Journal*, Vol. 65.

Hyett, N. / Kenny, A. / Dickson-Swift, V. (2014): Methodology or Method? A Critical Review of Qualitative Case Study Reports, in: *International Journal of Qualitative Studies on Health and Well-Being*, Vol.9.

ILO (2017): Employment in the Public Sector by Economic Activity, available under: http://www.ilo.org/ilostat/faces/wcnav_defaultSelection;ILOSTATCOOKIE=QJnrMLWOcolLX9KDemA2onXYpAJKY5eFlhvfT7pX_mtQddA7f4ZU!-834607540?_afrLoop=9881535563143&_afrWindowMode=0&_afrWindowId=null#!%40%40%3F_afrWindowId%3Dnull%26_afrLoop%3D9881535563143%26_afrWindowMode%3D0%26_adf.ctrl-state%3D7ho85ex5y_4, accessed on 20th of March 2017.

Jackson, G. (2009): Actors and Institutions, University of Bath, School of Management, Working Paper.

Jackson, T. (2017): Prosperity without Growth. Foundations for the Economy of Tomorrow, New York.

Jeong, B. (2015): The Developmental State and Social Enterprise in South Korea. A Historical institutionalism perspective, Seoul.

Johnson, C. (1983): Miti and the Japanese Miracle. The Growth of Industrial Policy, 1925–1975, Stanford.

Jones, L. P. / Sakong, I. (1980): Government, Business, and Entrepreneurship in Economic Development: The Korean Case, Cambridge.

Jung, J.-Y. (2011): How a Powerful Bureaucracy fell: The Abolition of the Economic Planning Board in South Korea, in: *Korea Observer*, Vol. 42.

Jung, J.-Y. (2015): Financial Liberalisation and Institutional Incompatibility: The Unresolved Dilemma of the Korean Economy, in: *Politics*, Vol. 35.

Kang, D. C. (2003): Transaction Costs and Crony Capitalism in East Asia, in: *Comparative Politics*, Vol. 35.

Kang, Y. (2008): Case Study: Adaptive Implementation of the Five-Year Economic Development Plans, KDI School, Working Paper Series, Working Paper 08–14, Seoul.

Kaufmann, D. / Kraay, A. / Mastruzzi, M. (2010): The Worldwide Governance Indicators: Methodology and Analytical Issues, Brookings Institution.

Kazakhstanskaya Pravda (24th of January 2017): It's time for business to respond to State Support – Nazarbayev, accessed under www.kazpravda.kz/en on the 24th of January 2017.

Kazakhstanskaya Pravda (22nd of February 2019): Bakythhan Sagintayev made a statement upon Government resignation, accessed 22nd of February 2019 under https://www.kazpravda.kz/en/news/society/bakytzhan-sagintayev-made-a-statement-upon--government-resignation.

Kellogg, P. (2017): Gods outside the Market. Central Banks, China and the Emergence of Neoliberal State Capitalism, in: World Review of Political Economy, Vol. 8.

Kim, E. M. (1997): Big Business, Strong State: Collusion and Conflict in South Korean Development, 1960–1990, New York.

Kim, S. (2016): Global Capital, Business Groups and State Coordination: The Changing Profile of Chaebol-State Relations in South Korea, in: *Socialist Studies*, Vol. 11.

Kim, S.-Y. (2013): The Rise of East Asia's Global Companies, in: *Global Policy*, Vol. 4.

King, V. T. (2008): The Sociology of Southeast Asia: Transformations in a Developing Region, Honolulu.

Kisoudis, D. (2015): Goldgrund Eurasien. Der neue Kalte Krieg und das Dritte Rom, Leipzig.

Koh, F./Koh, W.T.H. (2002): Venture capital and economic growth: An industry overview and Singapore's experience, in: *Singapore Economic Review*, Vol. 47, Research Collection Lee Kong Chian School of Business, accessed on the 14th of November 2018 under https://ink.library.smu.edu.sg/cgi/viewcontent.cgi?article=1037&context=lkcsb_research.

Koh, F./Koh, W.T.H./Tschang, F. (2003): An Analytical Framework for Science Parks and Technology Districts with an Application to Singapore, Paper presented at the Conference "Science Parks and Incubators", accessed on the 15th of November 2018 under https://pdfs.semanticscholar.org/1ffc/6a8322a017e54d79bd7740135e8e14415805.pdf?_ga=2.109310598.223117793.1542264964-422123748.1542264964.

Kohli, A. (2004): State-Directed Development. Political Power and Industrialization in the Global Periphery, Cambridge.

Kommersant (16th of August 2018): Minpromtorgy sverchdochodi ne nuchni, accessed under https://www.kommersant.ru/doc/3714376?from=four_business on the 16th of August 2018.

Kommersant (5th of February 2019): AFK "Sistema" i Baring Vostok naraschtschivayut doli v riteilere, accessed under https://www.kommersant.ru/doc/3874019 on the13th of February 2019.

Kröll, M. (1966): Walter Eucken und die Theorie der Wirtschaftslenkung, in: Jahrbuch für Sozialwissenschaft, Vol. 17.

Krueger, A. (1974): The Political Economy of the Rent-Seeking Society, in: *American Economic Review*, Vol. 64.

Krug, B. (ed.) (2015): State Capitalism, Cheltenham.

Krugman, P. (1994): The Myth of Asia's Miracle, in: *Foreign Affairs*, Vol. 73, accessed 6th of March 2019 under https://www.foreignaffairs.com/articles/asia/1994-11-01/myth-asias-miracle.

Kuo, E. Y. C / Low, L. (2001) Information Economy and Changing Occupational Structure in Singapore, in: The Information Society, Vol.: 17.

Kurlantzick, J. (2016): State Capitalism. How the Return of Statism is Transforming the World, Oxford.

Kwon, H.-j. / Yi, I. (2009): Economic Development and Poverty Reduction in Korea: Governing Multifunctional Institutions, in: *Development and Change*, Vol. 40.

Lai, C. (2018): Economic Nationalism in South Korea and Taiwan: Examining Identity Discourse and Threat Perceptions towards Japan after the Second World War (1960s–1970s), in: *Journal of Asian Security and International Affairs*, Vol. 5

Lai, K. P. Y. / Yeung, H. W.-C. (2003): Contesting the State: Discourses of the Asian Economic Crisis and mediating Strategies of Electronics Firms in Singapore, in: *Environment and Planning A-Economy and Space*, Vol. 35.

Lall, S. / Teubal, M. (1998): "Market-Stimulating" Technology Policies in Developing Countries: A Framework with Examples from East Asia, in: *World Development*, Vol. 26.

Larson, J. F. / Park, J. (2014): From Developmental to Network State: Government Restructuring and ICT-led Innovation in Korea, in: *Telecommunications Policy*, Vol. 38.

Lee, A. S. (1989): Case Studies as Natural Experiments, in: *Human Relations*, Vol. 42.

Lee, C. (2009): The Rule of Law and Forms of Power: Theorizing the Social Foundations of the Rule of Law in Korea, in: *Korea Journal*, Vol. 49.

Lee, E. (2008): Singapore: The Unexpected Nation, Singapore.

Lee, S.-C. (1991): The Heavy and Chemical Industries Promotion Plan (1973–79), in: Cho, L.-J. / Yoon, K. (eds.): Economic Development in the Republic of Korea. A Policy Perspective, Honolulu.

Lee, Y.-S. (2018): Law and Development: Lessons from South Korea, in: *Law and Development Review*, Vol. 11.

Li, K.-W. (2002): Capitalist Development and Economism in East Asia: The Rise of Hong Kong, Singapore, Taiwan and South Korea, London.

Li, L. / McMurray, A. / Sy, M. (2018): Corporate Ownership, Efficiency and Performance under State Capitalism: Evidence from China, in Journal of Policy Modelling, Vol. 40.

Liebman, B. L. / Milhaupt, C. J. (2016): Introduction: The Institutional Implications of China's Economic Development of China's Economic Development, in: Liebman, B. L. / Milhaupt, C. J. (eds.): Regulating the Visible Hand? The Institutional Implications of Chinese State Capitalism Oxford.

Lim, H.-C. (2010a): Korea's Developmental Alliance: State, Capital and the Politics of Rapid Development, in: *Pacific Affairs*, Vol. 83.

Lim, H.-C. (2010b): The Transformation of the Developmental State and Economic Reform in Korea, in: *Journal of Contemporary Asia*, Vol. 40.

Lim, H.-C. / Jang, J.-H. (2006): Neo-Liberalism in Post-Crisis South Korea: Social, Conditions and Outcomes, in: *Journal of Contemporary Asia*, Vol. 36.

Lim, L. Y. (1983): Singapore's Success: The Myth of the Free Market Economy, in: *Asian Survey*, Vol. 23.

Lin. L.-W. (2017): Reforming China's State-owned Enterprises: From Structure to People, in: *The China Quarterly*, Vol. 229.

Liow, D. E. (2011): The Neoliberal-Developmental State: Singapore as a Case-Study, in: *Critical Sociology*, Vol. 38.

Liow, E. D. (2011): The Neoliberal-Developmental State: Singapore as a Case Study, in: *Critical Sociology*, Vol. 38

Lombard, M. (2017): Government Intervention in OECD Member Countries: Equity at the Expense of Efficiency?, accessed 15th of March 2017 from: https://editorialexpress.com/cgi-bin/download.cgi?db

Losman, D. L. (2010): The Rentier State and National Oil Companies: An Economic and Political Perspective, in: *The Middle East Journal*, Vol. 64.

Low, L. (2001) The Singapore developmental state in the new economy and polity, in: *The Pacific Review*, Vol. 14.

Low, L. (2006): The Political Economy of a City-state Revisited, Berkeley.

Luttwak, E. N. (1993): The Endangered American Dream, New York.

Luttwak, E. N. (1999): Turbo-Capitalism. Winners and Losers in the Global Economy, New York.

Mahoney, J. / Goertz, G. (2006): A Tale of Two Cultures: Contrasting Quantitative and Qualitative Research, in: *Political Analysis*, Vol. 14.

Mantzavinos, C. (2004): Individuals, Institutions and Markets, Cambridge.

Markus, S. (2015): Property, Predation and Protection. Piranha Capitalism in Russia and Ukraine, Cambridge.

Markus, S. (2017): The Atlas has not shrugged: Why Russia's Oligarchs are an Unlikely Force to Change, in: *Daedalus*, Vol. 146.

Markus, S. / Charnysh, V. (2017): The Flexible Few: Oligarchs and Wealth Defense in Developing Democracies, in: *Comparative Political Studies*, Vol. 50.

Marx, K. (1993): Das Kapital. Kritik der politischen Ökonomie. Erster Band, Berlin.

Mason, E. S. / Mahn, J. K. / Perkins, D. H. / Kim, K. S. / Cole, D. C. (1980): The Economic and Social Modernization of the Republic of Korea, Cambridge.

Mauzy, D. K. / Milne, R. S. (2002): Singapore's Politics under the People's Action Party, New York.

May, C. (2014): Die Kultur des Kapitalismus in Brasilien, Indien und China, in: Nölke, A. / May, C. / Claar, S.: Die großen Schwellenländer. Ursachen und Folgen ihres Aufstiegs in der Weltwirtschaft, Wiesbaden.

McFaul, M. (2001): Russia's Unfinished Revolution: Political Change from Gorbachev to Putin, New York.

Meadows, C. S. / Hyle, A. (2010): Procedural Methodology for a Grounded Meta-Analysis of Qualitative Case Studies, in: *International Journal of Consumer Studies*, Vol. 34.

Milhaupt, C. J. / Zheng, W. (2015): Beyond Ownership: State Capitalism and the Chinese Firm, in: *The Georgetown Law Journal*, Vol. 103.

Minns, J. (2001): Of Miracles and Models: The Rise and Decline of the Developmental State in South Korea, in: *Third World Quarterly*, Vol. 22.

Mirza, H. (1986): Multinationals and the Growth of the Singapore Economy, London.

Musacchio, A. / Lazzarini, S. G. (2012): Leviathan in Business: Varieties of State Capitalism and their Implications for Economic Performance, Working Paper 12–108, Harvard Business School.

Musacchio, A. / Lazzarini, S. G. (2014): Reinventing State Capitalism, Cambridge, MA.

Musacchio, A / Lazzarini, S. G. / Aguilera, R. V. (2015): New Varieties of State Capitalism: Strategic and Governance Implications, in: The Academy of Management Perspectives, Vol. 29.

Naseemullah, A. / Arnold, C. E. (2015): The Politics of Developmental State Persistence: Institutional Origins, Industrialization, and Provincial Challenge, in: *Studies in Comparative International Development*, Vol. 50.

Noland, M. / Pack, H. (2003): Industrial Policy in an Era of Globalization. Lessons from Asia, Washington.

Nölke, A. / ten Brink, T. / Claar, S. / May, C. (2015): Domestic Structures, Foreign Economic Policies and Global Economic Order: Implications from the Rise of

Large Emerging Economies, in: European Journal of International Relations, Vol. 21.

North, D. C. (1981): Structure and Change in Economic History, New York.

North, D. C. (1990): Institutions, Institutional Change and Economic Performance, Cambridge.

North, D. C. (2005): Understanding the Process of Economic Change, Cambridge.

North, D. C. / Wallis, J. J. / Weingast, B. R. (2009): Violence and Social Orders. A Conceptual Framework for Interpreting Recorded Human History, Cambridge.

OECD (2017): Employment in the Public Sector, available under: http://www.oecd-ilibrary.org/docserver/download/4215081ec022.pdf?expires=1490006340&id=id&accname=guest&checksum=ECFD8FD989DC878C5B9D-6C781FE19430, accessed on 20th of March 2017.

Ortmann, S. / Thompson, M. R. (2018): Introduction: The "Singapore Model" and China's Neo-Authoritarian Dream, in: Kai, Y. / Ortmann, S.: From Sweden to Singapore: The Relevance of Foreign Models for China's Rise, in: *China Quarterly*, Vol. 236.

Pang, E. F. / Lim, L. Y. C. (2015): Labor, Productivity and Singapore's Development Model, in: *The Singapore Economic Review*, Vol. 60.

Park, E.-Y. (2009): The Rule of Law in the Republic of Korea, in: *National Taiwan University Law Review*, Vol. 6.

Peebles, G / Wilson, P. (2002): Economic Growth and Development in Singapore. Past and Future, Cheltenham.

Pereira, A. A. (2004): State entrepreneurship and regional development: Singapore's industrial parks in Batam and Suzhou, in: *Entrepreneurship & Regional Development*, Vol. 16.

Pereira; A. A. (2008) Whither the Developmental State? Explaining Singapore's continued Developmentalism, in: *Third World Quarterly*, Vol. 29.

Phillips, S. / Yeung, H. W.-C. (2003): A Place for R&D? The Singapore Science Park, in: *Urban Studies,* Vol. 40.

Praxisbuch (2015): Praxisbuch Interviews, Transkription & Analyse. Anleitungen und Regelsysteme für Qualitativ Forschende, Marburg.

Pirie, I. (2008): The Korean Developmental State. From Dirigisme to Neo-Liberalism, New York.

Pirie, I. (2018): Korea and Taiwan: The Crisis of Investment-Led Growth and the End of the Developmental State, in: *Journal of Contemporary Asia*, Vol. 48.

Pollard, V. K. (2011): State Capitalist Analysis – Before the Russian Revolution, in Reaction to Stalin's Consolidation of Power, and after the Cold War, in: Pollard, V. K. (ed.): State Capitalism, Contentious Politics and Large-Scale Social Change, Leiden.

Pollock, Friedrich (1973): Aufsätze zum Staatskapitalismus, Rotdruck.

Purcell, T. F. (2017): The Political Economy of Rentier Capitalism and the Limits to Agrarian Transformation in Venezuela, in: *Journal of Agrarian Change*, Vol. 17.

Quimpo, N. G. (2009): The Philippines: Predatory Regime, growing authoritarian Features, in: *The Pacific Review*, Vol. 22.

Ragin, C. C. (2013): New Directions in the Logic of Social Inquiry, in: *Political Research Quarterly*, Vol. 66.

Ragin, C. C. (2014): The Comparative Method. Moving Beyond Qualitative and Quantitative Strategies, Berkeley.

Rajah, R. (2012): Authoritarian Rule of Law. Legislation, Discourse and Legitimacy in Singapore, Cambridge.

Regnier, P. (2000): Singapore, a Global City-State into the Twenty-First Century?, in: Henke, H. / Boxill I. (eds.): The End of the 'Asian Model'?, Amsterdam.

Resag, J. (2017): Feynman und die Physik: Leben und Forschung eines außergewöhnlichen Menschen, Heidelberg.

Rigg, J. (1988): Singapore and the Recession of 1985, in: *Asian Survey*, Vol. 28.

Ro, S.-T. (1994): Korean Monetary Policy, in: Haggard, S./ Cooper, R. N./ Collins, S./ Kim, C./Ro, S.-T.: Macroeconomic Policy and Adjustment in Korea, 1970–1990, Harvard.

Rodan, G. (1989): The Political Economy of Singapore's Industrialization: National State and International Capital, Houndmills.

Rodrik, D. (1996): Coordination Failures and Government Policy: A Model with Applications to East Asia and Eastern Europe, in: *Journal of International Economics*, Vol. 40.

Rodrik, D. (2007): One Economics, Many Recipes. Globalization, Institutions, Economic Growth, Princeton.

Rodrik, D. (2014): Green Industrial Policy, in: *Oxford Review of Economic Policy*, Vol. 30.

Schein, E. H. (1996): Strategic Pragmatism. The Culture of Singapore's Economic Development Board, Cambridge.

Schiek, S. (2010): Politik, Öffentliche Verwaltung und Modernisierung in Kasachstan, in: Staat oder privat? Akteure und Prozesse zwischen Staaten und Gesellschaften in Osteuropa. Beiträge für die 18. Tagung Junger Osteuropa-Experten, Bremen.

Schiek, S. (2013): Widersprüchliche Staatsbildung – Kasachstans konservative Modernisierung, Baden-Baden.

Schneider, B. R. (2013): Hierarchical Capitalism in Latin America: Business, Labor and the Challenges of Equitable Development, New York.

Schneider, H. (2012): State Capitalism and Globalization – A Challenge to Whom?", in: *Illiria International Review*, Vol. 2.

Schotter, A. (1981): The Economic Theory of Institutions, Cambridge.

Schumpeter, J. A. (1942): Capitalism, Socialism and Democracy, New York.

Schwak, J. (2019): Dangerous Liaisons? State-Chaebol Co-operation and the Global Privatisation of Development, in: *Journal of Contemporary Asia*, Vol. 49.

Seawright, J. (2016): The Case for Selecting Cases that are Deviant or Extreme on the Independent Variable, in: *Sociological Methods & Research*, Vol. 45.

Seow, F. T. (2006): Beyond Suspicion? The Singapore Judiciary, New Haven.

Sim I.J.L. (2011): Does State Capitalism Work in Singapore? A Study on Ownership, Performance and Corporate Governance of Singapore's Government-Linked Corporations, University of Queensland

Simon, H. / Egidi, M. (eds.) (1992): Economics, Bounded Rationality and the Cognitive Revolution, Aldershot.

Singh, A. / Zammit, A. (2006): Corporate Governance, Crony Capitalism and Economic Crises: Should the US Business Model replace the Asian Way of "doing Business"?, in: *Corporate Governance*, Vol. 14.

Skocpol, T. / Finegold, K. (1982): State Capacity and Economic Intervention in the Early New Deal", in: *Political Science Quarterly*, Vol. 97.

Smelser, N. (1976): Comparative Methods in the Social Sciences, New Jersey.

Smith, A. (1776/1910): Wohlstand der Nationen, Köln.

Soest, C. v. / Grauvogel, J. (2016): Comparing Legitimation Strategies in Post-Soviet Countries, in: Brusis, M. et. al (eds.): Politics and Legitimacy in Post-Soviet Eurasia, Houndmills.

Song, B-N. (1997): The Rise of the Korean Economy, Oxford.

Spak, H. J. (1997): Transformationsökonomie: Aspekte und Bestimmungsgründe am Beispiel der Systemtransformation in Polen, Berlin.

Stark, M. A. (2012): The Emergence of Developmental States from a New Institutionalist Perspective: A Comparative Analysis of East Asia and Central Asia, Diss.

Straits Times (2017): Civil Servants to get one Month's year end bonuses as Economy does better, accessed 29th of November 2017 under http://www.straitstimes.com/singapore/civil-servants-to-get-one-months-year-end-bonus-as-economy-does-better

Streeck, W. (2009): Re-forming Capitalism: Institutional Change in the German political Economy, Oxford.

Suh, C.-S. / Kwon, S.-H. (2014): Whither the Developmental State in South Korea? Balancing Welfare and Neoliberalism, in: *Asian Studies Review*, Vol. 38.

SWFI (2017): Institutional Investor Profile, available under: http://www.swfinstitute.org/; accessed on 28th of February 2017.

Tan, K. P. (2007): Renaissance Singapore? Economy, Culture, and Politics, Singapore.

Tan, K. Y. L. (2012): Goh Keng Swee in Politics and Parliament, in: Chew, E. / Kwa, C. G. (eds.): Goh Keng Swee: A Legacy of Public Service, Singapore.

Taylor, I. (2002): Botswana's Developmental State and the Politics of Legitimacy, Paper prepared for an international Conference by the Political Economy Research Centre at the University of Sheffield.

Taylor, I. (2014): Emerging Powers, State Capitalism and the Oil Sector in Africa, in: *Review of African Political Economy*, Vol. 41.

Thio, L.-A. (2012): Between Apology and Apogee, Autochthony: The "Rule of Law" beyond the Rules of Law in Sinapore, in: *Singapore Journal of Legal Studies*.

Thio, L.-A. / Tan, K.Y.L. (2009): Evolution of a revolution: Forty years of the Singapore constitution, London.

Thompson, M. R. (1996): Late Industrializers, late Democratisers: Developmental States in the Asia-Pacific, in: *Third World Quarterly*, Vol. 17.

Treisman, D. (2012): The Return. Russia's Journey from Gorbachev to Medvedev, New York.

Treisman, D. (2016): Russia's Billionaires, in: *American Economic Review*, Vol. 106.

Tsui-Auch, L. S. (2004a): The Professionally Managed Family-ruled Enterprise: Ethnic Chinese Business in Singapore, in: *Journal of Management Studies*, Vol. 41.

Tsui-Auch, L. S. (2004b): Bureaucratic Rationality and Nodal Agency in a Developmental State: The Case of State-Led Biotechnology Development in Singapore, in: *International Sociology*, Vol. 19.

Turok, B. (1980): Zambia's System of State Capitalism, in: Development and Change, Vol. 11.

UNDP (2019): Human Development Report, accessed 26th of February 2019 under: http://hdr.undp.org/en/data.

Vahabi, M (2016): A positive Theory of the predatory State, in: *Public Choice*, Vol. 168.

Vakulchuk, R. (2014): Kazakhstan's Emerging Economy. Between State and Market, Frankfurt.

Vallier, K. (2019): Rawls, Piketty and the Critique of Welfare-State Capitalism, in: *Journal of Politics*, Vol. 81.

Vasil, R. K. (2000): Governing Singapore: Democracy and National Development, Sydney.

Vennewald, W. (1994): Technocrats in the State Enterprise System of Singapore, Working Paper No. 32, Asia Research Centre on Social, Political and Economic Change Murdoch University Western Australia.

Vogel, E. F. (1991): The Four Little Dragons: The Spread of Industrialization in East Asia, Cambridge.

Voigt, S. (2009): Institutionenökonomik, München.

Von Alten, F. (1994): The Role of Government in the Singapore Economy, Frankfurt.

Vu, K. M. (2011): Sources of Singapore's Economic Growth, 1965-2008, Trends, Patterns and Policy Implications, Lee Kuan Yew School of Public Policy, Accepted Paper, accessed on the19th of December 2018 under: https://www.researchgate.net/publication/252067815_Sources_of_Singapore's_Economic_Growth_1965-2008_Trends_Patterns_and_Policy_Implications.

Wade, R. (1990): Governing the Market: Economic Theory and the Role of Government in East Asian Industrialization, Princeton.

Wall Street Journal (2017): China Puts Electric-Vehicle Eggs in Battery Basket, 16th of March 2017.

Walter, A. / Zhang, X. (eds.) (2012): East Asian Capitalism: Diversity, Continuity, and Change, Oxford.

Wang, J. H. J. (2018): Innovation and Government Intervention: A Comparison of Singapore and Hong Kong, in: *Research Policy*, Vol. 47.

Wang, J. H. J. / Yeung, H. W.-C. (2000): Strategies for Global Competition: Transnational Chemical Firms and Singapore's Chemical Cluster, in: *Environment and Planning*, Vol. 32.

Wee, J. C. N. / Chua, A. Y. K. (2013): The Peculiarities of Knowledge Management Processes in SMEs: The Case of Singapore, in: *Journal of Knowledge Management*, Vol. 17.

Welch, C. / Piekkari, R. / Plakoyiannaki, E. / Paavilainen-Mäntymäki, E. (2011): Theorising form Case Studies: Towards a Pluralist Future for International Business Research, in: *Journal of Business Studies*, Vol.41.

Whitley, R. (1999): Divergent Capitalisms: The Social Structuring and Change of Business Systems, Oxford.

Williamson, O. (1985): The Economic Institutions of Capitalism, New York.

Wilson, P. (2011): Introduction, in: Wilson, P. (ed.): Challenges for the Singapore Economy After the Global Financial Crisis, Singapore.

Witt, M. A. / Kabbach de Castro, L. R. / Amaeshi, K. / Mahroum, S. / Bohle. D. and Saez, L. (2018): Mapping the Business Systems of 61 Major Economies: a Taxonomy and implications for Varieties of Capitalism and Business Systems Research, in: *Socio-Economic Review,* Vol. 16.

Wong, S. H. (1992): Exploiting Information Technology: A Case Study of Singapore National Computer Board, in: *World Development*, Vol. 20.

World Bank (2002): World Development Report 2002. Building Institutions for Markets, Washington.

World Bank (2008): The Growth Report. Strategies for Sustained Growth and Inclusive Development, Washington.

World Bank (2016): Worldwide Governance Indicators, available under: http://data.worldbank.org/data-catalog/worldwide-governance-indicators; accessed on 20th of November 2016.

World Bank (2017): World Development Indicators, available under: http://data.worldbank.org/data-catalog/world-development-indicators; accessed on 28th of February 2017.

World Bank (2019a): Governance Indicators, accessed 26th of February 2019 under: https://datacatalog.worldbank.org/dataset/worldwide-governance-indicators.

World Bank (2019b): World Development Indicators, accessed 26th of February 2019 under: https://datacatalog.worldbank.org/dataset/world-development-indicators.

WTO (2016): World Tariff Profiles, available under: https://www.wto.org/english/tratop_e/tariffs_e/tariffs_e.htm; accessed on the 28th of February 2017.

Yeung, H. W.-C. (1998): The Political Economy of Transnational Corporations: a Study of the Regionalization of Singaporean Firms, in: *Political Geography*, Vol. 17.

Yeung, H. W.-C. (1999): Regulating Investment Abroad: the political Economy of the Regionalization of Singaporean Firms, in: *Antipode,* Vol. 31.

Yeung, H. W.-C. (2000): State Intervention and Neoliberalism in the Globalizing World Economy: Lessons from Singapore's Regionalization Programme, in: *Pacific Review*, Vol. 13.

Yeung, H. W.-C. (2005): Institutional capacity and Singapore's developmental state. Managing economic (in)security in the global economy, in: Nesadurai, H. E. S. (ed.): Globalization and Economic Security in East Asia: Governance and Institutions, London.

Yeung, H. W-C. (2007): From followers to market leaders: Asian electronics firms in the global economy, in: *Asia Pacific Viewpoint*, Vol. 48.

Yeung, H. W.-C. (2011): From national Development to economic Diplomacy? Governing Singapore's Sovereign Wealth Funds, in: *Pacific Review*, Vol. 24.

Yeung, H. W-C. (2014): Governing the Market in a Globalizing Era: Developmental States, Global Production Networks and Inter-firm Dynamics in East Asia, in: *Review of International Political Economy*, Vol. 21.

Yeung, H. W-C. (2017): State-led Development reconsidered: the Political Economy of State Transformation in East Asia since the 1990s, in: *Cambridge Journal of Regions Economy and Society*, Vol. 10.

Yew, L. (2014): Asianism and the Politics of Regional Consciousness in Singapore, Abingdon.

www.ingramcontent.com/pod-product-compliance
Ingram Content Group UK Ltd.
Pitfield, Milton Keynes, MK11 3LW, UK
UKHW021829100926
8556IPUK00004B/235

9 783631 849088